THE TAPESTRY OF PLANETARY PHASES

*Weaving the Threads of Purpose
and Meaning in Your Life*

Christina Rose

The Wessex Astrologer

Published in 2011 by
The Wessex Astrologer Ltd
4A Woodside Road
Bournemouth
BH5 2AZ
England

www.wessexastrologer.com

ISBN 9781902405711

A catalogue record of this book is available at The British Library

Cover design by Tania at Creative Byte, Poole, Dorset

By the same author
Astrological Counselling: A Basic Guide to Astrological Themes in
Person to Person Understanding
The Aquarian Press, 1982. ISBN 085030301X

"*Absolutely superb. It lifts the whole practice of astrology out of the 1930s and for the first time makes it credible in the field of counselling. Its whole tone and presentation make it impossible now for anyone not to take this area seriously.*"

Charles Harvey, President Astrological Association of Great Britain

"*An exciting and exhilirating discovery which includes many example sessions of the author's work with clients, focussing on depth understanding. Christina comes through as a very warm, caring individual who is flexible and open to discovering what issues are most important to her clients. She encourages personal power and responsibility which is essential in the healing process. I give this book my highest recommendation*".

Maritha Pottenger, United States

"*Excellent and articulate*"   Howard Sasportas

"*Reveals the author to be a sensitive, caring and wise person with a sensitive, caring and wise use of astrology.*"

Bernard Rosenblum, M.D., New York

"*Lucid, inspired, yet practical... describes with clarity fundamental though complex concepts of holistic thinking now finally filtering down into the actuality of astrological work...distinguishes the aims of the contemporary astrological counsellor from the traditional role of the oracular and somewhat authoritarian style of 'readings'. Detailed transcripts of actual counselling sessions make fascinating reading and merit careful study by anyone wishing to work in this field... a book that addresses itself to the real-life situation of working with clients and as such it is revolutionary*".

Melanie Reinhart, Journal of Astrological Association of Great Britain

"*The author knows her territory... she emphasizes the value of communication with the client, rather than the shopworn technique of interpreting the hapless client's destiny and, to help the professional astrologer evolve toward a more interactive style. She provides transcripts as illustration of how to proceed. It all adds up to an enlightening book – a must for the practising astrologer*".

Richard Nolle, Horoscope Magazine

"*An excellent book for anyone in astrological counselling... she discusses the hows, the whys, the common errors, giving help to clients in real, not theoretical, situations. Highly recommended*".

The Key, United States

"*Especially impressive and touching is the broadness of outlook, the warmth and caring flow through the dialogues, and the absence of stiff mechanical dogmatism. This book is like a burst of sunshine after a long and dark rainy day in astrological literature*".

Marjolaine Burnand, Switzerland

For Daniel, with love

The heavens declare the Glory of God
And the firmament sheweth His handiwork

Psalm 19 v.1

Acknowledgments

I must first acknowledge the work of Dane Rudhyar (1895–1985) who set down an essential understanding of the Lunation Cycle in 1967 which inspired not only me but several others at the time who added their insights to the basic material. Chief among these were Marc Robertson, Alexander Ruperti, Michael Meyer, Virginia Ewbank and Joanne Wickenberg, whose works appear in the Bibliography to this book. Although I may depart, here and there, from any or all of these authors in order to offer my own perspectives, I do so only with respect for their initial writings which have indisputably spurred me to work with the essence of the phase-cycle and witness its myriad outworkings both in my own life and that of other people.

In any life there are key people who emerge at transformational points along the way and I am especially grateful to the following for enabling me to turn to these junctures and go through –Tom Broadley, B.J. Wilkinson, Malcolm Saville, Francis Collier Rose, Irene Wilberforce, Ella Cree, the Rev. Denis Duncan and Renata Symonds.

Several good and sturdy friends have either soothed my brow or kicked some other part of my anatomy into action as this book unfurled; none more so than Jenny Humphrey and Stephanie Collins. Without either one of you I suspect this book might have been a task too far and I am so very grateful for the unfailing love and support you have shown me. Among other friends and professional colleagues my thanks go to Sandra J. Levy whose attentive reading of excerpts has greatly assisted in the weaving of this book's threads, as well as Elizabeth Lewis and Kaz Chapman for editorial assistance. Also to Michael Harding and Chester Kemp for their observations on initial chapters and technical monitoring of astronomical and diagrammatic content.

More than anyone, however, I owe a deep debt of gratitude to all those who have worked with me as clients and/or students over the years and who have shared their lives with me so openly. Thank you all for being my real teachers.

Contents

Introduction

But for one day, a change of gender and certainly a sturdier pair of legs, I might have been a famous footballer. As things go, the illustriousness of that particular incarnation went to a certain Mr. Terry Venables, one time Manager *inter alia* of the England, Australia and Barcelona teams, who was born on the New Moon of 6th January 1943, the day before I came into the world.

"Born on a New Moon..." – ah! An evocative phrase, transporting us into an alluring sense of mystery, fascination, a promise of something to be discovered. What does it say about us to be born on this or any other kind of Moon? And why, as with the poet Keats, do we find that it "moves our hearts so potently"?[1] From as far back as we can chart human history, mankind has looked into the great celestial arc in wonder, bewilderment, fear, awe and questioning as the Moon weaves a pattern of different faces – from New Moon, to Crescent, to First Quarter, Gibbous, Full Moon, Disseminating, Last Quarter and Balsamic – on her voyage through the night skies before disappearing from view, only to re-emerge and trace the same steps month after month in eternal perpetuation. Superstitions, legends, folklore and myth from all around the world have evoked lunar images as inspirational, instinctive to the understanding of rhythmic growth, death and resurrection into new hope and life. From earliest Palaeolithic images of the Moon Goddess chiselled in rock,[2] through to lunar divinities spinning fates, agricultural planting cycles in accordance with the phases, suspicions and even studies to show increased incidences of crime, right down to modern day overnight radio phone-in presenters who can be heard pleading with their production team "Oh for heaven's sake, is it a Full Moon or something?! – I've got nothing but nutters phoning in here tonight!" the pattern of the Moon seems filled with immense power and meaning in our lives. And now, according to a recent news announcement,[3] scientists and artists are combining to build a Lunar Clock alongside the River Thames as a monument to reflect the changing phases. A curator of London's Science Museum is reported as saying "Isn't it about time that we looked up and out to those natural time cycles of this spinning rock? It is these that we human beings are wired to…".[4]

Indeed we are. One way or another, the passage and patterns of the Moon are embedded in everyone's consciousness and, sooner or later, whether we are enfolded in the arms of a lover on a moonlit beach, stepping into our own back yard with a telescope or simply taking Fido for his nightly 'walkies', there can surely be few among us who would not wish to awaken more to the simple yet intriguing pattern of the Shining Lady of the Night and have a deeper connection to her meaning in the *actuality* of our lives. Astrologers have become more accustomed over the last thirty years or so to including some understanding of the cycle, although it is still not as much to the forefront of their work as many in the profession feel it might be. This may be partly because earlier commentaries appear (on the whole) to have been written in somewhat abstruse and/or purely theoretical terms and it is only in comparatively recent times that shifts have begun to occur to bring it into more personal and practical understanding in the day-to-day application of astrology. What do these phases look like, sound like, *feel* like in the actual lives of people? How much of a grasp do we *really* have of them in the unfolding of our experiences? How can we bring them more into a clarity of understanding in an accessible way, one which will make a difference to our self-awareness and onward development?

Whether one has an attendant interest in astrology, is a dedicated student or indeed a seasoned professional, it is in order to address these issues that this present book is offered as a platform from which we can deepen our attunement to the eight-fold cycle, not only of Sun/Moon but also several other planetary pairings (for instance Saturn/Moon, Mars/Venus, Jupiter/Mercury) and thus derive a more direct connection with the ever-changing, ever-cyclic, evolutionary impulse of the Cosmos.

When Dane Rudhyar first set down astrological meanings for the Lunation Cycle in his 1967 book of that title (although he had been writing on the subject for quite some years prior to this), its impact upon me, as a new emerging astrologer at the time, was one of some relief. Up until then I had felt dissatisfied with what I experienced as a rather wooden and linear approach to astrology in terms of interpretations of planets in certain positions 'up there' doing something to me 'down here' and my life as running from past to future in a straight predictable line. I was not alone of course but part of a growing band searching for something more growth-oriented, organic, transformative and *alive* in astrology rather than reducing it to a somewhat dull taxonomy assembled for static definitions and conceptual analysis alone. In this respect Rudhyar's work provided the focus for three key realizations: one was to give recognition to the celestial space itself as reflective of a deeper (or higher) sense of Being; the second was to give conscious attention to the interconnectedness of everything within that space, whether or not any relationship between them was obvious; the third was to discern more consciously the ongoing cycle of creation-to-dissolution which underpins all that we experience and which is depicted so markedly in the passage of the Moon in the night sky. In other words, working with the phases was to 'enter' the astrological heavens in awareness of unfolding life reflected in its perpetual cycles.

That approach to an astrological understanding in people's lives is not only extant but seems increasingly to be needed. The global proliferation of astrological knowledge, particularly over the last 20 years or so, has seen us go beyond endless debate as to whether astrology is true or not, or works or not. Anyone who has utilized it for any length of time knows it works: more pertinent is how we live it from within us and apply its insights to grow and transform effectively in our lives. The human race today seems to be in something of another evolutionary shift where people search for something more reliable and sustaining other than the torturous processes of the materialistic and mechanistic world alone. Bureaucratic political systems and/or media-manipulation seem only to add to the pressures upon individuals to align themselves with some kind of other 'compass' by which they can derive both meaningful sense and less aggressive values in their lives. Part of this crescendo as we progress further into the 21st century may well be an even greater return to the organic motions and mysteries of the universe that have provided awakenings to mankind throughout the centuries.

When we look upwards into the heavens from earth, we see sun, moon, stars, planets etc. However, if we metaphorically enter that sky-space, as if taking a walk through the heavens (rather than defining ourselves by seeing it as a separate externality), we enter a realm of relationship to the fundamental rhythms of our lives from a greater dimension of awareness. In the celestial we are absorbing into our innermost selves all that envelops us, the very atoms of our bodies forged from the same elements as the stars. We can place ourselves responsibly at the centre of *all that* within which we 'live and move and have our being' as the Bible puts it. The eight-fold cycle of the Sun/Moon relationship traces this infinite space and we may say it is intrinsically who we *are* as opposed to the everyday identity we carry around through our actions, outlooks, conditionings, hopes, fears, quests. Indeed, such a perspective also, usefully, enables us to approach an understanding and acceptance of our lives from a witnessing observer position, as opposed to being only and continually mentally caught up in the small self's needs, conflicts, resistances and frustrations. J.C. Tefft sums it up eloquently when he writes:

> "… most of us … continue to go about our daily affairs in fundamentally uninspired fashion; ignorant of and therefore indifferent to the transcendent potential in conscious awareness embodied within us…. As a result, a significant amount of Cosmic Energy is lost in the building and expanding of self… The consequence is that an Awareness in Consciousness that is other than self is not only ignored, but also prevented from coming forth"[5]

Whether one wishes to refer to this awareness as linking us to Infinite Consciousness beyond Form, Eternal Life, a Higher or Real Self, Oneness, God, or anything else is a matter of preference borne of the religious, psychological, spiritual, philosophical and cultural orientations we have come through in our personal experience. More prosaically, others access this field by using words such as 'context' or 'paradigm', or simply a 'shift of awareness', which are also useful aids to inner understanding. Ultimately, however, it cannot really be labelled and defined but only experienced.

D.H. Lawrence, who felt that one of the greatest imaginative experiences the human race has ever had was that of the Chaldean experience of the living heavens, spoke passionately for an inner astrological experience by entering the magnificence of the celestial and its "living, roving planets":

> "In the astrological heavens … the whole man is set free, once the imagination crosses the border. The whole man, bodily and spiritual, walks in the magnificent fields of the stars and the stars have names, and the feet tread splendidly upon – we know not what, but the heavens, instead of untreadable space … To enter the astrological sky of the zodiac … is truly imaginative, and to me, more valuable … It is the entry into another … kind of world, measured by another dimension. And we find some prisoned self in us coming forth to live in this world … the sense of being the Macrocosm, the great sky with its … profoundly meaningful motions, its wonderful bodily vastness, not empty but all alive and doing"[6]

My experience of working with the eight-fold cycle of phases over the years is, primarily, that it does indeed enable us to access this essential space within which all that presided at our birth emanates, each of us shafts of consciousness through which the Universe can know and express itself. The phases assist in tracing the *contextual* threads underlying the surface *content* (outer manifestations) of our lives. Thus they enable us to stand back a little before plunging straight into static definitions of a chart factor. While honouring what we experience (i.e. the content – events, characteristics, situations, places, people), we are afforded a more spacious vantage point from which to consider the nature and purpose of those factors and the interplay between them within the whole. Since this awareness is not reasoned out mentally we use analogies, symbols, metaphors which carry an organic life of their own into the sense-consciousness of mind, body and spirit. Several such pathways will be employed throughout this book to take us into a felt-sense understanding of the phase cycle, one such being that of a tapestry.

In the same way that we look up into the sky to discern the positions of planets, but then go beyond those forms to enter the sky-space itself, so too we may walk into an art gallery or museum and see before us a magnificent tapestry. Upon it may be woven a unicorn here, two jousters in battle over there, a lady on a white horse, pomegranates, landscapes, a flowing river perhaps… Behind them all lies the raw canvas, little glimpses of which we may also see if we are not preoccupied with what emerges in pictorial form upon it. Likewise, in astrology, we usually focus on what appears (Venus square Mars perhaps) and proceed with an interpretation, but we may not take into account the larger context within which these energies seek expression through the consciousness of the human individual. The phases of the lunation cycle are the celestial backdrop (the canvas) upon which the thread (of Venus/Mars) is being woven. By catching ahold of this thread and tracing it through the canvas (our own innate substance), we are connected to a deeper meaning for our interpretation, one that holds a purpose behind it. Additionally, we may more readily discern the choices and pathways open to us.

The metaphor of weaving is not a new one of course; in lunar mythology, we are given the image of a spindle with the Moirae (the Three Fates) who spun the mysterious thread symbolizing the course of life and destinies of the human beings. Mircea Eliade alikens the waxing/waning hemispheres of the Moon to the shuttle of the weaver passing to and fro:

"By its mode of being, the moon 'binds' together a whole mass of realities and destinies. The rhythms of the moon weave together harmonies, symmetries, analogies and participations which make up an endless 'fabric', a net of invisible threads… That is why the moon is seen in so many traditions personified by a divinity … 'weaving' the cosmic veil, or the destinies of men".[7]

And later, still speaking of the Moon:

"Not for nothing is she envisaged in myth as an immense spider … for to weave is not merely to … join together differing realities (cosmologically) but also to create, to make something of one's own substance as the spider does in spinning its web."[8]

Likewise, everything in astrology, as in life, works in a cycle unfolding not in isolation but as part of an overall process. Each zodiac sign, each house, each aspect, every one thing is part of numerous threads in an interconnected web and nothing operates simply by itself without touching upon the whole. "Thou canst not stir a flower without the troubling of a star" wrote the English poet, Francis Thompson, exquisitely and simply capturing our awareness of all things being linked as One. The story of Indra's net in Eastern mysticism similarly carries the same theme of interconnectedness. The palace of the god Indra was said to be covered by a vast network of jewels, each so arranged that it reflected the images of all the other jewels – a total interrelatedness where everything is contained in everything else, in turn reflected the new physics of today and, astrologically, at its most emblematic in the ever-cyclic relationship of Sun/Moon.

As we trace the threads of the phases woven through various people's lives in this book, we can begin to see interconnections in the birth chart we might otherwise miss if we were only interpret its separate parts. There are three main ways in which this can arise: first, astrologers are accustomed to looking at planets in pairs, but usually only when there is an aspect between them. If there is none, the tendency is to disregard any relationship as existing between those planets. One may hear a person say "No, I have no aspect in my chart between Mars and Saturn" and that may well be so; yet the Mars and Saturn positions will fall within a phase in the overall cycle and therefore there is indeed *a most important relationship between them*. Secondly, we may fixate upon zodiacal *positions* of planets and see no pertinent difference between one chart and another containing the same soli-lunar signs. Yet there may be a vast reservoir of inner meaning we may again miss if we fail to engage with their *relationship* in the phase-cycle. For example, two people may present for counselling, each with Sun in Aquarius and Moon in Taurus. Ordinarily the astrologer would interpret these sign placements with perhaps little or no differentiation between the two people. Yet Person A may have Sun on 12° Aquarius and Moon on 3° Taurus (thus 81° apart in Crescent Phase) while Person B has Sun on 7° Aquarius with Moon on 19° Taurus (therefore 102° apart in First Quarter phase). Two people, each fundamentally Aquarius/Taurus, neither with any conventional aspect between Sun and Moon, but each coming from different contexts for developing their inner being and substance through these signs. A 'sameness' juxtaposed with a 'differentness', perceived only via the phase-cycle. One will carry forward the thread of inner effort and perseverance (Crescent) while the other will be more naturally attuned to the next interconnected stage, that of externalizing energy into the outer environment (First Quarter). The third way in which phase relationships can be useful to highlight interconnections which might otherwise be missed is where there is a lack of specific birth time. This is especially important in respect of the Moon since she travels, on average, some 13° per day. While this puts her actual position in doubt without a birth time, it is not sufficient (usually) to vary the phase relationship to another planet since each phase spans 45°. If, on occasion, the Moon appears as a possibility at the end of one phase and the beginning of another, then there is a choice to be considered by the astrologer and the phase can often be more clearly determined as the relationship and dialogue with the client is built up.

While the lunation cycle deals only with the Sun/Moon relationship, the phases derived from this pattern can in fact be applied to *any* planetary pairing (with the exception of Sun/Mercury, Sun/Venus and Mercury/Venus since these planets are never far enough apart from one another in the solar system to form a complete 360° cycle). In this book I shall be developing five main sets of planetary duos utilizing the personal planets (up to Saturn) and focusing upon polarities. As well as tracing who and what we can most naturally be and become (Sun/Moon), we must also take into account as inhabitants of planet Earth the fact that we develop within certain boundaries and limits (Saturn/Moon). We are also charged to develop perception (Mercury), evaluation (Venus) and submit these to being energized in the outer world (Mars) so that we grow (Jupiter). Jupiter/Mercury and Mars/Venus phase relationships will therefore also be covered, together with the fifth pairing, that of Saturn/Jupiter which focuses upon our inner aspirational compass when it comes to consolidating ourselves as individuals in structured societies – working for a living, aspiring to goals, building careers. Part II of this book carries delineations for each of these sets taking them through all of the eight phases of the cycle, utilizing client examples as well as examining the lives of well-known people past and present. While other pairings (such as with outer planets) will also be covered, it is my hope that at least the five main sets of pairings can be useful to astrologers when working with their clients, accessing the essential threads of meaning in the same customary way they already take stock of main planetary positions and aspects. Doing so enables the consultant and counsellor alike to deepen their understanding of the context within which the human individual is developing and broaden their appreciation of the variations of astrological principles when brought into manifestation in a person's actual life.

Finally, I must address the sub-title of this book and the question of *meaning* and *purpose*. Ordinarily when we use these words they tend to suggest something we are striving for, a quest we endeavour to reach. Examining the birth chart with its signs (representing needs to be fulfilled), houses (representing our goals) and planets (what we need to do or be in order to bring all this to fruition) does indeed enable us to decipher these quests – but they are *secondary* purposes. They seem overwhelmingly important to us in our day-to-day lives, where we want to establish this, conquer that, achieve xyz. But they come and go like clouds (or indeed planets) in the sky – here today, gone tomorrow. Our *primary* purpose lies in the infinite celestial itself – the ineffable sky that always lies behind the clouds – of which we are the living embodiment. It is a constant inner energy field – one composed, paradoxically, of change and experienced in the perpetual cycle of unfolding phases. The Sun/Moon and other planetary phase relationships are key access points to being able to embrace the vision and live this dimension of Being within us.

So where does all this leave me and Mr. Venables? What is the connection between us? Well, none at all on the level of secondary purpose. His is to be a famous football manager, mine to be an astrological counsellor. Now of course it may be that Mr. Venables knows a good deal about astrology, I have no idea, but I can assure you I am unable to reciprocate in *his* field of endeavour since (as my five-year old grandson will readily attest) when it comes to kicking footballs I am complete rubbish. What Mr. Venables and I *do* share (along with millions of others born around the same time) is the primary purpose of developing New Phase Capricorn/Aquarius as a fundamental essence of our life growth and development within the Whole, each of us weaving (shaping, directing) the threads as befits our individual patterns.

Working consistently with the eight-fold phase cycle enables us to refine the birth chart into main themes which lie at the heart of our lives. They throw into sharp relief awarenesses of ourselves which our conventional charts may not readily yield and thus afford a clear guide to in-depth understanding – and indeed a greater acceptance – of ourselves and our place within the Totality.

Part I

The Lunation Cycle

I: The Rhythmic Dance of Sun and Moon

All life begins in darkness. The fertilized seed in nature – be it of plant, animal or human kingdom – begins its journey hidden from view. It must then anchor itself firmly, break through to the light of the world, grow, flourish and reproduce itself before once more descending back into the darkness from whence it came.

This cycle of creation-maintenance-dissolution is one of eternal repetition and underpins all realms of experience. Buddhist teachings speak of *impermanence*, where something arises, stays for a while and then disappears or dissolves. "Each instant is not a static for as soon as it arises, it moves towards its own cessation."[1] Similarly in biological terms, we speak of natural rhythms *of production, storage* and *discharge* occurring in all living organisms. Wherever we look we find our lives reverberating to this ever-recurring cycle and, astrologically, its most graphic representation lies in the changing face of the Moon. Emerging from the darkness after conjoining the Sun, she first appears to us as a slim crescent, then a half-circle, gradually increasing in light as she journeys to maximum development and stands fully illuminated in the solar light. Thereafter she journeys back down displaying diminishing stages of light until once more she becomes a slim crescent, then slips back into the unseen… until a few days later the cycle is renewed as she once more aligns herself to the Sun.

It is not, of course, the Moon alone tracing this pattern of alternating dark and light in a never-ending story, but rather her relationship to the Sun (whose light is reflected) and to the Earth. As the Earth orbits the Sun, the Moon is also moving around the Earth and reflects the sun's light to us from their relative positions as we see them. I suspect that part of what so compels us in this pattern is that instinctively we know that we are witnessing a symbolic triad of relationship between ourselves and our two Luminaries. We feel at one with the steady unfolding tableau of darkness to light and back to darkness – a coming out of, then disappearing back to, no-thingness; beyond rational explanations, something from deep within the core of us is stirred up into recognition and familiarity of being enfolded by this Moon, this Sun, as they eternally lead us through the rhythmic dance of connectedness, symbol of wholeness and ongoing life.

The Synodic Month

There are fundamentally three types of 'month' (periodic cycle measured by the moon) used astrologically: The *sidereal* month is the time taken for the moon to make a complete revolution of the earth. It tracks the position of the moon relative to the background of the stars (Latin, *sidus, sideris*, a star, constellation) taking note of where it is at any given time and measuring how long it will be before it reaches that point again. On average this is 27.3 days and we are familiar with this as reflected, for instance, in the human cycle of ovulation.

The *tropical* month is calculated against the backdrop of the ecliptic (apparent path of the sun around earth), on either side of which lies the zodiacal belt with its attendant planetary rulerships. This measurement also traces the position of the Moon and barely differs from the sidereal month in duration, but it does link us to an attendant correlation between the zodiac cycle and lunation cycle in terms of meaning, a factor which we shall see reflected as we progress in the following chapters to our understanding of the unfolding phases.

Meanwhile, the earth is also orbiting the sun and it is not until another 2.2 days have passed (i.e. on average a total of 29.5 days) that the moon is in the same position relative to the sun and together they form a conjunction (a New Moon). This is the *synodic* month (Greek, *synodos* – a meeting or a coming together along a way, as in ecclesiastical circles where the word 'synod' is used to describe an assembly of the governing body of the Church). It is therefore the measurement from one New Moon to the next. The important factor to note is that since it tracks, not the *position* of the moon, but her *relationship* to the Sun and Earth, it is this cycle with which we are primarily concerned for the purposes of this book. The synodic month (also known as a 'lunation') is that which takes us into discerning the essential make up of this trinity of Sun/Moon/Earth, the basis for the entire 360° cycle of phases.

Two Hemispheres

In the following diagram, we can see that at New Moon (when Sun and Moon are aligned on the same side of the Earth) the side of the Moon turned toward Earth is in darkness, receiving no illumination from the Sun's light. Therefore we do not see a New Moon, whereas at Full Moon (when the Sun and Moon are on opposite sides of the Earth) the side of the Moon turned towards the Earth receives the full light of the Sun.

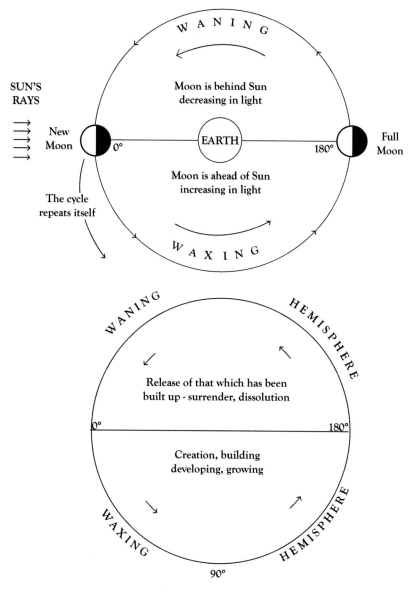

Two Hemicycles

The first half of the cycle (lower hemisphere) runs from 0° (New Moon) to 180° (Full Moon). This is essentially where *energy is built up* after initial commencement (0°) until it reaches its point of maximum development (at 180°). This is the **Waxing Hemisphere**. As you sit reading this paragraph, take a deep breath in, filling your lungs to capacity. The commencement of your breath we can equate to 0° and the point at which your lungs are fully expanded is represented at 180°. As you started to exhale, the commencement of your breathing out was 180° and, as the air flowed out through your nostrils, your lungs gradually emptied back down to 0° again. This reflects the **Waning Hemisphere** which is one of *releasing that which has been built up*. Another deep breath in, and you repeat this regular cycle over and over – creation to dissolution. In modern day parlance we could say it is the rhythmic 'default setting' for our lives. It is a cycle we also experience in the physical body with its patterns of waking/sleeping, the diastolic/systolic rhythms of the heart, the ebb and flow of blood through veins and arteries. In addition, a really good intake of breath will also see your abdomen rising, then falling as you breathe out again.

Synonymous with this twofold pattern and in terms of the human individual's development in life, the first half of the cycle (waxing) represents an increasing endeavour *to move out from the past, building up energy within to establish a new form of life* and its culmination is at Full Moon. The overall theme is of being pushed from within to develop forwards. It is a time for beginning things. The second (waning) half of the cycle represents movement outwards, *releasing energy into the environment and sensing the needs of the future*. The overall theme is of being pushed from behind by accumulated energy from the first hemisphere, to continue and complete the entire cycle. It is a time for letting go, dispersing, disposing of, ending things. This basic analogy will be expanded as we continue looking into the cycle in terms of four quadrants and then eight phases.

At this point, however, it is important to note the dividing line of 0° – 180° (New to Full). This constitutes a *crucial demarcation* between the two different meanings of the hemispheres. Once 180° has been reached, the degrees then *decrease* back down to 0° again, as shown in Figure (a). Some commentators continue the cycle beyond 180° by increasing the degrees incrementally by 45° to the maximum 360° (as shown in Figure (b)). However, I feel this is to lose sight of the all-important difference between the two hemispheres and the crucial New and Full Moon points which differentiate them.

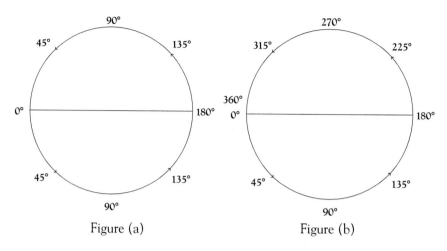

Figure (a)   Figure (b)

Starting from 0°, once the 180° position has been reached, no further development is possible – that which has been built up *must* now be released. (Note of course how, once your lungs were filled to capacity, you could breathe in no more – you *had* to breathe out). This, too, enables us to identify the essential nature of any cycle in life – it has a beginning, a middle and an end. Something begins, we sustain it for a while, then it must disintegrate and dissolve. If we resist the disintegration we are not allowing the cycle to go through its natural process of unfoldment (from creation to dissolution) and thus we arrest any transformation which is endeavouring to occur. We need to let things go when dissolution calls (180°) because only then can new things arise (the next 0°). Your intake of breath *had* to be exhaled, not only because you would go blue in the face or bust a gut (!) but full expiry leads to a new in-breath arising, ensuring ongoing life.

When dealing with Sun and Moon (or any planetary pair), if the Moon (or quicker-moving planet) is in the waxing (building up) hemisphere she is *x* number of degrees *ahead* of the Sun; if in the waning (letting go) hemisphere we would speak of her as being *x* number of degrees *behind* the Sun.

Four Quadrants

Here again we see the cycle of creation-maintenance-dissolution. Creation and growth take place in the first two quadrants, while the 180° Full Moon point marks not only the fullness of developing, but also the commencement of dissolution which then takes place over the final two quadrants. Again we see that 180° is therefore both a completion point (of building) and a

The Four Quadrants

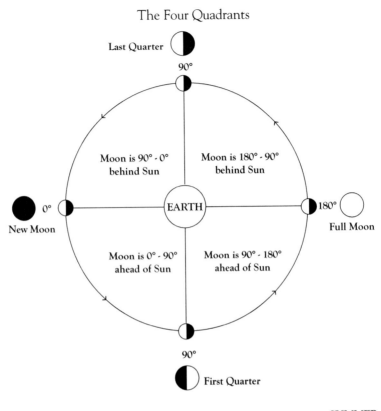

Last Quarter

90°

Moon is 90° - 0° behind Sun

Moon is 180° - 90° behind Sun

0°   EARTH   180°

New Moon   Full Moon

Moon is 0° - 90° ahead of Sun

Moon is 90° - 180° ahead of Sun

90°

First Quarter

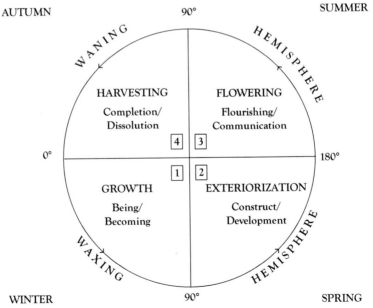

AUTUMN   90°   SUMMER

WANING   HEMISPHERE

HARVESTING   FLOWERING

Completion/ Dissolution   Flourishing/ Communication

4   3

0°   180°

1   2

GROWTH   EXTERIORIZATION

Being/ Becoming   Construct/ Development

WAXING   HEMISPHERE

WINTER   90°   SPRING

beginning point (of releasing). The two 90° angles mark definite transition points between:

Creating/Building (1) – to – Externalization/Fulfilment (2)
Fulfilment/Flourishing (3) – to – Completion/Dissolution (4)

To revert to our breathing analogy, as you begin to inhale no one else particularly knows about it – until they *see* you (and possibly hear you) at the 90° turning point expanding your chest while holding the deep intake of air. This is akin to moving from Quadrant 1 to Quadrant 2 in the Waxing Hemisphere. Then, as you begin exhaling (at 180°) you can be seen and heard releasing the air in your lungs until at the 90° turning point in the Waning Hemisphere it becomes quieter in its dispersal as the breath dies away. This is moving from Quadrant 3 to Quadrant 4.

In the world of nature, Quadrant 1 would equate to a new seed in the soil while Quadrant 2 represents its growth above the ground (in the exterior). Quadrant 3 sees the flowering plant while quadrant 4 witnesses its withering and dying … to re-seed at 0°. Thus we may also equate this quadrature to the four seasons (in the northern hemisphere) of Winter (when growth starts underground), to Spring (when the shoot appears above the soil), Summer (full blooming) and Autumn (Fall) when the plant is harvested or gradually depletes back down into the earth from whence it came, dispersing its seeds for the future.

Following this analogy through to human development, the first (or Winter) quadrant represents the essential being or 'coming into play' of the two planetary principles concerned. It comprises energies which are **instinctive** and **automatic**. The second (Spring) quadrant would be the emerging functioning of the two planetary principles in the life. It is governed by **breaking through to the exterior**. The third (Summer) quadrant marks the **full functioning and effectiveness** of the planetary principles in the outer environment and the fourth (Autumn/Fall) quadrant is representative of the **influence which has arisen** as a result of the interaction of the two planets, the **fruits of their functioning** leading to new cycles of further development.

Eight Phases

Keeping in mind the essential twofold division of Waxing/Waning (marked by the demarcation of New 0° – Full 180°) and also the two 90° transition

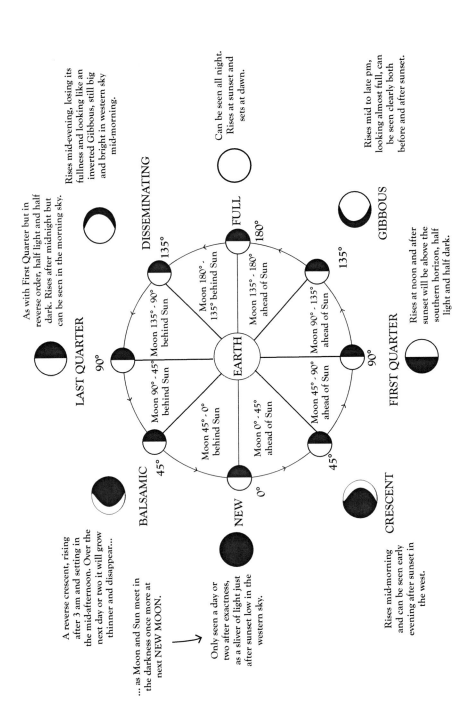

Rises mid-evening, losing its fullness and looking like an inverted Gibbous, still big and bright in western sky mid-morning.

Can be seen all night. Rises at sunset and sets at dawn.

As with First Quarter but in reverse order, half light and half dark. Rises after midnight but can be seen in the morning sky.

Rises mid to late pm, looking almost full, can be seen clearly both before and after sunset.

DISSEMINATING

FULL

LAST QUARTER

GIBBOUS

Moon 180°- 135° behind Sun

Moon 135° - 90° behind Sun

Moon 180°- 135° ahead of Sun

Moon 135° - 180° ahead of Sun

135°

180°

135°

90°

EARTH

Moon 90° - 45° behind Sun

Moon 45° - 90° ahead of Sun

90°

Moon 45° - 0° behind Sun

Moon 0° - 45° ahead of Sun

FIRST QUARTER

45°

0°

45°

BALSAMIC

NEW

CRESCENT

Rises at noon and after sunset will be above the southern horizon, half light and half dark.

A reverse crescent, rising after 3 am and setting in the mid-afternoon. Over the next day or two it will grow thinner and disappear....

... as Moon and Sun meet in the darkness once more at next NEW MOON.

Only seen a day or two after exactness, as a sliver of light just after sunset low in the western sky.

Rises mid-morning and can be seen early evening after sunset in the west.

The Eight Phases

The phases of the Moon are shown for Northern Hemisphere. In the Southern Hemisphere each 'shape' of the Moon would be seen in reverse to those which appear here.

points of the quadrants, the diagram shows further division of the cycle by 45° increments to provide us with eight phases:

The degrees of the circle *decreasing* back down to 0° after the opposition point matters also in terms of dealing with aspects in the phases (which will be covered more fully in Chapter 4). To speak of increasing the degrees after Full Phase (i.e. making Disseminating Phase 225°, Last Quarter 270° etc.) would be to lose sight of the known aspects and their conventional degree-values used in astrology. The 45° incremental divisions which yield the eight phases mark important 'alert' points. These, too, will be discussed more fully in the chapter on aspects, but for the moment we can see that they mark the divisions between New and Crescent phases, First Quarter and Gibbous phases, Full and Disseminating phases and Last Quarter and Balsamic phases.

It should be noted that some texts refer to the Disseminating Moon as a 'Waning Gibbous' and to the Balsamic Moon as a 'Waning Crescent'. The word 'gibbous' derives from the Latin for 'hump-backed' which aptly describes what we see of this protuberant-looking Moon, while the word 'balsamic' I believe may derive from ancient ceremonies for the disappearing Moon at the end of the cycle, when incense (sweet-smelling resin from the balsam tree, used as a healing balm in medicine, also for perfumes) and herbs were burned at the dying of the light and heralding the dawning of new creation (the New Moon following).

The meaning of the eight phases will be more specifically addressed in our next chapter where we will begin to build a familiarity with the cycle as a whole in terms of its manifestation in actual life. But first, we may also look at further divisions of the Moon's cycle, above the basic eight-fold pattern, which some astrologers prefer to use.

Further Phase-Divisions

Although one could in theory divide the cycle into any number of phases, some raise the query as to why it is not a twelve-fold cycle (as with the zodiac signs) while others favour a 28-phase division reflecting the 28 day cycle of the Moon's revolution of Earth. In putting forward an eight-fold division, Rudhyar was very clear in his differentiation between the *position* of a planet (e.g. Sun in Aquarius in the 5th house) which is the usual basis for the twelve-fold division of a chart, and the *relationship* of that planet with another celestial body (e.g. Sun 109° apart from Moon). The latter tells us nothing about the position of the Sun and Moon, only about their relationship, which in turn is based on arc distance between them in the 360° cycle and upon which the astrological aspects are based. The overall space, or part, taken up by that relationship (i.e. 109°) constitutes the *phase* (in this case either First Quarter or Disseminating) which we see from Earth.

A twelve-fold division of the celestial sphere more befits a classification of planets when we are concerned with their *position* in the sky in sidereal or tropical month measurement, but in the lunation cycle (the synodic month) it is the *relationship* between two planets with which we are concerned, and, as stated, for this Rudhyar adhered to an eight-fold division. All of these start with a twofold, then four-fold division (the equator, yielding two hemispheres, then the intersecting ecliptic yielding the equinoctial and solstice points). The twelve-fold system (positions of planets) then sub-divides each of the resultant 90° quadrants into 3 x 30°, while the eight-fold system (of phase relationship) divides them into 2 x 45°. These latter non-astronomical bisections at the midpoint of the four quarters are points of maximum intensity, or what Rudhyar called points of "significant confrontation" (and I earlier referred to as 'alert points'). More lucidly, the resultant eight phases gives us the eight *main depictions* of the face of the Moon as we repeatedly see her on her monthly journey through our night skies.

In the East, sometimes a 27-fold or 30-fold division of the Moon's cycle is used, though also the 28-fold cycle, again as mentioned earlier. Some astrologers, such as Bernice Prill Grebner[2], offer a combination of meanings for the fundamental eight phases together also with a 28-fold division based on the Mansions of the Moon used by ancient astrologers, which are sub-divisions of the zodiac each Mansion spanning 12°51'26". William Butler Yeats published A *Vision* in 1925 tracing a 28-fold cycle. Although Yeats was well versed in astrology, rather than astrologically or astronomically based A *Vision* seems to be derived from his immersion also in mystical philosophies and esoteric studies. Channelled via his wife through automatic writing and occasionally in a sleeping-state, it is a complex multi-faceted series of images, presented through poetic and esoteric descriptions of polarities spiralling in a gyratory cone-like sphere, tracing the soul's evolution through life and the evolution of the world through history. Busteed and Wergin[3], writing in 1976, were inspired by Yeats', as well as Rudhyar's, work and added their own empirical studies. These two writers assigned to the 28 phases an altogether different system of division, i.e. 4 phases of 30° each plus 24 smaller phases of 10° each. Then, in 1988, Martin Goldsmith, also drawing upon Yeats, Rudhyar, Busteed and Wergin, presented his own symbolic key to the Moon Phases[4], utilizing the same divisions as Busteed and Wergin but adding his own researches and clairvoyantly-derived pictorial images for each phase.

While some of this may be a little bewildering, in choosing how many phases to work with much can depend on what you are you seeking to understand from them, as well as your general approach to astrological study. I have found the work of the aforementioned writers fascinating to explore when working with my own personal life processes and they may well be helpful to the reader engaged in ongoing avenues of spiritual and psychological development. However, for some it can also be a reality that clarity of understanding emerges more readily from simplicity than complexity. Especially if you are working with astrology every day, to then add more and more ideas, information, symbols and images to a fundamental pattern may be to clothe it with outer bulky garments which can shroud it from view altogether. More pragmatically still, to the professional consultant, who must already handle daily a welter of factors to be borne in mind when working with clients, I would offer the suggestion that the eight-fold cycle is sufficient to provide you with a basic tapestry of contextual threads which, as you survey and relate them to the subject of the chart, will yield much insight and guidance even before you commence your own way of reading the chart as a whole. Moreover, I would certainly echo the words of Busteed and Wergin when they say "written examples are not nearly as convincing as living examples"[.5]

Finding the Phases in the Birth Chart

Although most computer programmes today will show the Sun/Moon phase both natally and by progression, and other planetary phases can follow, even with only a basic knowledge of the astrological chart, it is possible to discern them for yourself. Several writers have suggested various ways of so doing; these range from drawing a phase wheel of eight 45° sectors using a compass and protractor and superimposing it over your chart form to 'read off' planetary positions, to assembling a Moon Phase and Aspect Wheel (both Jinni and Joanne[6] and Demetra George[7] offer some particularly clear methods including diagrams). However a simple method is **to take the slower-moving planet first (e.g. Sun) and place it as if it were at 0° (or as if you were placing it on an Ascendant).** Then imagine a line running straight across from it (to 180°). For instance, if your Sun is on 24° Scorpio, you would imagine it thus:–

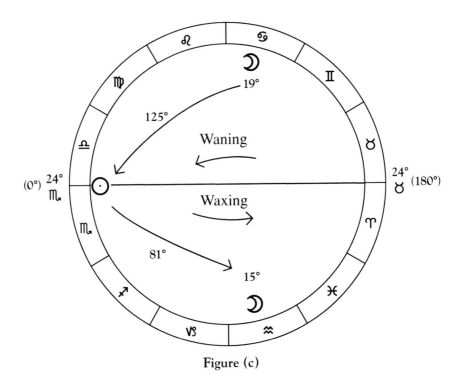

Figure (c)

Then look at where the faster-moving planet is (Moon) – if it falls in any of the signs in the lower hemisphere (from 0° – 180°) it is ahead of the Sun and waxing; if in a sign from 180° back down to 0°, it is behind the Sun and waning.

Using the following table of phases to read off the appropriate phase according to the number of degrees apart the planets are, we can now see in the diagram that, with the Sun on 24° Scorpio, if the Moon is on 15° Aquarius, it is waxing and in Crescent phase (it is 81° ahead of the Sun). Alternatively, if the Moon is on 19° Cancer, it is waning and in Disseminating phase (125° behind the Sun).

The Table of Phases

	Phases	Faster Planet is:
W A X I N G	New	0° – 45° ahead of slower planet
	Crescent	45°– 90° "
	First Quarter	90° – 135° "
	Gibbous	135° – 180° "
W A N I N G	Full	180° – 135° behind slower planet
	Disseminating	135°– 90° "
	Last Quarter	90° – 45° "
	Balsamic	45° – 0° "

A Little More Phase-Finding …. just to help get into your stride in finding the phases by sight and simple mathematics:

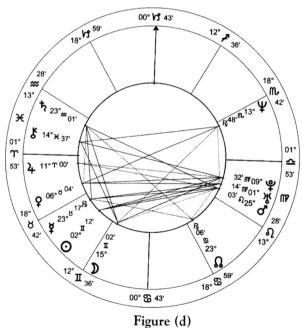

Figure (d)

In the previous chart, again *always locating the slower-moving planet first:–*

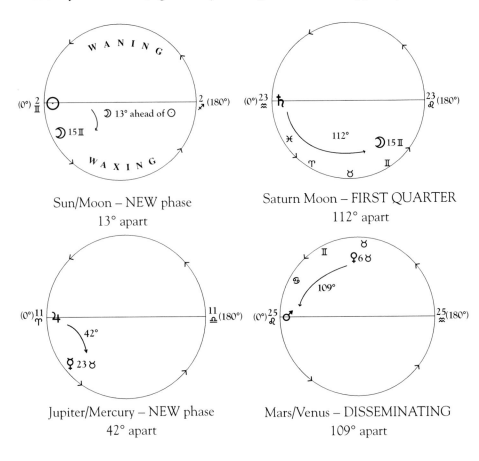

Sun/Moon – NEW phase
13° apart

Saturn Moon – FIRST QUARTER
112° apart

Jupiter/Mercury – NEW phase
42° apart

Mars/Venus – DISSEMINATING
109° apart

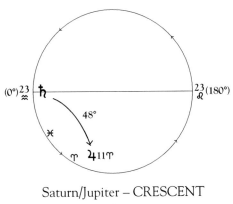

Saturn/Jupiter – CRESCENT
48° apart

Just by tracing these five main phases alone, we can already glean that, with four of them in the waxing hemisphere, the foundation of this person's life is composed of *building up and developing*, Mars/Venus alone being in the waning hemisphere and ready for *release*. Therefore, an overall emphasis on applying oneself, working to establish something yet a flowing (Disseminating) capacity for creative and relating energies to be communicated/shared.

Finally, the following diagram shows each of the eight phases first depicted by its main theme (or thread of meaning) – Spontaneity, Effort, Assertion etc. Underneath that is a *type* of person this general theme might give rise to (an instigator, worker, fighter etc) and thirdly each phase carries a description of the kind of energy or characteristic manifestations we may see arising (instinctive presentation, persevering effort...). These we will explore more closely in the next chapter.

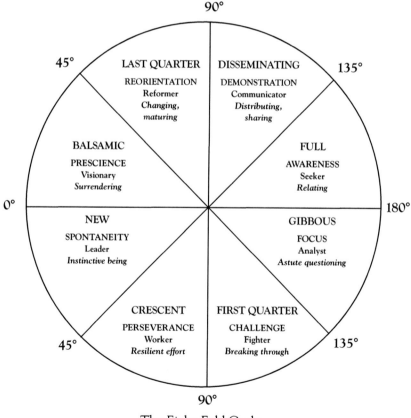

The Eight-Fold Cycle

2: The Cycle in Action

I cannot now recall the exact source, but I once heard of a letter from an elderly widow to the editor of a horticultural magazine, in which she wrote *"Sir: Since my husband died, I have buried myself in the garden...."*

Well, I know what she means! While I cannot claim any great expertise as a gardener beyond general pottering about and basic maintenance, nevertheless there is something about the gradual tempo and motion of the unfolding horticultural dance through the changing seasons that concentrates the mind and being into a simple acceptance of nature's cycles. No matter how much we may wish it otherwise, we simply cannot plant a daffodil bulb in September and expect it to flourish by Christmas. In the northern hemisphere we must await the Spring and the return of the Sun over the equator from south to north before we can herald the arrival of those delightful trumpet-headed blooms. So too with the phases: we must flow with the natural rhythms of each, allowing ourselves to be at one with the emergence of an inner quality of simple *being* at New Moon, not pushing or insisting upon it for, by definition, we would have to be further along in the cycle (at Crescent or First Quarter) where such energy is a more natural occurrence. Similarly we must tread carefully, surmise, question and consider at Gibbous, dispense and share what we contain at Disseminating, surrender our gifts at Balsamic... and so on. There is much to be appreciated in the wisdom of the earth's rhythms and transitions from first germination to blossoming to wilting to regrowth.

It also sometimes crosses my mind that the study of botany might have a few things in common with that of astrology. The botanist takes a specimen plant or flower, places it upon a laboratory bench and submits it to examination for its more particular properties – analysis, classification, notation. Similarly the astrologer sets up a chart, scrutinizing and collating different areas of intellectual interpretation and deductive reasoning. But how very much more meaningful and alive both studies are when we work with the actual living, growing, changing, unfolding life that is the plant or the individual person. In the delightful Nasrudin stories as recounted by

Sufi teacher, Idries Shah, the incomparable Mulla was approached by a man who had studied at many metaphysical schools. Wanting to prove that he was eligible for discipleship he poured out in detail where and what he had studied over the years.

"I hope that you will accept me, or at least tell me your ideas" he said, "because I have spent so much of my time in studying at these schools".

"Alas!" said Nasrudin, "you have studied the teachers and their teachings. What should have happened is that the teachers and the teachings should have studied *you*. Then we would have something worthwhile"[1]

Growth to Dissolution: The Plant in Nature

It is in that spirit of accompanying the *living* manifestation and learning from its unfoldment that we can now combine the phase meanings we have discerned thus far and place them within the context of the generic life of a plant. Metaphorically 'burying ourselves in the garden', we can follow the plant's pathway and become aware of its analogous reflections in all that we see, hear, sense, discern in the fundamental life threads woven by the human individual.

The core descriptions of the phases which follow by analogy with plant growth enable us to acquaint ourselves with the essence of each, upon which we will gradually expand as we progress through the following chapters of this book, more especially in Part II where we will witness them in the lives of people. Rulerships suggested to accompany the phases must be utilized flexibly; there is no definitive start point for each – moreover not all astrologers conversant with the Lunation Cycle are agreed on such correlations. However, in practice, a phase may be equated to (for instance at Full Moon) Cancer as an accompanying rulership but as it expands, beyond (say) 30°, it will gradually take on the hue of a secondary Leo quality. Additional understanding of how a phase is operating in the life of a person can be discerned by noting where the accompanying rulers (sign and planet) are positioned in the chart as a whole. For example, that Full Phase person may have Cancer on the 6th house cusp and Moon in the 10th house, lending a focus upon work and career directions as being the areas of life to which the phase quality is most directed, whereas another Full Phase type may have Cancer on the 4th and Moon in the 7th, directing us more toward establishing an interior sense of belonging and the development of relationships as key objectives in the life.

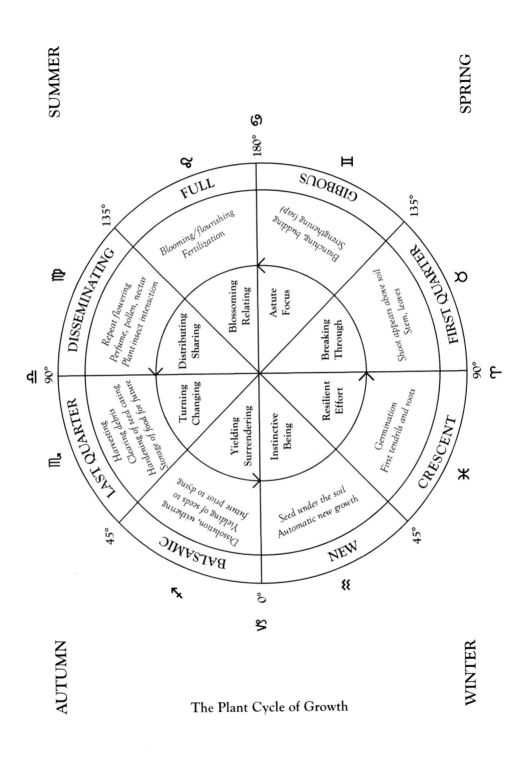

SUMMER

SPRING

AUTUMN

WINTER

♋ 180°

♌

♍ 135°

FULL

DISSEMINATING

Blooming/flourishing
Fertilization

Repeat flowering
Perfume, pollen, nectar
Plant-insect interaction

♎ 90°

LAST QUARTER

Harvesting
Clearing debris
Hardening of seed casing
Storage of food for future

♏

Distributing
Sharing

Blossoming
Relating

Astute
Focus

Turning
Changing

Yielding
Surrendering

Instinctive
Being

Resilient
Effort

Breaking
Through

45°

BALSAMIC

Dissolution, withering
Yielding of seeds to
future prior to dying

♐

0°

♑

NEW

Seed under the soil
Automatic new growth

♒

45°

CRESCENT

Germination
First tendrils and roots

♓

90°

♈

FIRST QUARTER

Shoot appears above soil
Stem, leaves

♉ 135°

GIBBOUS

Branching budding
Strengthening (sap)

♊

The Plant Cycle of Growth

NEW PHASE

The seed is under the soil – teeny tiny, yet containing multitudes. It holds within all it needs to fulfil its potential to become the mature plant. It is at one with its environment, standing at the doorway of embracing the world of form. Rudhyar equated 0° New Phase to the Spring equinoctial point (0°Aries) but I depart from this view for there is no propulsive energy here such as we associate with Aries/Mars. The seed does not jump up and down in the soil excitedly exclaiming "Yippee! Look at me! I'm going to be a great big sunflower! Just watch me go!" As we saw at the beginning of Chapter 1, life begins in darkness – and in New Phase the seed is hidden underground, simply and quietly resonating the 'such-ness' of its being. Yet neither is it doing nothing, for intense inner energy in the form of resilience is being generated as a foundation of the unstoppable impetus of nature. Enfolded in its casing, I equate this seed point more with 0° Capricorn (the Winter solstice point) when in nature the life cycle commences deep under the soil. Reliant upon its intrinsic properties, it may be comfortable and steady, or indeed very vulnerable, in its experience of becoming established (Capricorn/Saturn). The soil may be too cold, too dry, or slugs, snails, and other predators may disturb its bedding. It's a tricky business being a seed. Yet every new beginning contains the potential for the full complexity of life experience. The seed is at the start of an epic journey and fully committed to meeting it.

Similarly in the human individual, the threads to be woven for those born in this phase are those of an instinctual approach to life. This is an unspoken dimension of being, not composed of conceptual analysis. There is inner anticipation, even a sense of wonder, but nothing is planned or premeditated, nor is there deliberate outward physical striving – rather a spontaneity, an 'is-ness' which meets life in whatever form automatically, coming from a context of commitment. Whether the experience is sturdy or vulnerable, sustenance is drawn from reliance upon innate hardy qualities arising (Capricorn/Saturn) and developing in their own way, an acceptance of natural timing and a forward momentum to meet life.

Themes: automatic and instinctive participation, wonder, newness, spontaneity and commitment.

CRESCENT

Following the initial absorption of energy in the previous phase, the now-swelling seed finds its protective husk beginning to crack and germination commences. In a bid to make its way forward to growth, the seed now cautiously sprouts some first tiny underground tendrils and roots. Considerable tenacity and striving is at the centre of this activity and the going may sometimes be tough – after all, there may be obstacles in the soil to be overcome (stones, boulders, rocks) if the thin, wormlike rootlets are to burrow sufficiently to absorb nutrients and moisture in their quest to anchor themselves. Charles Darwin alikened this stage to a 'brain' in the plant which somehow knows to directs these little roots slowly but constantly downwards, firmly into the soil, tasting it as they go,[2] for the soil itself gradually releases its nutrients to them. Viennese biologist, Raoul Francé, spoke of the tendril finding a 'perch' even out of an obstacle by winding itself around so firmly, like a corkscrew, it would be hard to prise away.[3]

In human life, the purpose of being born with the Sun/Moon in this phase is to weave threads of resilience and determination in merging with and adjusting to (Pisces/Neptune) new circumstances. The overall life stands as an expression of the twofold theme of (a) breaking out from the past (the seed casing) and (b) forging a way ahead with stoicism and innovation (Saturn/Uranus/Aquarius) in order to secure a threshold in life and build roads ahead.

Themes: effort, perseverance, adaptation, establishment, endurance.

FIRST QUARTER

Here we meet the first appearance of the green shoot above the surface of the soil. The plant now puts down some stronger secondary roots to burrow deeper still, while at the same time developing the opposite and complementary thrust *upward*, surging toward the light. Spring is indeed sprung and thus I equate *this* phase to the Spring Equinox (0°Aries), the time of year (northern hemisphere) when we begin to see new shoots peeking above the ground for the first time. As this stage unfolds, the plant must exert much energy (Aries/Mars) to develop a stem and formation of first leaves. The 16th century German mystic, Jakob Boehme, able to see and experience through different dimensions, spoke of being able to mingle with a plant, to feel its life "struggling towards the light". In sharing the simple ambitions of the plant in nature he also spoke of "rejoicing with every joyously growing leaf"⁴. So there is a sense of 'triumph' here in keeping with the theme of surging through, but it should also be noted in nature that there can be nothing haphazard about the onward growth. The stem that grows must be sturdy. This is also a crucial transformation for the plant, a point of no return. Hitherto it might have withered at any time (e.g. not able to break from its casing at Crescent Phase nor able to form anything more than weak stringy tendrils to secure itself). At this 90° waxing square the plant is indeed out in the light, and open to sun and rainfall which it needs to sustain it ever onward. But here also there is transition from the inner warmth of the underground soil to colder air and drying winds, so the shoot must also acclimatize itself to this exposure and press on.

This phase is synonymous with the challenge to present oneself in, and make a mark upon, one's world. **This** *is where propulsive energy is required (Mars/Aries correlation) – energy which underpins the establishment of a more definite road forward away from the past. Greater assertion, pushing and striving for emergence in one's exterior world characterize the tapestry being woven. Yet unrestrained energies can detract from the sturdiness of the individual's development and be hazardous to the potential ability to meet the challenges of life.*

Themes: action, assertion, challenge, daring, decision, impact.

GIBBOUS

At this stage foliage has appeared, yet at the same time there is a slight ebb in the vitality of the plant as it 'approaches the runway' to its flowering. Here, even more than in the last phase, we are shown that nothing is haphazard. Writing on nature's patterns, Philip Ball describes the succession of leaves along a stem as tracing three different kinds of spiral, each leaf displacing the one below it by a more or less constant angle and at regular intervals. It is surmised that the plant 'selects' such geometric adaptations in order to gain maximum exposure to sunlight.⁵ How very ingenious! – a reflection perhaps of the Geminian co-rulership here. In the ebb or withdrawal of energy (synonymous with the steadying Taurus rulership) it is as if there is a contemplative step on the part of the plant in order that a higher manifestation of energy can take place to ensure the well-being of the eventual flower – a sort of *'reculer pour mieux sauter'* as it stands at the doorway of the important task just ahead. This is a stage of sap rising which is lifeblood ('security' – Taurus) to the buds forming yet the plant may also be subject to pests and disease, for as buds appear so do the insects. Some may be welcome while others are a nuisance; if these are sufficiently overcome, just prior to blooming there can be a slight 'quickening' (Gemini) as the plant prepares itself to open its buds.

These themes are synonymous with the human individual developing an awareness and consideration of possible difficulties to be encountered notwithstanding that one has already achieved a great deal. Focused care, caution and assessment are the hallmarks of what is needed at this stage of the phase cycle and a balance of energies that can discern when and how to move forward with precision, timing, know-how… ensuring nothing is left to chance in order to reach a goal.

Themes: Learning, discerning, assessment, precision, focusing, consideration.

* * *

At this point we have reached the culmination of the first half of the cycle. As we saw earlier, planetary pairings in waxing phases are built up for personal development, integration and effectiveness to underpin the ongoing life, whereas those in waning phases need to be expressed, spread and shared with both the immediate and wider environment. For the plant, it has reached the fullness of its growth (waxing); now it must announce itself and interact with its surroundings (waning) commencing with:

FULL PHASE

If all has gone well for the plant in its previous stages of development, here it will reach a glorious culmination of the first half of its cycle of life. It is now in beautiful bloom, fully engaged with all aspects of its surroundings – soil, air, sun, winds, rain, wildlife, especially insect life by which it will become fertilized, and it flourishes in its place of belonging (Cancer rulership). In the summer we draw back the curtains one morning and what was the day before a plant, seemingly standing very still with its preciously enfolded buds, now dominates our view and we announce "Oh look! The sunflowers are out!" Stark recognition of a magnificence (Moon, ruler of Cancer, stands opposite the Sun). Yet this completion point also means the plant commences the second half of its cycle – the letting-go (waning) where eventually it will meet dissolution. Here the plant uses its flowers to attract pollinating insects in order to reproduce itself, its fertilization at this stage ultimately carrying the life of the plant's genus ever forward.

For the individual person this phase correlates with the need to develop conscious awareness of one's full being in relation to the surrounding environment and all that it contains, including other people. Needs to flourish and interact combine with needs for recognition, illumination and integration of purpose, principles and meanings. Tapestry threads to be woven are those of interconnectedness on personal, sociocultural and transpersonal levels.

Themes: Completions/new beginnings, relatedness, reflection, awareness.

DISSEMINATING

The plant thrives through secondary blooming providing constant display for all to admire (Leo) while generously dispersing its perfume and continuing its interaction with insects and other forms of wildlife. Some plants are even known to display a communicative intelligence at these two stages (Full and Disseminating) – only opening themselves to a certain type of bee, for instance, and closing down if some other winged insect should fancy his chances instead! Some even radiate a kind of light to guide the chosen bee in – he gets to have his own illuminated landing-strip! The height of summer is a very busy (Virgo) time in nature when growth is still rapid, flowering repeats itself, and now too begins the process of carrying forward tiny organs of fertilization, symbols of creative new life. There is an ebb-and-flow motion here – flowing in the sense that the inner fruits begin to swell, ebbing in that the plant contracts into a design by way of formation of the seed within the fruit – a tiny speck of organized matter (again Virgo) – to be carried forward to the next stage of the cycle.

The Disseminating phase within the human individual is mirrored in a capacity to communicate with one's surroundings and share what one has learned and understands as meaningful, gathered up from previous activities and interactive experiences. The need is for life to be fluid, freely moving along so that what one has to disperse and share can be distributed without hindrance.

Themes: Distribution, sharing, communication, involvement, participation.

LAST QUARTER

Autumn (or Fall) signals a change of direction. The growth and flourishing seasons are drawing to a close and the plant must now be harvested (or proceeds to natural withering and hibernation). Just as Aries/Mars was synonymous with the new thrusting shoot at First Quarter, here at the opposite point the attendant Libra/Venus rulership reflects a balance of essential values and productivity being 'stated' in the world. We witness the plant (certainly a deciduous tree) making its presence felt by one final glorious display of autumnal colour as it turns to the closing of its cycle. This is balanced by the fact that it is a season of much produce for food as well as debris to be cleared up (all those autumn leaves) and perhaps used as mulch for the new growing season to come. Very importantly the plant also stores food for the hardening up of the seeds it is carrying which will soon be yielded for that oncoming new cycle.

Last Quarter threads to be woven in human life consist of turning points to be made, propelled by the past from which one has come. We can look back observing all that has gone before but we cannot keep a grip on some old continuity. In this phase we must weave a thread of recognition of the 'springboard' from which we have emerged which now points us on to a diversionary path. There exists an inner call to stand and/or speak out as the embodiment of all that we have become and are, conveyed through values (Libra/Venus) we stand for – beliefs, philosophies, thoughts, ideologies – firming them up to express them in our environment.

Themes: reorientation, diversion, development of maturity in the outer world, promulgation of individual values.

BALSAMIC

The plant at its stage of senescence and dormancy now returns into the ground dispensing its seeds – these will be carried into the soil by insect life, transported on the backs and in the fur of small animals or borne on the winds and rains of winter. This is a phase of transformation leading onward to new growth and discovery. The hitherto plant-in-its-cycle must now be relinquished (Scorpio/Pluto) and commit its last vestiges to that future growth (Sagittarius/Jupiter) as it approaches hibernation/dying. In the natural world fields will now lie fallow, divested of what has gone before, yet the dark underground soil is subject to renewal of nitrates plus other minerals and bacteria over a season before the entire cycle commences *de novo*.

This phase is synonymous with the yielding of inner attributes skills, insights which can live on and serve the world – whether or not this is within the lifetime of the individual concerned. That which is yielded comes less from direct action as it does from unseen layers of inspirational energy. Our weaving of a Balsamic thread enables us to surrender the past and submit to inner transformations; this in order to release the potential of new life to come and serve the spirit of discovery by which it is brought into being.

Themes: sensitivity to future potential, surrendering one's gifts, inspiration, vision.

* * *

Unfoldment in Human Life

Taking this eight-fold pattern of growth, we can apply it to a person, an activity, or a life cycle – indeed anything by way of analogy in order to grasp the flow and quality of energy from one phase to the next and over any length of time. For instance, we can look at the phases as **Eight Types of People** and see how each might behave and react in a certain situation. For this, we might suppose that the local Health and Fitness Centre has started up a course for those who want to learn to swim for the first time. A well-qualified instructor is on hand and has given the class an introductory talk, demonstration and answered questions, and now they are ready to enter the pool itself:

New Moon Type

He slips automatically into the water, with its gentle undulating movement, feeling a sense of wonder at how it supports his body and ripples around his limbs following his every movement. He lets the water 'take' and enfold him, even allowing his head to become submerged, instinctively knowing to hold a deep breath while this lasts. He is fascinated by all the possibilities that swimming can open him to and is glad he came.

Crescent Type

She stands hesitatingly at the edge of the pool, unsure of whether she is quite ready for this experience. She peers into the water and it all looks a bit… well… *wet*. Not to mention deep. Part of her wishes she'd never come, but she's here now so might as well plough on. Gingerly she extends one foot then the other into the water and grips the pool-rail while gradually submerging her body. As she perseveres further into the pool, some of the others in the class hold out a hand to encourage her forward.

First Quarter Type

Like the Crescent type, he too feels a little unsure but is determined this pool of water is not going to get the better of him. Besides, since signing up for it he's been mentally and emotionally working to prepare himself inside for this swimming course and he can't chicken-out now. He jumps in with two feet and makes a big splash, then thrashes his way through, arms and legs flailing, to get to the other side. Having made it, his head jerks triumphantly out of the water and he looks all around – oh boy, it felt good to get through.

Gibbous Type

She stands at the edge of the pool sizing up the situation with her formidable mind. She endeavours to assess the depth of the water at different intervals along the entire length of the pool and asks the instructor questions about the temperature of the water. Maybe she has even brought along her own thermometer. She also takes careful note of how many other people are in the pool and where they are positioned so as to choose a point to enter the water and have a clear path in front of her to practise swim-strokes until she perfects them.

Full Moon Type

He feels glad this course has finally started up and has come along to it with quite a few of his pals. Hey, it's going to be great to meet up each week in this way and all learn together. He also becomes aware of how big and wide the pool is and in his mind's eye he revels in the possibility of soon being able to power his way through the water completing several lengths, and becoming an accomplished diver. Maybe the Centre will even hold Swimming Galas – maybe he'll win a prize or be awarded a special Certificate with his name embossed in gold lettering.

Disseminating Type

She too feels very ready to enter the water along with all the others; she likes the feeling of them all learning together, helping one another and sharing their experiences as well as exchanging ideas for getting better at the various types of strokes. Besides, it's great that the Instructor is on hand to answer questions or make suggestions. Oh yes, there's quite a lot to learn, but it's also great being part of a group endeavour. Maybe they'll even do synchronized swimming shows soon.

Last Quarter Type

While the other members of the swimming class are starting off at the comparatively comfortable shallow end, he figures that if he is really to be a good swimmer he must be prepared to go just that one bit further and enter the water where it is deeper. He might even do so from a diving-board. He remembers when he was little and loved paddling in the sea with Mum and Dad. He knows if he can 'make it' with the more grown-up stuff now this will properly sustain him as a strong swimmer and, who knows, he might even go on to be an Instructor himself one day.

Balsamic Type

She glides into the water like a fish, letting go the cares of the day. She holds in her mind's eye wonderful visions of how beneficial this is to her whole mind-body-spirit and wonders why she never thought of learning to swim before. But now that she's taken this first leap, not only can she commit herself to it more from now on but she can also bring her children along to see if they might enjoy it too. Maybe she'll write a poem about the whole experience when she gets home and add it to the collection she is hoping to publish soon.

* * *

In terms of tracing the phase meanings through a **Life cycle,** we might take an example of something that happily occurs somewhere in the world every day: two people meet and fall in love:

New

They have just met and all is a mixture of excitement and relative ease, even if mixed with little flutterings of vulnerability. All their senses are heightened – 'Moon' rhymes with 'June', everything feels wondrously alive and they feel special. It seems anything and everything is possible now that they have found each other. Neither of them has to think about, analyze or put effort into the relationship as it carries itself along automatically by its brand newness and magical quality. Both of them simply enter spontaneously into it and feel committed to going forward.

Crescent

After they have known each other for a while and the relationship has become a little more established, they begin to find that some of the initial automatic attraction between them is 'settling down' (or even wearing off!) and they are aware they need to make adjustments to accommodate each other. They might, for example, discover things about their partner that they dislike or find difficult, so they need to begin working at the relationship with rather more effort.

First Quarter

So far, the relationship has sprung into being and then developed, perhaps with a little bit of effort by both parties. They have been together for quite a while and now feel more commitment to the relationship. Just as in nature there is a thrust at the Spring equinox to the seeking of a mate (birds, for instance, strut their plumage and sing their sweetest songs), here too in human life there is a need to express that urge openly and more obviously in the world. For our couple, this might be the stage at which others get to see that these two are indeed 'an item' and/or it may be the point at which they decide to get married and announce it to their folks.

Gibbous

Marriage has brought a whole new set of challenges to them both and time has to be spent learning to live together. This involves paying attention to developing routines and working out ways in which to make the marriage not only viable but an ongoing success. There can be a lot of strain at this stage as each of them has to learn to fit individual needs with joint ones; there may also be a certain amount of juggling with arrangements concerning careers/workloads and time spent together... not to mention assimilating the 'in-laws'!

Full

Two things can occur here; either there is a failure to adjust, the marriage will fall apart and they will decide to go their separate ways, or they both become even more consciously aware of the purpose of their coming together. Let's suppose, for the sake of example, that they are now indeed fully pledged to mutual love and support, so much so they decide to bring children into the world. It is the ending of their life as a couple and the beginning of their life as parents.

Disseminating

Having developed consciousness of purpose, their marriage will now be guided by this and, together with their growing children, they develop an even further understanding of themselves individually, of each other, and of their children. They may also become more known in their locality as the XYZ Family who live down the lane at Number 22 and are noted for their involvement in and contribution to the community.

Last Quarter

The purpose established at the completion point (Full Phase) is losing its initial meaning. Time is passing and their children are now grown up; the patterns, beliefs and attitudes by which, as a couple, they have lived for so many years do not seem so applicable any more. This can be a difficult transition time and requires a complete change of attitude. This may be another point at which the relationship could end and the two people set off on different roads. However if the marriage remains then perhaps, released from the responsibility of caring for children, they decide to do something quite different but that holds possibilities for the future… like setting up in business together.

Balsamic

By now as a couple they are reaching retirement age. This is a period of forward thinking. Life slows down a little and they need to be sensitive to the new way of living that is ahead of them, even though they cannot yet see it very clearly. They might, for example, consider going to live abroad in the sunshine for their remaining years. Additionally they may put into operation plans for their ultimate departure from earthly life, for the well-being of their children and grandchildren and so as to assist with the growth and unfoldment of those future lives …

Relationship of Faster and Slower Planets

Earlier we noted that two planets in a phase-relationship are expressed in terms of the slower-moving planet *first* (i.e. Sun/Moon, Saturn/Moon, Jupiter/Mercury etc.) To examine the relationship between the two more closely, imagine that an aeroplane taxis on to a runway in preparation for take-off on a long-haul flight. It is, and will remain, in contact with the control tower for instructions. The pilot will have to use his own initiative in many situations during the flight, but he will be dependent on the control tower for navigational data, weather forecasts, instructions on handling any engine troubles, cruising height, plus when and where to land... and so on.

As a metaphor this illustrates the constant dynamic between two planets as they move through the complete cycle of eight phases. The aeroplane is representative of the faster-moving planet (e.g. the Moon) while the control tower represents the slower planet (e.g. Sun). Although the faster planet has a great deal of freedom and independent movement, *it is always acting under the instructions of and subject to the slower planet*. As an example of this, we might use, as a third analogy, a situation in which there is a teacher (slower planet) and a pupil (faster planet) in a one-to-one relationship: perhaps an expert classical musician is training a young pupil as a concert pianist. We need to presuppose some existing ability on the part of the student to play a piano before work begins but, tracing the same essential themes of each phase of the cycle as before, this time we can also bear in mind the dynamic interplay between the two planets themselves:

New
The pupil is eager to get started. He has considerable enthusiasm for this new training and the teacher allows him a period of time just to get the feel of things and be free to experiment and 'play' in every sense of the term.

Crescent
The teacher decides it is time for the pupil to get down to some serious work and directs him from his own experience. The pupil may find this process a little irksome as the effort involved places some restriction on his own freedom of expression and the long hours of practice makes it all rather tedious. Tsk!

First Quarter
By now the pupil has considerable grounded ability under his belt and the teacher decides he is ready to give a public concert. The pupil may be eager to do so, but even if he feels reluctant the teacher pushes him into it since he judges that for this pupil to 'make it' as a concert pianist sooner or later he has to commit himself to the challenge of the outside world.

Gibbous
Having come through his public performance, the pupil is much more aware of the mistakes he has been making and is also more willing to listen and learn from the teacher. He goes back over and thoroughly digests what he

may only have skimped on before. He realizes at this stage how much there is to do to perfect his techniques in order to succeed.

Full

Here the teacher is less directive, much more inclined to leave the pupil standing on his own feet in order to develop a full realization of what his music means to him. The pupil feels thrown back on his own resources as the teacher adopts the technique of being onlooker, fully engaged but with no interference, as the pupil carries out more performances and collects due applause.

Disseminating

By now the pupil has developed a deep conviction of what he wants to do and is playing the piano fluently, expressing his own feelings. He finds himself sought out by many venues and gives as many concerts as he can; nevertheless his performance is still strongly influenced by the maestro-teacher.

Last Quarter

The pupil realizes fully that he must develop his own unique style rather than simply translating that of the teacher. The latter assists him, perhaps by pointing out how he is limiting himself by holding on, perhaps rigidly, to things he has been taught but which are no longer appropriate to the pianist he is truly endeavouring to be in his own right.

Balsamic

The teacher knows that, at this level, he has little or nothing more to teach his young charge. The pupil is reaching for new forms of expression that are more and more becoming uniquely his own, that he can take into developing his future career.

...At the next New Moon, the pianist might receive an invitation to perform internationally, perhaps with full orchestra, thus taking his career to a whole new level. And so another round of the phase-cycle commences...

* * *

We have assumed in these examples that all goes well, or reasonably well, at every stage of the cycle, but in human life terms of course it may not. Whether we are examining the cycle in terms of personal inner development or outer experiences, nothing in the astrological chart is a 'given'. There is nothing to say that a First Quarter phase person *will* rise to challenges or that a Disseminating person *will* be a good communicator and all we have to do is sit back and wait for it to unfold, for these are fundamental contextual threads required to be woven through the embodiment and consciousness of the person concerned in their developing life.

We also need to be aware that sometimes we live out our main phases very well, while at other times we may exhibit difficulties or go 'out of phase' altogether if intervening themes of the chart as a whole should impinge and we feel pulled this way and that. In these circumstances, understanding the phases can assist both astrologer and client working as a team to use them as a 'direction finder' – helping the client to get back on track with his or her intrinsic self. An example of this might be someone who is putting a lot of impatient emphasis on achieving celebrity as a desirable way of life (synonymous with Full Phase) – yet their natal Sun/Moon is Gibbous. When they can *come from* the essence of focused consideration, and developing know-how (Gibbous) and thus be more properly who they are, there is frequently a quieter acceptance, a composure... which *then* enables them more freely to access the path into the goal that is sought (fame etc). We can see something of this occurring in Emma's life in Part II under Crescent Phase (pp. 100-1). When people can take a little time to 'come home' to their essential selves when faced with a difficulty, it may not immediately provide them with the answers they were hoping to find, but it is often the case that they will report feeling much calmer and heading forward more readily than they otherwise would have done. It is a little like putting on a pair of shoes that actually fit, instead of hobbling around in those that may look appealing but are actually crippling your feet every step of the way.

A third possible interruption to the flow of the cycle is that difficulties can arise if the actual living out of a phase is weakened by other factors; for example initial emergence at New Phase may not be strong enough to survive the sustained effort necessary at Crescent stage. Crescent may not feel sufficiently committed to move through the challenge of First Quarter, and Full Phase may feel particularly vulnerable if it becomes apparent there is no purpose or meaning in what it is doing or being. In our earlier examples, the couple in love may not make it through the trials and tribulations of their Gibbous phase, our concert pianist might throw a distinct 'wobbly' at Full Phase when he finds himself seated at a grand piano in a packed Royal Albert Hall ... not to mention that any one of our swimming class might harbour repressed memories of near-drowning in childhood and find, when it comes to it, they can't follow through. Accompanying conventional chart factors will of course enable the astrologer to broaden the possibilities for interpretation, as will discussion with the subject of the chart.

Again, those from whom we have learned about growth in nature throughout the ages – from Hippocrates to Paracelsus to Goethe, on to Darwin, Rudolf Steiner, Luther Burbank, Peter Caddy (Findhorn), Sir David Attenborough and so many others – all have endlessly shown us that true understanding emerges not solely from being intellectually cloistered in ideas nor trying to apply fixed formulae, but through relationship, interaction, communion with the *living* plant, animal, tree ...

3: The Role of the Moon

When I was a child, my mother would quite often send me out on little shopping errands to get last-minute things she needed in the kitchen. Her purpose might have been to bake a cake or simply supper for that evening, but off this little dutiful Capricorn would trot and bring home the flour, eggs, butter or whatever it was, in order that the task could be completed. Inconsequential though this little scenario is, it serves as a metaphor for the first part of looking more closely at the Moon's role in the unfoldment of the phases. As a *mediator,* her essential role is to dispense the solar light to each planet in turn after birth as she travels quickly through the zodiac in a month, while the Sun travels but one of the signs in the same timespan. Yet at the same time, she also 'collects up', as it were, the essence of those planets in turn, through the individual's unfolding life experience, in order to bring them home to the Sun at their next (New Moon) meeting, just as I the child brought home what I had been charged to collect and laid the bag at my mother's feet.

In Chart A overleaf we can see that after birth the Moon will pick up in turn first Neptune, then the North Node, Mars, Jupiter, Saturn, Uranus, Chiron, Pluto, Mercury and finally Venus in order to complete the purpose of the Leo Sun. Quite a full 'bag of shopping', i.e. the several steps to be taken on this person's road forward to development. In Chart B, however, before returning to the Sun the Moon has only to collect up Mars/Node, Chiron, Saturn and Mercury as main factors to be incorporated into the individual's being.

These planets in sequence after birth will be experienced in the early months/years of life (with the Moon by progression travelling approximately 1° per month) but will also be recapitulated some 29½ to 30 years later when the progressed Moon returns to the same point. Depending on how long we live, we may go through three progressed cycles, each one calling forward similar themes albeit along differing spirals. One client reported an extremely early but very clear memory-experience of being a small baby lying in (what she took to be) a pram, on a warm summer's day, kicking with her little legs and arms. She can remember feeling the warmth of the Sun and indeed knowing 'Sun' as well as knowing she was a very small being. She could hear children playing around her, their laughter and squeals – she knew 'children', 'laughter', 'play'. Suddenly a bee buzzed around her face. *She knew to stop kicking and be still.* She heard one of the children say "Oh look there's a bee buzzing round the baby's head" – she knew these words, she knew what they meant. She knew to stay still some more. A woman came, wearing a black dress with a pinafore and carrying a cloth. She knew this was **not** her mother. The woman flicked the cloth at the bee and it flew away. She (the baby) knew she could continue kicking. (Later in life, in discussing this with her mother she was able to identify that she had been left in the care of a neighbour in the village – the woman with the pinafore – while her mother had to travel into town for the afternoon, the one and only time this occurred apparently). While she retains no other memory below the age of three, this stands out very markedly in her experience. In this person's chart, strikingly the Moon met with a Mercury-Pluto opposition at around seven months old. Here we have an accessing of a deeply penetrative soul intelligence, an unmistakeable knowing, albeit in an entity so tiny. She profoundly *knew* 'bee', buzzing, 'pinafore' 'cloth' and who her mother was *not!* Each time the Moon (or any major planet) has activated that opposition by progression, she has encountered experiences where serious decisions are required based on deep interior cognizance. On every occasion, she has found herself staying very still, listening deep inside, surrendering to inner promptings... and then unerringly *knows* what to do.

For the native of Chart A, at somewhere around two months old there would have been resonance to a Neptunian theme (Moon meets Neptune in 2°). As an even smaller baby than our previous example, and especially with the involvement of the Moon, this would undoubtedly have been absorbed through the neonatal bonding to mother. In this particular case the mother had to leave her home to evacuate into the countryside with her baby as this birth took place at the outbreak of World War II. Her husband had been called up to serve in the army and as a consequence she felt very lost, sad and isolated, all synonymous enough with Moon/Neptune 4th house. By progression, when the Moon first conjuncted this same point for the subject of the chart at the age of 27½ years she was married with two small children. Her husband entered into a catastrophic business deal which resulted in the bank foreclosing on their house, which they then had to vacate and live with relatives for a while until they could rebuild

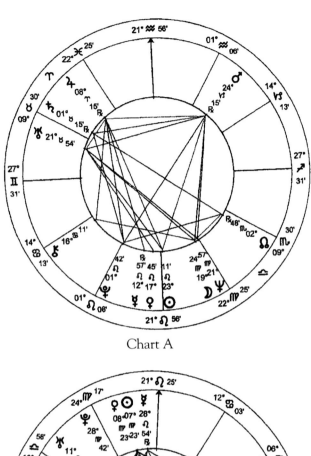

Chart A

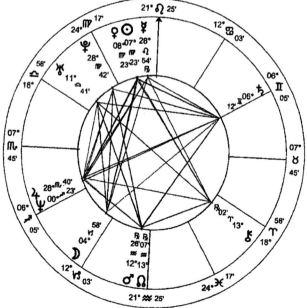

Chart B

their lives. Yet another reverberation of loss and readjustment in her sense of belonging/containment (4th house). In Chart B the Moon would meet Mars and the North Node in the 3rd house in 38° = approximately 3 years 2 months (nothing is known of this), then travel on to meet Chiron in 99° = c. 8yrs 3 months (again nothing is known) and thereafter Saturn in the 8th house in 152° or c.12 yrs 8 months. At 12½ years old the individual experienced the sudden death of his father.

It can clearly be useful to go back over what you can remember (or discover) from your early life and track the times when the Moon met each planet in sequence. The accompanying manifestation – whether on an outer or entirely inner level, and ranging all the way from relatively inconsequential to major turning points – will have underpinned and illuminated your continued unfolding psychospiritual development as only you ultimately can experience and describe it. Of course, it may be a little more complicated than I have hitherto depicted since when the Moon meets up with any planet it is also triggering the whole structure of connectedness with other planets (for example by aspect patterns as well as moving through different phases in relation to the Sun). In practice an astrologer would open up the planetary issues as a whole in order to trace understandings – and lend clarity to the meaningful threads woven in our lives.

Planets Before and After Moon

On one of my childhood shopping expeditions I was asked to get bread, cabbage and eggs. Just as I got to the front gate, my mother called out to me from the doorway *"Whatever you do, **don't come home without the eggs!!!"*** **EGGS** became emblazoned in the forefront of my mind as if written by a fiery sword. My entire survival rested upon their acquisition; after all if I failed I would have no home to return to, I'd be an outcast, abandoned, orphaned… aaargh! Once more bypassing the story itself, the point of it is again analogous to the Moon's role in that *the first planet to be met by the Moon **after** birth constitutes a major direction or quality for development in your life*. It is a first priority; it is the "don't-come-home-without-it" planet! If you were born in or near New Phase, it is quite likely this will be Mercury or Venus since they are never far from the Sun (and the Moon is conjunct or has only recently pulled away from the Sun). Otherwise this first meeting by the Moon can be with any of the inner or outer planets. If it is Venus, then developing a sense of inner worth, clear evaluation, pleasure or love will always be important in the forefront of your life; if Mars, then activating drive and energy will be uppermost, Saturn may point you to a specific road of conformity, hardiness, duty or limitations to be met, while Uranus will lead you through paths of innovation, independence, or to somehow stand out. (People with Moon first meeting Uranus often feel compelled to be or do something notable in the eyes of their society for instance). Whatever the situation, this is the planet that most forms the crux of your individuality and unfolding destiny; it must be prioritized as undeniably necessary for you to understand within yourself, develop as best you can and finally 'bring home' from your sojourn in this incarnation.

The last planet to be touched by the Moon **prior** *to birth marks a quality which you can most fall back on.* Having only just left this planet before your entry into the world, it is the one the Moon most 'recalls', as it were, as she begins her journey through your life. It is already inherent within you, whether you conceive of this as being by heredity, prenatally-absorbed experience or reincarnational residue, and you will seek to recapitulate it. In Chart B, that of the child whose father died, we can see that the Moon last touched the Jupiter/Neptune conjunction prior to birth. Therefore qualities of inspiration, encompassing a wider realm beyond the individual self, or meeting with illusion, delusion, idealism, mystery or discrepancy – any or all of these may form a predisposition to which this individual would readily reverberate. This conjunction was to be triggered by the Moon's meeting with Saturn at the age of 12½ as it partakes of a more detailed T-square structure involving Saturn and the Sun. His father was a noted professional in an exceedingly high-powered field and the death occurred not only as an undeniable blow but also in mysterious circumstances, giving rise to much speculation (Jupiter/Neptune) amid the grief.

In the chart of Sir Winston Churchill, we can see that the last planet touched by the Moon prior to birth was Uranus (the capacity to stand out, make a difference, be notable). The first planet to be met ('don't come home without it') is, unsurprisingly, the god of war (in the first house moreover – the war leader). The first meeting of Moon and Mars would have been early in his life (around 4 years 9 months = 57° apart), then by progression some 29½ years later at around age 34 and again 29½ years later still at around age 63-64. Given that Mars is the ruler of the 7th house (relationships/alliances), it is apposite that at 34 he became a cabinet minister under

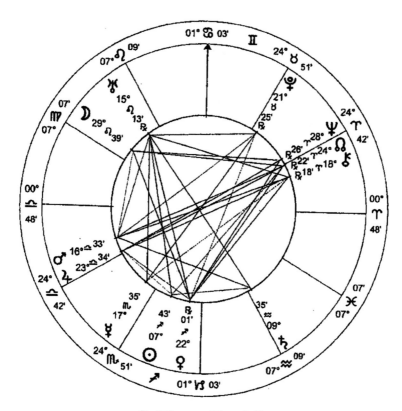

Sir Winston Churchill

Asquith and also married his wife Clementine. At 63/64 he was in the run up to the outbreak of the second World War but also dealing with the drama of another alliance, i.e. that of the King who abdicated in favour of marrying Wallis Simpson. So, tapestry threads of negotiating, relating, balancing, fighting to appease and bring peace (Libra) and seeking beneficial outcome (conjunct Jupiter) can be traced in the cyclic sweep of this Moon in service of an explorative (Sagittarius) Sun, handling many things at the same time (3rd house) and whose ruler conjuncts Mars as the priority planet to be developed and brought back home.

Planetary Containments Within Sun and Moon

Probably for most of us shopping in today's world is a matter of driving to a supermarket, filling up a trolley, loading it into the car and off home. We might even have made a list of things we need and tick them off as we go. So 'eggs, flour, sugar, butter etc' when translated analogously to the birth chart become whatever planets our natal Moon meets in turn after birth, as we have seen. But perhaps like me you have gone round the supermarket with such a list and just as you are reaching for the flour from the shelf you realize that you have plenty of it in your kitchen cupboards already – ah yes, now you remember, you bought some from that nice farm shop just last week. And maybe you even recall that you also bought a dozen eggs from the same place... so they too can be deleted from the list. *These are things you already have in store.* Synonymously this applies to planets which appear sandwiched between the positions of the Sun and Moon since they were last conjunct. They represent qualities you already have 'on board' within you and can draw upon (especially the last one, as we also saw earlier). Planets positioned *after* the Moon, between it and the Sun to which it is returning, represent qualities yet to be developed, especially the first one as we have also seen; it is the incarnational intention of the individual to bring those planets to life. So, in Chart (1) below the waxing Moon in New Phase has already 'gathered in' the essence of Mercury, Venus and Uranus but is yet to develop Pluto (as first planet), Saturn, Neptune, Chiron, Jupiter, Node and finally Mars. In Chart (2) the waning Moon in Full Phase has already

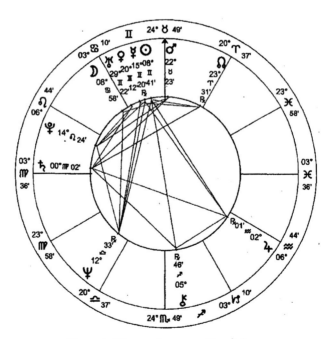

Chart 1: Planets between Sun/Moon

'on board' (since last meeting the Sun) Chiron, Jupiter, Mercury, Mars and Venus; yet to be collected up are North Node, Uranus, Saturn, Pluto and finally Neptune.

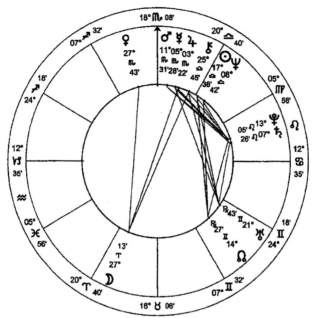

Chart 2: Planets between Sun/Moon

Planetary energies already 'on board' within us are all soul-memories, as it were, again whether absorbed during our gestation period or from a wider series of incarnations and/or ancestral-hereditary links. Since it can be deeply revelatory to touch into such meanings in our lives, the intriguing work of three writers in particular comes to mind as valuable aids to understanding; one is Judy Hall who examines the birth chart in terms of past lives and reincarnational themes in *Karmic Astrology*;[1] the second is Tad Mann (A.T. Mann) who traces the period from conception to birth, then on into childhood, maturity and old age in *Life*Time Astrology*[2] from a timescale perspective also outlined in the earlier work of the third person, Rodney Collin, a pupil of P.D. Ouspensky, in *The Theory of Celestial Influence*[3]. Given that this perspective gives weight to the 9th house cusp as conception point (and reverting to this in Churchill's chart) it is heralded by the position of Pluto in dynamic T-square aspect to Mercury and Uranus and we are at once in touch with his capacity for powerful oratory as being already 'on board' at his birth and ready (crucial even) to be brought over into life.

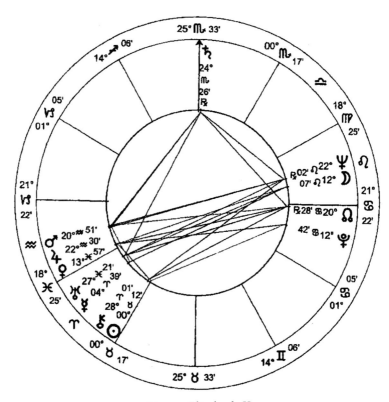

Queen Elizabeth II

In the Queen's chart, we see that since last connecting with the Sun the Moon has already collected up Pluto in the 6th house. The capacity for a hard working and demanding life of service would seem to be a powerful karmic thread she was predisposed at birth to step into and rely upon. It is not an 'ingredient' she has to 'go out and get'. The first planet to be met after birth is the impressive Neptune in Leo, standing in opposition (full illumination) to a rising Mars/Jupiter conjunction in the 1st house (again leadership) and flowing by T-square into the focal solidity of Saturn at the MC which (unsurprisingly in the Queen's case) we associate with duty, conformity, serious determination/dedication and reserve – also reflective of the 6th house Pluto.

Less famous examples include one person whose Moon formed an exact trine to Mars some 2° (2 months) prior to birth. At that time his mother experienced tremendous weariness, over and above the normal tiredness at this advanced stage of pregnancy. On attending for a medical check-up it was found she had quite a serious *iron* (Mars) deficiency and needed a booster injection. We may surmise that this was an experience of the baby also receiving much needed energy to help him through. As an adult, discussing his relationship to his mother he described her as "a great source of strength, I always feel stronger after talking things over with her". Another client was conceived by parents who had been living together but did not particularly want to bother with the formality of marriage. The Moon opposed a Sun/ Venus conjunction approximately five months prior to his birth at which point suddenly the parents, joyously awaiting the arrival of this child and wanting to give it all the love and stability they possibly could, changed their minds and married amid much support and congratulation from their wider families. Joy and wellbeing were thus absorbed by the gestating entity leading to an incarnation where feeling secure in the certainty of being loved and cherished is his happy destiny.

Taking note of planets before and after Moon may often additionally help us to hone in with far more precision on the meanings of chart patterns which might otherwise remain concealed to our understanding. For example, if you were to ask the average astrologer to comment on a chart with Libra rising, the Sun in the other Venusian sign of Taurus and a Moon-Jupiter conjunction, they would probably come up with something off the top of the head which all sounds quite pleasant and benevolent. If you were to add that the person was born in Sun/Moon Disseminating phase they might even add that there would be important communication skills to be lived out. What then do we make of the chart of Adolf Hitler (shown overleaf) – someone to whom we hardly ascribe the words 'pleasant' and 'benevolent', although he was of course very commanding and 'successful' as a communicator, the judgment of Libra rising admitting of no variance within, or evolvement from, his own fixed viewpoint (Venus Taurus 8th square Saturn Leo 10th).

Consider, however, that at the moment Hitler was born the Moon had already collected up Mars, Venus, Neptune, Pluto, Chiron, North Node, Saturn, and (like Churchill) finally Uranus, thus bringing in a prior experience of these planetary energies. If we did not know whose chart this is, we might raise a little questioning about the Neptune/Pluto conjunction – a generational factor of course, but its 8th house position and the fact that it is aspecting the commanding 3rd house Moon/Jupiter might well have us questioning its potential for inflationary ruthlessness in communicating and decision-making, as well as the establishment of self-worth and importance

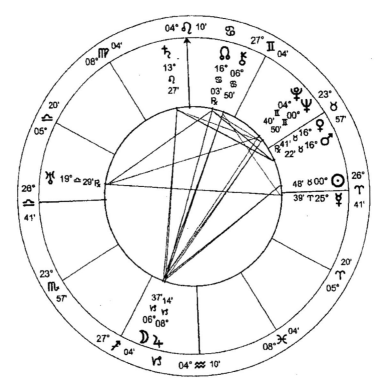

Adolf Hitler

(rulers of 2nd and 5th). We might also give clarity to possible prior issues of pain/wounding concerning zealous beliefs, philosophies, causes to espouse, being brought into the present incarnation (Chiron 9th) and wonder about all of these factors in the light of needs for supremacy and control of a 10th house Saturn (ruler of Moon/Jupiter 3rd). All in all we would zero in more noticeably on the sheer dominant power and demand of that 3rd house Jupiter to be fulfilled since, of course, it lay immediately before him for this incarnation (first planet out from the Moon and moreover ruler of the 3rd house). Hitler certainly did not 'return home without it'! Post-birth, only Mercury remains to be brought back home to the Sun; it is ruler of the 11th house (the society around) and 9th house (establishing a place in that society through formulation and pronouncements of own philosophies). In focal opposition to the easy-to-fall-back-on Uranus, Mercury may again point to brilliance in communicative performance for revolutionary purposes but so too does it engender the potential for disorder, disarray, utter fragmentation … of a home, or homeland (Uranus ruler of 4th).

The New Moon Before Birth

Astrology is a study of cycles which are repetitive in their structure but their underlying contexts differ as each builds on the previous one, tracing a spiral of shifting meaning with each commencement occurring at a different point. A New Moon in Gemini one month will be followed by a New Moon in Cancer the next and a New Moon in Leo the next... and so on. As she travels through the phases we have seen that the Moon seeks to fulfil her mission of bringing to life the purpose of the Sun through the embodiment of the incarnating individual. It follows that the potential of this whole cycle, begun at New Moon, is one we need to identify beyond simply knowing which particular phase of it we were born under. It is a gateway through which each of us is born as an expression of the universal whole and required to take our part within the emerging eight-fold story. Imagine that you have joined a ballet troupe and are allotted a certain role in a performance. It could be the *waltz* part perhaps, or a more vibrant *mazurka*, a mellifluous *prelude* or a triumphant *finale*. Whether or not you are a principal dancer or one of the chorus, essentially you are not separate from the whole ballet but a necessary exponent of its entirety (which might go by the name of *Swan Lake, Coppelia, Les Sylphides...*). Similarly, you may be born in Crescent, Gibbous, Last Quarter or any phase, yet you are a vital component of the whole unfolding purpose started at the New Moon which preceded your birth.

Calculating the chart for this New Moon Before Birth will enable you to touch into its meaning. Since it occurred before you actually came into the world (unless you were born exactly *on* it) Rudhyar advocates setting the chart on an equal house basis and placing the Sun/Moon conjunction on the cusp of the first house.[4] It is the sign in which the New Moon occurred and its main aspect patterns with which we are concerned, as indicators of what is coming into being and into which you would ultimately step and take your place. However it is also important to note that *if that New Moon falls on or very near to a planet in your eventual birth chart, then that natal planet will provide a key channel for you to develop the main purpose and direction for your life* – coming out from the past yet rooted in the new potential that you embody. In the case of the young boy (Chart B earlier) whose eminent father died (possibly through foul play), the New Moon before birth fell on the 28th degree of Leo. In the eventual birth chart some eleven days later this point was to be occupied by Mercury, ruler of the 8th house

Saturn and also conjoined to the T-square between Saturn/Jupiter/Neptune (triggered at his father's death). Moreover the Jupiter/Neptune conjunction in the New Moon Before Birth chart sat exactly on the 4th house cusp (often signifying the father, also end of life) with Saturn occupying the 10th (parental axis). As an adult presenting for consultation this person, voicing his avowed intent to get to the bottom of how and why his father died, described his memories of him as "a somewhat fascinating man, cloistered in an alluring world of academia and professional work which was all a bit of a blur to me, so from that point of view something of a remote figure ..." This is synonymous enough with Jupiter/Neptune and Sun/Saturn yet, in view of the Jupiter/Neptune as the last planets having been collected up by the Moon at birth and also made focal through the New Moon before birth, these would seem to be key incarnational themes the soul needed to experience in its evolutionary impulse through this life.

The Sabian Symbols

A further way of giving added meaning to lunar and other planetary positions in their cycles is to explore symbolic degree meanings. In the annals of astrological history there have been several such collections by which insight may be derived to give the seeker after meaning some substantiation of their experience. By whatever means such degree symbols are obtained, they can be tested out when exploring particular points of reference in the Lunation Cycle. The Sabian set were clairvoyantly obtained in 1925 by Elsie Wheeler working in tandem with the astrologer Marc Edmund Jones who later brought them into published form[5]. Their meeting for this purpose in San Diego has been chronicled by Dane Rudhyar in *An Astrological Mandala*[6] together with a reformulation of the symbols for each degree of the zodiac. More recently, Lynda Hill has brought the symbols up-to-date in her eminently readable work, *360 Degrees of Wisdom*.[7]

There can be considerable ambiguity with many of these degree meanings, as both Jones and Rudhyar conceded, although Rudhyar went on to propose that greater clarity could be found by looking at them not in isolation but as part of a series of sequential degrees through the cyclic process. We may easily miss the truer significance of something if we concentrate upon one factor alone, but when viewed from a wider context we get the bigger picture. Of great importance in my view is that we should not endeavour to grasp symbolic images too literally and apply them wholesale as glib interpretations upon an astrological client. Far better to allow space for the person to absorb them spontaneously in their own context of time. When we refrain from *imposing* a meaning on someone, we leave them free to find their own. Perhaps it is as an expression of this that Lynda Hill ends each of her commentaries with the wise query 'What does this SYMBOL say to *you?*'

If the commentary on a degree symbol seems a little tenuous to you, then taking into account additional keynotes of the preceding and following degrees can lead to expanded realizations. The symbol for the opposing degree and sign can also be considered and even those for the emanating 90° points to provide a fuller framework. Additionally the degrees accentuating each of the phases, particularly the New Moon before birth but also the unfoldments of these cycles by progression, can reveal an illuminating quality or purpose pervading the life. I recall a time when I was experiencing a great deal of stress, wondering how on earth I was going to find the stamina to get through. I had a dream of a very elderly, frail man walking towards me, holding something out in his hand and announcing that he was my great-grandfather. On awakening I realized that I had not given a great deal of active thought and attention to this my ancestor although I knew he was a Victoria Cross winner and had also been awarded a Distinguished Cross Medal, all in the same week. He died 30 years before I was born so my knowledge of him was both family-anecdotal and sparse. Yet I also knew that in the dream what he was holding out to me were his two medals. I immediately cleared my desk and began trawling though all the various cycles, progressions, phases etc. of my own chart, until I realized that there had been a long series of planetary activity focused upon the 23rd degree of Capricorn. So I went to the Sabian Symbols. And nearly fell off the chair when I read "A soldier receiving two awards for bravery in combat..."! So ambiguity though there may be on the one hand, on other occasions the meanings of the Sabian cycle can be arresting in their acuity, evoking startling recognition and giving rise to much-needed encouragement for a person to get to work with an unfolding inner process.

In the Queen's chart, we noted the positions of both Pluto (12° 42' Cancer) and Saturn (24° 26' Scorpio). Rounding these up to the next full degree, we find commentaries as follows:

13 Cancer – *A hand slightly flexed with a prominent thumb*
This speaks of the thumb as symbolic of the will and that individuality

expresses itself through strength of character. This therefore implies meeting life with steady determination.

25 Scorpio – *An X-ray photograph*

The symbol speaks of insight and responsibility in structural, functioning frameworks.

It seems unquestionable that determination and steadiness of bearing are hallmarks of the Queen's presentation of herself to her world, together with her duty in submitting to and maintaining the ongoing structure and system of the British monarchy.

In Churchill's chart, we find Uranus, last planet met by the Moon, on 16 Leo and the first planet (Mars) on 17 Libra. Additionally, Pluto on 22 Taurus sits commandingly at the conception point (9th house cusp) as we saw earlier:

16 Leo – *The storm ended, all nature rejoices in brilliant sunshine*
17 Libra – *A retired Sea Captain watches ships entering and leaving the harbour*

Given the scenes of jubilation on the streets of Britain in 1945, any further comment on 16 Leo would be superfluous. As to 17 Libra, having completed his mission as war leader Churchill did not immediately return to power but seemed to step back 'to take a calm and objective view' (the keynote for this symbol). And indeed, in his chart, after meeting Mars as first planet, the Moon next comes to Jupiter (opposite Neptune) – a more expansive and philosophical outlook of stillness and contemplation for what had been victoriously struggled and fought for.

Finally – and I promise you *mes enfants* I am really not making this up:
22 Taurus – *White dove flying over troubled waters*

Says it all. But, for completeness, the commentary speaks of inspiration arising in the individual in overcoming crisis. Considering that the conception point hoisted the potent Pluto opposite Mercury and squaring Uranus, it was of course through the sheer power of his oratory and insight that Churchill inspired a nation to fight on the beaches, never surrender and to reach for its finest hour.

4: Aspects Within the Phases

Aspects are a main feature of working with the Lunation Cycle because they mark a *high point of energy within each phase*. They point to an important factor to be developed, or a step to be taken by the individual in order to bring the phase to fulfilment. Additionally, like the cycle itself, they reflect a *relationship*. Rael and Rudhyar state "Some life task or function that cannot be performed by either planet's function alone must be developed by both together"[1] This highlights the two planets working as a team and takes us back to our analogy of the aeroplane and Control Tower (pp 29-30). There we saw that although the lines of communication between them are open all the time (the phase) there are specific moments when the tower will radio the pilot and vice versa. These 'moments' are analogous to the aspects and the *type* of aspect shows the nature of the task to be undertaken. The teamwork between the planets and the step itself are in service not only of the background phase but the entire cycle from creation-to-maintenance-to-dissolution... or in our present analogy, from inception to duration to completion/landing of a long haul flight.

Usually when astrologers consider aspects, it is only the angular distance between planets that is noted together with whether we ascribe notions of ease or difficulty to the aspect derived. However, by far the most crucial element to understand is that, since we are dealing with a cyclic process from 0° to 180° and back down to 0° again, *an aspect occurring in the waxing hemisphere (where energy is built up) will have a totally different function and meaning to the same aspect occurring in the waning hemisphere (where energy is released)*. It is to be lamented that this understanding has been bypassed by all but a few of the world's leading astrologers over the years who, to echo the late Charles Harvey's words, "continue blind-eyed"[2] to treat a sextile or square in one hemisphere as being the same thing as a sextile or square in the other.

A further point to bear in mind is that an aspect cannot be considered as an entity in itself. The entire cyclical nature of life which astrology traces so expressively is apt to be lost by approaching it as a single factor since, in the process, we lose sight of its purpose within the whole. I remember Howard Sasportas often saying "there's no such thing as a straight line in the universe" which we can perhaps use as a reminder that each aspect must be understood as being part of a thread of continuity, interconnected within the ever-spiralling cycle. As such it is a natural outworking of the aspect which precedes it as well as a natural prelude to the one that follows. Bil Tierney sums it up eloquently in his excellent book on aspects when he writes "...like signs and houses, aspects can be seen as defining meaningful phases of relationship following an orderly sequence within a more encompassing cyclic experience".[3]

As to *types* of aspects, astrologers throughout the ages have largely considered them as good, bad or perhaps indifferent – older terms such as 'malefic' or 'benefic' having been supplanted in more modern times by 'favourable', 'unfavourable', 'major/minor' or 'hard/soft' etc. Again if we think of the two planets as working together then, as in any partnership, there can be moments of confrontation or tension as well as moments of harmony and clarity. The control tower may become exasperated with the pilot if he does not adjust his altitude when called upon to do so; the pilot may feel irritated with the control tower if diverted to an unexpected runway for landing. Yet if we would allow ourselves to refrain from immediately assigning some kind of 'credit-rating' to aspects, it is possible to see their vital role within the entire cycle whatever mental concepts and emotions we may harbour about them and whatever their manifested outcome.

One of the greatest truths in astrology was stated by Charles Carter in his book on Aspects where he pointed us to "That which is unitary above becomes many below; the trend of manifestation is always toward increased diversity...".[4] In other words, there are innumerable ways in which we may bring an aspect to life, but in working with the phases it is the underlying context of meaning standing behind the aspect's function with which we are concerned. From this perspective, even those habitually regarded (even condemned) as 'bad', 'difficult' or 'negative' may, in the countenance of them, yield a purpose which is wholly beneficial, even miraculous. Consider the caterpillar who submits to a dark descent into chrysalis, doorway to transformation as 'butterfly'; or the oyster who must periodically undergo the intense irritation of sand in its shell yet which gives rise to a new form in creation. It is human nature to want to run away from negativities yet going through such gateways awakens us to new realizations about ourselves we may not have experienced by any other route.

Although differences exist between astrologers as to precisely which aspects they use in practice, most agree on the fundamental twelve-fold division of the 360° circle which produces the series of aspects interspaced at 30° each. Starting from 0°, this yields the conjunction, semi-sextile, sextile, square, trine, quincunx and opposition. The eightfold division into phases generates the 45° semi-square and 135° sesquiquadrate, while the quintile series (72° quintile and 144° biquintile) are increasingly advocated for inclusion by today's astrologers. In leaving out other aspects which many find of value (e.g. septiles, noviles etc.) this does not imply that I consider them of less consequence; simply that I do not have sufficient long-term experience of them from actual client work to present a comprehensive or authoritative view. Additionally, to include too many aspects into the eight-fold phase cycle would be cumbersome. However, any aspects can of course be considered against the background of the respective phases in which they arise.

Unaspected Planets

The prevailing view leans toward regarding an unaspected planet as representative of something in us that is unintegrated or constitutes some kind of 'lack' since it is not related to anything else in the chart. However, from the perspective of the Lunation Cycle, no planet is out on a limb since it is automatically in relationship with any other planet by dint of the fact that it stands within the ever-connected web of phase-relationship.

The absence of an aspect may point us to there being no specific significant step to be taken by a particular planet *in tandem with another planet*. It is akin to being in a marriage where one person may do things as an individual without their partner necessarily being equally involved in the task, yet the overall relationship of their marriage remains. Being unaspected does not mean that there is no significant task to be undertaken *at all* by the planet – there is, and it is a task it must do alone and resolutely. But this does not necessarily constitute a negativity or debilitation. I am rather more inclined to the view that if there are no conventional (or lesser-known) aspects, then perhaps it is because they are not needed. The purpose underlying such a planet is to be fulfilled through a *concentrated* existence, unperturbed by extraneous factors which might deflect it from its task. While it is not part of its remit to partner-up with another planet to perform a significant function, it does fulfil its mission by standing in its own stead, *enabled* (rather than disabled) by its very singularity.

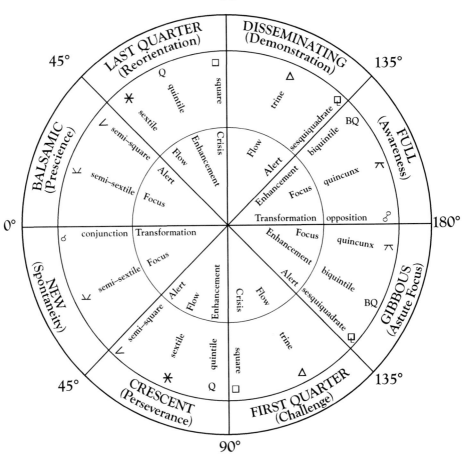

The Cycle of Phases – The Cycle of Aspects

Eleven Aspects – Six Categories

The diagram above shows the eight phases of the Lunation Cycle with the main 11 aspects I have put forward superimposed within. From this it can be seen that each phase contains two or three aspects totalling 20 such steps in the cycle as a whole. To these I have added my own reconceptualized understanding of their function (i.e. 'alert' points or 'flow' points etc), each of which we shall then trace in terms of their inner purpose.

Becoming accustomed to identifying the aspects in this way enables us to see them more clearly as an overall cyclic process *as well as* being high points of energy in each phase. We may look upon them as potential qualities reflected in our charts and bestowed upon us at birth, but we might also consider the word 'potential', i.e. **capable** of being brought into existence. They are *required* of us: it is we who must develop and live them.

I have arranged the overall total of 20 aspects into 6 categories of purpose (Transformation, Crisis, Focus, Alert, Flow and Enhancement) and they are distributed throughout the eight phases, as follows:

HIGH POINTS OF:	ASPECT(S)	APPEARANCE WITHIN PHASES
Transformation	Conjunction & Opposition	At the start of New and Full, thus also marking the division between the Waxing and Waning hemispheres
Crisis	Squares	First and Last Quarter Gateways, marking the Quadrant divisions of the Cycle
Focus	Semi-sextiles & Quincunxes	New and Balsamic Phases (the semi-sextile) Gibbous and Full Phases (the quincunx) Each appears on either side of a Transformation point
Alert	Semi-squares & Sesquiquadrates	Gateways to Crescent and Balsamic Phases (the semi-Square) and to Gibbous and Disseminating Phases (the Sesquiquadrate)
Flow	Sextiles & Trines	Within the Crescent and Last Quarter Phases (sextiles), either following or preceding an Alert Point; trines appear within First Quarter and Disseminating where they follow or precede Crisis Turning Point
Enhancement	Quintiles & Biquintiles	Crescent and Last Quarter (quintiles) occurring just before or just after a Crisis Point; Gibbous and Full Phases (biquintiles) occurring just after or just before Alert Point.

Voyage Through the Aspects

While the various manifestations of aspects will be more specifically seen in the actual lives of people in Part II, for the moment we can trace the fundamental significance of each, noting both their essential hemispheric differences as well as viewing them sequentially around the cycle.

The Conjunction (Orb allowance 8°)
Point of Transformation/Regeneration

A conjunction is not, strictly speaking, an aspect since the two planets are not glancing at one another as if across a room, but *are* together in alignment, as in an embrace. Consider that you are walking through an airport lounge and you see two people locked in a great big hug. Now, is this a Departures Lounge where one of them is about to leave on a journey and their hug is a farewell-till-we-meet-again? Or is it an Arrivals Lounge, where one has just come off a flight and the shared hug is a delightful "Hello! I'm home! Good to See You Again!" The first would be a *separating* (New Phase) conjunction – the Moon is about to take her leave of the Sun and journey around the chart. The second is the *applying* conjunction of the Balsamic Phase where the Moon has completed her circuit and is returning to the Sun. Two totally different connotations for the conjunction, reflecting the two different phase contexts within which they occur as well as the transition point between the background hemispheres of Waxing and Waning.

A conjunction marks a point of *transformation* either via a completion (Balsamic) or an initiation (New). It is a powerful resonating-energy arising deep inside, requiring us to relinquish something of the self and its experiences (Balsamic) or submit to new beginnings through a sense of automatic commitment (New). In terms of sequential unfoldment, the Balsamic conjunction is given to assimilating its resources before relinquishing them in the service of a new impending purpose ahead, while the New Phase conjunction is intensely charged with that new purpose which must now be embarked upon. Both conjunctions are self-contained, occurring as they do in the 'dark Moon' part of the cycle and both are given to operating instinctively at this 0° point of regeneration as one pathway ends and another begins... just as the seed starts new growth following its relinquishment by the old dying plant.

At the waxing New Phase conjunction the planets are in relationship for the purpose of beginning something and there is an inner allegiance to instinctively following through. The significant steps taken or inner drives to be developed are those of spontaneity and unpremeditated expression. This may sometimes contain an element of confusion or idealism since there is not yet an ability to distinguish the self from that within which it is contained as simple Being. Yet the thrust is ever onward. This an aspect of *Instinctive Initiative and Impetus.*

The waning Balsamic conjunction marks a doorway on to something-to-be-born, forged from the total energies of the cycle it has come through. These will now serve the future, the planets being together as a vehicle to carry this out. Steps taken are those of submission or surrender, denoting a pull toward inner vision, leading to a potency for onward manifestation. The capacity for stimulation and transmission of one's inner gifts exists but failure to yield 'seeds for the future' may arise as apathy or escapism. It is an aspect of *Creative Vision and Renewal.*

The Semi-Sextile – 30° (Orb allowance 2°)
Point of Focus

As with the conjunction the semi-sextile only occurs in New or Balsamic Phases, its meaning thus emanating from those contexts. It is a point of *focus* that requires us to notice at a deep, but soft 'felt-sense' level, something which we may either find a little disturbing or a little intriguing. Like a gentle herald whispering in our ear that 'something's up', it is apt that it occurs in the dark lunar phases where outer activity is diminished for this means there is space for us to be inwardly attuned. Consequently our consciousness is raised (perhaps only momentarily) above the ordinary and everyday, for here we must balance action with moments of stillness in order that the 'something which is up' can capture our attention.

The fact that this aspect falls sequentially either just before or just after the conjunction point (transformation and regeneration) serves to notify us that whatever the 'something' is, it matters very much; hence the requirement truly to focus upon it and suspend peripheral considerations for a while. If we miss it (or dismiss it) at first, it tends to filter up into our awareness in some other way. As a prelude to an ending (Balsamic) or as signatory to a beginning (New) it carries a quality of intermittent little promptings some of which you grasp instantly, others come and go until they emerge as more of an open realization.

The waxing New Phase semi-sextile denotes that whatever was begun (at the conjunction) is now burgeoning into preliminary growth. It accentuates a *Perception of Growing Possibilities.* For the seed in the ground, it is the 'warmth that swells the grain', plumping up and heralding the fact that it's on its way to becoming the plant. In a chart it will show realizations and abilities starting to be stimulated within us, a dawning sense of potential qualities and skills for overcoming the past to follow a new path. The planets involved need to be gently cultivated for the significance of this aspect is one of gradual emergence. If the prompting is missed or if vulnerability is high, its potential may manifest only at the level of half-baked attempts.

The waning Balsamic semi-sextile carries awareness that soon there will be no light in the night sky as the last remnants of silver crescent disappear. The Moon is travelling once more to unite in hidden mystery with the Sun. As opposed to the waxing semi-sextile which denoted a burgeoning, here there is diminishment and surrender. As the plant submits to the inevitability of its last seeds being yielded, by the same token the seeds have to release the plant – take their leave of the very host that has brought them to this place and must soon die, as they will live on. It is an aspect of *Yielding to What Is To Be*. In a chart it can denote a prompting to give of our abilities as a pathfinder for the good of the whole and to assist in the new formation of energy. If resisted, we may balk at the loss of an old pattern and display resentment or a refusal to abrogate self-will.

The Semi-Square – 45° (Orb allowance 6°)
Alert Point

Both semi-squares in the cycle occur at gateways to a phase: the waxing semi-square at the doorway to Crescent and the waning semi-square at Balsamic. Both I have termed 'alert points' since again we are required to notice something (as with the semi-sextile), but here it is more than mere soft focus which is brought to bear. The power of the gateway means we are veritably jolted into recognition of an important step to be taken at these portals. We must wake up and pay attention to what needs to be done. It may have real nuisance value, an irritating or arduous quality – we frequently do *not* want to do it and may feel sulky and resentful that we are even required to. Strangely, however, once the encounter is made, there is a growing inner determination to continue with what lies before us and see it through. The main difference between the hemispheres is that planets in the waxing semi-square must put decided energy into pushing forward to meet a pathway, whereas those in the waning aspect have to be alert to the need to step back.

As the gateway to Crescent Phase, **the waxing semi-square** denotes effort and perseverance seriously required so that what was established (at the conjunction), then focused upon with a realization that it is growing (semi-sextile) must now start to be definitively *anchored*. It marks an *Encounter with Reality*. The planets must function with persistence through toil, trial and error, as in the seed's task of establishing first roots. Staunch potential for endurance grounds the planetary energies into a significant tenacity. If there is insufficient stamina to overcome the past, the 'alert' may be met with hesitation and resistance in a bid to hold on to what is known. If refuted altogether, there can be entrenched inertia, thus depletion of the planetary energies.

At the waning semi-square the alert goes out signalling that all that has been established in the past must soon be released (gateway to Balsamic). The planets involved serve to open us, perhaps abruptly or even sorrowfully, to what we need to let go rather than stay identified with. The fully grown plant has been harvested and from here will be taken on to the natural completion of its life cycle. In a chart, the planets need to function through *Diminishment of Outward Impact*. Their relationship is one of refraining from direct action, instead being impelled to release their energies to help mark out a future pathway. There is often a sense of inner dedication to whatever this is and less seeking to have personal influence upon the environment. There can be irritability if we make continued attempts to steamroller our way through, for life really requires that we relent a little, operate from attunement to being part of a whole and use the planetary energies to offer experience, knowledge and wisdom to be dispensed onward.

The Sextile – 60° (Orb allowance 6°)
Flow Point

This aspect carries a certain fluidity. Occurring as a high point of energy within the background context of either Crescent or Last Quarter phases, it either follows or precedes the Alert Point of a semi-square – so there is either an ability to structure (waxing) or de-structure (waning) one's life to allow matters to flow forwards. We either reach out more easily into the environment after the struggle of the Crescent semi-square or, having turned to a new pathway (Last Quarter) we divest ourselves of extraneous material – issues and activities once vital to us – and reorient ourselves to a reorganization of abilities.

At the waxing sextile, having sequentially moved from a new beginning (conjunction), first awareness of it at semi-sextile and then the eyes-wide-open experience of having to work at and anchor it at the semi-square, the sextile which follows denotes *Reaching Out and Interaction.* Like first tendrils drawing sustenance from the soil, this aspect is a high point of energy accentuating the need for merging and interchange. The significant task of the planets is to build connections, develop versatility, mental agility, communication and discovery. If the ease of flow is too much relied upon (or raced after), the effortful purpose of the background phase can be lost and the result can be superficiality or a scattering, rather than directing, of one's energies and skills.

At the waning sextile in Last Quarter where the emphasis is reorientation, the flow of the sextile assists the redirection to meet a new path forward. In the cycle of aspects, this sextile has received the enhancement of mature creativity (the prior quintile) and looks to the impending alert point of the Balsamic semi-square. The planets' task here is to effect a rearrangement of outlooks, ideas, visions and strategies for future development, in particular those borne out of experience. It is a high point accentuating *Reorganization and Clearance,* just as harvest time is a culminating point of productivity yet also involves a sweeping-up of debris from the old cycle. If the potential is not recognized, there can be an element of giving up on things or not wishing to be bothered.

The Quintile – 72° (Orb allowance 2°)
Point of Enhancement

Derived from the division of the 360° circle by 5, this aspect (together with the biquintile at 144°) has become rather more focal in recent times, perhaps largely through its basis of the 5th harmonic and the work (notably) of John Addey[5] and David Hamblin[6]. From these and other insights together with my own experience of witnessing them in people's lives, they seem to operate initially at a level beyond (or above) the ordinary consciousness of the mind-identified self. Frequently there is an inspiration or creative impetus to do, be, strive for something, or alter direction whether or not it goes against some grain. For this reason, I have placed them within the phase-cycle as *Points of Enhancement or Enhanced Development.*

Quite *what* is enhanced will be dependent on the phase position of the aspect, for there are a total of four within the cycle: two quintiles (arising just before or just after a Crisis Point, highlighting the Crescent and Last Quarter phases) and two biquintiles (arising just after or just before an Alert Point, highlighting the Gibbous and Full phases). This in itself leads us in the direction of the higher state of awareness being either a necessary prelude or aftermath to some important life juncture. We see parallels occurring in many kinds of explorative psychospiritual avenues, such as in Roberto Assagioli's work on psychosynthesis[7] where it is around critical stages of awakening that new self-realization and transmutation occur. Similarly in Buddhist teachings where 'citta' holds a deep resonance of understanding through an awakened heart-mind, as described by Jack Kornfield who speaks of its 'diamond-like' clarity.[8] All these factors make this aspect worth dwelling on a little.

What for instance do we mean by 'creative'? For many it is equated with innate talent and artistry belonging to the worlds of the painter, musician, poet, writer etc. At a deeper level, however, it also describes both a quest and a vision for bringing something new into existence with perseverance and coherence. This deeper sense was proposed by the existential psychoanalyst Rollo May[9] as 'a necessary sequel to our being' and needs to be aligned with courage. For Dr. May (echoing Sartre, Kierkegaard and Paul Tillich) this meant moving ahead despite anxiety or despair, developing assertion not as rashness, pride or bravado but as an inner commitment and dedication to a quest. John Addey directed us to an intense energy in developing specialized fields of activity but also the potential for the abuse of such power, while David Hamblin speaks of a sense of style and "the creation of order out of chaos".[10] Dennis Elwell[11] suggests that the power of the quintile lies mainly in "effective willing" to bring a creativity into being and also points to the dangers of over-estimation and pride while Tierney[12] notes that quintiles are "apt to originate from a deeper resource within" and that they "allow us to grasp a holistic overview" and bring "a rare perspective into sharper focus". This comes closer to my own sense of these aspects, as does Charles Harvey's understanding of Mind and its production from instinctive "knowing"[13] which I take to mean as opposed to the ordinary incessant stream of our everyday thoughts.

While all of the works cited merit careful study in building up a fuller understanding of this aspect, it seems to me overall that we rise above thinking and go beyond words at a quintile level since something requires our complete attention, our willingness and readiness to 'see' penetratingly and be exquisitely ready to follow its non-formulaic promptings. Indeed it occurs in the charts of creative people of all kinds who periodically are inspired in a brief moment to follow such inner realignments, coming from whatsoever direction and howsoever induced. We stir ourselves into an awake readiness in order to turn some kind of inner-illuminated corner, enhanced by an incentive that arises beyond words or explanations and is untouched by individual aggrandisement.

The quintile is therefore often one of impending creative breakthrough. The number 5 is also associated with the pentagram in ceremonial magick, symbolizing the power to command, subdue and harmonize the elements of creation and bring about changes in conformity with the will. In this context, Elwell also speaks of matters rebounding upon us if we make precipitative attempts to grasp and possess a result as some kind of dominant trophy to satisfy ego demands. In such a scenario the aspect may manifest negatively, impairing the creative act and diminishing its authenticity to power us forward. And to return to Rollo May, he reminds us that there are many kinds of courage we need to summon up as we meet creative points in our lives, not the least of which is the willingness to align ourselves with the unknown – that for which we have no precedent, no ready-beaten path, no guide; truly facing the stirrings of some enhanced quality being brought into existence.

The waxing quintile in Crescent Phase represents an *Enhanced Incentive to Aspire* to a goal. Sequentially, the plant has gone through anchoring itself (at the semi-square) and has discovered its capacity to both meet and draw upon nutrients released from the soil (sextile). Here at the quintile, the pull is toward its immediate future (the turning point of the First Quarter square where it will become the shoot above the ground). This aspect contains high potential to draw upon deeper skills arising from within (of which we may possess only an outline awareness) but the accompanying enhancement is one which *powers* our way forward. Like Archimedes before us we might leap up suffused with lightning realization and a strengthened will or, more simply, feel a surge of inner-connectedness with a timeless moment of understanding. Through such experience the purpose of the planets is summoned into existence by the very spur of the aspect's incentive.

The waning quintile *follows* rather than precedes a turning point. Here the plant puts on one last magnificent show of colour and vibrance before beginning its descent toward dormancy. Planets in this aspect hold within them a turning point already achieved which must now be manifested in the environment as a clear statement. It marks a *Release of Enhanced Maturity*. It accentuates the ability to create a specific platform from which to produce or pronounce something. Inspirational insights, philosophies or talents can provide a liberating forward movement into new endeavours. Over investment in personal advantage can, however, impair its possibilities. In the evolutionary cycle of aspects, this one is on its way to meeting the waning sextile where (as we saw earlier) things must be reorganized in preparation for the waning semi-square where individual impact cannot be retained ad infinitum but must be yielded for the good of the whole.

The Square – 90° (Orb allowance 8°)
Crisis Point

When the Moon reaches the First Quarter square in its movement from darkness towards light, away from the Sun, it crosses the orbit of the Earth. From now there is not so much push from within (the conjunction) to develop but rather a pull towards the opposition and the light of the Full Moon. At the Last Quarter square, the reverse is the case and the Moon moves from the light, diminishing back down into darkness. The Moon's change of appearance to a half-lit circle at both these 90° points is spoken of by Rudhyar as a symbolic 'cutting through' or cleavage[14] and, with his co-author Rael, as Crisis and Decision Points (de-cision – cutting in half; Gk. *crino* – to decide).[15]

These are indeed junctures of major decision and change – and this is the significant function to be achieved in either hemisphere. Both are moving from the past to advance forward, but they do so in different ways – one meeting a challenge (First Quarter) the other turning to a diversionary road (Last Quarter). Both are phases of action and in both there are urges to break through: one is a break-out into individuality (First Quarter) while the other is a break-through into maturity (Last Quarter). Their importance is also derived from the fact that they form the gateway not only to those phases, but also to the four quadrants of the entire cycle. Thus, like the conjunction and opposition points, they are Major Thresholds. As myth and legend show us, Thresholds constitute doorways of departure or reconciliation, passing some physical feat or knowing the right question to ask. In *The Hero with A Thousand Faces* Joseph Campbell wrote of acknowledging the transition from a known to an unknown, complete with risk and sense of danger in crossing boundaries, yet with the capacity to develop competence and courage by which such fears can fade. We may cringe or quake at the mention of 'crisis' yet if we are able step back and view this dynamic in our lives from an observational vantage point (as opposed to getting caught up in the detail or drama), we are also able to see that when we have turned to and assimilated these transitions they have been crucial to our growth and transformation notwithstanding any pressure or strife.

At the waxing First Quarter square the plant, having passed through the enhanced surge at the quintile, now pierces the crust of the earth's soil. A monumental breakthrough accentuating a high point of release from the past. Fear and courage run in tandem as what is known is relinquished and a new road struck out upon. It is an aspect of *Empowerment through Challenge*. The planets combine in self-assertion and strong will to repudiate outworn and stultifying conditions. Through them we take a stand as an undeniable vehicle through which forward advances can be made. Yet this convergence of planetary energies also requires us to proceed *solidly* and with circumspection – just as the plant must develop a *sturdy* stem to accommodate leaves and buds (the oncoming trine). Failure to meet the challenge can result in feeling blocked and thwarted.

The waning square at Last Quarter is likewise a threshold, gateway to the Reorientation phase and final quadrant of the cycle. Like the waxing square, old ways of being no longer fit and a change has to be made via the planets involved, but here their purpose is to dispense outwardly what they hold within. This aspect needs to move from the past not by a repudiation of it but by incorporating its experiences as a means by which to develop the planets' significance on one's own specialized terms. It accentuates self-reliance and a willingness to change with the tides of life for there is much to be shared, spoken out for (or even against) that would move one's own and others' lives forward. It marks a *Springboard to Maturity*.

The Trine – 120° (Orb allowance 8°)
Flow Point

The two trines in the cycle appear in First Quarter and Disseminating phases, therefore accentuating either meeting challenges or communicating/ sharing what you know and understand. Both aspects are capable of being utilized productively, creatively, with an overall sense of *flourishing*, thus the capacity for success also exists in both whether in tangible material terms or via inner development and growth. The main difference is that in the waxing hemisphere the planets involved need to be cultivated and developed onwards to fulfilment; in the waning hemisphere the planetary abilities are already in place but need to be demonstrated and matured.

The waxing trine although a point of flow, is nevertheless still one of action since this is still First Quarter phase. Sufficient onward commitment to whatever one is doing or being needs still to be maintained to allow for positive manifestation. This is an aspect of *Onward Growth and Flourishing*. The plant, having established itself outwardly and resolutely at the prior 90° square, now begins to exhibit some little 'embellishments' – we usually call them leaves. Planets in this aspect carry the capacity for working to reach success and its rewards. Often manifesting a stylish quality, they combine for accomplishment as an *ongoing* mission rather than resting on any laurels at the first flash of success. Failure to maintain the energy of this First Quarter phase can undermine the possibilities either by taking success for granted or through unwillingness to put in the work to get there.

At the waning trine in Disseminating phase there is similar flow and ease. Just as the plant at this stage establishes a network with the wider ecosystem around – sun, rain, winds, insects etc. – so too the planets involved spread their energies into the environment, displaying, demonstrating, sharing, communicating. Secondary blooming and young fruits beginning to ripen also have their parallels in that this aspect may contain a good measure of both style and competence. As an aspect of *Demonstration and Communication* there are abilities and skills within the planets but since it is approaching a need for maturity (the oncoming Last Quarter square) they need also to be forged from the furnace of our own individual lives rather than merely replicating those we have gathered up from elsewhere.

The Sesquiquadrate – 135° (Orb allowance 2°)
Alert Point

The combination of a square plus a semi-square points us not only to breaking through something but also an accompanying jolting-awake quality. This aspect forms the gateway to either Gibbous or Disseminating phases and both sesquiquadrates symbolize the need to rise out of habitual ways of being and be extremely attentive to what is next needed. The main difference between the hemispheres is that the waxing aspect awakens us to the need for diligence and scrupulous care in seeking and discovering, whereas the waning sesquiquadrate calls for us to be vigilant in conveying an adeptness in that which we have developed, to communicate it out to the best of our ability.

The waxing sesquiquadrate marks the entry point to Gibbous phase. As an alert gateway it is synonymous with the growing plant getting down to the serious business of developing further foliage and buds. Energy must now be focused assiduously notwithstanding that all sorts of impediments exist (e.g. predatory insects). It is an aspect of *Seeking and Discovery*. The planets combine in an arresting sense of attention, probing and discernment to bring something to light and learn from mistakes. It marks a high point of learning, mastering detail, establishing insight. If overdone there can be an irritable harrassing quality; if bypassed, a sense of being an alone outsider borne of the awareness of wanting to discover but failing to give energy into the search.

The **waning sesquiquadrate** represents an equivalent Alert Point with similar power to be prodded into an awakening. Having bloomed (Full Phase) the plant in nature now stands at a threshold where it must extend itself further into the environment, acting as a catalyst by sharing its resources – petals, scent, pollen, fruits, etc. So too the function of planets in this aspect is to spread and share what we know, have been taught or shown and contain within us. It is an aspect of *Communication of Capability and Proficiency*. It needs to be lived out among others in the wider world taking care to hear their views also, even if they do not match our own.

The Biquintile – 144° (Orb allowance – 2°)
Point of Enhancement

How is it that a fully grown human can step outside in gale force winds, a torrential storm or raging blizzard and be buffeted to the ground … yet the tiniest flower with delicate petals remains rooted and sturdy through it all? Inexplicable though much of it is to the strictly scientific mind, plants are capable of the most striking ingenuity, construction and survival. They have been shown to contain an awareness of intent and perception of the future as well as anticipation of the Sun-Moon phases. The smallest among them, hidden under the earth in the cold of winter, will know when the Vernal Equinox is due and begin their journey upward, generating their own heat to melt the snow as they go – a feat they share with many members of the animal kingdom.

Similarly the stages of the cycle containing the biquintiles reflect ways in which we most tap into and release qualities and activities which further the development of something (waxing Gibbous) or enable it to flourish openly (waning Full). And, just as we witness in nature, sometimes these abilities or knowing-perceptions arise from an all-pervading consciousness the mind cannot necessarily pin down and quantify. Following on from the sesquiquadrates which marked high points of attentive energy, the biquintiles represent points of *resolve*, the planets combining in order to either assemble, gather together and bring a precision to something (the waxing aspect) or perform, or speak out for, that which has been so ordered and arranged (waning).

The waxing biquintile represents an enhanced resolve to bring things together to reach a better conclusion. Following on from the deft ability of the preceding sesquiquadrate to discover through attentiveness, this aspect brings into play qualities of arrangement, design or assembly, with ingenuity and an appreciation of efficient functioning. For the growing plant, sap is now rising now to feed its developing buds, synonymous with this aspect being *An Enhanced Spur to Development*. The planetary energies combine in imagination, resourcefulness and perseverance. Over-emphasis can mean there is a frenzied and fastidious quality to this (given the context of the background phase) and a tendency to get stuck in that, rather than working through to a completion.

The waning biquintile in Full Phase is *leading to* a sesquiquadrate, as opposed to its waxing counterpart which had just left one. This aspect represents the need to develop an *Enhanced Realization of Meaning*. Here there is awareness of the full range of one's inner capabilities (the plant has bloomed prior to this point and is still flowering). This aspect needs to give cognizance to the future and approach it with integrity. The planets involved feel strongly impelled to display a clarity of organization and vision, reflecting upon and focusing into a purpose that will be long-lasting in the wider environment. If this is not understood, it can emerge more negatively as 'pontificating', perhaps wanting to be the centre of attention (Full Phase) and call all the shots, (albeit under a subtle 'Let's All Agree We Do As I Say').

The Quincunx – 150° (Orb Allowance 3°)
Point of Focus

If, dear reader, your housekeeping skills bear any resemblance to mine, then somewhere in your home you will have a very untidy cupboard (or attic) – a glory-hole full of all kinds of junk you have chucked in there over the years. Old pictures, toys, shoes, half-used tins of paint, the silver candlesticks your granny left you when she died, that old exercise bike you swore you'd use every day... Now let's suppose that someone in the family calls you saying they are going to hold a special dinner party and they thought maybe granny's candlesticks would look good at the centre table... "Any idea where they are"? they ask. Oh *groan* –wherever could they be? Ah yes, *oh groan again* – in that glory-hole. No two ways about it – you are going to have to clear it out.

This idea of clearing out a cupboard was first mooted in relation to the quincunx aspect by the American astrologer Zipporah Dobyns (who, more pertinently to her nationality called it a 'closet-clearing' aspect).[16] Like so very many of Zip's insights, I have found this an extremely useful analogy in tracking quincunxes in my own clients' charts over the years, both in relation to the well-known 'awkwardness' that can ensue from two planets in this relationship and also in understanding the two *types* of quincunxes. It also enables us to see the quincunx in its setting as part of the sequential process of aspects occurring just prior and just after it. The relative who phoned about the candlesticks we could say is synonymous with the prior sesquiquadrate (commencement to Gibbous phase), alerting us to the need to seek and discover. A week later, you get another phone call: "Any luck finding those candlesticks yet...?" Tsk! – you haven't even started to look have you? – here is the biquintile, the resolve that builds up following the alert – "I *really must* turn that cupboard out". That leads to the Gibbous quincunx, then on to the opposition, with the Full Phase quincunx after that. The main difference between these two quincunxes is that the waxing aspect is synonymous with the *instigation* of the cupboard-clearance whereas the waning quincunx reflects the subsequent *rearrangement* of the cupboard, (after the opposition 'completion' point). In the human individual this would be reformulating one's attitudes and actions in the light of developed awareness.

At the waxing quincunx, the time has come – you open the doors to the cupboard and turf everything out, sorting it as you go. You now have three piles at your feet – things you definitely don't want to keep and can take to the charity shop, things you might keep as you never know when you're going to need them and, thirdly, important things you want to hold on to. This is an aspect of deep focus in order to see clearly what you are dealing with, *Sorting Priorities and Making Adjustments*. It can take a lot of work (understanding) to sift through this-and-that, or this-versus-that, but the aspect requires us to start making adjustments to something that is malfunctioning or muddled within us. There is a need for clarity between the planets involved, getting down to the business of understanding each one and making the necessary adjustments to reach a better level of compatibility between them.

At the waning quincunx, again there is sorting and prioritising to be done but it is now in the light of clarity we have reached (at the Full Phase opposition). Here we find workable ways of proceeding – in our cupboard analogy, of the three piles at your feet only two remain since you've dumped what you didn't need. Now you start to replace the items in the cupboard, starting with the least important items first (since those can go at the back) and then the most important items last so that from now on they will be at the front and readily to hand. This is an aspect of *Rearrangement and Establishment of New Order* – what needs to be retained and what needs release. Different experiences and aspects of our nature are reflected upon (Full phase). Just as we now relate to a new tidy cupboard and vow not let it deteriorate into the old muddle, so too there is a conscious monitoring of our inner attitudes so that they flourish effectively.

The Opposition – 180° (Orb allowance – 8°)
Point of Transformation/Regeneration

This is a point of both completion and a new beginning. We have come to the end of the waxing hemisphere and thus the building up of energy and action from within. The plant has bloomed (or not) and we have found our candlesticks (or not!). As a point of completion, it is not always synonymous with fullness and success in the way our minds may wish – the plant may bloom, but weakly, or fail to bloom at all (in which case there is an ending and dying) and Granny's candlesticks may have to remain a mystery a while longer if we failed to find them. We are placed at a point of full consciousness of *what is* and a need to align ourselves with that, whatever value-judgments or emotions we may assign to it.

It is also a point of balance, the entire axis being akin to the "awareness continuum", spoken of by Fritz Perls in Gestalt Therapy. In the universal cycle we have entered the span toward dissolution which eventually will give rise again to something new being created. It can be difficult to process this opposition point since it seems part of the human condition to have many preferences as to the way we want life to be, or think it *ought* to be, and balk at an outcome which does not fit those choices. We are also apt to be decidedly resistant to allowing dissolution to occur even though we may know it is in the nature of all things that nothing is fixed and permanent forever. The opposition is then experienced as a dichotomy, a conflict between diverse factors pulling against one another, again which we respond to with intolerance, feeling out of alignment with the world around.

If we consider two children on a playground see-saw, they are indeed in 'opposition' – as one goes up, the other goes down, then vice-versa. But if we were to move them towards each other along the horizontal plane of the see-saw, we would see them as closer together with less motion and therefore less disparity. When planets oppose one another we may fly wildly from one to the other, yet the purpose of the aspect is to bring the inner meanings of the planets into a steady settled point of no resistance, allowing them simply to be in this balanced counterpoise. Here we know 'up' because we know 'down' just as we know 'day' because of 'night' or male/female, I/You. The recognition of opposites then becomes a seeing of them as one whole and the aspect can be integrated as a unity (or polarity). Both oppositions in the cycle (in waxing Gibbous and waning Full) carry these implications through the planets and signs concerned and both tend to be developed through our interactions with others. What we see as opposite and do not accept lies within ourselves, we attract to us; then gradually as awareness grows we see 'the other' not as a separate outsider but as a reflection of something within.

Both oppositions are apt to overdo things, stretching themselves to fullest expression to reach a unifying sense of awareness. The main difference between them is that the Gibbous opposition is intensely focused and striving (like the plant with one final thrust to bring the buds to full bloom) and therefore may try over-hard to reach a result, while the Full Phase opposition requires full cognitive, sensory and emotional awareness of how the planets involved are interacting in the person's overall development (plant in full bloom), but more negatively can denote putting on too much of a show of things. On a more positive level the main hemispheric difference is that the waxing opposition is reflective of final and particular preparation of something, while the waning aspect denotes the ensuing presentation and experience of it (akin to putting the last flourishing touches to a special culinary dish then setting it triumphantly upon a table for consumption).

The waxing opposition arising in the final stages of Gibbous Phase carries an implication of highly focused energy in the service of completing something. The planets are intensely, earnestly focused on their shared mission and purpose and much may be riding on it in the overall life. There exists a capacity to present something to the world at large which offers a spur to Life and enlightenment. It is an aspect of *Striving to Fulfilment* and carries possibilities of bringing insight and industry into an integrated whole, although over-emphasis may evoke too much assiduous industry and the 'over-egging of a pudding' ...

The waning opposition in Full Phase is synonymous with vigilant acceptance of 'what is'. Denial through resistance in favour of other preferences disrupts the awareness which is the purpose of this aspect. The Moon stands fully illuminated by the light of the Sun, with Earth poised between them and completion has been reached – an 'is-ness' which can be in no doubt. It also carries a theme of 'the fullness of being', i.e. feeling highlighted by our interaction with others and learning to share with them in balanced give-and-take ways. Through the planets involved we can experience opposites as a central dynamic of wholeness within and are led to participation among others in order to integrate polarized drives and qualities. It is an aspect of *Realization and Awareness*.

These aspect commentaries are not of course intended to provide a comprehensive coverage of all possibilities *but are 'pointers' to the essence of each aspect*, set within the backdrop of the eight phases. By catching ahold of the initial thread of meaning (the phase), we can individually follow the aspect and its nature ('flow', 'alert', 'focus' etc) through and witness its outworkings in our own life experience. Many interpretational texts offer insight on more definitive outcomes and manifestations and these can be of assistance as additional guidelines as long as their findings are not applied too mechanically. Any writer can only offer a perspective borne of their own consciousness as it is in the moment, yet tracing the astrological cyclically by listening to and witnessing it in the actual experience of people carries its own authenticity.

5: Planets and Pairings

There is broad agreement among astrologers on the essential meanings of the planets which, very briefly, might be summarized by saying that the Sun represents our central purpose, while the Moon is how we carry that out; Mercury is how we perceive and think about things, while Venus denotes how we establish our values. Mars is synonymous with how we go after what we want, Jupiter is how we seek to expand and develop our lives onward and Saturn is how we set boundaries for ourselves. The outer planets (Uranus, Neptune and Pluto) are of a different order, signifying our transpersonal and collective experience and, if we are individually aware of them at all, they could in turn be said to denote new perceptions which challenge old patterns of being (Uranus), a need to transcend the physical world of form and embrace an all-encompassing unity (Neptune) and a compulsion to submit to vaster, deeper life experiences which transform our lives irrevocably (Pluto). With these planets we touch into our *unconditioned* state of being and, through their gradual emerging levels, an understanding of our evolutionary path through life. We shall revisit these planets more specifically in Chapter 11.

While there can be a tendency to look upon planets from a separatist standpoint and equally to race for an interpretation of their 'effect', from the perspective of inner understanding we need to go beyond placing them in a particular location (in the sky or in our charts) but experience them as living principles residing in each of us. Symbolically interacting with one another in their natural sequence within the solar system, each leads into or 'informs' another to give added colouration to the way we instinctively express them. In their order out from the Sun, Mercury's perception and acquisition of knowledge feeds into our Venusian capacity to assess matters on the basis of feeling. Sometimes these two interact well, while at others they can be at odds. Suppose, for example, we are walking along the High Street and we come across a shop selling ice-cream. Following Mercury's perception of it, our Venus judgment could be that a large helping of that chocolate-and-raspberry-ripple might go down rather well right now. But then Mercury reasoning may tell us exactly the opposite – or at least point out that our judgment is not compatible with our other Venusian value, that to risk putting on weight from eating ice-cream is unattractive and unhealthy. The example is a trivial one, but although the Mercury function is one of mobilizing us into concretely noticing something and the Venus function is pleasure seeking and pain-avoiding, if left to run amok inside us we are capable of making all sorts of contradictory decisions and operating from fluctuating modes – such as wanting to enjoy as much ice-cream as possible while at the same time wanting to be slim!

Synonymous with these two planets being between Sun and Earth, both Mercury and Venus are interior functions. Nobody knows about our perceptions or evaluations until we take action to convey them outside of ourselves. We do so through Mars which, as the first planet out from the Earth, is our drive to energize and achieve the purposes of Mercury and Venus by taking exterior action. We go into the shop and buy ice-cream, thus for the first time someone else (the shopkeeper) knows about our thoughts and desires. Having indulged ourselves, with the Jupiter function we feel satisfied and have achieved an expanded sense of self. Even if we chose not to buy ice-cream because it seemed unhealthy, Jupiter can be experienced as self-congratulation that we have taken care of our bodily needs wisely and feel better about ourselves as a result. Saturn within us needs to ensure that the growth attained via Jupiter becomes a settled part of us and we reach a *stasis* – an inner structural knowing of limit. We know when to stop eating ice-cream as we feel full. We might of course ignore this and continue with Jupiter, buying *more* ice-cream, even adding another flavour… **then** we stop because we are now feeling bloated or even nauseous.

While we can trace the planets' basic functions symbolically from perception to evaluation, to action, to satisfaction, to the boundary of completion, following their natural order of orbit around the Sun, in reality they do not necessarily function sequentially but are subject to fluctuations or difficulties in our awareness at any time. Saturn, for instance, might intervene at any time … perhaps at the Mercury stage where we are feeling so 'down' that day we don't even notice the ice-cream shop. Or at the Venus stage to convince us that we have no business buying any at all since we don't deserve it! Or at the Mars stage, we find to our chagrin that just as we step into the shop, we find we've come out without any money in our pocket.

Five Core Functions

When it comes to the cycle of phases, each planet can be paired up with any other in order to examine their purpose (as a duo) in terms of the phase they occupy, with the exceptions we noted in the Introduction. For example, if you wanted to explore your propensity toward joy and abundance you might look at the Jupiter/Venus phase; or if you were considering your capacity for innovation borne of striking new insights you might look at your Uranus/Mercury phase... and so on. Following Rudhyar's initial teachings on the Lunation Cycle, a few other commentators around that time (notably Robertson[1], Ewbank and Wickenberg[2]) adapted and extended it into other main combinations and applications. For practical purposes, however, there are five main sets of planetary pairs which form a fundamental platform in our lives and are derived from the personal planets (Sun out to Saturn), these being synonymous with our individual and social development. They are **Sun/Moon, Saturn/Moon, Jupiter/Mercury, Mars/Venus** and **Saturn/Jupiter.**

While their various manifestations will be seen more specifically in people's lives in Part II, for the moment we can trace these five in terms of their recognized functions from the perspective of traditional astrology's teachings, based on the interconnectedness of the seven planets known to the ancients and the twelve zodiacal signs. From the dawn of recorded astrological history, the pattern of the heavens which became woven into Man's understanding emanated primarily from the two 'Great Lights' (Sun and Moon, ruling Leo and Cancer respectively). This is shown in Diagram 1 with the five planets in their order of motion around the Sun determining the rulership of the signs flowing into each hemisphere. Thus the Sun and Moon each rule one sign and each of the planets rules two, in a shared spectrum of meaning. The signs are alternately of positive (+ masculine) or negative (– feminine) polarity, the Sun ruling the hemisphere from Leo to Capricorn (Day) and the Moon ruling Cancer to Aquarius (Night).

Extending out into each hemisphere (starting from Leo/Sun) we find Virgo, Libra, Scorpio, Sagittarius and Capricorn, ruled respectively by Mercury, Venus, Mars, Jupiter and Saturn. And in the hemisphere from Cancer/Moon, we come to Gemini, Taurus, Aries, Pisces and Aquarius, also ruled respectively by the planets from Mercury to Saturn, denoting a connection of shared likeness of one thing to another. We can also see their pairings by polarity as facets of an opposing continuum working toward wholeness.

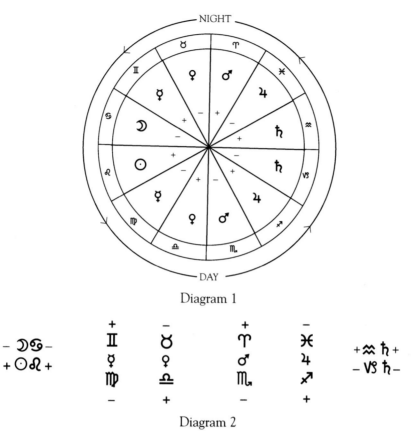

Diagram 1

+   −   +   −

− ☽♋ −   ♊   ♉   ♈   ♓   +♒ ♄ +
+ ☉♌ +   ☿   ♀   ♂   ♃   − ♑ ♄ −
         ♍   ♎   ♏   ♐

        −   +   −   +

Diagram 2

Diagram 2 depicts the same order of seven planets/twelve signs drawn in linear style, showing the Sun and Moon each in polarity to Saturn, with Mercury and Jupiter connecting the feminine signs of Virgo/Pisces and the masculine Gemini/Sagittarius, while Venus and Mars connect the masculine Aries/Libra and feminine Taurus/Scorpio, again reflecting the pairings by rulership and polarity seen in Diagram 1. This is also depicted by Rudhyar in his book *The Astrology of Transformation* (Chapter 3).

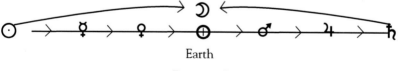

Earth

Diagram 3

Diagram 3 represents the planets' order of motion from the Sun, with Saturn as the boundary planet. The Sun/Saturn polarity is implicit in the Sun/Moon, Saturn/Moon pairings with the Moon as mediator to the earthed individual as receptor. On either side of Earth, we have Mercury as the first planet inward from the Sun, in polarity to Jupiter as the first planet inward from the boundary of Saturn. Venus is the first planet *inwards from* the Earth *to* the Sun, while its polarity Mars is the first planet *out from* the Earth towards Jupiter and Saturn. In this overall system we can also see that the masculine planets (Saturn, Jupiter, Mars) are paired with the three feminine planets (Moon, Mercury, Venus). Saturn/Jupiter as a polarity represents a further pairing where the planets concerned are *successive* in orbit in the solar system and Rudhyar suggests this type of linking represents significance in terms of the *work* which together they accomplish through their complementary drives,[3] in this case of expansion and contraction in individual and societal development where we augment our sense of being, while maintaining a reality of the environment, culture and times in which we are functioning (the boundaries).[4]

The seven-fold development of planets as inner functions of the human individual has frequently been compared to the famous Shakespearian "All the world's a stage" speech from *As You Like It*[5] which traces the seven ages of Man and carries an allusion to the cycle from Moon ("the infant mewling and puking in his nurse's arms") to Mercury ("the whining schoolboy… creeping like a snail, unwillingly to school"); then Venus ("the lover… sighing like furnace, with a woeful ballad"); on to Mars ("a soldier … sudden and quick in quarrel"), Jupiter ("the justice in fair round belly") and finally Saturn ("the lean and slippered pantaloon with spectacles on nose"). So from these stages of development in human life together with our understanding of the planets, we can begin to see that when we pair them up they are of particular significance at the core of our development. Each pairing is made up by the planets working together in an intrinsic polarized pull to be blended into a synthesis through effective functioning in human life.

The combination of **Sun and Moon** shows how we are innately equipped to bring the purpose of the entire birth pattern into being. We operate instinctively with this combination in terms of the phase they occupy since together they represent our inner drive to do and be that which we most need as an overall creative intention for our lives and to which we feel predisposed.

The combination of **Saturn and Moon** refers more to a structured identity we build (alongside Sun/Moon). Here we define our boundaries as we experience them from the nature and content of the world around us and conform to those limits through workable participation with our environment and adherence to its expectations.

Jupiter's combination with Mercury represents our capacity for perception, movement and expansion; it brings together Mercury's transmission of the solar purpose, with Jupiter's drive to extend it (from Mars) to the boundary of Saturn. It reflects our communication, mobilization and understanding, to grow, reach fulfilment and decipher further meaning.

Mars/Venus as a complementary pair is reflective of the inner drive to establish and externalize our preferences and experience pleasure (the feminine principle of Venus), spontaneity and activity (the masculine drive of Mars) whether by personal creativity and/or in feeling-participation with others. Personal assertion is blended with emotional interchange to achieve a balance of needs/desires with others.

And finally the **Saturn/Jupiter** pairing reflects the overall soli-lunar purpose being conveyed onward to a concretized actuality. In order to render all of the above functions viable and sustaining in our lives, we must shape ourselves to fit into wider social frameworks and adapt by working to underpin our lives and take our place.

While these are, at this stage, overviews of the planetary-pair meanings, they will be augmented at the start of each set of delineations in Part II. For the moment, we have arrived at five core functions, each of which can appear in any of the eight main phase-relationships and this can be diagrammed as on the following page.

Astrologers of course have their own individual ways of working with a chart. Sometimes (nay, even often) it varies from one client to another according to different needs and questions under consideration. While the conventional chart yields a vast amount of information to put the individual more in touch with his or her universe, the phases provide an additional and unique set of identifiable threads weaving their way through and affording a clear guide to a deeper understanding. For comparatively little extra work the process of chart exploration can be rendered more meaningful and specifically pertinent to the client by their inclusion. Having set up the chart, simply list the five main pairs and their phases alongside and consider these *first* as contextual parameters within which the chart as a whole is to be expressed. Any repetition of phases can be noted (e.g. are there two planetary-pairs in Disseminating, or three pairs in First Quarter, therefore

Phase-Relationships

Planetary Pairs

SUN/MOON

The inner drive to do and be that which inside you feel you want and need - the ability to go for what you want in a manner which feels most natural and comfortable to you in order to live out your intrinsic sense of purpose

SATURN/MOON

The inner drive to conform to the expectations of the world around you and all it contains - to do and be what you feel is required of you, which feels extremely compelling, even binding, in order to construct a steadfast sense of identity

JUPITER/MERCURY

Your capacity for reaching out into the environment, communicating and expressing yourself by words, movement, shared understandings, navigating your way through the world and developing connections

SATURN/JUPITER

Your capacity for building structures in society by which you can pursue goals and secure a place of standing through work, career, finances - creating a platform for your potential in the outside world

MARS/VENUS

The way you express yourself as a creative, loving, sexual being ready to relate. The capacity to attract others and be attracted to them as well as developing inner resources, talents, skills

Phase-Relationships

NEW

Functions spontaneously, instinctively, in unpremeditated ways, simply being as it is meeting life in automatic participation

CRESCENT

Perseverance, resilience and endurance combine with innovation and a capacity for onward movement

FIRST QUARTER

Assertion, striving and challenging qualities prevail and action springs in unconsidered ways in order to break through and press forward

GIBBOUS

Discernment, scrutiny and focused consideration give rise to precision, care, assessment and learning

FULL

Awareness, relatedness and the seeking of meaning give rise to flourishing, illumination, completions and transitions

DISSEMINATING

Fluidity, free-movement, smooth flow of energies gives rise to involvement, participation and communication with the surrounding environment

LAST QUARTER

Action based on considered outlooks, building maturity of decision and effecting transitions in societal outlooks

BALSAMIC

Inner awareness of future potential and enabling such to come into being. Functioning from unseen realms of understanding

Diagram 4

specific emphasis on these qualities to be developed). We can also note whether an aspect exists, thus alerting us to significant tasks to be lived to bring the phase to fulfilment. The phases may also contain other planets, adding further meaning to what needs to be expressed, plus the first planet and last planets met by the Moon can be noted as to a main quest being sought in life and the inherent qualities with which it is met.

A familiarity with the phases also enables us to decipher a deeper meaning than is ordinarily to be had from interpreting factors in isolation. Many people seem to approach their chart as if they were the victim of it as opposed to being its emissary. Finding they have a Mars/Pluto conjunction occupying the 12th squared by Saturn, all manner of mayhem lodges itself in their minds, fuelled often by set interpretational texts. But is it a New Phase conjunction or a Balsamic one? And is the square to Saturn a First Quarter or a Last Quarter? – are there other planets contained within these phases? What are the other supporting phase-relationships – how do they link in and weave an emerging portrayal of this person's life-path with its very important conjunction purpose to be lived? A student in an astrology class once told me that with his Moon Venus/Saturn/Neptune T-square, he was forever lonely and longed to meet a special partner. He had read all the books on this aspect-structure from which he was convinced that unrequited love was his hapless lot in life. When we examined the phases, Neptune was in the 5th in Full Phase to Moon Venus 11th, in First Quarter square to Saturn in 9th and the Saturn/Moon was also First Quarter. So – much potential for forward thrust and the seeking of awareness for his creative 5th house potential. Enquiring what he did for a living, it emerged he worked in the film industry primarily as a screenplay writer. Being ignorant of this career role, I asked what it entailed – what were the conditions he needed in order to fulfil his talents as a screenwriter to their highest? And the answer was "mainly space, a little bit of tranquillity now and then, nothing hassling me so that I can fully concentrate and be open to inspiration". Well, he may not at that time have yet found the dream girlfriend (though I gather he did later) but here was a glimpse of a deeper purpose peeking through the T-square, previously held only as a negative and limited concept by which he defined himself.

Part II

Planetary Phases in the

Individual Birthchart

Planetary Phases in the Individual Birth Chart

If we were airline pilots placing ourselves in the cockpit of a jumbo jet for a long-haul flight, we would expect to find before us a control panel of instruments – buttons, switches, dials, lights etc. This flightdeck contains everything we need to enable us to take the aircraft along its flight path, to its destination. I doubt that we would do anything other than engage with it, fully, finding out everything and checking every switch, dial, light, how they function, what they are essential for and how they are interconnected – *and we would use them to fly the plane*. It takes time and dedication to learn how to pilot a jet aircraft… but so too does full living and discovery of ourselves as individuals of meaning and purpose. The analogy may be a loose one, but the astrological map is somewhat akin to the flight control panel, guiding and assisting us to fly the 'craft' each of us calls 'my life'.

While much astrological practice may focus upon the giving of information along the lines of characteristics and events, understanding ourselves goes beyond the mere adoption and espousal of a set of ideas. In order to turn information into self-knowledge, it is the meaning lying behind outward manifestations that lead us to deeper understandings through inner experience of ourselves as the embodiment of cosmic principles and thus allows for our ongoing growth and development. The delineations which follow for planetary phase relationships are offered as a pathfinder to the underlying threads of meaning. Since the phases refer to an overall context within which your life can best develop, they refer to the essence of your being rather than necessarily definitive outcomes or manifestations, although examples of the latter will be shown.

There are of course many possible avenues along which each thread may be ultimately woven and it is in symbolically taking ahold of the thread itself and following it – (i.e. instinctual development in New Phase, persistence and effort in Crescent, challenging/endeavouring in First Quarter etc.) – that we can relate it to our own specific experience. Sometimes our understanding may be immediate, while at others it amounts only to an inner felt-sense identification. But the very act of touching the thread, however tentatively, may well be sufficient to spiral it up into awareness just as the soft plucking of a harp string in an otherwise silent chamber gently but instantly commands our listening attention.

Accessing the five core functions of the planetary pairs through the eight phases can provide a formidable platform for such inner work. People usually resonate to a phase if they are allowed the space to consider and explore its presence from their own intrinsic self-knowing rather than if they are presented with it wholesale as an intellectual appraisal. From the various descriptions and examples given, allow yourself to weave through the planetary phases of your own birth chart to enable such clarity to take its place in your consciousness, in its own way and its own time. In the process of so doing, you may well come up with understandings of each phase/pairing that are wholly new yet vital and central to your nature, therefore of undeniable meaning and purpose.

6: The Sun and Moon

Finding a satisfactory definition of the Sun's meaning in a chart is never easy, largely because it is so all-encompassing. Neither is the task helped by the popularity of 'Sun-sign astrology' which implies that its function is a matter of everyday characteristics somehow plonked upon us at birth. The Sun, as the centre of our solar system, provides the necessary sustaining energy to keep all the other planets going. It is therefore the integrative life force that enables us to be alive, inspires us to go on living, to be full of purpose, strength, capability. Representing a purposeful release of willed inner power, its key attributes are creative energy, vitality and wellbeing. Additionally it symbolizes a sense of *ongoing* fulfilment within us simply *because* we are individuals seeking to express and actualize all of our potential. As the fundamental psychological drive to express fully the purpose and meaning of the individual life it corresponds very closely with the way we define the sign of Leo and the 5th house.

The Sun itself is of course too powerful, too hot, to sustain physical and biological life; it needs something to take its light and power to Earth, to each of us as the individual embodiment of its principles. It needs the Moon to reflect, soften and mould its power so that it is available for development by us to fulfil the needs of the sign it occupies and achieve the experiences and goals of its house position, as well as its aspects to planets. These are all reflections of the Sun's purpose residing within us.

Through the Moon we develop a flexible but automatic pattern of feeling, action and thought, hunting out and collecting up experience as we convey the Sun's purpose. While thinking and action have their place in the Lunar function they have to be integrated into what is primarily a feeling response. Clear, detached thinking is not the province of the Moon, yet nevertheless decisions are made at very deeply rooted, feeling-dominated levels that contain both our *earliest* decisions and our ongoing *instinctive* reactions. Often our instant response patterns, such as in an emergency, contain the tendency to follow habitual lines and an automatic sense of being contained and safe. These also give rise to root decisions in life stemming from a sense of familiarity through emotional, cultural and familial origins. Defined in this way, the Moon is closely allied to the needs of Cancer and the 4th house.

The Moon also mirrors the rhythms of our life, our physical body and our habitual sensory/emotional experiences (just as we observe the Moon move and make perpetual pattern changes through the sky-space around us). Yet while we feel secure in connection to its customary rhythms, if we rely too much upon Moon we can become far too bound up in these needs, all too easily running back into a desire for comfort, security and sensual satisfaction, but which may become indolence and stagnation. We have to go beyond the Lunar orbit, out to the furthest planets to explore and live them all – and, through Moon, bring them home to the Sun.

When we put Sun and Moon together as a pair, we might perhaps imagine that we are standing at the centre of a vast central storehouse of energy such as a giant power station. A power station is simply that – a station generating vast power, but taken on its own its energy is not specifically directed... until something is connected to it, to distribute the power and channel it through to functions of lighting, heating etc. The Moon metaphorically plugging into the Sun at each of their synodic monthly meetings (New Moon), brings the solar impulse to life through form (the embodiment on earth) whereby outlets for expression (represented by the planets in the entire solar system) can be developed. As we have seen, in taking this unitary power and reflecting it to the earth, the Moon is a focal indicator of our pathway, moreover by dint of her swift movement as the only heavenly body which, by progression, returns to its own natal position during a lifetime (whether once, twice or three times).

In our identification of a power station (or central engine-room), we can further think of this powerful Sun/Moon combination operating as a kind of continual background reverberating 'hum' within us. Resonating to it instinctively in rhythms and reactions, we share this in common at biological levels with all other living creatures on the earth. In the human individual, consciousness depicted by Sun/Moon is a vital welding of inner energy and the means within us to carry out what we need to do and be as a central pathway. It is through whatever phase they occupy at birth that we are able to trace a thread of this essence, bring it to life and have it flourish. Nevertheless, it is possible for Sun/Moon to receive interference from, and sometimes domination by, other planetary pairings (such as Saturn/Moon) as well as other conventional chart factors and these should be borne in mind in coming to an understanding of their central phase-relationship in the eight-fold cycle.

Overall, and as we saw initially in Chapter 5, the Sun/Moon phase constitutes an innate drive to put into operation and fulfil that which we have the potential for, that which we profoundly want to do and be from our centre, to carry forward the life-force as purpose and meaning for our incarnation, how we seek to develop that, what it may entail and how we essentially go about it.

Sun/Moon New Phase Moon is 0° – 45° ahead of the Sun

Becoming

> "A sower went out to sow his seeds … some fell by the wayside… some fell upon stony ground…"   [*St. Matthew Ch.13 v.3*]

Consider the seed in the ground. We hope that it is in a fertile garden, tended by those who will ensure it receives the right soil and nutrients. Or lovingly laid in its own seed-tray in a warm greenhouse, thus open to the same advantageous start in life. On the other hand, it may have been borne on the winds after separating from its host plant, billowing hither and thither, until it eventually lands in a meadow where it has to find a niche among other seeds and plants as best it can. Maybe it has only managed to land in a crack in the pavement or in one of Alfred Lord Tennyson's "little crannied walls" high up in a crumbling ancient ruin where soil is sparse … just enough to gain a foothold perhaps. As St. Matthew tells us, there are many kinds of beginnings for the little seed as it starts out on the pathway to find its place in the sun.

Whatever its beginnings, we know two things about the seed: first, it has a thrust towards Life – the way is *onward, forward*. Secondly, it holds within all of the potential to become the fully-flowering plant of its particular genus (a sunflower or poppy perhaps) as well as the potential to live on and disperse more seeds into the future. It simply carries the full possibility of 'sunflower-ness' or 'poppy-ness' as its inherent path and its journey is commencing. Correspondingly, those born with the Sun and Moon in New Phase carry within them an automatic drive to be and become that which they intrinsically *are* and can be. Their lives are developed in unpremeditated, uncontrived ways, operating on the spur of the moment, imbued with a sense of sustained inner purpose and meaning. They know deep within that coming from this instinctive impulse their spontaneity of being carries its own order and composure, as it does in all of nature.

This is the standpoint from which New Moon people *need* to meet life, simply submitting to experiences rather than trying to map things out in advance or getting hung-up on outcomes for this will rarely, if ever, be satisfactory or effective for them. Acting from the heart (which also draws other people to them) they may not always be aware of their considerable impact, often appearing unobtrusive and unassuming. Overall, their way of being in the world emanates essentially from a basic human warmth and additional signature of goodwill they seem to stamp on everything. This will usually be felt despite any other strained approaches and I agree with Michael Meyer who states that this type "responds to relationship instinctively".[1] Indeed, they are often those to whom complete strangers feel both safe enough and compelled to tell their entire life story. They can charm a roomful of people by radiating a gentle humility or dazzle that same room with joyful humour. However obvious, or however soft and intangible, there is often a sense of stylish or charismatic presence about this person, a certain '*je ne sais quoi*'...

Yet there is a resilience being constellated in dedication to a mission... a 'seed' knowing it is at the commencement of an epic journey and needing to develop hardiness, especially where there is little or nothing to latch onto except creation (wholeness) itself. Sometimes it can be difficult for them to quite understand that they exist in the world at all, since identification with that world would mean an identification with form – the physical and material as an objective concept. Since its awareness lies in simple being, then 'existence' (Latin – to stand out) is a separation from the original state, the start of differentiation and this does not commence in the cycle of development until a little later on after the conjunction is through. It is not others of which they are oblivious so much as their own form-identified selves and there can also be difficulty in being aware of their own feeling-motivations, such that they frequently seem to be operating out of an idealism or naivety before they can put it into a more concrete experience and make the necessary adjustments. Sensing things at a deep interior level and in a way that defies logic, this may take the form of indulging in fantasies or dreams which may sometimes cover up their real feelings. Or there may be a 'fudging over' of the realities of a situation before addressing key issues, usually because there is an underlying need for time/space for the surrounding dynamics to sink into the person's awareness before being able to deal with them. The key inner tone is one of something that has to be made manifest in order to live the full extent of their being. It may in fact be several things, such as a bundle of innate skills or a dedicated and purposeful direction – not that the individual will necessarily think of it in such clear terms; more often it arises simply as a deep feeling that one wants to *give* so much out to the world. They may not precisely know how and where this is all going to come into actuality. Some may leave it sitting at the level of fantasy, but the essential purpose is to make it a living reality by directing the imagination into creative activity.

Some commentators have spoken of this phase as being go-getting and plunging into life, full of confidence or high animation but I have not necessarily found this to be so. It *can* be the case where, for example, there are other threads of meaning impinging on the Sun/Moon which would lead one to suppose attendant vigorous energies and the more thrusting development of a pugnacious self. But the spontaneity of New Phase is not necessarily physical and expressed in obvious ways, for as we saw in Chapter 2, the seed in the ground is not raring to go, breaking out from its casing instantaneously, but primarily rooted in being-ness. In fact, many New Moon people have a sort of 'on/off' quality about them as if they either want to be *totally* involved in what they are doing or being, or they cannot be bothered with it at all. You may never know quite what has flipped the switch and indeed neither may they. Inner questions not only of security and belonging but also of motivation and enthusiasm may arise for them in this respect, particularly if we take the word 'enthusiasm' to its Greek root of *en*, in, *theos*, a god – or 'God-inspired zeal'.

In this connection, much will depend on environmental factors and the entry point into life itself, as we also saw in Chapter 2. If I were a seed in a fertile garden I imagine I would have considerably more zeal, howsoever inspired, for the pathway ahead of me than if I were quivering in but a scratchy piece of earth halfway up a cold mountainside! So the on/off quality may also emanate from a deep avenue of tentativeness of the 'Shall I or shan't I?', 'Will I live or will I die?' kind. All that new beginning for the seed, all that potential to be unfurled, yet *anything* could happen: it could get dug up by mistake even in a fertile garden, or trampled underfoot especially if it has secured its beginnings in but a tiny fissure of concrete; it may be pecked from the soil by a passing bird or have landed in a part of the meadow where it is overhung with larger plants and trees bearing down nothing but dark shade upon it and preventing its access to the light of the Sun. And yet *still* the path is forward. This kind of energy is reminiscent of Paul Coelho's description of the "warrior of light" whose dreams carry him forward and who knows "there are moments when one should act and moments when one should accept. The warrior knows how to distinguish between these moments".[2] This is a warrior of inner intelligence, faith, confidence (*con*, with – *fidence*, faith), again as opposed to the warrior of power and adversity emanating from a thrust to fight in defence or offence. Deep down there is an unspoken (perhaps unacknowledged) self-reliance in New Phase types, notwithstanding an accompanying vulnerability.

Part of the vulnerability is that recognition is a major factor in their lives and they can lose energy and interest very quickly if it is not forthcoming. It is particularly difficult for them to be ridiculed or humiliated and if the New Moon person is met with utter frustration, s/he can find this intolerable and 'switch off' completely or at least be extremely disinclined to try again for the validation needed. If the vulnerability is high, then in the same way that a seed in the ground may be swamped and choked off from flourishing by mightier plants or weeds, so too the New Moon type may be relegated, squashed aside and mistreated by other people who operate at more acquisitive or challenging levels, and thus be rode roughshod over. Some may 'bunker down' into their Moon only (by sign and house), in a virtual cocoon of hibernation, living this out while leaving the rest of the chart largely as what Charles Carter called a "dumb note". In the process they may create something of a barrier around them in fear of utter demolition and out of instinctive self-protection. Alternatively they may create a way of life in which they are forever billowing in the wind like a lost tossed seed, never landing anywhere much. Conversely, the more stoic amongst them will embody principles of flourishing and growing in spite of harrowing, painful conditions.

However, while we all need to feel the warmth of the Sun on our face, to bask in the glow of recognition, yet in New Phase I have not especially found that this is of the overt egotistical variety with its attendant need for bells-and-whistles and trumpets blaring. Again that may be present if other chart factors support the notion of such satisfaction being sought, but overall it is not a major feature of the New Phase *per se*. If it exists, it is usually projected within a context of child-like innocence, playfulness, fun, rather than any bigotry or caustic arrogance. Alternatively, those who do occupy a famous 'stardom' role in life very often do so within the fundamental context of a rather more contained or 'cocooned' existence, such as may be afforded by a family or entourage around them who offer protection, safety, privacy. Otherwise many New Moon types are masters of self-deprecation, preferring to keep a low profile or even be reclusive. This may be particularly the case, where the conjunction of Sun/Moon is close (as for example in Queen Victoria's chart where it falls in the 12th house), reflecting the fact that we do not see a New Moon as it is obfuscated for a few days both prior to and after the conjunction. And sometimes, even if the limelight appears and the New Moon person is invited to step into it, there can be bemused astonishment coupled with a self-effacing desire to 'get it over with as soon as possible', rather as if the initial seed feels unsure it can quite take all that light suddenly shining upon it since its very being emanates from the darkness. Some may step out into a spotlight yet feel guilty or even act self-punitively in the face of recognition and praise. Such was the case with one client, an amateur actor who was suddenly asked to take the lead role; on the way home after the first night, wherein he had been much hailed, he managed to start a monumental argument with his wife over the most trivial of matters, thus (in his words) "making sure my moment of glory was thoroughly ruined and I could retreat to obscurity!"

It is more a need for simple validation that is crucial for this person. Where this is not available, many find their experience of manifesting creativity in the world is a poignant, sometimes burdensome, or lonely one. In the process this phase type can feel that although the world is not particularly supportive of its creativity as it is being unfolded, it is all too ready to grasp its results – or as another New Moon client put it to me "I feel my life is a constant stream of being taken from until I am drained and withering". They can feel very 'hassled' by a world which expects something from them all the time (a little like impatiently waiting for seeds to show the first signs of growth – how long are they going to *take*?!) But the 'seed' of course has its own inner design and timing and for this they need periodically to return to the interior to access who they intrinsically are and from which the validation sought can really spring.

The derivation of 'recognition' from Latin *recognoscere*, is to 're-know' oneself. Gurdjieff spoke of "self-remembering" – recalling the essence of your being – and this is a lunar state, developing understanding not from the concrete mind and knowledge (which is the province of Mercury) but as an inner absorption. Thus, again, periods of quiet introspection are required for New Moon people in order to reconnect with their purpose and if they are not to succumb to frustration, stress or feelings of emotional exile. Many have a deep affinity with nature, animals, plant life, all residing in simple being. From this, the need for validation – regardless of the fact that it may be shot through with vulnerability – arises as a seeking to share something precious that is emerging from within. Not being much given to superficialities and 'small talk', the need to re-know oneself can also mean that many periodically attend retreats or simply find a place in their day-to-day lives to create a sacred space for reflection. Others still may concern themselves in fields such as psychotherapy, astrology, spiritual teachings, for inner exploration and awareness of others. Many are singularly adept at being what Carl Rogers called "congruent", i.e. able to enter into another person's frame of reference and bring warmth of understanding, as opposed to seeing another person solely as an object for evaluation and interpretation from an aloof and conceptual standpoint. Existential psychoanalyst Rollo May comes under this phase, as does James Hillman, former director at the Jung Institute in Zurich, together with New York psychiatrist M. Scott Peck. Like James Hillman, Dr. Peck was a prolific writer, also with an ability to get straight to a moot point (the Sun/Moon phase contains a Mercury/Mars conjunction). His best-selling *The Road Less Travelled* begins with the statement of startling and truthful simplicity: "Life is difficult".[3]

As emblems of a new beginning, many born in this phase are singularly good at instigating things, taking the lead without necessarily being able to identify a discernible road ahead. This is not through conscious planning and directing, simply an inner resonating to something that feels like a 'must do' or 'must be'. Only later does it emerge that it was a precursor for an innovative step forward. They also know they have to take this road and set something upon it, even though inwardly they may feel pulled by patterns from the past holding them back. Even if they are not 'upfront' leaders of anything, they often stand for something that represents a turning point or evokes a fresh start in the spirit of whatever age or culture they inhabit. William Wilberforce was born with the phase in Virgo, the Sun end being in exact quincunx to Uranus. Mercury was the first planet to be touched by the Moon after birth and this planet opposes Uranus; thus both luminaries focus upon freedom as a key tenet, reflected in his life through the abolition of slavery. Queen Victoria was cited by Rudhyar[4] under this phase on the basis that her name was given to a whole era. The era itself, of course, stood for many beginnings – in industrial, scientific and political fields. Victoria personally was a 'hidden seed' in her isolated and restrictive upbringing until she became Queen and even then she disliked the pomp and circumstance associated with her position. She notably kept herself hidden from view for long periods, particularly after the death of Prince Albert, operating from behind the scenes but through ('cocooned' by) a powerful prime minister such as Disraeli. A further example is Elvis Presley (Sun 17° Capricorn with Moon 44° ahead in Pisces) to whom we give leadership status when we speak of him as "The King". Beyond the vivacious presentation of his talent (mostly represented by attendant threads in his chart), Presley exuded an interior lonely vulnerability coupled with quiet humility. The Sun and Moon border the New and Crescent Phases, thus signifying the fusion of innate creativity with the capacity for struggle and effort: a pivotal figure standing at the gateway of, and a foundation for, the building of a new era of Rock and Roll. Yet he was also cocooned within an entourage and especially his manager who never allowed him to tour the United Kingdom. The singer Annie Lennox comes across as a fusion of charismatic 'presence' and dedicated creativity; she exudes a way of being which seems automatically to convey that her gifts are hard won and worked for, plus an unmistakable reservoir of private emotional depth (Sun/Moon New in 4th house Capricorn).

New Phase people may also go through 'dormant' periods, yet nevertheless always open to new beginnings. Sir David Attenborough writes of the excavation of an ancient settlement in Japan which had been a harvest-store during the Yayoi Period (c 300 BC – AD 300) where in one pit there were still some grains and seeds. Most were blackened and dead, but among them lay one seed which looked different to the rest. It was planted, watered and astonishingly sprang into life. It was a beautiful magnolia.[5] So just as a small seed even after thousands of years is capable of answering the thrust toward life, New Phase people may be low-key, barely noticeable, even 'off the radar', yet spring up into creative life again. There is also often a quality within them that leaves a lingering trace, long after we have met them, even after they have died. Again we meet this in the iconic Presley, who is not only written and spoken of as "The King Lives!" but whenever one hears of him he always seems to have "just left the building"...

The automatic quality of the New Phase can be particularly reflected closer to the conjunction and may be found in those whose lives follow a set and designated road, such as Prince William born on a New Moon eclipse and whose pathway is obvious and automatic by dint of his birth and the future role to which it is leading. On a familial level, the New Moon person may emerge, literally, as a new 'thread' being introduced to the ancestral line, or as representative of a different individuality, perhaps taking the line on to a new perspective from what hitherto was a set pattern the family had settled for.[6]

Unless one is born exactly on a New Moon, there may be other planets in the space between Sun and Moon. These will highlight additional innate or early-absorbed themes, becoming a main focus as the person grows, either impinging negatively upon the basic quality of the phase or indeed enhancing it. In fact, since the phase is essential pliable in nature, this type may be very easily deflected from its simplicity, latching on to powerful containments, or aspects to Sun or Moon or both. Saturn, for example, may emerge as a stiff formality, expectation of limitations or a solid concreteness, while Pluto may herald a thread of suppression, needs for power, intense control or deeply embedded emotions and Mars may have this person functioning with more obvious outward vigour. It might also be noted where Capricorn falls in the chart for both this sign and its ruler are synonymous with the time of year when the seed is underground and can be useful in helping a person identify where and how they may be seeking to anchor themselves in life for onward participation.

The chart of Muhammad Ali shows Sun/Moon New Phase opposing Pluto in Leo ("I am the Greatest").

The Leo Ascendant describes the need to project himself as an individual of supremacy in his chosen work (the ruler, Sun, in the 6th house). Notably, the late Howard Sasportas (himself a highly creative, pioneering and charismatic New Phase type) spoke of the 6th house as being "the place of blossoming into precisely what we are meant to be".[7] Pluto is not only opposite the Sun/Moon New Phase and their midpoint but in turn completes a T-square with Mars in Taurus, reflecting his physical prowess. It is also worth noting that the first planets met by the Moon after birth are Mercury

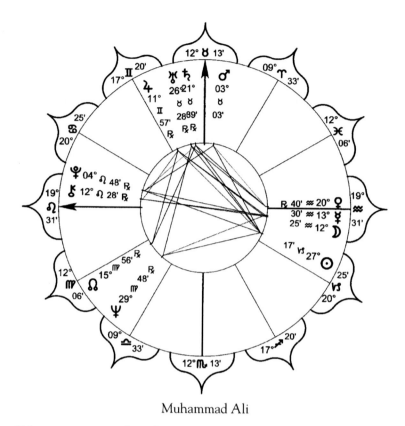

Muhammad Ali

and Venus conjoining the 7th cusp – the flow of chatter and taunting banter with opponents, the alacrity, the dancing movement, the inner need to stir up his world (Venus, ruler of 10th, square Saturn/Uranus in 10th), all portrayed through the New Phase context of playfulness, charisma, good humour, carrying himself with the endearing "Float like a butterfly, sting like a bee".

Once the 30° semi-sextile point has been reached the impulse to be and do is felt a little more immediately such that it becomes 'graspable' to talk about yet may not be altogether full of clarity. Those in the later stages of New Phase often convey a mixture of both an awareness and wonder at their standing on the brink of something. This then forms the context within which they weave their threads of creative being and the astrologer is in a key position to help them gradually verbalize what this brink may consist of and take first steps into meeting it. Working with those born under this phase requires us to be aware that they are led by their own inner promptings, however unreasonable these may seem. Theirs is a way of being not designed to fulfil mental concepts of logic and reasonableness but must follow its own dimensions. This can certainly be augmented by the astrologer who helps them validate their experiences through meaningful dialogue. They are often assisted by tracing imagery, such as being an actual seed in the ground – what kind of seed are they, where are they planted? Identification with the animal kingdom is also frequent – "I feel like a mole burrowing away underground, trying to tunnel my way through, and people hate it when I unexpectedly come up for air in their carefully manicured lawn!" said one client who was grappling with issues of relating to work colleagues who objected to his truth-seeking and open honesty about things. Overall it is the spontaneity of being within the New Phase type that always carries its own elucidation.

Sun/Moon Crescent Phase Moon is 45° – 90° ahead of the Sun

Anchoring Building

> "Always remember that striving and struggle precede success, even in the dictionary."   [Sarah Ban Breathnach]

The now–burgeoning seed has to expend effort into breaking through its outer casing and establishing itself in the soil. In the words of Pema Chodron[8] it could "freak out or settle in". Both are possibilities in this phase. In order to render itself secure in its setting so that it can go forward further and become the shoot above the ground, the emerging seed must encounter its surroundings by putting out some first tendrils and little roots. Slowly and gradually these initial anchorings are extended and spread as the new plant struggles to fix itself in *terra firma*.

People born in Crescent Phase primarily need to develop qualities of earnest effort in unfolding their lives. Theirs is a pathway of building something up, patiently, carefully, persistently, to keep working at it come what may. Unlike the New Moon type, the ability to tolerate frustration is very high here; in fact frustration, difficulties – and yes, mistakes – are often regarded as par for the course. It is also important to note the two main movements in this phase: the first is the breaking away from the seed casing and the second is the struggle forward into the path ahead. Over and over again one finds Crescent people breaking away from a past set of circumstances in order to build up what they have come into life to do and/ or be. The ability to trust one's instincts is not automatic here as it was in New Phase, so there is a tendency for the Crescent type to need some kind of definite pattern to fall back on while at the same time pushing forward to establish something new. While they turn their faces willingly to the road of persistent building, yet they often need to know that there is something solid beneath their feet – be it a home, a partner, set of friends, a particular faith; something that grounds and anchors them, just as those first roots do for the plant as it pushes on to an eventual chink of light. This may be particularly where the past consisted of some kind of cherished certainty or belonging, for example leaving a family or even a homeland as part and parcel of their overall mission to become architects of a new future.

Some Crescents may find this path all too wearisome and instead get stuck in inertia, although the sheer boredom of this may provide the necessary prompt to 'try, try and try again' in life. However, if there is an utterly resistant response to the call to move forward, it can mean they are totally caught up in, and prefer to remain with, what is already solid and known from the past. The repressed energy can then arise in other ways, such as physical debility, overly-dependent attitudes or a constant 'woe-is-me' air of tedium. The lack of effort can also lead to a turgid or superficial lifestyle where little holds any consequence or meaning – the safe plodding job requiring no particular drive or skill, nor even the need to stand up and be counted, but nevertheless produces the monthly paycheck. But whatever the actual manifestation, the main issue here seems to be a tendency not to take risks if possible so as not to lose what has already been gained.

The persistence within this phase can mean that some Crescent types can seem a little 'heavy', demanding, blunt or entrenched. Sometimes this takes the form of being very materialistic or possessions-oriented, or they seem personally to loom large in every situation as if in a takeover bid. The basic tentativeness of the phase can make it difficult for them just to let go and enjoy themselves. It is as if there is always something they have to be beavering away with, always something that has to be checked out, there's an important task at hand and it *cannot* be left, of that they are adamant. Indeed, if we bear in mind the young plant still in the darkness under the earth yet with new little roots growing, the task is indeed important. It *has* to anchor itself, no two ways about it if it is to progress through its full life cycle. But from another perspective, the potential for dogmatic, steamroller attitudes may need to be addressed if they present difficulties. One young woman reported that whenever her Crescent Phase mother-in-law came to stay, she would stomp around the house checking out every vase, every picture, every last set of silver teaspoons she had ever given the couple on their marriage, and if she could not see them would demand to know where they were! More positively, however, the bluntness can mean that they are apt to be utterly straightforward in their determination, shooting straight from the hip and 'telling-it-like-it-is'. A good example of this dynamic came from legendary Hollywood star, Bette Davis, (born with Sun in Aries in the 5th in Crescent phase to Moon conjunct Pluto in Gemini). On personal levels they are often experienced as good buddies, people you can rely on to see a job through; super troupers.

Functioning at their highest, Crescent phase people are found playing a pivotal and fundamental role. They may literally be doing the spade-work, building foundations for something that will serve the needs of, and be answered by, many other people. The solidity with which it is delivered similarly sets an example to others who also seek to develop their lives with resilience, such that they often turn to a Crescent type for inspiration and support. 'Sheer guts' might be an apt description, though some may occasionally see it as intransigence or even foolhardiness. I am reminded of The Fool in the Tarot pack, one depiction of which is a young man with his bundle of experiences over his shoulder about to step out over what looks like a precipice and a dog at his feet yelps to hold him back. Yet the card carries the intrinsic meaning that there is an opportunity to create a new way forward in life, all possibilities are open and the only way to discover what this new path holds is to tread it. Even though it may sometimes seem that the path of the Crescent Phase is slow, arduous or even boringly plodding, if we go below surface interpretations we discover those of stamina who painstakingly *stay the course* and do what needs to be done, anchoring it all as a reality. The challenge and the commitment to the task within this phase makes it possible for them to carry on almost indefinitely, even in the face of obstacles, defeats and setbacks. Working at its best, the major threads to be woven are those of professionalism, dependability, conscientiousness and endurance. Very often we may find them living out a role as actual builders, or architects, or skilled craftspeople, artisans, who master their resourcefulness and accomplishments. But whatever they do they live by knowing *what* they are doing and *why* they are doing it, coupled with a determination to complete whatever is theirs to contribute to the world.

When the Sun and Moon are nearer the 60° sextile aspect in this phase, there is often a distinct ability to relate to the environment. Rael/Rudhyar[9] describe this as indicative of reaching for opportunities for further growth and development. It correlates with the plant utilizing its first tendrils to stretch further into the soil around which, in turn, releases nutrients to it. Wildlife, such as those helpful chaps called earthworms, assist in the process opening up aerated channels enabling the nutrients to flow and ease the passage of roots through the soil. Likewise, as this individual makes known whatever they are patiently developing, they attract the support of others. Nearer the quintile aspect there are enhanced and courageous elements to the 'reaching out' and 'communicating' and the past in a person's life also has much less of a pull. Often there are drives to devise newer roads out of old ways of doing things and bring in a more enlightened approach. One example of this was Maria Montessori, born with the Sun/Moon in sextile containing Mercury in the 3rd (education). She was to focus her strong and practical desire to help children (the Moon rules an innovative Mars/Uranus conjunction in Cancer and Saturn's practicality is focused into the 5th) to develop their self-creating process of absorbing knowledge and understanding. Thus she gave rise to what is now known worldwide as the Montessori method which gives recognition to a child's natural ability to teach itself untrammelled by the thoughts/directions of adults. The Sun is in Virgo, highlighting the Mercurial/3rd house theme of education, highlighted further still by a quincunx (reorganizational) thread to Chiron in the 9th (the teacher) which opposes Mercury in the 3rd.

Rudhyar said[10] that every individual is born "in answer to the need of humanity at a definite time and place". If the need of humanity on 15th January 1929 was for a soul of Sun/Moon Crescent perseverance, effort and struggle in pursuit of a noble cause, then this was surely generated in the birth of Dr Martin Luther King whose life proclaims loudly the highest manifestation of this Sun/Moon phase. In his chart the phase contains both Mercury in 10th house Aquarius and Venus in 11th house Pisces. These represent two major qualities inherent in Dr King and exemplified throughout his life via his empowering and electrifying oratory (Mercury Aquarius 10th) and the strength of his spiritual ideals (Venus Pisces in the 11th/Aquarian house).

Their positions also denote the direction of these ideals into addressing injustices and championing social causes and, notably, the Moon end of the phase is Piscean ("I have a dream…"). Attacked, threatened, imprisoned and bombed, Dr King's persistent and fervent determination to build a better tomorrow for those suffering in the turbulent face of segregation in the American south undoubtedly earned him his rightful place in history as a man of undaunted conviction, compassion and purpose.

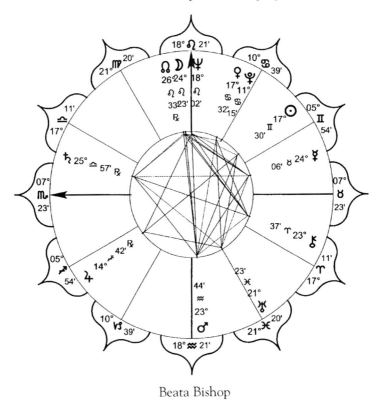

Beata Bishop

Beata Bishop is a psychotherapist, astrologer, writer and long-time survivor of a life-threatening cancer. The Moon in Leo is ahead of the Sun in Gemini by some 67°, at the sextile aspect emphasizing the capacity to reach out, discover, and avail oneself of support from the environment within the context of effort and struggle. In 1979 she was at the height of her career as a successful journalist, having established a home in London after leaving her native Hungary in 1948. So it was with rude shock that she discovered during a routine medical examination that she had a malignant melanoma. What had started as a small brown spot, to which she gave as much attention as one would to a freckle, now became much darker and was spreading. She set about her own researches (Sun 8th house Gemini, Scorpio rising, Pluto cusp 9th) and discovered that she was suffering from one of the most lethal of cancers. Things were to go from bad to worse.

Several months of surgery and skin grafts followed, only to find a year later that the cancer had spread into her lymphatic system. Devastated, she felt drained of all life particularly on being informed that without further surgery her life expectancy ranged between six weeks to six months. The words 'setback' and 'frustration' so common in the lives of Crescent types do not even begin to come close to what Beata must have felt. Yet this most persevering and conscientious of women moved ever forward. With help from her friends she phoned around everywhere (the sextile) looking for help, insights, *anything...* until somebody said "Why doesn't she try the Gerson therapy?" Dr Max Gerson, an orthodox doctor, had published *A Cancer Therapy – Results of Fifty Cases* in 1959 which set out precise guidelines for treating cancer nutritionally and by drastic detoxification.

Beata travelled to the world's only Gerson Clinic in Mexico (this in the face of many people who thought she was mad – a 'Fool'). Her Gemini/Scorpio spirit quickly alighted on the two central tenets of Dr. Gerson's teachings which were that a degenerative disease exists on the basis of (a) toxicity of the body and (b) deficiency of nutrients. Notably the Moon end of the phase is opposed by Mars, ruler of the 6th house of bodily health and one of the rulers of her chart. Both the Sun and Moon aspect Neptune, ruler of the 5th house of vibrant life which itself contains Uranus calling for transformational insight (square Gemini Sun). Daunted by the long haul it would require, yet not wilting in determination, Beata learnt the theory and practice of the therapy to clear the accumulated toxins. There followed two gruelling years of this regime, reducing its intensity only very slowly and gradually.

Beata has not let up on her commitment over the past thirty years. In 1985 she published a book recounting the story of her healing journey[11]. More recently she co-authored another[12] with Charlotte Gerson (daughter of Dr Max Gerson). She has worked unceasingly to promote the value of addressing and treating a cancer not necessarily through removal, irradiation or chemotherapy, but to look beyond the tumour to see it as a symptom, one such being nutritional deficiency and bodily toxicity so rife in the unhealthy diets of our world today. Her remarkable journey has recently been enhanced by the setting up of a further Gerson Centre in her native Hungary, a very fine accomplishment in the furtherance of this important healing path. Several tapestry threads can be traced in Beata's life: initially leaving behind a past (her native Hungary) putting down new roots to build a home in England, working hard to anchor herself in a career through which she communicated with her environment; then submitting herself to the onerous path of facing her imminent death and overcoming this through sheer guts, an adamant, questioning mind and persistence to find another way.

The patient building quality of this phase can easily be submerged by a modern collective responding to instant gratification and superficial quick fixes. Mounting debt crises beset the lives of many who became swept up into a 'wanting-not-waiting' culture, particularly in the mid-1990s onwards, with its *cri du coeur* of "Live for Today!" As the credit card wagons rolled, crushed under their wheels were the spirits of many a Crescent soul with needs for consolidation and courage but who were instead pulled by the climate of an opportunistic business culture. Emma was born with Aquarius rising, a dynamic Jupiter/Pluto square plus Venus/Uranus trine, with an additional strong Sagittarian emphasis, all within the context of Sun/Moon Crescent. Young, vibrant and incredibly beautiful, she lived an exciting life as a fashion buyer, travelling constantly all over the world. Indeed fixing an appointment proved very difficult because of her calendar/itineraries, but she finally made it, out of breath having just flown in from New York and sat across from me in a rather comfortable armchair ... but one upon which she just perched on the edge. At any moment I expected her to jump up and announce she was "leaving on a jet plane"....

A subsequent appointment was of the same order – arriving breathless, edge of the seat, full of next exciting plans.... and yet ... there was something else... something unsettling about all this. I had to do a considerable amount of looking at whether this was not just plain little old Capricorn me feeling a mite dull in the face of such glitz and glamour. But then she phoned again, sounding tired and jaded. She had a few days free and wondered if we could talk. She arrived, sat on edge of seat etc. ...yet was somehow quieter. When I addressed this, she said that she was very exhausted, her job was meaningless yet felt she could not let up on her schedule with its spiralling costs she could barely keep track of as she did not want to let her parents down. It seemed they had considerable pride and emotional investment in this most beautiful of daughters with her dynamic successful life. Picking my words carefully, I described Crescent phase. As I finished, with a query as to whether her tiredness may be an expression of something within her needing to live a life not of frenetic activity but one of more considered construct, she sank (for the first time) well back into the comfortable armchair, her hand came up and ran itself back through her long mane of beautiful hair and she said, *very very slowly*: "You – don't – know . . . how – utterly – relieved – I am... listening to that... *God!*"

Gradually she began to unfold (again building every word carefully) a story of how she truly wanted to leave England and set up home in Europe. It emerged that she had a plan to build a horticultural centre on a plot of land she had seen for sale on one of her many journeys. She was hesitant since this meant leaving home and parents yet she was fired with a commitment to this task, especially as she had plans for a small animal holding which would be an educational centre for children too. As she spoke, I heard a young Crescent phase woman eminently equipped to work hard at something she believed in and build it up brick by brick if necessary. Her endearing caution coupled with inner conviction, plus a need to ease her way out of a way of life she increasingly found ill-fitting – these were the threads that spoke out the essence of Crescent Phase.

Finally – and perhaps a little surprisingly – under this phase we also have one Mr. Francis Albert Sinatra. Notions of effort and struggle probably do not immediately spring to mind here, for one is surely usually first transported by the magical 'Come-Fly-With-Me'[13] delights of a 5th house Jupiter (ruling the Sagittarian Sun) in Pisces, Mars in 10th house Leo, Neptune charismatically conjunct Leo Midheaven.

But the Crescent phase (Sun/Moon 76° apart) is there, with the creative enhancement of the quintile already incorporated into his being, and I feel there are two main tapestry threads of building and struggle which we can trace. The first is derived from many moons ago when I sang for a while with a main London Choir; once or twice we were reminded in rehearsal of the value of timing, phrasing and enunciation. So some of us met up in little groups, spending whole afternoons listening to various soloists, but certainly Sinatra, on the basis that if we were in need of a masterclass where every word, every phrase, every key change is not just merely well sung but also beautifully *crafted* – well, who better? This was a man with impeccable timing and phrasing... and the ability to hone even a single word in such a way that it *anchored* itself in one's heart and memory everlastingly. So the building of superb craftsmanship was one avenue conquered by Sinatra throughout his legendary and enduring career.

The second thread we can trace is in his emotional life. Yes, there are the threads of initial struggle and effort to establish himself in the early years (1930s to 40s), working as a delivery boy or waiter, and yes his career stalled on several occasions and he constantly picked himself up to make repeated comebacks. But it is the positioning of Venus and Uranus, together with North Node in the 4th house of belonging, contained within Sun and Moon, which leads me to look more for threads of feeling difficulty to be overcome. Venus is in Capricorn opposing Saturn ('None but the lonely heart…'[14]). Roy Alexander[15] says of Sinatra "It is a substantial part of his magic that he conveys so well the feelings of being lost, vulnerable and deprived of love". Along with the struggle of inner loneliness notwithstanding outer creativity and world-conquering success, Uranus conjunct the North Node and in gibbous quincunx to Saturn seems to speak of an impregnable emotional determination and needs for freedom to build something carefully, further exemplified in the lyrics to 'My Way'[16] which might almost be an anthem to a Crescent struggling spirit imbued with striking individuality.

Sun/Moon First Quarter Phase   Breakthrough
Moon is 90°–135°   Challenge
ahead of the Sun

> "The ultimate measure of a man is not where he stands at moments of comfort and convenience, but where he stands at times of challenge and controversy."   [Dr Martin Luther King]

Having anchored itself in Crescent Phase, the plant has broken through the ground and is in the light. With an almighty thrust it now stands at a new gateway of vibrant new life. This phase is synonymous with the appearance of the waxing Moon when it has reached a half-circle with its dividing line between dark and light – as Rudhyar points out, a cutting in half, or 'decision'. Perhaps you can remember a time in your life when you pushed your head above some kind of parapet. It probably meant you were answering a challenge, putting yourself out there, standing and fighting for something new and different. When this arises we may not know whether the world will applaud us, or biff us on the nose; no matter, we break through anyway. And it all "happens pretty fast!" as Ferris Bueller found on his famous Day Off.

Instant decisive action is indeed the keynote of the First Quarter person. As opposed to the New Phase energy which sprang from a fundamental spontaneous warmth, here it derives from an impatience to handle the physical, material world. This person *has* to get going and keep moving. S/he may not feel vital and alive unless attacking some kind of problem, getting something started, or even breaking something up. The movement is not one of gradual easing forward as in the Crescent phase, but requires a veritable Butch Cassidy and The Sundance Kid *leap* over a precipice. At their most vigorous, these people will act first and think about it afterwards, bulldozing their way through if necessary to get things done and bring an idea or action to life. There may not always be a clear-cut end goal in view, but there is an all-or-nothing commitment. The basic drive is to start something and see what happens, handle the consequences as they arise. There are myriad ways of these themes being manifested in the life of any one individual and of course they may be modified by other (perhaps more sedate) threads within the chart. But, overall, this phase carries the potential for developing qualities of immediate response, improvisation, development of fast reflexes, opportunism.

In order to achieve this, the past needs to be repudiated in some way so that a corner can be turned and a new road forged ahead. Some may find this difficult or be resistant to the turning point. In such cases, they can spend an inordinate amount of time and energy complaining about their situation (and the past), yet repeatedly fighting with it, dragging up past events, people, situations for complaint, thus generally feeding more energy into it. Others may try to ignore such things altogether, yet nevertheless walk around with a terse air of contained anger like a bee trapped in a jam-jar. If, instead, they can lift up a little and explore the nature of the 90° turning point here, the energy previously utilized to keep things intact can then be released to be woven into a new future.

The driving ambition of First Quarter people is often accompanied by a need to prove themselves to the world, ruthlessly if necessary, and they are sometimes uncomfortable with the realm of feelings which they sense might just get in their way. In short they can simply dive in with all guns blazing, no matter what, to destroy some existing pattern they deem is *outmoded*.

One has to credit them for their bravura in repudiating the past, even in the face of resistance from many around. However, the lack of clarity as to ways forward once something has been dispensed with is worth dwelling on consciously if they are not to trip themselves up and jump brazenly from a frying pan into a fire. The energy available is synonymous with, for example, a political activist who may clamour loudly and bravely for the overthrow of a government, but be much weaker when it comes to knowing what is going to replace it. Similarly the First Quarter type may barge straight into a situation but have no exit in view – as we saw in 2003 when the First Quarter George W. Bush along with his supporters led an invasion on Iraq in defiance of many voices of dissent around the world.

The bust-out-of-jail quality to this person is sometimes presented as if their very life depends on it. This may be connected to early life experiences (such as warring factors in the early family environment), or even birth itself. Janov, for example, found that impulsive types were "running off a birth sequence", i.e. part of the need to plunge ahead in life without considering consequences was that *not* to do so could recall the trauma of near-death due to stoppage of the natural birth process.[17] Controversy there may well be, but in this phase there is very little tolerance of frustration – "Don't Stop Me Now!" – and, as we have seen, there is a large danger of acting prematurely. Whether this is perceived as 'barging in' or 'being forthright' is a moot point but in either case there is just an imperative to go with the power of the impulse. Again Janov found that this may equate to where the about-to-be-born makes a last ditch attempt to get out of the womb, the plunging quality of the birth becoming an imprinted prototype for later ways of being.[18] Since the emphasis is upon action and not consideration, a sense of timing, tact and discretion are therefore not features of this phase and if the action is ego-driven to a high extent there may even be bids for domination being played out. And if you do attempt to hold back First Quarter types, far from being able to switch them off (as you might do very easily with New Phase) you are likely to provoke them into even more frenzied activity!

In jumping in with two big feet, it has to be said that in some cases there may also be hints (even large dollops) of arrogance, plus an array of very definite opinions thrown at, or dumped upon, you until you feel you have been hit with the proverbial brick. However, if you are a First Quarter type and have read thus far, stay with me because it does get better! As always, other threads in the overall chart may of course modify this and, to be fair, I have known many First Quarter types who are mortified if it is pointed out to them that they are hogging the floor to the detriment of others, or that they are being unnecessarily heavy-handed or destructive. From a positive perspective, we *need* First Quarter energies to keep us on our toes. After all, we could just coast long in an old pattern and not even know we are being suffocated by its sameness and lack of life. It would be like drifting along a lazy river in a little boat – all very pleasant, but we need the vibrancy of First Quarter to take the helm, yank the tiller, set the boat on a new course when it looks like we could be headed up a creek without the proverbial paddle.

Self-doubt is something that practically everyone suffers from but nobody cares to admit. There is a sense that it is a negative which must be swept aside and, as a result, few may explore it for its value. This can certainly be the case in this phase where, as we have seen, the energy is set gung-ho toward acting with apparent fearless conviction. However, more positively it can also be the case that those who *do* take the time to be compassionate with themselves and acknowledge their anxiety (which is certainly present at this 90° turning point) have more openness and flexibility about them, which in turn leads them (perhaps more easily) onto new paths in life. It may well be that for some First Quarters the more tension and anxiety they feel, the more we may see them surging forward with smoke fairly billowing out from behind them but compassion comes from the heart – and the French word for 'heart' (*coeur*) gives rise to our word 'courage'. Indeed for the First Quarter type, self-doubt – if they allow themselves to embrace it – can be a crucial cornerstone, and mark of, their bravery in meeting a challenge.

Being especially adept at clearing away old debris from the past and plunging in First Quarters may often be found in some arena where they get rid of something that is dying on its feet. Or, if it is dying because it has not received sufficient stimulation then this is the person who can jerk it back into new life. They have a great capacity for stirring people into action, although not always appreciative of those others' feelings or preferences. During times when I was retained as a counselling astrologer in corporate situations, I found very many of those in management/strategy situations who displayed the most in terms of go-getting creative ideas were First Quarter types. They faced everything full-on, took several bulls by horns, demolished outworn ideas and showed a flair for turning things around to have a more telling impact. These were not people who were content to stand around 'umming and erring', nor did they walk around their offices with impressive-looking sheaves of paper, flow-charts, reams of statistics and report memos with boxes to be ticked. They just wanted *to get on with it* and make a difference. As such, they were seen as contributing immeasurably to their corporate calling and regarded as born managers.

For the counselling astrologer working with a First Quarter type there may be frequent discussions along the lines of "How will you actually implement that?" or "What's your way forward here – and what needs to happen next?" or "If you don't want to go down that road anymore, what are the options… and where do they lead?" or just a plain and simple "What are you actually doing this *for*?" As we have seen, treating a First Quarter person with indifference or hostility, or (even more futile) trying to change them, will provoke an upsurge of their determination or defiance. Since their crucial drive is to clear the ground of whatever they experience as an obstacle, working with them is akin to being a gardener eliminating weeds from around a new shoot peeking out into the light for the first time so that it has the required space to push through further and grow. When the phase nears the 120° trine aspect, the energies are more free-flowing and laced with an easier sense of security, less agitation, more grounded inner assurance that one is on a road to success.

In another business setting I was asked to comment on a situation which had got out of hand and which seemed to centre around two main protagonists, both of whom wanted to have high impact and be seen as 'Numero Uno'. Person A was born with Sun and Moon 95° apart and Person B with them 128° apart. Both were valuable employees, contributing skills and insights which set them far beyond others in the company (who nevertheless had other attributes). When I met them, Person A's energies were very upfront, go-getting, *seriously* ambitious and a little bit 'grand' (a lot of Leo/Jupiter in attendance). He was indeed impressive, knowledgeable and highly focused especially in areas which were not immediately noticeable but required action, yet each time he appeared he would look around expecting everyone to respond as if an Imperial Majesty had entered the room. Person B was similarly driven, focused on specifics but had an altogether more secure way of presenting himself (his Sun/Moon phase had passed the trine aspect). Additionally, he had an emphasis on 7th house Libra and his enterprising skills were largely centred on encouraging others in his team to add their own insights. His greater ease of being meant that he was also a good listener. In both cases, the first planet met by the Moon after birth was Uranus. In Person A's chart this lay in the 7th house and the experience of the department at large was one of being somewhat 'zapped' by him if they did not fall immediately into line with his wishes and treat him with due deference. In Person B, Uranus fell in the 3rd house where it seemed to be lived out via bright ideas, a wanting (often a slightly irritable impatience) to share them with others (trine Mercury in 7th Libra also), see them acted upon and receive feedback.

The situation was eventually resolved with the suggestion that in order to deal successfully with the actual goals of this company, a separate department could be created and headed up by Person A. This might involve a grand title and a hike-up in salary, but it would give him a department ('a Kingdom') of his own. Its remit was to ensure that the company as a whole, under his public relations leadership and spokesmanship, took its place at the forefront of the particular field of endeavour. Person B could also be validated for his insightful and interactive skills (with or without grand title – I did not get the sense from him that such things were important). One way to do this would be through the set-up of a special training and management department where people on all levels could come together to share views, decide on strategy and keep the wheels moving on track, again to ensure the company's leadership in the field. And periodically both the PR department (Person A) and the Training department (Person B) could submit their proposals to the board. Additionally, and on the basis that those who are at the forefront of something are not always the best exponents of it, this allowed some freeing up of a space for others to rise through the ranks and have their own contributions aired. A garden can accommodate many varied wonderful plants.

Sport is an arena in which these energies often find their best expression. A key example is tennis champion Roger Federer born with Sun on 16° Leo in square aspect to the Moon ahead on 21° Scorpio. The First Quarter phase incorporates the positions of Venus, Saturn, Jupiter and Pluto. The Federer hallmarks are of style, adeptness and precision (Venus rises in Virgo) in that if you focus closely on each shot you can clearly see the open, honest, battling First Quarter energy, totally intent upon its goal; yet if you sit back and watch him from a position of simple enjoyment, you could be forgiven for thinking you were at the ballet instead of Centre Court, Wimbledon. Venus also rules the 2nd house of inner resourcefulness and in this house we find both the hardiness of Saturn (ruling both the 5th house of sport and the 6th house of the physical body and stamina) together with the zeal and focus of Jupiter and Pluto. This arrangement adds up to a sense of what I believe sports people call being 'in the zone'. Federer of course is a skilled master borne of typical First Quarter determination to break through and have unquestionable dynamic impact, in respect of which the conjunction of Moon to Uranus first after birth appears simply (if you will forgive the pun) to serve the final Ace.

Perhaps a little more surprisingly, the Queen is a First Quarter type. We are accustomed to her public persona as an exemplary portrayal of Saturn conjunct a Scorpio Midheaven, a deeply engraved sense of duty to her calling and station in life, yet also one from which she will not be deflected. In this connection the First Quarter phase encompasses Pluto in the 6th house which we also saw in Chapter 3 was already 'collected up' by the Moon at birth. Nevertheless, small peeks behind the scenes of royal life also show a more animated personality beneath the formidable exterior. One television documentary showed her dealing with her daily dispatch papers, fairly zipping through them with few, if any, hesitations, until they were cleared, completing the process with one hand clapping against the other with a 'right, that's *that*' flourish. The Mars/Jupiter conjunction in the 1st house square to the Saturn conjunct Midheaven, gives additional emphasis to a 'lets-get-on-with-it' determination and further aspects of First Quarter energy were revealed in a seemingly-insignificant anecdote reported in a biography of, Prince Edward.[19] Apparently one evening the Queen and Prince Charles were in the sitting room at Buckingham Palace, with the corgis, and the Queen was idly pulling out bits of fluff and dirt from the dogs' coats and flicking them into the open fire… where they spat and crackled as each one fell. After a while, this began to irritate Prince Charles who finally protested, "Oh really! I wish you wouldn't *do* that!" The Queen looked up, briefly… and then, true to First Quarter (which dislikes being curbed), promptly escalated the process, picking and flicking even more assiduously than before!

The British comic genius, Tony Hancock, was born with Sun in 10th house Taurus in First Quarter phase with Moon in 1st house Leo. The phase incorporates a Venus Pluto conjunction in the 11th house and Neptune rising just prior to the Moon in the 1st house.

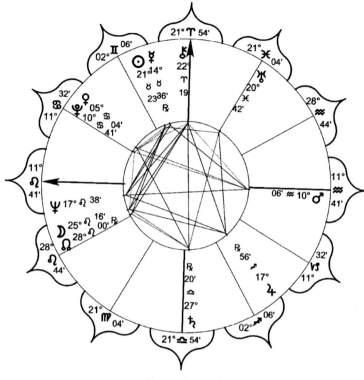

Tony Hancock

   Hancock (as he is affectionately referred to) was best known for his radio
and television programmes *Hancock's Half Hour* during the 1950s and 60s.
During a personal inner life containing much loneliness, alcoholism and
despair, his was a path of seeking to build a life of stability and rootedness
(Taurus) while needing to be seen (1st house) as a charismatic leader (Moon
Neptune) and be the centre of attention (Leo). He had a typical First Quarter
lightning-quick grasp of situations and would plunge unhesitatingly into
things, frequently bypassing the need to look at detail (from his scriptwriters
for instance) in a bid just to rush ahead in imposing, dramatic ways. There
is a wide opposition of Venus/Pluto to Jupiter in the 5th (humour, being
in the limelight) which in turn is trine the MC (wanting fame and glory).
His First Quarter impatience and fighting qualities came particularly to
the fore however, if he felt anyone was upstaging him. It is believed that
deep down he really always wanted to be an actor and it is likely that
Hancock's inner emotional difficulties, including the insecurity of Venus in
Cancer conjunct Pluto, may have been what led to many intense feelings

of jealousy, defensiveness (Venus also aspects a lonely 4th house Saturn) such that he would often ensure that anyone he saw as a 'competitor' was quickly sidelined, which this phase is also apt to do. Yet it was also perhaps this Cancerian-Saturnian 'lostness' of him which carried emotional appeal and warmth (Moon/Neptune/Leo) and made him one of the best-loved of British comedians despite the rather fraught context.

It is also the case that there are many First Quarters who are enchantingly ready for every challenge going in a wholly delightful, if somewhat bamboozling, way. Here we may find the 'loveable rogue' full of banter and 'mouthiness'. Fictional characters often portray that which we would know about ourselves more clearly than a living person, for as Richard Bach points out, they are often "more real than people with bodies and heartbeats".[20] An example would be the hilarious 'Del Boy' character in the British TV comedy *Only Fools and Horses*, superbly portrayed by actor David Jason. This is a character who takes on whatever assails his senses as a way of moving through, going beyond, meeting whatever the world throws at him, all in a bid to 'get there'. "This time next year", he tells his laconic younger brother Rodney, "we're gonna be miwwionaires!" In the same vein, Jason also memorably played Pa Larkin in the TV adaptation of H.E. Bates' *The Darling Buds of May*. Both these fictional characters are archetypal 'cheeky chappie' heroes who challenge the world not in aggressive, fighting style, but by coasting their way through, fuelled by the qualities of opportunism, improvisation, fast movement and just sheer bravado.

On a non-fictional level, when The Beatles returned from their first tour of the United States, they asked the First Quarter John Lennon, "How did you find America?" "Turn left at Greenland" came the forthright, impudent reply.

Sun/Moon Gibbous Phase Moon is 135° – 180° ahead of the Sun

Focus/Analysis Discernment

"The degree of freedom from unwanted thoughts and the degree of concentration on a single thought are the measures to gauge spiritual progress."   [*Bhagavan Sri Ramana Maharshi*]

"There is guidance for each of us, and by lowly listening we shall hear the right word."   [*Ralph Waldo Emerson*]

Now that the shoot has its head above the ground, it is not only viable but thriving. Its stem/leaf structure is in place and, importantly, buds now reveal themselves in readiness for the forthcoming full-flowering. Consider a time in your life when you had built something up and then you found yourself on the threshold of almost 'getting there'. As you came round the final bend, so to speak, there was a need for deep focus and concentration – Have I left anything out? Do I need anything else here? Supposing I do this – what will happen? Maybe I shouldn't have started this … or maybe I should … can I handle it? If the natives of this phase were to have a motto it might be 'look before you leap' for there is a sense in which they are primarily concerned with acquiring as much information as possible *in order to move towards a result*, always wanting to ensure that the right thing is being done, nothing is out of place or left to chance.

Those who are parents will know (or recall) the endless stream of "Why?" questions your darling offspring sprang on you, relentlessly, day in and day out, usually between the ages of two to four years. And as each question was answered it generated further questions. If so, you will understand the energy and need behind Gibbous phase to build a life in which information, knowing, understanding, seeking out all the whys and wherefores, is such life-blood to this person, just as it is to the small child who is endeavouring to figure out how s/he fits into the entire scheme of things. Acquiring 'know-how' and developing techniques is a need that moves from deep within them to find out what works and then function in life accordingly. If at the same time it is allied to any *cautionary* looking-before-leaping, then this person may well appear to move forward in life with some trepidation as if negotiating a minefield.

The phase commences with the alert point of the waxing sesquiquadrate, denoting the capacity for discernment and discovery. Gibbous types are more often than not extremely well-informed people, on whatever level. They are found in situations where intellectual analysis, research and formulaic methods are required, such as in academic or technological settings; alternatively they may simply be collectors of more superficial ideas or techniques, but with no less incisive focus. Often they have a 'nose' for ferreting out detail, a forensic mind that can sleuth anything down, a commitment to intellectual honesty and precision upon which they base their findings and are prepared to stand or fall. Whatever the actuality, their need is to locate an inner methodical, systematic rhythm to proceed in life.

At this they frequently excel, but it is also an arena in which they can just as often become stuck. When this occurs, there is usually an additional perfectionist thread weaving its way through their being, such that they can become over-anxious and 'pernickety' if anything is out of place or does not conform precisely to the method they had constructed with such deep consideration. Sometimes this may manifest as them being 'right' while you are 'wrong', for they have researched it and you have not. Tread carefully, for it may be true! Alternatively, on a general level, there can be a kind of brooding analytical mentality which seems to be fuelled by much anxiety and doubt. Sometimes this may be borne of an earlier life where certain controls, rules or beliefs were rigidly maintained, such as in an orthodox religious background or one of high propriety; thus the person feels anxious not to 'transgress' or make mistakes, which leads to the wary treading over eggshells. If getting it absolutely completely utterly right or perfect is high on their internal agenda they can indeed be fastidious to the nth degree.

I have found this phase to contain many paradoxes (as indeed does all of life) but while there is considerable flexibility in the Gibbous type, yet they can be most inflexible once they have alighted on a particular system that is seen to work. They can certainly generate a great deal of action in life, although very often it is a mere peg for them to launch into endless prior discussion of it followed by equally endless analysis and justification afterwards. Partly this is highlighted by the kind of inner dialogue suggested in the opening paragraph – that could be followed by "Oh, you see, I knew it was the wrong thing to do! You should have stopped me! Why didn't they tell me that it would turn out like this? Well I was only trying to help. I've done my best, what more do you expect?"... and so on and so forth. Here the mind is like a chattering monkey, making incessant noise (*yadda, yadda yadda*), when really what is required is "freedom from unwanted thoughts" as spoken of by Ramana Maharshi.

When their need for questioning and analysis is overdone it becomes worrying, fussing, or over-control; it may also be filled with an expectation that others should operate from the same compulsive methods to accomplish in their lives as they do. In the process they may fail to see the uniqueness of another individual but simply apply a perfectionist view of how they *should* be (to fit in with the system). The issuing of moralistic edicts might be another manifestation but, conversely, if the workings of their not-inconsiderable minds are not understood because they have become overloaded or engulfed by them, they may sometimes even be viewed as muddled, dithering, or incoherent. However, it can also be argued on behalf of the Gibbous type that it does take a searching ability to root out detail for something to be excellent. This points us up rather more in the direction of being creatively immersed in intense focused experience or 'the degree of concentration on a single thought', rather than the chattering mind, again as spoken of by Ramana Maharshi.

And so on the one hand we have the Gibbous energy which is second to none when it comes to finding out the details of things, how it all works and how to keep things in order to ensure continued proper and efficient functioning. There may be a highly skilled drive to develop new techniques and systems, such as in computer expert Bill Gates, born with the phase from Scorpio (Sun) to Aries (Moon) just past the waxing quincunx, an aspect so very geared to sorting out, analysing, prioritising. On the other hand, there may be too strong an adherence to method, procedures and cerebral analysis such that they may be applied relentlessly, worryingly, leaving no room for manoeuvre, nothing out of place. Occasionally this is even translated into appearance (e.g. the 'well-scrubbed' look, or make-up skilfully applied, all is perfectly colour-co-ordinated). It may also be seen in systems of communication, especially in today's world where we might come across Gibbous as Hi-Tech/Laptop Man or Woman who, for every occasion, proceeds on the basis of analyzed information, logging on, keying in, pressing 'enter'. Questioning and finding out can, however, come from levels other than mental constructs and the more flexible type of Gibbous is awake to the fact that looking, watching, listening can also often take us directly into what is needed to be known, as the quotation from Emerson points us to.

The Taurus and Gemini positions in the overall chart can offer further threads to explore as to how and whether these patterns are woven into a meaningful focused actuality, particularly since the phase is partly about moving forward cautiously, deliberately (Taurus) and utilizing the incisive mind to know what is right and what is not, having questioned to find out (Gemini). The drive to understand and synthesize different elements into a functioning whole may take many Gibbous people along routes of personal self-exploration, and here psychology, philosophy, spirituality, may be key pathways. Others may shine in mathematics, astrophysics, engineering, information technology. But whatever avenues are taken, they are those which call forward the need to perfect skills and techniques as well as the capacity to sharpen their insight to take note of detail. Sometimes one may find them as intrepid explorers or journalists bravely reporting from a war zone – surely a situation in which you would need to look before you leap! A case in point is Kate Adie, former BBC chief news correspondent, born with the Sun Virgo in Gibbous Phase to Moon Aquarius, who is renowned for her crisp, efficient and detailed despatches from conflicts in Albania, Yugoslavia, Rwanda, China, Sierra Leone and the Gulf War.

Often the need to acquire workable techniques can mean that this person is best suited to situations in which they can be encouraged to develop along a pathway where learning by trial and error is a theme. They are supremely adept at fitting things together like a 100,000-bit jigsaw but since the 'error' bit may worry them they could find life more harmonious – and it would give them more leeway – if they are (for example in a work situation) in some kind of apprenticeship. Here they can function alongside another person acting as mentor who either answers the questions or helps them delve for their own understandings. In this way if errors are met, overcoming and moving through them is more likely for a Gibbous type who has steady, practical guidance from another, rather than being just on their own where they are likely to feel they have to devise another system since the first one was not perfect!

Books! A joy to the Gibbous type, especially those which help them research things further and wider to feed their appetites and fascinations. Many people born under this phase have also told me of early life experiences where, alongside books, their ability to be intrigued by something and follow it through to understand its workings were fed by (for instance) a first physics lesson at school, or a favourite uncle who bought them a telescope for Christmas. One client told me of a time when she was eight and her mother had given her a good 'telling off' for something she had not actually done (but her sister had and did not own up). Furious at this injustice, she went out into the garden and took it out on an old china bowl that was just lying there filled with dry earth. As she kicked it, the bowl turned upside down and shattered… revealing an ants' nest, complete in every detail and with the colony functioning as a total industrious whole. She has never forgotten sitting in awe at the precision with which these small creatures had built their several compartments for eggs, food storage etc, and the little corridors along which they now all scurried in response to their kingdom being kicked over. A deep respect for rhythm, order, precision, hard work, cohesion, concentrated effort – and even ants – has remained with her all her life, and these qualities are manifested in her career as a teacher of mathematics and as an amateur astronomer.

The pioneering naturalist and ecologist, Gilbert White, was born with the phase from the end of Cancer to early Capricorn. He meticulously observed the cycles of natural wildlife through the seasons in elegant detail. The phase contains the quick and profound perception of a Mercury conjunct Mars square to Saturn in Scorpio and his book *The Natural History of Selborne*[21] was to inspire Darwin in his biology studies. White was a quintessentially English county vicar whose writings (largely through their informality and warmth as opposed to being presented as an academic tome) have shaped our view of the rhythm and relation of human beings and the natural cyclic life; above all they remain influential for their deeply perceptive observations.

With the Gibbous phase, we must remember that its central meaning is in part a preparatory one. It marks the final phase of the waxing hemisphere, but we have not reached the 'main music'. The plant is as yet only in bud but not yet full bloom. If the Sun and Moon are near the 144° biquintile, there is often a key ability in any field where efficient techniques are required, to arrange, devise, put things meaningfully together. There is a certain inner *resolve* to this aspect, a capacity to bring elucidation to whatever is being worked on. Where the phase reaches towards the quincunx, there is the capacity to actually get down to the business of sorting out, making something coherent and workable (as in the case of Bill Gates). Rael/Rudhyar refer to this aspect as a "last chance" point (i.e. before the 180° opposition which marks the end of the waxing hemisphere and thus all that has been built up preceding it).[22] They make a further striking analogy to a student having to hand in an exam paper when the bell rings for time being up! Whether or not you have completed all the questions, the signal has come to finish and you must stand or fall on what you have produced. As the opposition orb is entered, from bud to full bloom, the Gibbous type may become obsessively hung up on outcomes, perhaps brooding that a goal ahead may not be perfect, or indeed see that all that really matters *is* the goal ahead and they have 'given it their best shot'.

Conscientious Gibbous Types are disinclined to rush haphazardly into life, their questioning nature usually taking the form of deep inner ruminations and experimentations. Although often sticklers for precision, their flexible quality can be encouraged, for example by helping them to see that there are 'many ways of baking a cake' rather than getting bogged down in one method only because the recipe book says so. Skilful, quick and sharp, the more goal-oriented among Gibbous types may need to check out from time to time that they are not bypassing deeper observations (i.e. those which lie beneath or beyond the intellect alone) otherwise there may be a tendency to arrogance in the maintenance of a powerful position or a tendency to set oneself above other people, recognizing only the desire for control. However, once they have decided on a way forward they can be very decisive, accomplished and insightful.

As we consume our daily supply of pasteurised milk, sip a beer or maybe slip into something comfortable and silky at the end of the day, we might consider our connection and indebtedness to the man whose chart appears overleaf, i.e. that of Louis Pasteur, eminent French research chemist and biologist, whose discoveries swept away the fatal anthrax disease in cattle, epidemics of chicken cholera, deadly rabies in dogs and who demonstrated that beer, wine and milk turn sour due to exposure to micro-organisms in the air. Additionally, his identification of parasitic infections among silkworms saved the prosperity of that industry from being entirely wiped out, not only in France but in silk-producing countries the world over.

There are several striking threads we can follow in the understanding of his Gibbous purpose in life. First, the phase contains *all* the other planets, bar Mercury. Thus it would seem he incarnated with prior experience of everything he needed, leaving Mercury as the key direction for his life (the first and only planet to be collected up by the Moon – in Gemini moreover – after birth before returning to the Sun). Standing at the entry to Capricorn and in the 3rd house (the development of his enquiring intellect and processes of discovery) Mercury rules both the 9th house of the higher mind and 11th house of social creativity, innovation and transformation of his society/culture. Jupiter – as the last planet touched by the Moon prior to birth and therefore a quality he could rely on – is the ruler of this heavily tenanted 3rd house and he was indeed deeply focused on his work, always determined to devise more and more tests to reach a sound conclusion. I doubt if our modern day phrase 'thinking out of the box' existed in Pasteur's time (even in French!) yet, often in direct contrast to what most others around him seemed to believe, Pasteur held to his awakening ideas with

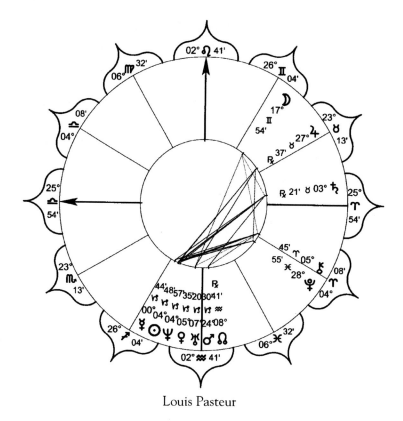

Louis Pasteur

deep determination. In this context the Sun end of Pasteur's Gibbous Phase includes a conjunction to Uranus giving free rein and independence to his probing mind. It is also conjunct Neptune – singularly apt for a man who was to research putrefaction via airborne (3rd) bacteria and progress to insidious (Neptune) diseases, developing vaccines to eradicate them.

Neptune is also ruler of the 5th which in turn contains Pluto, capable of radical creative discovery. While working on the rabies germ among animals (but not humans) a child (5th) who had been bitten by a rabid dog was brought to him. Knowing the child would certainly die if he did not take a risk with his as yet untested vaccine, Pasteur embarked on a series of inoculations on the child, who survived and regained full health. Three years after this event Institut Pasteur was founded for the development of vaccines. Pluto is vividly conjunct a 6th house Chiron with its themes of woundedness, healing and an audacity to persevere, both squaring the Sun end of the phase and trining the Leo Midheaven. Again most apt for a revered conqueror of disease and whose discoveries inspired the later work of Joseph Lister in the development of antiseptic surgery. The Moon end of the phase finds her on the midpoint of Saturn square to Midheaven. Pasteur certainly had to fight his corner and/or work alone on many occasions as well as run the gauntlet of those who would mock his findings in the scientific press of the day (Gemini). However, this set-up (together with the aforementioned planets in Capricorn) also speaks to me of long, arduous, painstaking, careful tenacity and a profoundly concentrated mind. He was noted for his adherence to work as his constant source of inspiration; indeed, one even detects a hint of Gibbous-type obsession in that his dying words were "What are you doing here? One must work!"

Seemingly another nose-to-grindstone worker is former British Prime Minister, Gordon Brown. Born with a cluster of 12th house Pisces planets on the one hand and a Moon conjunct Pluto in Leo straddling 5th/6th cusp on the other, he is perceived as a man whose demeanour can switch from a warm well-lit smile to a granite-jawed dourness and control in a split second. Importantly from the point of view of the Gibbous phase, he is spoken of by those who have known him over a long period of time as a man of impressive ability to probe through a plethora of information (such as a large pile of newspapers) and deliver a concise analysis of its content within an exceedingly short space of time. Such sharpness of intellect and apparent focused obsession is something that Dr. Anthony Storr pointed to as co-existing in an individual where there are needs for control and a propensity for vigilance;[23] thus it seems apposite that Mr. Brown was a minister in (and eventually presided over) what was often seen as an over-surveillant and over-regulatory government. The apparent swing between sensitivity on the one hand and control on the other may also be a reflection of the Cancer/Capricorn IC/MC axis of the chart and whatever were his early internalized family patterns and experience, such as his known religious upbringing (also Pisces, Neptune conjunct Saturn ruler of MC, Pluto conjunct Moon ruler of IC) where compassion may alternate with patriarchal authority.

If ever there was someone serving an 'apprenticeship', it must surely be Prince Charles. Hearsay would also have it that he is pretty exacting in his day-to-day life, wanting things to be 'just so', but at a deeper level he is a man of focused insight as befits his Gibbous phase containing Chiron, Mars and Jupiter. Though it need hardly be set out (for it is well documented) Charles is frequently outspoken on many issues not only for which he feels a deep passion as befits his Scorpio Sun and rising Pluto, but which he has also taken time and careful study to look deeply into for himself.

Jupiter is accentuated in a conjunction to Mars (co-ruler of the Scorpio Sun) occupying its own sign of Sagittarius and opposing Uranus. Together, these planets point us in the direction of an enterprising thread, particularly as the 11th house seeks to be *socially* creative and Jupiter, as co-ruler of his 9th house, leads us to think in terms of the development of his views, beliefs, philosophies, particularly as they may enlighten the wider community. Since it is not customary for the British monarch (even in-waiting) to speak out personally on issues of great importance, Charles develops avenues created by his own enterprise (Mars/Jupiter/5th), encouraging young people (5th) to receive training (apprenticeship = Gibbous) for their goals, via The Prince's Trust. In addition the development of organic farming seems to be reflected in the Moon end of the phase in Taurus, in a Capricorn house and trine to Saturn in the 2nd (ruler of 6th), thus adding an Earth thread of setting things down on a concrete platform. This also contains a good deal of sensitivity for the Earth signs (in my experience) have much more of an aesthetic quality to them than most of the traditional textbooks would lead us to believe. He has also focused much insight on the development of natural medicine, architecture, our relationship to plant life, involving himself in shared philosophies, outlooks and reaching for amelioration of society's condition. He speaks eloquently on such matters, often collecting criticism (i.e. standing or falling on his earnest inquiries). It seems fitting that the Sabian Symbol for the New Moon before Charles' birth (which was in fact an eclipse – often a portend of someone who is to take a prominent role in the world) is 9° Scorpio. This is offered as *A Dentist at Work* and speaks of the need to develop inventiveness and technique (*so* much a feature of Gibbous) in order to ameliorate the ills of society.

Overall, if one is looking for a specialist organizer, who can sift, delve, catalogue and scrutinize the component parts of something, right down to the most important detail – and come up with a result that fits a bigger meaningful perspective, then the Gibbous type is precisely what is needed. But it needs to be blended with flexibility and sensitivity if one is not spiral off into a forest of complexity where none needs to exist, generating endless paperwork. As if to underline the point, I turned on the radio during a break in writing and heard a news item that an up-to-date manual for police recruits had been published, containing a 93-page report on the subject of…

(wait for it)… *How to Ride a Bicycle*. Eh? Ninety-three pages! I mean, what is there to say? – sit on saddle, grab handlebar firmly, check brakes, put feet on pedals, push off, keep pedalling. *N'est-ce-pas?*

Sun/Moon Full Phase
Moon is 180° – 135°
behind Sun

Awareness
Seeking

> "The Sun pours its light upon everything: a diamond will sparkle magnificently, a decaying fish will decay more quickly."   [*Dane Rudhyar*]

The Moon is directly opposite and totally illuminated by the light of the Sun and, symbolically, the plant is now in full bloom. It is also in ongoing relationship with its surroundings, both receiving and giving. Continuing to absorb nutrients from the earth as well as sunlight upon its face, it releases its perfume into the environment attracting to it other forms of nature who avail themselves of its pollen (or take up residence) thus providing for fertilization and eventual reconception as new seeds. This metaphor enables us to understand that Full Phase illumination represents an intense engagement with life in the human individual. Correspondingly, the need is primarily to develop conscious awareness of what one is doing and being. Whereas the New Moon's energy was unconditioned and spontaneous, the Full Moon cannot avail itself of this, for here one is at maximum revelation and there is no retreat. One is 'out there' for all to see and relate to – *and for all to be seen and related to* – thus there is also maximum seeking of experience through interconnectedness at personal and socio-cultural levels.

This phase marks the end of the waxing hemisphere of the lunation cycle with its development through instinct, perseverance, effort, challenge and discrimination. This completion point also contains the recognition that it is also the beginning of the (waning) return journey. The Moon looks to the Sun for maximum light that is the means by which the continuation of the overall purpose can be ultimately achieved, a yearning for her return to the Sun and the joyful solace of her task completed. Thus there needs to be full integration of solar and lunar principles, a fertilization, a synthesis or union of purpose. Speaking of this relationship in *The Moon: Myth and Image*, Jules Cashford states:

"A fundamental polarity is thus set up between Sun and Moon such that their differences are magnified and, by the same token, their reunion longed for as a reconciliation of cosmic principles, so that all that is separate and alone shall be healed and made whole."[24]

A plant may bloom either triumphantly or weakly according to its prior journey from seed, yet each stretches itself to its greatest ability to flower (full meaning and purpose) before continuing its pathway. Especially since the Sun and Moon are positioned in a compelling and magnetic relatedness in this phase, they represent a fusion of energy which is most often played out and experienced through *human relationships*. Whether we are bathing in the warm waters of friendship or romantic love, or battling the stormy seas of enmity and strife, here we have the knowing of something by dint of its polarity and, through the experience of 'otherness', we reveal our inseparable oneness. Approaching an understanding of the phase from this perspective, it is not often one finds Full Moon types living an entirely solitary life. Indeed they will usually place an *immense stress* on this department of their lives, sometimes even feeling that they can hardly function *except* in the context of a relationship. The need is for a partner, whether in co-operation or adversity, to reflect qualities which are actually within oneself but cannot see. This is so for us all, but becomes a particular theme at Full Phase where awareness is a key need. If this is developed, then there is access to a consciousness not ordinarily available in the small self's busy, needy world, giving rise to a more balanced approach in relating generally. Going beyond the conditioned need for fulfilment of ourselves through another person we may instead look to our interactions with others as capable of being illuminated by a timeless dimension of being. The spiritual teacher Eckhart Tolle speaks of this as love being "the recognition of the formless in the other – which is the recognition of yourself in the other".[25]

One of the main difficulties which can arise is that the person may be quite unwilling to acknowledge the need for such awareness. Without such recognition the personality can be instead very moody, unreliable, lack stability in some form, or appear to be unfocused, immature or divorced from reality. Unlike the opposite New Phase which responds spontaneously, Full Phase finds this difficult; instead s/he may over-react to difficulties by either withdrawing (drooping, like the flower only weakly blooming) or indeed the opposite, i.e. being over-assertive and blocking off sensitivity to other people's needs (a more overblown blooming). Without awareness Full

Moons can get caught up in some over-stimulated notion of themselves, which can often mean looking for something or someone to illuminate them and by which to feel gloriously fulfilled. Alternatively, if there is a diminished (wilting) sense of one's own being there can be an assigning of power only to the other. In this phase, therefore, there is a need to focus upon seeing another person as they are, rather than perceiving them merely as supporting characters in the drama of our own personal lives. A further (but relatively common) variation is where the Full Phase person prefers to stay in the cool shade of the mind/intellect alone, looking for outside reasons, rather than risk the glare of illumination of their inner world where enlightenment ultimately resides. Conversely, some make this a veritable feature of their life's journey, giving it full recognition via dedicated inner development and immersion in spiritual experiences.

In this latter respect Full Phase may also appear in the charts of those who live from a *knowing* which does not match up to the 'normal' (dysfunctional) human condition. What they see and understand is fully illuminated but may be regarded by the ordinary world around not as any transformational or spiritual emergence but as mentally ill and medicated in a bid to treat and/or suppress it. Yet as a deep search for an inner understanding and profound healing, when it can be honestly and respectfully related to and followed through, the true expression of the individual is able to emerge and fly free. Such a theme was beautifully exemplified in Virginia Axline's account of *Dibs*[26] which is a moving exposition of her work with a small child psychologically suffering inner fear and rage and deemed 'mentally defective'. His unfolding development through their interaction in play therapy bore such shining hallmarks of dignity, absence of criticism, assignments of blame or imposition of psychiatric labels that both were changed, Axline herself was eventually able to say "Dibs is the only real person I ever met... who could teach me what it means to be a complete person – and to even go beyond that".

There are many arenas in which these threads of soli-lunar energies are woven between 'self and other'. Human emotional relationships are the most frequent but we may also trace them through the vocation/career. It may not be the career itself, or the relationship itself, that is of prime importance to the Full Moon person, so much as the 'prop' it seems to offer. If it is not there, as we have seen the person stands unshielded, to be in stark open awareness of what actually is. If there is no actual relationship (or career) then this phase type may be found relating to *something* – be it a way of life, a belief system, or following another person as guru or teacher, all in a way in which s/he is propped up and pillowed by some kind of interface between self and total awareness. We all stand or fall in terms of whatever Sun/Moon phase we have incarnated into, but where this is in the full light of the Sun the consequent glare can be experienced as overwhelming, or indeed fully entered into and therefore oblivious to all else around it. This might be (for instance) a feeling of being surrounded by so many images, sounds, sights that one feels a veritable rabbit caught in the glare of headlights, or indeed that one is a Super Shining Star.

In personal relationships, I have met many people who were in situations where they wanted to be looked after, protected by, or indeed protective of, a partner. A fear of living autonomously can lead to an unrealistic dependence on another person, even becoming so enmeshed that they wish to be totally absorbed by the other. Meanwhile, that 'other' may either have a fear of losing *their* autonomy through such intense intimacy, such that one eye may be kept on the exit-door ready to make a bolt for it, or they assume a role of authority which must be pleased or obeyed. These dynamics may manifest as expectations of being held by the partner in some kind of dramatized or reverential light, seen as 'divine' or as a god/goddess and 'worshipped', or looking for a partner who required this. On the other hand, some relationships were those where each of the partners (both shining stars of one kind or another) seemed to want to eclipse one another. But so too can there be relationships where the individual's own shining abilities bloomed *through* the experience of difficulty and struggle via a partner, awareness developing through relating as 'confrontation'. A leading actress came to see me at a point where her eleven-year marriage to a physically abusive husband was in the last throes of divorce stage. She said "I always wanted to be an actress ever since I was a little girl, but I was a snivelling little scaredy-cat most of my life… and d'you know, it was through being married to Jack that I managed to find the guts in me, the strength in me, to thrust myself out there… I couldn't have had a better teacher". In other words, while she did not herself physically retaliate in this relationship, she developed an awareness of the 'fight' within her own being, mirrored to her via the adversarial 'other'. Similar threads may be traced in the life of 'Simply the Best' Tina Turner where the Full Moon forms a T-square to Mars in the 7th house.

Quite often I have met Full Phase people who want to be on some kind of 'stage' in life, and this may be achieved by dint of a partner who is conversely held 'in the wings', even swamped altogether if the need for stardom is exaggerated. I have additionally met those who were in a partnership with someone accomplished or successful, but while they themselves dabbled a bit with something of their own, such as a hobby, their own needs for stardom were gathered in only vicariously through the partner. If the need for shining stardom is not high in terms of outer world recognition, then quite often Full Moon types are found in relationships where each of them (and as a twosome) 'shine' in respect of those around, such as family and friends. This may be the couple who have a home to which all are welcome, the door is always open, the air is one of joy. There may also be themes of great generosity for no recompense here, just as the plant in full bloom will give of its beauty and release its heady perfume whether or not there is any passer-by.

In terms of career, generally speaking Full Moon types are not especially geared to the mechanics of anything. They respond much more to indefinable notions – qualities rather than quantities – and will feel out of place in any situation which emphasizes hard-nosed facts and figures. However, unless the person is willing to confront the need to build self-awareness, any perceived lack within them may be sought in terms of its polarity on to a career role, often in overblown terms. As in personal relationships, they may look for something which they feel will complete them in terms of what they inwardly sense might be missing. As such, they may opt for an escalated presentation of themselves and seek a career which will fit this, or ultimately be found to stand as its opposite. Someone might believe they are the world's most magnificent opera singer and audition for La Scala... where they will pretty soon find out whether what they believe is true, or whether they had better get a job waiting tables in one of Milano's pizzerias!

They will also often look for positions where they can be at the forefront and looked up to. This may well involve uniting with others (or another) to bring to light that which they could not have done alone. Being somewhat prone to histrionics, again there may be a liking for presenting oneself in inflationary ways, demanding attention or indeed basking in the reflected light of those they deem to be powerful. Otherwise there is a seeking for some kind of general illumination by which they could feel boosted into full aliveness. Publicity, stardom, celebrity status are often sought and enjoyed or they are known for something dramatic, exotic, flamboyant or sweepingly stylish (such as British textile designer Zandra Rhodes born with the Sun end of the Full Phase conjunct Mars and Neptune in 'designer' Virgo and trine dynamic Uranus) and Coco Chanel (she of the Little Black Dress which always has impact and shines on through every era) or the legendary Michael Jackson with his spectacular dance movements, the masterly precision of Sun/Pluto in Virgo combining with the expressive fluidity of the opposing Moon in Pisces – meticulous to mellifluous.

Sometimes they are found in situations where special clothing can be worn to enhance them (e.g. the theatre) or where the wearing of a uniform is required, perhaps with added regalia/medals. They may also pursue fields where they can win awards, commendations or qualifications, perhaps collecting a string of impressive letters after their name. Still others may be found in rather more pomp and circumstance situations, among the elite VIPs or titled people, or at least wanting to associate with those who are regarded as part of some 'higher echelon'. Some may adopt a different name, one that has a ring of grandeur or stardom to it. In more ordinary, but still shining, circumstances some carry out perfectly ordinary jobs but manage to stay in the limelight by acting as the office buffoon or court jester while others might in fact do very little but adopt an important-sounding job title and just enjoy swanking around a bit!

On a more inner level, the full-illumination thread of this phase may be exemplified in the intense, aware focus as often only a small child can portray, intent on the wonder of discovering a worm cradled in an upturned leaf. From a position of profound self-awareness they follow an inner calling which takes the form of a shining dedication to a cause greater than themselves, placing it at the forefront and following its vision. Or combined threads of meaning are lived out, where they are at the forefront of something *and* in relationship within the context of developing their own inner vision. Such was the case with Krishnamurti who came to world recognition from a young age having been 'discovered' by Annie Besant and C.W. Leadbetter of the Theosophical Society. He was adopted by Mrs Besant who founded the Order of the Star with the young Krishnamurti as its leader. Brought to England, he was raised among the aristocracy and educated privately, in preparation for presentation to the world as spiritual saviour/avatar. Through this alone we have several Full Moon themes – being thrust into the light (stardom... with its own Order moreover) and seen as divine, being in impressive, elite, situations where the accent is on participating in higher echelons, and of course being at the forefront of something wondrous, fully illuminated. Yet, when it came to it, the far-understanding Krishnamurti eschewed all claims to his presentation as guru to be placed before hungry followers looking for enlightenment. Through him came the illumination of truth as that which can only be discovered from within oneself, rather than expecting it can be given to you by another. Here too there is a departure from mechanistic approaches which would have had him expounding on particular philosophies or religious outlooks and presenting interpretations; instead an embracing of understanding through the mirror of relationship.

Following one's own insight, faith and trust in something, through a welter of perplexities and difficulties (until one is inspired through some means inexplicable to the everyday mind) is also seen in the life of visionary William Blake to whom creativity and originality took precedence beyond the conventions of visual art and the mathematical thought processes of his time. A visionary from childhood, Blake's prophetic self-expression and powerful imagination aligned itself to the revolutionary nature of his times, underpinned by a fervent sense of spiritual duty. "*I will not Reason and Compare: my business is to Create*".[27] The Moon in his chart first meets Neptune by progression at about thirty-three months old, roughly the time at which Blake is first reputed to have experienced visions. Sun/Moon form a biquintile aspect within the Full Phase, in relation to which Robertson speaks of what one can accomplish through meaning which can "leave your mark on this world".[28] Rael/Rudhyar also speak of quintile series as emanating "a world-transforming energy"[29] and I see this aspect as one of inner resolve to bring something creatively to life. Thus we have the visionary, who through spellbinding authenticity as artist and poet, gives his vision form, his whole creative spirit being fertilized with the substance of the age in which he lived. Neptune sits on the cusp of the 2nd house, aptly echoing the sense in this phase of being out of place with facts and figures. Blake was unable to follow in his father's hosiery business footsteps as he simply had no head for trading, book-keeping, or the mechanics of pounds shillings and pence.

In terms of relationship, Blake remained married to Catherine Boucher for forty-five years. Catherine was inordinately nurturing and supportive of her husband's needs (Moon Cancer) even learning herself how to paint and draw sufficiently to be able at least to assist him in his work. Yet for all their closeness she could not entirely be a kindred spirit for the mystical, visionary Blake by entering into or debating his ideas; indeed there are few intimate friends for such an unusual spirit, a factor which so frequently leaves one in an outer world of some isolation (Moon Cancer 12th opposes Venus in Capricorn) while the relationship is with one's inner world. This dynamic also highlights his early life experiences of visions which were (initially) met by being beaten. For little children experiencing such phenomena it is an intensely lonely and isolated place if their attempts to exteriorize the awareness are met with harsh brutality and denial. Blake *could* have lived out a life of adherence to tradition (Mars/Saturn opposition) just to curry favour and get along, yet he could not and would not kill the spirit that informed his urge to articulate his creativity in his own individual manner. The Moon end of the phase trines Uranus in the 9th house (freedom, innovation, inspiration) while the Sun is conjunct Jupiter (both the natural ruler of the 9th and ruler of Pisces on 9th cusp) in the personally creative 5th house.

Where the Sun and Moon are at the 150° quincunx in this phase, the need is to develop a conscious monitoring of one's inner processes, although there can also be a tension borne out of holding on to the past (which may be seen in a romantic light) rather than focusing on the stark realities of the present. There may be a wistful, slightly enigmatic quality about this person but it may also be experienced as infuriating if they embellish or 'embroider' matters in order to conform to an idealized notion. If, however, they are more concentrated, they may be shining beacons for others. Where there is the 144° biquintile this may be manifested in terms of a special proficiency in what they do, be it creative or more intellectually-orientated. There may be accent on the delivery of something that has been brought together and understood (as in Krishnamurti's life). Negatively, however, if the need for stardom contains egoic needs soaring to stratospheric heights, there may be an arrogant overblown quality to the delivery which may then appear unfocused or pontificating.

Though it is difficult to separate fantasy from historical fact in much that is said of her, Mata Hari's chart shows the phase containing the positions of Neptune, Pluto (in a powerful T-square with Jupiter and Uranus) and Venus. Therein lie the threads we associate with known themes of her life as a person of glamorous and powerful mystique, a courtesan and exotic dancer, who met her end via execution by firing squad at the age of forty-one.

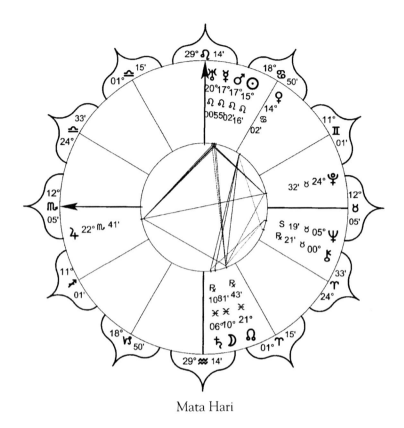

Mata Hari

Born in Netherlands as Margaretha Zelle, after an initial affluent childhood her life became absolutely circumscribed by relationships – initially of those around her and then her own. Her parents divorced and died while she was still young, which meant she had to go and live with her godfather. She became a kindergarten teacher, but the headmaster became flirtatious with her and she was sent instead to live with an uncle. While still very young, she was married to an army officer (a man in uniform!) who turned out to be a violent alcoholic and divorce followed. Having also become interested in Indonesian culture and joined a dance company, she then went to Paris and became a circus horse-rider, giving herself a titled name (Lady Macleod). A woman by all accounts of quite some mettle (Moon Saturn conjunct, Sun Mars conjunct) she struggled through to earn a living and pretty soon won fame as an exotic dancer and was a contemporary of other leaders of the movement (such as Isadora Duncan) who looked to the East for inspiration. Her fame, mystique and flirtatiousness won many admirers and she became mistress to a millionaire industrialist. Continuing to be immersed in eastern sacred dance, she embellished her image by pretending to be a princess of priestly Hindu origin. Elevating exotic dance to respectable status she quickly became world famous and entered into relationships with those in further high-ranking and influential positions and in very many countries, including politicians and royalty, who indeed propped and pillowed her in a luxurious lifestyle.

However as the War approached her reputation began to be seen in a different (opposite) light, as dangerous, promiscuous, dark, wanton. It is unclear whether she was set up for the spy charges of which she was ultimately tried, although she had earlier admitted to working as an agent for French military intelligence. But this may have been out of an ideal and overblown (Full Phase) need to sound and present herself as more intriguing. She was executed in Paris in October 1917 and it will not be until 2017 that historical documents can be unsealed which will reveal the full facts of the trial of Mata Hari.

Sun/Moon Disseminating Phase
Moon is 135° – 90°   Distributing
behind Sun   Dispersal

"Communication leads to community, that is, to understanding, intimacy and mutual valuing."   [Rollo May]

The plant is in its second or third blooming and, while a few petals may fall, there is still the relationship to its surroundings, while first young seeds are wafted through the air like tiny parachutes fluttering to their destinations. In the same way that a plant will disperse its nectar and pollen to be carried off by the bee so that an outcome can occur, so too in this phase it is the collation and distribution of what one contains that is of prime importance. There has been no further expansion on the part of the plant (and thus, by analogy, the personal, individual self) since the Full Phase opposition. What one is alerted to now (at this second sesquiquadrate in the cycle) is the need to extend the self into the surroundings *by participation*. These are people who need to present themselves in such a way that who they are and what they can do becomes 'aired' (disseminated) to others. In fact, this is the phase of the *natural communicator*.

Expression in this phase is characterized by a conscious certainty of who one is and that one is doing and being the right thing. There is a comfortable and fluid way of interacting, a need for them to feel they are doing something for others and that there is therefore interconnectedness. While gathering up all their ideas, knowledge, information or abilities and relaying these to all around, there is also a liking for life to be kept moving, flowing, like a river, unhindered by obstacles if at all possible. Frequently these are very knowledgeable people who simply want to speak out for what they have learned, understand, or who have alighted upon as an idea or way of life which holds their attention so thoroughly that there is little that could stop them from wanting to take it out into the marketplace and convince others of its worth. Usually both amiable and sociable, there is great delight in using their mental and physical skills either in obvious communicative fields (such as journalism, education, broadcasting) or in performance fields (such as theatre and sport) or indeed in salesmanship since they often have a way with words that is capable of getting anybody interested in anything.

In practice, working with Disseminating types can be a little like negotiating a swimming-pool; there is a shallow end where you can splash about happily and playfully, the deep end where you can reach all manner of profundities and understandings, and the gradient slope in the middle where you are free to swim for either 'shore' so to speak, as circumstances and moods dictate. The shallow end person mostly knows what s/he knows, everything is contained in a few feet of water and there is no particular need to venture further out. The middle-depth type of Disseminating is more open to the fact that there are wider issues to consider, while those at the deep-end are far more willing to take what they know and submit it to a searching pursuit of purpose, sharing their skills through demonstration and performance.

Not entirely comfortable with long-term or heavy projects when swimming in the shallow end, this type prefers to keep things moving along so as to be able to get on with the next thing. There is something of an adventurous and light, even 'frothy', optimistic spirit here; very chatty (even gossipy) they can ramble on a bit, delightful though it often is. like a fluttering butterfly. Some will trim their sails to suit whichever wind is blowing, keeping everything light and inconsequential. However, when they swim out a little deeper, this may also translate as an *impatience* once they see a road forward. They can become 'tetchy' when they cannot see something happening that their minds tell them *ought* to happen or, conversely, see something occurring that they feel is out of kilter. They may also show a disdain for being told anything or having things explained to them. So they can hassle, even become fanatical, in a bid just to proceed ahead. This can be particularly so when they have alighted on an idea that they feel *works* (whether it is their own idea or extrapolated from elsewhere). It is better for them if they can concentrate on their own thinking, however, since a mere latching on to information from derivative channels can dull the freshness of their communicative abilities. If this is the case, there could be a tendency toward becoming encapsulated in concepts or stereotypical views that limits their undoubted capacity to stay open to examining matters further (go a little further into the deep end). The position of Virgo and its ruler Mercury can yield further pointers as to this person's drive to channel understanding and skills into their environment.

A key factor to which one needs to be alert in this phase is that there can be a propensity to overdo things and become engulfed. The fact that other people may not be the same as them or have different interests or outlooks may be entirely overlooked. They may have very profound understandings but it is possible for them to get so carried away on the wings of their ideas that they can be in danger of getting into dogmatic positions of 'always knowing best' or *believe they have the exclusive truth on something* and this of course can lead to intolerance. Fine communicators though they so often are, nevertheless it is possible for them to 'talk down' to people (however unintentionally). The vocal emphasis is such that it conveys that you ought already to know what is being said to you and in fact it should be patently obvious even to an idiot... which they may be implying you are! More generally, in day-to-day discussions, this might manifest as difficulty in letting another person speak without hindrance, constantly anticipating your next word or, even more infuriating, stealing your punch-line. At its absolute worst this phase type may be over-pontificating or zealously evangelical. Both Gladstone and Disraeli, Prime Ministers to Queen Victoria, were born in this phase and both had strong oratorical abilities. However, Disraeli was rather more of a debater, while Gladstone came across with a dogmatic, crusading quality such that Victoria once famously complained of him "He addresses me as if I were a public gathering!"

"Silence is the element in which great things fashion themselves" said Thomas Carlyle, but some in this phase (rather like Full Phase) are unable to tolerate aloneness or disconnection from others for any length of time. The main difference between the two is that Disseminating puts more emphasis on reaching out to a wide circle of people rather than one central relationship. Being lively, articulate and with a love of meeting people for the exchange of ideas, there can be a tendency to fill every conceivable space with activities, people, events, perhaps as an avoidance of the 'deeper regions of the swimming pool'. Some clients articulated this as worries about what they might find… possibly unexamined beliefs or fears they might be harbouring which they would rather not get involved with. They just like the river to flow freely, not be a raging swirl.

Others, however, simply adopt 'positive only' outlooks. While it is part of the delight of this type to be able to apply a light geniality to everything, here difficulties can be met with a tendency to jolly things along and gloss over them, again perhaps in a bid not to be overwhelmed. Some may even seem incapable of understanding negativities and could be dismissive of weakness or despair in others' lives. In a few cases I have found this phase to be short-fused, even patronizing, about other people if they have never had these experiences personally, even carrying an air of cool, detached pride or superiority concerning that. Alternatively there can be a strong need to 'fix' them in some way, perhaps with reason and logic as a 'solution', and if that fails to work then they might revert to soothing platitudes such as 'try hard not to worry'. Nevertheless, while for the most part they feel more comfortable keeping things at factual, light levels, other factors in the chart pointing to a more profound willingness to relate can moderate this considerably. For when they do allow themselves moments of stillness, Disseminating people can be inordinately sharp in insight, both about their own and others' lives.

Those born under this phase may not always show early signs of being good communicators. Language may come later than most in babyhood/childhood, or there may be speech impediments or other difficulties associated with expressing oneself. Nevertheless, and especially as we move into the depths of the Disseminating swimming-pool, it is often to be found that encoded in these difficulties are the threads of being which come to fruition as a fine orator, writer or spokesperson, such as Winston Churchill who spent a childhood of stammering and stuttering. One client went through one of those agonizingly lonely childhoods where he was to be seen and not heard, brought up alone by two ultra-disciplinarian parents. Nevertheless as he grew he developed a very keen observation of people, situations, the way their minds worked, the nuances of their feelings through facial expression and body movements, however subtle. He subsequently became a successful teacher, then journalist and award-winning cartoonist.

Baba Ram Dass, formerly Harvard professor Richard Alpert, researched psychedelic drugs in the 1960s with Timothy Leary, and was thrown out of that institution amidst much controversy. He journeyed to India, found his guru and his calling to explore the nature of consciousness. His 1971 bestselling book *Be Here Now* became a spiritual touchstone for many in that era. His stories, writings and explorations have continued since, although he suffered a stroke in 1997 which left him with speech asphasia. This he worked through therapeutically, producing the further publication *Still Here* in 2000 and *Fierce Grace* (a film concerning his life and the experience of his stroke).[30] Ram Dass was born within orb of the waning trine where ability is accompanied with a sense of flow and enjoyment of one's surroundings, the people one meets and equally fluid expression of communicative gifts. Sir Arthur Conan Doyle, was born with the exact trine from the 12th to 9th houses and a Mercury/Pluto conjunction sleuthing away in the 12th house of mysteries. Although he followed a medical career, he had discovered his talent for storytelling while still a boy at school, an ability which included brilliant deductions of logic and analysis. The Sun end of the phase is conjunct Uranus and had just risen at birth over a Gemini Ascendant, while the Moon is in Aquarius 9th. From his schooldays onwards he was always able to draw to him many friends among whom he found much inspiration and learning from shared ideas. Indeed, some of them ended up in posterity, as characters in his novels.

The chart of Yehudi Menuhin is a rich composition involving three T-squares plus a Grand Trine in Air. The Disseminating Phase encompasses all of these factors since the Moon sits at one point of the cardinal T-square (Moon opposite Saturn, square Jupiter), the Sun sits at one point of the dissociate T-square (North Node opposite Neptune, square Sun) and Uranus, contained as it is within the phase, sits at one point of both the fixed T-square (Mars opposite Uranus, square Mercury) and the Grand Trine in Air (Venus, Uranus, Midheaven). Here indeed was a man of communication, primarily through his musical genius. The Sun/Neptune square particularly seems to pick up on his quoted regard for music as being "a kind of prayer made audible". In addition, Menuhin was also an educator, the school at Stoke d'Abernon in England and the International Competition, both bearing his name, being world-renowned and the springboard for many of today's leading musicians.

The official website[31] describes Menuhin as a "driven communicator", with an ability to "buttonhole" people – factors with which I would certainly concur from my own personal acquaintance with him during one period of my life. Everyone needed to be on their toes when YM was around since he would look into everything, making sure that all was moving forward cohesively, indeed like a flowing river. He was also something of a mimic and (totally undetectable) hoaxer who could adopt a voice, even an accent, which could have been from any culture or gender and never seemed out of place – a manifestation perhaps not only of the hypnotic effect of Sun/Neptune which can slip itself into any imaginative identity but also of the Moon end of the phase where it is in Gibbous phase to Saturn. This represents a careful, even exacting need for everything to be properly done, and the ruse would be to phone people up 'incognito' to ensure that they were handling things competently. But again it was always within the context of ensuring an overall forward movement and flowing completion of the task in hand, rather like the composition of a beautiful symphony. He spoke eloquently of the need for tolerance among people (Neptune occupies Cancer 7th) and, alongside his genius as violinist and conductor, he was also a gifted speaker and lecturer, addressing audiences throughout the world with grace and geniality not only about music but also on matters of self-development, relatedness between nations, and shared cultural learning.

Finally, sometimes, the waning trine in this phase can accompany a life where there may be too much ease and this can have its own drawbacks. Marc Robertson referred to "a subtle kind of hell" where a person lives what other people might conceive of as an ideal lifestyle, perhaps of great comfort or privilege, but one is bored rigid because there is little to strive for or feel connected to. Then they feel they are drifting aimlessly... *unless* they can align themselves with something they do earnestly believe in, are moved by and want to speak out for. Because if anyone can do this, it is a Disseminating type.

The circumstances of Prince Harry's life are such that many would consider it an ideal existence. However, there is a challenging square from the Sun in the 8th to Mars (the soldier) in the 11th (society at large) ruling

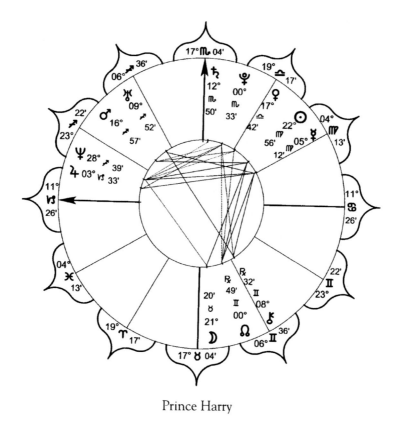

Prince Harry

the 3rd and 10th houses of movement and outer goals, combining assertion and commitment. With Sun and Mercury in Virgo and Moon also in earth plus Capricorn rising, he is in all probability a competent man, able to cope with practicalities. Additionally, the Sun is in the 8th house, not a position where anything is taken at face value, much more a vibrant, intense energy that wants to discover for itself through interacting with others (Disseminating). However, as we have seen from his life so far, every now and then he meets the frustration of wanting to get out there and get on with it, but the country's need to preserve and protect his person and position denies him this. Perhaps it is a little like trying to play a Rachmaninoff Piano Concerto with one hand tied behind your back (although whether Harry personally experiences it as such I do not know).

Be that as it may, it is the *Mercury* position in the 8th (and contained within the Sun/Moon phase) which leads me to surmise whether there is not also an assiduous probing mind (and Pluto is in 9th), one that is capable of speaking out with an easy ability on whatever preoccupies him and to which he feels committed (8th) and earnestly wants to share (Disseminating). This is also one of those charts in which the first (and last) planets touched by the Moon could be important additional indicators of life purpose. Since last meeting the Sun, the Moon has travelled past Venus, Pluto, Saturn, Uranus, Mars, Neptune and Jupiter, so these are incorporated within Harry at his birth. The Moon's next port of call … *is Mercury.* Along the way it picks up North Node/Chiron opposite Uranus, so I would expect him quite early in his life to have incorporated a sense of being his own individual person, not necessarily always fitting in with surrounding conformities, and these form a T-square to the Mercury.

The last planet touched by the Moon was Jupiter, representing a competent, reliable quality (Capricorn) and here in 12th house it suggests a compassionate person, again able to inspire a confidence that he has a practical handle on things. Additionally, these qualities could be directed into life via amelioration (Jupiter) of any situations of suffering (conjunct Neptune 12th) where these qualities are required. (The Neptune/Jupiter phase in this chart is New and could be said to represent a need to experience a sense of unity with something larger than himself to which he can dedicate his powers of endeavour). Together with Mercury quintile the Midheaven (an enhanced ability to communicate), crucially *Jupiter and Mercury are also in Disseminating Phase* (see Chapter 8) thus a double emphasis on his potential role as a natural communicator.

It is therefore possible that we may yet see this soldier prince emerge wearing a different 'fighting' hat (sorry, crown), as some kind of outspoken, eloquent and compassionate practical campaigner for a cause (possibly an alternative, 'maverick', one) in which he utterly believes. He has a father who is no stranger to speaking out on issues which have concentrated his heart and mind, plus he was born of a mother (Sun/Moon Disseminating cusp) who, prior to her death, was emerging very clearly as someone prepared to speak out for matters that concerned her. So these threads may be pointing us to a deep triad of meaning and purpose between all three people. While Harry already does, of course, lend his energies to charitable enterprises[32], somehow one has the sense that there may be more within the nature and innate skills of this young prince than he has yet had opportunity to reveal.

Sun/Moon Last Quarter
Moon is 90° – 45° behind Sun

Reorientation

"Two roads diverged in a wood, and I –
I took the one less traveled by,
And that has made all the difference"

[Robert Frost. The Road Not Taken]

The plant has completed its series of bloomings and is fading. The finalisation of all that it contained is approaching, but importantly at this stage it must be gathered in and harvested in order to be productive. This phase is directly opposite to First Quarter where the 'de-cision' saw the lighted half-circle of Moon moving *away from* the Sun, breaking out into the world and taking on the challenge of her purpose. Conversely, here at Last Quarter the illuminated half-circle now *faces* the Sun to which she is returning.

It was characteristic of the First Quarter individual to meet life by taking direct action regardless of whether or not the end-goal was clear. There, the need was to break out and repudiate the past even in the teeth of resistance. At Last Quarter, the end-goal is clear (the return to Sun and completion of the mission) – but there is a reticence to take action. In this phase the individual functions at a slower capacity and whatever action s/he does take emanates from a *growing inner pressure* to do so, rather than in the spirit of instantaneous aliveness. Here the reorientation needs to be made not so much from repudiating the past, nor getting stuck in it, *but using it in order to move on and place oneself at the mature helm of a new future.* There is at least one major turning point within their lives – or even a crisis (as meaning opportunity for transformation) – which will identify them as an individual standing in the world in their own right, by the very taking of this road when it appears. In this way they can be forerunners of something transformative arising.

To return to our analogy of an aircraft and control tower (Chapter 2), we could say that this is the point at which the tower communicates with the pilot directing him to set his bearings for an eventual landing. However the pilot, originally on course and heading for Heathrow, is now instructed to reset his instruments for he is being diverted to Edinburgh. It introduces a pressure – there he was, cruising happily toward a destination on a flight he has done a hundred times before, but now he has to take a different course. It's a nuisance he could do without... but somehow, deep down, he knew it all along. Last Quarter people often initially develop their lives along established acceptable patterns – maybe nothing special, out-of-the ordinary or remarkable, but functioning adequately well in a step-by-step way. At the same time, this pattern might weigh upon them and inwardly there is a sense of 'something else' that is their ultimate calling. It may even have an inevitability about it. Quite often this road will emerge (if it has not before) around the age of thirty (just after the first Saturn return) or around thirty-five to thirty-six (when Saturn squares itself) or nearer toward the mid-life period (thirty-nine to forty-four years) and the Uranus half-return. If this is given recognition then the movement is one of launching themselves into a maturity where there is nothing between them and the real world out there. Nevertheless, due to the accompanying pressure, it is often the case that there can be a reluctance to take this diversionary road until one *has* to, it becomes an imperative or one can do no other. Sometimes it might be refused altogether.

The crucial need for Last Quarters is to propel themselves into the outer world by expressing their own values and establishing an individual place in their society. The plant's seeds are infused with energy and toughened up in their casings in preparation for their ultimate dispersal (there is much to be distributed into the environment). The host plant submits itself to a harvesting which will re-route it into other 'produce' (as wheat is to bread). In the previous two phases there had been a certain free flow of energy in relating to the environment and sharing information and skills, but now this turning point stands as a more definitive and productive goal to be presented. Last Quarters do so by *establishing a channel through which they can be seen and heard as a living embodiment of a set of ideological beliefs, or definite systems of thought, philosophies, truths.* To this end they will seek to create a specific concrete platform from which to operate in their lives. This then becomes what they are most known for, identified by, regardless of what had hitherto been their pattern of life. When this dynamic is functioning unimpeded, they could be forgiven for feeling that they are living at something of an oblique angle to everyone else. The accompanying hesitation may mean they are waiting for the timing to be right or the drive itself has not yet matured sufficiently to be assigned a place in the open world. Nevertheless this thrust towards change is slowly gaining momentum.

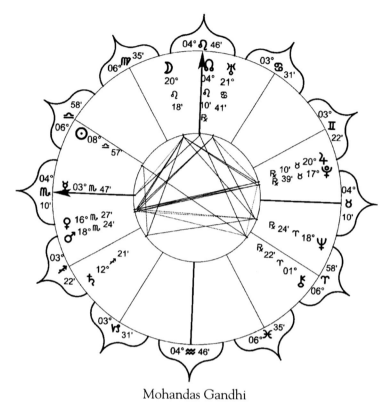

Mohandas Gandhi

For Mohandas Gandhi, the turning point came when, as a young – not especially successful and very reluctant – lawyer (and pretty penniless to boot) he was nevertheless asked to assist in a South African legal case. Ordered off a train there in which he was travelling first-class, Gandhi was faced with whether to take on this confrontation or simply cave in and return to India. He said 'yes' to his turning point, and in the process found himself and his life calling, becoming a fighter for the rights of all people through peaceful protest and non-violence, initially as leader of the Indian community in South Africa. The Last Quarter phase is at the waning sextile, thus the capacity to meet and achieve specific goals through radical outlooks and reformulations. The Moon occupies the 10th house and last met both Uranus in the 9th and its own North Node (conjunct Midheaven). Thus he brought into this life an inner drive to do or be something notable that constitutes change and breakthrough, plus the courage to stand up for one's beliefs and maintain a resolute position even if it feels you are standing alone. The turning point came from being a lawyer (9th) in a foreign country (also 9th). The Moon end of the phase forms a T-square with Venus and Mars opposite Jupiter/Pluto signifying his powerful and resolute maintenance of a non-violent disobedience policy, irrespective of numerous experiences of arrest, imprisonment, ill-health, always championing the cause of the individual (Sun opposite Chiron 5th) and taking this all back to his homeland (Uranus rules the 4th house) and its eventual independence in 1947.

The lives of two former British Prime Ministers also reflect this contextual thread of a turning point being reached by which they were to take their place in the outside world. Margaret Thatcher was born with Moon in Leo in the 9th house 51° behind the Sun in Libra in the 11th. Having originally followed a fairly sedate course in life of studying to be a biochemist, then a lawyer, she entered politics at the age of thirty-four, became leader of her party at the age of fifty and suddenly emerged as the first woman British Prime Minister four years later; she won three successive election victories, in the process collecting upon her shoulders much in the way of either praise or opprobrium. Similarly, her successor, John Major (whose birth time is not known but who was born with Sun in Aries in Last Quarter phase to Moon in Capricorn) was a young man with little in the way of formal educational qualifications, had failed as a bus conductor, then became an insurance clerk, then on to working in a bank, until he too entered politics at the age of thirty-three, rapidly climbed the ranks to become Chancellor of the Exchequer under Thatcher until she left office and made him her successor. He went on further and unexpectedly to win a second term in office. In Thatcher's case the irrevocable turning point of this phase is all the more telling since it contains Mars in a T-square with Jupiter and Pluto (of which Sun is also at the apex), highlighting the drive, power and control with which she is associated. But in both Thatcher and Major we see the threads of an initial ordinary life leading to a distinct diversionary path, each of them seeking to be the personification of a set of ideological beliefs and living this out in upon the very concrete platform of parliament, as leaders no less.

Barack Obama (born with Moon in Gemini in 4th house, 69° behind Sun in Leo in 6th house) of course became the first ever African-American President of the United States. His very campaign password was "Change" reflecting Last Quarter coupled with Aquarius rising, its rulers in exact waxing quincunx and moreover he was elected under a transiting Saturn/

Uranus opposition. It is also interesting to note that the toughening up of the seeds at this harvesting stage of the plant-cycle represents a self-perpetuating strength to be lived on into the future. In the human individual this quality can emerge as a stalwart drive to challenge old structures and instigate a new powerful road forward, often in a way which will brook no argument. "There is simply no alternative," said Mrs Thatcher on one notable occasion and "The lady's not for turning" on another, while President Obama upon entering the White House called for a bust of Sir Winston Churchill which had long sat in the Oval Office to be removed and replaced by that of Abraham Lincoln.

Of course not everyone wants or intends to become President, or Prime Minister, or any other kind of leader, yet still this theme of a catalytic turning point marking the life remains. When it arises, the two main avenues of response are to accept and go with it, or it is refused. In the same way that I doubt Gandhi realized he was standing in a world-changing moment when a policeman threw him forcibly off a South African train, so too Last Quarters may not always know consciously, while it is arising, that they are on the brink of a turning point. The reorientation may not come in dramatic ways but simply in ordinary life situations. For example, quietly going about their lives, they then find that something needs to be confronted and they are the ones to do it. This may be with a person, an organization, a set of rules, a longstanding family dynamic, an ideology ... somehow Last Quarter person is most aptly placed to turn aside from what and who they have been, speak out and take a stand. This may be a relief not only to themselves but to others around who might also be astounded at this person's ability suddenly to produce a new juncture in the road, such that they might be heard to say "Gosh! I never knew he had it in him!"

Where this dynamic is met with ongoing reluctance, there can be a great deal of tension between how this person sees themselves and how they would like to be, but without any resolution of this they can spend a great deal of time forever getting ready to be and do something different... but never really doing it. Then they might live a façade, not really 'coming clean' (either with themselves or other people) as to what it is they most want to turn to in life, or indeed denying the fact that deep down they do not want to turn to it at all. Some hide their true intentions by not sharing goals or outlooks with those close to them for fear of 'stepping out of line', (which of course is precisely what they *are* doing and are supposed to do). In some circumstances, it may *appear* as if the Last Quarter person is diverting off on to a road of their own, yet in reality they may be following a societal (or other person's) path which only *looks* different (but is actually 'safe'), gathering it up and presenting it as one's own, yet unable truly to sustain it because it simply is not.

Those who think in linear rather than cyclical terms may especially not understand that the reorientation of something is leading to a new creation. They may forever get stuck in trying to maintain a status quo or appeal may be made that there is something which prevents them from turning to a new road. Like a horse that shies at a fence (which it is perfectly capable of jumping) their own inner fears may lead them to cook up all kinds of weird and wonderful explanations for why they can't make changes. Beneath it all may lie a need for continuity of the past, rather than maturing from it – but a plant in nature does not seek to bloom and bloom forever and never go through its natural cycle of harvesting, dying and regrowth. Failure to realign oneself along a different road when it arises can lead to difficulties (either physically, psychologically, or both) in 'leaving home' and entrusting oneself to the outer world. Usually such issues will become clear by the time of mid-life, (if not much earlier, which is usually the case) but some may balk at the trend well into their forties or fifties. Sometimes the only platform they construct is one of blame and anger at a world which calls for them to grow. Instead they sit, replaying vestiges of their early life dynamics in their own home-lives and/or work situations. While most of us have a few quibbles at least about our past and how it had the audacity not to be perfect, it is the *context* of the past that both serves a purpose and provides the launchpad – now we must make the leap.

An alternative response is one of only wanting to see things in a idealized light. But this can again be an enemy of necessary change. Some adopt visualizations, affirmations or positive thinking programmes by which they can convince themselves that their life is 'really and truly wonderful'. Of course such strategies can work reasonably well in some situations, but where they are utilized artificially to create a mentally-constructed picture being laid over an existing, *unexamined* (and much older) inner pressure seeking proper release, they frequently cannot be sustained. We surmount a negativity first by giving it full recognition and surrendering to its reality; only then can one begin alternatively to fill the space it takes up with more life-affirming ways of being. These are all very understandable, often poignant and very human responses, but the point of the phase is that change has to be made if this person is not to sink down into a life which would be, by comparison, mind-numbingly ineffective and mechanical. Here they would find themselves as just another machine chugging along the same old grooves as everyone else, or where they are constantly trying out new things but with little or no result and stuck in a rut. Life knows what it is doing and frequently produces a series of opportunities and turning points, many of which will not be taken up, or the person shrinks from the brink; they simply may not be ready. And then along comes something else, the pressure from within has reached a certain level and the person is spurred into action.

If, however, there is vehement refusal to turn from an established path and embrace change, then the energy of the phase can again erupt in intermittent spurts of condensed anger through which the person, perhaps having succumbed to a life of comparative banality, becomes a walking grievance-looking-for-a-cause. Sometimes the pressure of this leads to some kind of sudden, even shattering, experience by which they are jolted to turn around and look at their life through a wholly new perspective. Like The Tower card in the Tarot deck, this can ultimately be a complete transformation endeavouring to break through the upheaval, leading to an inner psychological and spiritual renewal. One Last Quarter man, angry with his aristocratic background for ousting him from its original pampered comforts to put him into boarding school at the age of seven, then on to public school and university, developed a life of constantly seeking for a world which would ensure his comfort and wellbeing, more especially his needs for childhood emotional nurturing from which he felt unfairly wrenched. When it became clear that no one could recreate the ideals he sought, he developed instead much volcanic frustration and a relationship with alcohol to a degree of severity that it almost cost him his life. Demetra George puts it very succinctly when she says of Last Quarter that "they tend to wear a mask of their old selves... while on the inside there exists a state of total anarchy".[33] Fortunately for this man this *was* his turning point and with great courage he faced it head on, eventually emerging with some very fine values of his own to put into the world, particularly his knowledge of classical music upon which he became a noted expert. A seed in nature accepts without demur that it is to be borne on a different wind to create itself anew.

Many Last Quarters are pulled into the outer world where they can use their heads and come from positions of command and organization. They are often excellent at finding strategies, solutions, 'ways forward'. The essential thread being woven is that of *promulgation* and for this they are often at the forefront of something where they can take an overview. Nearer the 72° quintile, the surge toward the new road is experienced as less of a fight usually because the individual is aware of an enhanced creative flow within (which might indeed be a key skill or innate talent) which they heed and follow. At the 60° sextile there can be a competent and fluent adaptation to life goals and an identifiable purpose the individual wants to achieve, plus a readiness to organize it. Around both these aspects there may be considerable emphasis on being able to revamp, restyle or reframe something so that it works better for the future. People in fields such as management consultancy, public relations or other training situations carry this ability to take something the way it was and 'have it work better' (which echoes the essential thread of this phase – of moving something into a maturity). Functioning at their highest Last Quarters are capable of leaving an indelible mark upon their world.

Sun/Moon Balsamic Phase   Surrender
Moon is 45° – 0°   Prescience
behind Sun

> "Nothing will remain long of the black stormy night
> Long ages have not been appointed for anyone to carry the cross;
> The glad dawn that shines yonder says that a fine morning is on the way."
> [*William Williams, Pantyceyln,*
> *Darkness Tends Towards Light,*
> *Llyfr Emynay a Thonau 513*]

The plant now surrenders back into the earth, bequeathing its final seeds to carry the cycle of growth to new life (at the forthcoming New Moon). Nature does not have a problem with dying and disintegration; it is at one with the totality of the life/death/life cycle present in all creation as a continuing spiral.

As in New Phase, Balsamic is not a context in which reason and logic are either prevalent or required. Like the plant, this person needs to surrender the past and turn to an awareness of what is to come. Tuned into the potential of all things as opposed to surface appearances, this type find life often means taking a leap in the dark led only by a visionary sense that it is leading to a purpose. For these reasons they may not fit in with the expectations of either their personal background nor their contemporary life for there is something else for which they are 'listening'. Just as when you hear a train rumbling in the distance before anyone else, or an ever-instinctive animal will move to higher ground prior to the eruption of an earthquake, so too Balsamics gear their understanding to meet this felt sense attunement to an unseen world, simply following its unfurling pathway in whatever way it is apprehended from within and then developing this into a legacy to be left.

When this capacity for inner vision is operating unhindered, the individual is not only led and inspired by it, but *galvanized into action by it as if drawn by a magnet*. If the Last Quarter type was a forerunner of a new future emerging, then the Balsamic type is the herald of it as something now at hand. When the vision of what they want to do, be, or contribute is powered forward, then the demand of Balsamic types is that they *become some kind of pathfinder or trailblazer*, providing a thread for others to pick up and follow on from. In the process many of the people they meet may be brief, short-term acquaintanceships, to whom they disperse the 'seeds' that are needed and then pass by. Thus they may be those through whom a new paradigm can arise. That which is endeavouring to come to life through them is, more often than not, something which the small self (with its needs for identity, satisfactory outcomes and recognition) is in the way of. So it is through a higher inspiration that it finds its path forward and its actuality may, or may not, be known within the lifetime of the person concerned. One might imagine that the chap who invented the wheel could have been a Balsamic type. Sitting in his Mesopotamian cave one night after a hard day rolling logs, he accessed something within, perhaps even inspired by the circular logs themselves. And the rest, as the cliché goes, is history. Such a person could never have known that many, many hundreds of years from his life the whole planet would operate on billions and billions of wheels, everywhere. His was the consciousness through which that which was to be seeded as the essence of 'wheel' could know itself in the universal whole.

If this context is not functioning clearly, or if the challenge is unrecognized then, conversely, this person may run the risk of becoming discontented, lacking in purpose, escaping into dreams and fantasies in an attempt to ward off the dullness, boredom and sheer apathy of life. In the process they can appear ineffective, lazy or useless, living with their head in the clouds, out of touch with practical needs or realities or perhaps seeking relationships of childlike dependency in expectation that someone else will deal with such things for them. Some may spend their lives eternally 'wanting something to happen', unaware of the power within to propel this into being for themselves. And if they are *deeply* disconnected from this context, they may even work very hard to keep it that way – repressed – usually by seeking to align themselves with some societal or world-view in an attempt to be in step with everyone else, or looking to be 'rescued' by something that would give them a sense of direction. Within this context also, they may hold on to their past history or deeply embedded beliefs, working and reworking these threads over and over in one tiny corner of the tapestry of their lives until they are knotted up inside. Balsamics are capable of giving their all to a cause, an art, a path forward but crucial to this process is the need to deal with the past. Just as in the preceding phase there was a need to move on, here too one must remain forward-looking. The past can be left where it is, energy withdrawn from constantly harking back to, or jabbing an accusing finger at, it and redirected instead into revealing and weaving trailblazing, awakening threads.

This road, as any other, may be strewn with its fair share of difficulties and obstacles. Apart from remaining stuck in the past, quite frequently I have met Balsamic people who seem to display an inordinate need for freedom although they are frequently not too sure what this means for them in actuality – sometimes it is merely the freedom to sit and do nothing all day. It emerges as a distaste for being pinned down by, or held practically accountable for, anything. The difficulty for them is that further than this they have been unable to go. They can then become 'out of phase' and feel very much a captive of their past, developing negatively-fatalistic beliefs that the whole of their life is a constant repetition of it. If they remain caught in this knot, they can again cave in to the world-weariness and apathy spoken of earlier. Here it is as if the disintegrating plant would say "Oh for heavens' sake just let me be a wilting sunflower, don't bother me with anything else. Seeds? You want seeds? Oh God I'm so tired... what do you mean you want me to be a pathfinder and trailblazer? – just leave me alone!" There may even be an attendant petulant "What's in it for *me* anyway?" Answer: Maybe nothing – or nothing tangible and immediate –

but there it is, this one last task and you are the vehicle through which it can come into being.

There are several roads which may be taken. One is just to stay with the apathy and shun all attempts to enter any deeper insights which take them beyond into new perceptions. Or, one *does* hear the call to be a pathfinder, but it is done half-heartedly because the conscious ego may still be stuck in the concept of freedom and 'what's in it for me', or else wants to be 'rescued' by some practical other who will take over and handle things. The third road is to turn to it willingly, *surrender* even though there may be a great struggle away from a past and much to be given out from oneself in terms of energy and commitment. Surrender does not imply giving up or giving in (as in defeat or passivity) but a natural yielding to the flow of how things are unfolding. At this point, as the dissolution is fully faced, the seeding of a future pathway is one to which the person is drawn, fascinated, enchanted, but also committed (attendant Scorpio rulership), such that any accompanying difficulties are but a mere corollary. New realizations become transformative and are coupled with compassion and understanding as threads to be woven for the good of the whole and a future to come. If they are put to use only to preserve some kind of status quo for the individual's personal satisfaction, then the Balsamic's expression in the world is apt to be seen as dull or a little stolid. Otherwise, and more openly, a call has come and needs to be bowed before in total acquiescence. Whatever is to be distributed from that emerges without the conceptual self necessarily having had anything to do with it. No song and dance required.

Carl Rogers, pioneer of the client-centred approach to counselling and psychotherapy, was born with the Balsamic Moon close to Chiron and 'returning home' within a day of birth to the Sun which was conjunct Saturn in Capricorn – thus, a deep inner potential to yield healing (Chironian) seeds which would serve as a solid platform (imminent New Moon conjunct Saturn in Capricorn) for that which was to be built up and flourish into the future. Reaching beyond techniques and the interpretational, theoretical and diagnostic values of the therapeutic relationship. Rogers focused more inwardly upon the 'space' within which such relationship takes place, most notably defining the qualities which need to be present in the therapist/counsellor. In the process, he yielded seeds which formed a powerful paradigm in the development of twentieth-century psychotherapy, augmenting the recognition that each person and each situation is new and unique and that the understanding of another person begins with an understanding of ourselves.

The visionary quality is one readily found where there is an accompanying sense of 'informing the future'. Bob Dylan, whose work dovetailed him into the social revolution of the 1960s, memorably informed us *'The times they are a-changing…'*.[34] He was born with this phase occupying the creative 5th house and containing both Jupiter and Uranus trine to Neptune in the 9th, adding to the innovative, flourishing, inspirational essence of both music and message. George Orwell, born with the Moon behind the Sun by only 0°12' in Cancer, and Neptune also conjunct the Sun in the 10th – his prophetic visions of political tyranny and oppressive totalitarianism have distinct signature in the chart with Pluto (conjunct the MC and opposition Uranus conjunct IC) being the last planet touched by Moon before birth. Dane Rudhyar, often referred to as a "seed man" and whose philosophical insights in astrology have inspired many to look wider and deeper, was born with this phase containing Mercury in Pisces square to Pluto. His first book, *The Astrology of Personality*, published in the mid-1930s, together with many of those that followed, still yield new and profound realizations for the astrologer of the 21st century.

Also in the literary world we find Ian Fleming, creator of James Bond, who always dreamed of being a writer yet did not begin doing so seriously until he was forty-three (although he was a journalist for Reuters for a while). Aquarius rises and its ruler Uranus is in Capricorn in the 12th house (suitably enough for a former Intelligence Officer which he also was). This within the context of Balsamic Sun/Moon forming a First Quarter trine to the 12th Uranus. Uranus in turn opposes Venus conjunct Neptune adding the piquancy, sensuality, glamour and excitement of his works. From *Casino Royale* to *Quantum of Solace* (and not forgetting *Chitty Chitty Bang Bang* along the way), these were indeed seeds dispersed which would multiply in the future 'thrills and spills' of world entertainment, through books, films, music. In similar vein, we find A.A. Milne (the phase containing Venus which forms a Grand Trine with Jupiter and Uranus in the 5th) who bequeathed the seeds of timeless delight to all children (from three to a hundred-and-three) via Winnie the Pooh, Christopher Robin, Piglet, Eeyore and my most favourite Tigger. We may also point to actors such as Sir Derek Jacobi (born with this phase in Libra, with a Mars/Neptune conjunction on a Virgo Ascendant – a meticulous and exquisitely focused artistry/sensitivity) who exemplify the theme by being able to step out of their own identity and enter a space wherein another being is characterized, clothed with words and actions and brought to life before us, in so compelling a way that this it becomes the iconic measure by which all future performances of the role are compared; this long after the actor has left the stage, taken off his costume and make-up and gone home to his own private personal self.

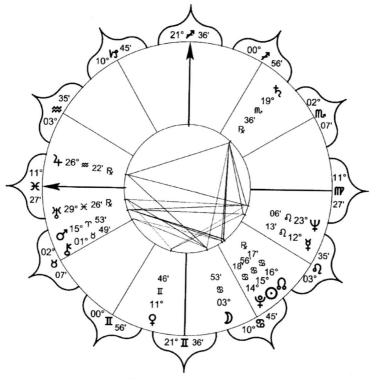

Elisabeth Kubler-Ross

Elisabeth Kubler-Ross was the first of triplets weighing only two pounds at her perilous birth. Strikingly, the Balsamic Phase contains Pluto. Additionally, both the Sun/Pluto end and the Moon end of the phase, are in aspect to Saturn in the 8th by trine and sesquiquadrate respectively, hence an association to Death. As she grew, Elisabeth knew she wanted to be a doctor but she was vehemently opposed by a tyrannical father who refused to help her and against whom she fought (Sun conjunct Pluto square Mars). Leaving home at eighteen, she struggled through war-torn Europe, part-volunteering, part working as a laboratory assistant while going to medical school. As a doctor she was particularly struck by the lack of caring afforded to those who were dying and this gave rise to her growing (Balsamic) realization that more could be done and understood concerning the dying process itself as well as the needs of the human being meeting it.

Her universally acclaimed book *On Death and Dying*[35] served as a groundbreaking force to change humanity's perspective of death, to revolutionize the way we care for our dying, affording greater dignity and understanding and removing taboos through open discussion of its various stages. And this, not only for the dying person but for all concerned, such as counsellors, therapists, healthcare professionals and indeed relatives/ survivors of the dying. She also researched near-death experiences and the nature of the afterlife. Though frequently lonely, unsupported and even ostracized, her compassion and hard work (Cancerian Sun/Moon and Pluto) shone through, making her very much a pathfinder and trailblazer in developing a compassionate, holistic perspective on the experience of death and its incorporation within accepted medical discipline.

But of course not all Balsamic types are Kubler-Ross's, Flemings or Rudhyars. They may not appear to be or do anything special 'out there' at all, simply living their lives in some kind of hinterland where their energies are more geared to privacy and contemplation. Positively there may be an inner contacting something of value, an awareness beyond words and descriptions, Tolle[36] has referred to such people as 'frequency holders', i.e. those who are anchored in their inner life, bringing a quality of stability and quiescence to world consciousness. Every so often, however, they may also emerge from the shadows and speak or act out what inwardly they fervently know to be right or true.

Negatively, however, we may sometimes find the 'drop outs', living on the fringes of active participatory society, lounging around in dismal resignation watching TV and funded by state benefits. Should they perchance present for any astrological work, more than frequently I have found that some kind of banner of a negative past needs first to be dismantled – even though it may be resolutely clung to as "Well, I can't help it" or "It's not my fault". Resting one's sense of being in a warped knot in the tapestry, it may take a little while for them to unravel, but when the process of discovery does begin, they listen for a future drumbeat to follow. Usually I have found that it helps such a person to focus on what *moves* them, what *holds* them, mesmerizes them, has them feeling a sense of awe. Asking such a question directly will not usually work, because the intellect will endeavour to respond – and what moves the Balsamic person is not contained within the intellect. Consequently putting things into words may be difficult and, as Storr has described,[37] it can be of more help if the person follows spiritual dimensions of understanding or any avenue where guided imagery or art, poetry, music or journal-work can be invoked to constellate the feelings deep within.

Living in attunement to an unseen world may of course be coloured by the environment in which the Balsamic lives and can have an especially hard time flourishing in a material culture. Much of the western industrialized world is approached only mechanistically, where circumstances and events arise and the only way of dealing with them (so the belief goes) is through planning, action, the development of reason and the collation of more information and technology. From this context, human beings are compelled to find answers through control and analysis. It is of course a world view which has reigned supreme for a very long time and is one into which human beings are consensually locked; from its perspective, the exploration of an inner landscape (let alone an unseen world informing the future) is regarded (if it is given *any* recognition) as of secondary importance or else is a matter for derision. Conversely we have seen an escalation of psychological and spiritual practices, together with a fusion of east-west philosophies, particularly over the last fifty years or so, which provide a counter-balance and indeed seem today to have placed us decidedly at the helm of distinct and growing evolutionary changes in consciousness where spiritual development emerges more and more as a value to be espoused.

For the strongly Balsamic individual, accompanying planetary phases (especially Saturn/Moon) will provide further clarification and a platform for discussion with the individual concerned. Additionally, the placement of Scorpio, Mars and Pluto in the chart can be informative as to the possible avenues for the shedding of an 'old skin' so that a transformation can occur. Sometimes this is recognized and yet almost missed if the person is caught up in societal norms: I recall a young woman client who appeared very fragile and morose, curled up somewhat defensively in a chair, with dark lank hair framing a pale, wan face. And yet as the session went along, I was aware of a sort of deep intent radiance that shone through her as a person. She had the Sun/Moon Balsamic with Mercury in 12th house Scorpio plus a focal Mars/Pluto/Saturn set-up, all which seemed to be reflected in her huddled, deeply cautious and tense timidity. However, when it came to discussing the Balsamic phase she suddenly moved! Sitting now totally upright, she spoke straight to me (as opposed to just sideways from underneath the lank hair). She told me of a novel she wanted to write, and indeed began to fumble in her bag for some dog-eared bits of paper which constituted her first chapter. As she read the first paragraphs to me, a few tears welled up at the back of my eyes. It was so incredibly beautifully written. It emerged that she had long wanted to write ever since she was a child, but had endured a background in which she was bullied by older brothers. Anything she did write, she would keep hidden for fear they would find it and humiliate her. This was a pattern she had recapitulated throughout her life, the bit of past that had become knotted up and reworked over and over. It said something for her courage that she was able to bring her dog-eared first chapter to our session. It also said something for the Balsamic energy being alive and well and about to come through…

We talked it over. Drawn by the magnet of her own Balsamic nature, she resolved to type it all out properly and see what happened from there…. *But then it was as if she 'blew it'.* She said "Right then, first things first. I'm going to enrol for a writing course at my local Adult Education Centre". "Why?" I enquired meekly, feeling a little 'thrown'. She looked at me with a mixture of astonishment and pity. She explained, somewhat painstakingly so that I would understand (!), that she had seen the course advertised and felt it would be a good thing to learn how to be a writer. Besides, one of her friends was going on it. "Why go to school to learn how to be a writer", I asked, "when the writer you're seeking is already resident within you? Not only that… she's knocking quite loudly at your door? Why not just let her in?" I did not want to push this – after all, and for all I knew, there were some perfectly good writing courses out there to encourage her and my own personal feeling that she did not need to step in line and mechanically do what everyone else was doing may have been just that – my own personal feelings and possibly prejudices. However, the upshot was that she started on the course, but after three weeks phoned to say she found it all too "boxed-in and stultifying", so was not going any more. Instead she just sat with typewriter, paper… and left the rest to the visitor knocking at her door. The call had come, she said 'yes' and to date stands as the author of three published novels.

Where there is a 30° semi-sextile in this last phase, the need to turn to the creation of a new future is accompanied on the one hand by considerable vulnerability, borne of feeling that one is caught up in a kind of hurricane of the past and unable to feel anything except frustration because of it. Yet, on the other hand, the fact that this semi-sextile has been reached also suggests that the individual has the necessary readiness to pause awhile, step outside the drama of his or her life rather than being distracted by or bound to it for this weakens our internal (and, for that matter, eternal) ability to be galvanized by our own acute powers of observation. The visions and ideals in the Balsamic phase may be ahead of their time, some people will readily accept them, others will not. Yet overall there is a compelling sense of wanting to step out onto a pathway, the results of which may not be immediately known. Rather than sit around waiting for someone else to do it for them, latter stage Balsamics particularly need to be guided by the promptings of their own inner spirit to establish this as yet unknown road. Our earlier examples are of those who have done just that. As a result they leave something behind them both during their life and after they depart it – for posterity, a legacy that shines on and on for those who are to come… new seeds to be sown.

7: Saturn and Moon

Saturn bids us make specific choices and develop self-responsibility for structuring our lives. Sometimes this may involve a sense of loss since making a definite choice implies, by its nature, a yielding up of other would-be options. Even on a simple level we can see this might be so – for instance, I have clearly made the choice to structure my time right now by writing this chapter. In so doing, I might well have sacrificed other possible options for my day – watching a favourite film, meeting a friend for lunch, reading a book. Choosing to structure time in pursuing a leisure activity is just as much Saturn as choosing to work upon a task.

Traditionally Saturn is associated with duty, obligation and necessity, but these too are usually the consequences of choice. The motivation is different but the decision ('I will do this rather than that') is Saturn in action. Following on from Jupiter in the solar system, Saturn's function is to achieve a *crystallization* of our expansion into the environment where we merge and co-operate with our fellow beings. To do so, we set up clearly defined, sometimes even rigid, ways of enabling this to occur. The face of Saturn which seeks concrete identity by conforming to the *mores* of our group is the Capricorn/10th house face where we establish social identity, following the rules and requirements of our environment. Here we attain a guarantee of protection as long as we stay in our allotted place, as it were, and it marks our social standing in the community. At the same time, we also develop structured realizations of our value as a creative social being. This is more synonymous with the Aquarian face of Saturn and the 11th house where we act more freely and individually to make a difference, through contribution to the community of which we are a part.

Each person starts off in life, as Rudhyar put it, "a small island in the vast ocean of mankind".[1] When we combine Saturn with our needs for belonging, containment and rhythmic familiarity (Moon), we see that as well as incarnating with central purpose (Sun/Moon) we also step into a world of form. We are housed in a physical body, subject to the gravitational laws of planet earth, are a specific gender, occupy a position in a culture, society, family, set of parents and are given a name. All these are boundaries within which we develop the means and will to become all that we may be. A newborn baby will reflect through its shining eyes the pure consciousness of Being but, as we grow, pretty soon we become aware of the physical-material world which holds us in containment. Primarily there are the significant people around, how they appear to us, how we sense and feel their being... and our own in relation to them. We discover the Saturnian norms, patterns and expectations which become vital to our ongoing stability *and survival* by incorporation of and submission to them as imperatives. Thus our central purpose becomes held within a construct of identity-definition.

We are long accustomed to viewing this planetary pair through the lens of parental/familial images and our early imprinted life experience which contains many tiers of reference. From these, we develop a whole array of responses and belief systems and hold them to be true in order to keep the pattern intact by which we can survive. This then becomes the formulated picture and cumulative history to which we respond, continually reconnect and even cling, in order to build a set and workable identity we can rely upon (even long after the circumstances in which that identity became so constructed have passed by). In other words, Saturn/Moon becomes so habitual and ingrained that we resonate to it compellingly. Examining this phase can help us decode these threads in which we may be unwittingly entrapped – whether they are threads of positivity or otherwise. Getting stuck in the phase can mean we never access other levels of awareness which would help us define our individual purpose more readily and develop an autonomy.

Everybody has a life story – and given half the chance most of us will tell it, complete with anecdotal flourishes and suffused with all the agonies, ecstasies and aspirations of our journey so far. Some have experienced very harrowing early life circumstances while others report only happy memories and feelings of gratitude. Wherever we personally feel ourselves to be along this continuum, identifying the threads we are weaving at Saturn/Moon level can assist immeasurably in both accessing and clarifying the inner sense of who we are endeavouring to be and become. Submitting to such awareness enables us to go beyond it and/or incorporate the potential of Saturn/Moon more meaningfully in line with our purpose. Or, as Howard Sasportas once neatly put it, before you can *disidentify* with something you first have to identify with it.

Saturn/Moon can be a comfort zone that we don't like to leave because we feel strange or uncomfortable outside of it (which we may then define as being 'wrong' because of course it is not fitting a conformity) yet we need to move out from it every so often in order to tread an individual path of maturity. At the Saturn/Moon level we not only have to find a way of being that conforms to our understandings built up from original conditions, but also build a road forward in order to serve the purpose of the Sun/Moon. But if our Saturn/Moon needs run counter to those of Sun/Moon, especially if they are squirrelled away out of conscious range, then Saturn/Moon phase may take over Sun/Moon, even obliterating its meaningful function.

Tracing our family and ancestral themes via the Saturn/Moon phase can enable us to experience the central tapestry-frame onto which we have initially harnessed our threads of development. The many pathways of thought which exist in our world approach this from different perspectives, for example seeing ourselves as a product of our parents' lives and characters by dint of being their offspring in a family matrix and wider ancestral lineage. From this perspective, things get propagated and passed down the line, the spirit of preceding generations weaving itself in as a causal principle to the core of our being and shaping our unfolding development. We may also perceive our incarnation as a matter of choice on the part of the evolving soul (when, where, who to be born to and for what purpose) – as in Plato's *Myth of Er*[2] – where the nature and significance of the parents/family are chosen as serving the unfolding purpose and meaning of the to-be-born. Whichever philosophical, spiritual or psychological perspective is adopted as a lens, it seems clear that when we are small we set down for our lives what we perceive as a marker for 'the way things are' which then becomes the premise upon which life is built.

While there may be drawbacks and difficulties to be encountered, there can also be a considerable amount of *wisdom* within this, borne of the inner structural acquiescence to limits that monitor us like an Internal Supervisor, bidding us to pause, step back, consolidate, know ourselves... closely. Consider a man with a Moon/Saturn conjunction in the 4th house opposite Mars in the 10th, both adversely aspected by Pluto in the 8th. All his life he has been cautious to the point of inaction and people complain that he is dull, timid and ineffective. Yet suddenly he has been offered a key career position which is both highly desirable and lies well within his capabilities, but he is full of fear about accepting it. If we were to sit with him as he surveyed his Saturn/Moon and allow a space for awareness to arise, we might find that he grew up in a harsh and tyrannical background where being fearful and timid *would have been a protective strategy*. He might tell you that when his very exacting, critical, irritable or violent parent(s) came home, he would stay huddled in his room very quietly reading books or getting on with something unobtrusively. How very astute of him then as a young child to ensure his ongoing survival in that environment by adopting this response. And as he makes further connection to the wisdom and strength behind the original decision to be cautious, he can perhaps begin to make a new relationship with this quality within him, rather than only succumbing to the world's present-day labelling of it. For one thing, he might discover that doing things quietly and unobtrusively is to do them carefully, meaningfully, with strength and determination … *as he took up his new job*. We might even discover that it leads him to profound and dedicated insight (which the new job may also be calling forward); thus we get a glimpse of what the aspect-pattern/phase was *for* all along.

The pulling power of Saturn/Moon is that we automatically turn to it when faced with anxiety since it represents how we feel most able to 'vanquish the foe' and survive. The past is not something to be erased as it is a part of our experience. It can be referred to as informative in order to give clarity to that experience, while also releasing the energy we pour into holding it intact and claiming it as a fixed, ongoing reality. When we incarnate and seek to operate within the Saturn-bound limitations of the space-time world, it is somewhat akin to getting caught up in a role. Some have alikened this to an illusory movie we are watching, of something that occurred a long time ago, we made a decision about, called it reality and have gone on living ever since. It is in observing and witnessing these dynamics at Saturn/Moon level that we can most reconnect with our deeper, more authentic and individual ways of being as a signpost to onward growth.

Overall, and as we touched upon in Chapter 5, the Saturn/Moon phase constitutes the drive within us to build an identity by which we can define ourselves, given that we are living within certain structures on planet earth. In that sense it is protective, life-affirming and directive. It also reflects how we develop a conformity – to do and be that which we deem is expected of us. Again, this may be protective but in addition may also consist of repetitive patterns from earlier life, including a battery of assumptions and attitudes we adopted then but may unwittingly adhere to and perpetrate long into adult life, whether or not they serve the purposes they once did.

Saturn/Moon New Phase
Moon 0° – 45° ahead of Saturn

When any two planets meet in New Phase, the energy is both automatic and powerful. With Saturn and Moon the urge within us to conform to what is expected is all-pervasive and often well-nigh impregnable. Identification with early life decisions, beliefs and images can be such that this person does not need to think about projecting an identity or way of life as they grow since – whether for good or for ill or a mixture of both – it is as if they have one ready-made. As a result, they usually present a very powerful, even charismatic, sense of who they are, borne of whatever norms have been engraved upon their experience. This is not to say it is necessarily a negativity, but one of the main hazards is that it can be very limiting. It can also be difficult for this person to recognize his/her patterns of being and stand aside from them simply because they seem as if set in stone, thus hard to access or get beneath.

It is possible that the person experienced tremendous control or excessive discipline by parental or other authority figures in early life, or indeed a key person was of such personality that it was overwhelmingly strong (positively or negatively) and the growing child automatically takes it on like the donning of a helmet. There may be close resemblances between the individual and a parental figure such that words, phrases or stances are automatically adopted and trundled out. Alternatively it may be that the aura of the family as a whole, or the particular society/culture in which the person was brought up, has the nature of a very dominant way of life. Again, whether positive or negative, not only does the person feel compelled to follow, but such patterns can have something of a wall around them protecting them from awareness and change.

Quite often the pattern might involve hard work, as in the life of former US President, Jimmy Carter who gleaned his pattern of industry from a stern father. As young as five years old, he obediently and relentlessly (the phase is in Scorpio, 1st house) applied himself to the family's peanut-farming activities, taking them into town for sale and returning home to his father with the money so earned. Later in his life, we see him applying these same arduous drives when he felt obliged to forego a career in the Navy and return to his family upon the death of his father and the near bankruptcy of the farming business. Working zealously to rescue the situation, he was eventually so successful that he became a valued member of various civic organizations, later Governor of Georgia and President in 1977. While of gentle and genial self-presentation (Sun Libra, Libra rising, Venus conjunct Neptune), the Saturn/Moon phase in Mr. Carter's chart is strengthened in its indomitable will, responsibility and patient toil by the Sun square Pluto (the Saturn/Moon ruler) and a Grand Trine linking Moon, Uranus and Pluto. These were moreover qualities he was similarly to display during his presidency particularly concerning his part in the Camp David peace accords.

There may be also be concrete adherence to positive qualities of strong determination, physical and psychological hardiness, clarity of purpose, responsibility, or a quiet controlled stoicism that just gets on with the job and makes a fuss about nothing. Alternatively, there may be an automatic acceptance of rules, rigid or singular outlooks, doing one's duty or the expectation only of oppression, burden, or hardship.

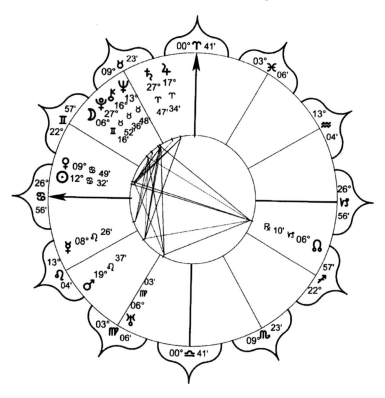

Emily Jane Popejoy

Emily Jane Popejoy was a young country girl barely out of school in 1896 when, like an Inanna descending into terrible tribulations before an Ereshkigal, she entered into 'service' in London's fashionable Kensington where her employer was a Mrs Nicholls. In keeping with this phase, Jane (as she was known) automatically accepted the societal context of her times and thus the expectation that young girls from 'ordinary' backgrounds should take employment in domestic service. It was the usual thing for them to do. It was her 'station in life'.

The phase contains Neptune, Chiron and Pluto as threads already woven into the tapestry at birth and awaiting exteriorization through life experience. Given the potential for suffering, vulnerability, wounding, alienation and life/death struggle contained within these planetary themes, what occurred in this young girl's life was indeed distressing in the extreme and ultimately fatal. Mrs Nicholls treated young Jane appallingly, criminally – systematically starving and beating her, sometimes dragging her by her hair in the street. On several occasions Jane begged bread from neighbours, pleading with them not to inform her mistress. She was worked extremely hard and paid one shilling and sixpence per week; without this she had no other means. She went from being a normal, happy and healthy girl of sixteen to a terrified, unkempt, scavenging wretch. Letters home to her family chronicled a happy life in Mrs Nicholls' home but alas it later emerged that they had been dictated by the latter, under threat of further ill-treatment. One year later, on Christmas Eve, Jane was rescued by what was known as the Travellers' Aid Society and transported back to her family home in Surrey where a doctor was immediately summoned. Her condition was truly pitiful – she could not stand nor walk and weighed only 29 kgs. Barely able to speak, she had broken fingers, a broken nose and her body was covered with bruising. Moreover she was in a state of acute, advanced starvation and suffering pneumonia. Her mother stayed constantly praying by her daughter's side, but two days later, after managing to inform them in her last breaths that Mrs Nicholls was responsible, Jane died. She was seventeen and a half years old.

In addition to the harrowing condition of the phase and the planets contained, we can also see that Jane's Sun/Moon phase is Balsamic (dissolution and the seeding of a future pathway) and contains the 12th house South Node conjunct Venus in Cancer. This seems to carry a particular poignancy, given what we know happened to her, for there is a signature of fearfulness through feeling unprotected or unloved, possibly as a residue of past life experience (12th) and met again via work situations and authority/employment (North Node 6th/Capricorn and the ruler, Saturn, in 10th). The North Node itself would seem to offer Jane the potential to apply herself and develop strength and resilience and with Venus conjunct the Cancerian Sun, one has a sense of her as a kind and caring person who wanted to do her best, perhaps 'be a good girl' and work hard. But, especially with its need for concreteness, any Moon/Saturn combination wants to be more than just kind; it wishes to be of actual, competent, use. So here we have young Jane, conforming to what was expected of her, utilising her caring gifts in someone's else's home and wanting to be of practical dedicated service.

There are times when something may not be entirely knowable except within the totality of all universal Life. Thus, like Charles Carter before us,[3] we may have many questions as to why this set of phases and aspects should have worked out so shockingly in the life of a young girl who, to all appearances, came from an ordinary loving family and had ventured out into the world of work as a hale and hearty young person, only to return but a year later so piteously broken down to the gates of her death. The outer planets and Chiron contained within the phase offer us a first signpost (as suggested earlier) but planets conjoining a nodal axis can also denote 'fated' meetings with others. Whether they are brief or long-lasting there is a quality to them that has us feeling that they are somehow meant. Here was a woman (Venus) – Mrs Nicholls – under whose roof and in whose care (Cancer) Jane was supposed to be as an employee (opposite Node 6th). Thus it may also be that this meeting with Mrs Nicholls was of a karmic nature, one which Jane (indeed perhaps both parties) had incarnated to make. While there is no information on her very early life (when the Moon would first have met South Node conjunct Venus) if we continue to track the Moon through the zodiac, it can be seen to conjunct the North Node in 6th house Capricorn (already noted as a symbol of her employment/employer) in 210° – correlating to 17½ years.

It is also possible that with Uranus, as ruler of the 8th in exact square to the Moon end of both Sun/Moon and Saturn/Moon phases in this chart, perhaps it was part of Jane's inner purpose, through her experience and her death, to be an *awakener* of the social dynamics of her environment (11th house Moon, ruler of the chart). Particularly if we consider the 11th as being the 2nd house from the 10th (earning from one's work) perhaps it was through this position as maidservant that Jane served to usher in major shifts, changes, transformations in the working conditions of her time. One cannot help but acknowledge that she has also served to both capture the attention and inform at least one astrologer before me (Mr. Carter, above) – and here she is again, true to her Balsamic Sun/Moon nature, offering us further seeds of understanding in our quest to understand cosmic threads of meaning. Along with meeting up with Mrs Nicholls for some possible unfinished business, perhaps these were all purposeful and valuable threads in the short life of Emily Jane Popejoy. (Mrs Nicholls was tried and sentenced at The Old Bailey to seven years' penal servitude for manslaughter.)

Somewhat surprisingly for Moon and Saturn, this phase may sometimes be found in people who appear to be either unusual or rebellious in some way, but when you follow the thread through it is usually to be found that in fact early concrete *expectations* of them were in some way unusual and they are merely identifying with and conforming to these. Great Uncle Timothy may have been a colourful hero or a bit of a wag and the child gets to be named after him, thus picks up that it is part of the package of being in this family that one becomes colourful, unusual, rebellious. Others in this phase follow a more conformist line, sometimes bearing names that have been carried down over many generations where each person has followed the same pattern in life – e.g. all the William Henry Thomases have been alcoholics, or church pastors, or politicians, anything... but they follow automatically, one upon the other, the set-out and structured road.

It may well be that these themes will come into play at the first Saturn return or again at age fifty-six, but may arise at any of the seven-year intervals of Saturn's transits whether to the natal Moon or any other planet. Where the New Phase reaches the 30° sextile there can be more manoeuvrability, such that the person may still present an identity taken on wholesale when young and yet at the same time show 'chinks' of being able to be a little more ready to examine their own feelings and intuitions, open up new pathways and do a little more of their own thing. Alternatively, and as the phase progresses to its 45° close, there may be some breaking through of the instilled pattern perhaps even becoming a little at odds with norms and rules, thus setting a newer purpose in train.

Overall, however, this phase can speak of a searing sense of purpose. Many books may speak largely of negative-only outcomes such as insufficient parenting, over-control, lovelessness, abandonment, deprivation etc. But such manifestations are by no means a given and, even if they are met, they point to an underlying purpose. Saturn/Moon serves to put you on your feet (as does the experience of abandonment, lovelessness, deprivation) and the astrological counsellor is in a key position to withhold the imposition of a set interpretation without also listening carefully to that client's own experience. When the inner qualities of this person are accessed they are often a pressing spur for them to carve a concrete, competent and meaningful path in life.

Saturn/Moon Crescent Phase
Moon 45° – 90° ahead of Saturn

In this phase, where the emphasis is upon effort, building and anchoring, there is correspondingly an underlying belief system that life must always consist of these things and the identity is constructed accordingly. Thus there can be a constant application of oneself, sometimes wanting to control and build life to set preferences rather than allowing it to unfold in its own way or just generally feeling that one's security always depends on relentless struggle. Key threads in this phase are therefore largely woven into patterns of what we might call The Worker and/or the Tryer... and sometimes a little bit of both.

The Worker is someone whose identity is built around practicality and conscientiousness in all that they do. Theirs is a way of being in which they just crack on and put a shoulder to the wheel. If there is a heaviness attached to this, they may be 'workhorses', pitching themselves right into (or even pitting themselves *against*) something, knuckling down to hard graft or else depleting into stuckness and exhaustion. From a positive perspective, the personal background may have contained avenues of struggle for noble causes, such as a specific ingenuity or durability. More simply the person experienced an ordinary hard-working background and/or there may have been early life experience of tough pursuits (one person's background involved a family devoted to mountaineering and cross-country running to keep fit). In addition I have seen this phase accentuated where there was at least one significant background person who was competent, yet perhaps a little too over-organizational and controlling. Whatever the actuality, the theme represents something of *a brisk call to apply oneself.*

This is a person who will strive to establish a key goal or take on the mantle of responsibility for the preservation of something (a way of life, a family continuity…) but generally they will work hard in order to bring a major task to fruition. Isambard Kingdom Brunel, builder of bridges and steamships, was noted for the monumental effort he put into all his undertakings, sometimes to the detriment of his health. The Saturn end of the phase (with Uranus for added innovation) conjuncts the Midheaven and opposes the Sun in Aries (he shone in many engineering 'firsts') while the Moon rises in Sagittarius, reflecting the breadth of his work and ability to take on widespread and ambitious projects.

Where there is a Tryer identity in this phase, the inner belief runs along the lines of life not only being a struggle, but in order to get anywhere it is going to be a tough ride and *you have to try very hard to make something of yourself*. No one in the early background may ever have actually said those words, but to the Saturn/Moon Crescent type the implication can be there. Almost invariably this type will give the impression of being under great pressure and working assiduously to 'Make It'. Huffing and puffing with the burden of it all (which of course they believe they must expect), there may be considerable preoccupation with any task in life, be it small or large, and an approach to it shot through with a sense of serious toil. In addition there can be great vulnerability, even resentment, because the belief that 'one must try hard to make something of oneself' necessarily implies that what is already there, within oneself as an individual, is not good enough. Thus they can feel 'flawed' and even more driven to work like the proverbial Trojan to prove the reverse and be found acceptable.

Sometimes the early environment contained themes of difficulty through illness either for this person or a parent/sibling, thus the accent was upon extra work and concern through care and attendance. Or the background conditions may have been those of struggle for financial reasons or such as exist in a war-zone. Sometimes significant people were locked in interpersonal conflicts and the child sees no other way of dealing with life except through struggle. Overall, whether the threads are experienced positively or negatively, one frequently meets those of this phase who are engaged in an activity, career, relationship or general way of life which they report as taking a great deal out of them. It may be objectively true that the situation is one requiring great stamina, bravery, or persistent effort, and the person may indeed be a conscientious worker. Yet at the same time there can also be a sense that this fits a prior constructed belief that has become habitual and is an unexamined set pattern to which the person automatically conforms.

Sometimes fear may arise in constant battle against something that always seems to get in the way or that has to be defended against, and there is never any 'let up'. One client was brought up in a village home in close proximity to a prison. A couple of riots and at least one break-out during his childhood led to constant locking of doors and windows by his parents, an habitual pattern of defensive control which he continued well into adult life, especially when he was alone in the house and even in the hottest of weathers. There can also be a great striving to reach objectives, but it is coupled with an emotional 'withholding', as if the person is functioning yet while always holding their breath. The expectation here is that the struggle may become too much, that one will not win, or that even if one does succeed it will not satisfy the inner need for self-approval, since there is still the motto 'you have try hard to make something of yourself' which, again, may never have been said, but which is forever spinning in their minds like a long-playing record.

Sooner or later in life, the Saturn/Moon Crescent person realizes that conforming to the negative pressures of this pattern is counter-productive to their true aims. When its futility is given full recognition, they feel more motivated to moving forward. I have witnessed many people working through these issues therapeutically, while others found their basic conformity to old frustrating patterns altered at moments of major life-changes, such as when they married, or emigrated or set off on an entirely new career path than the one they first started off with (which was probably full of excessive effort and eventual disappointment). By whatever means the breakthrough arises, there then follows a line of development which stands as a new presentation of themselves. This too may consist of a hard-working identity capable of earnestly reaching a goal, but without the attendant 'drag-down' of conformity to a belief in drudgery and exhaustion... nor indeed tripping over one's own feet in a desperate effort to hit one's head against yet another brick wall!

The movement onward can be particularly relevant at the 60° sextile where it is through connectedness with others that the individual comes to understand the inner pattern and establishing a different road ahead. Again s/he may toil hard but it will be in the service of bringing something to light as a result of such thoroughness (as in Brunel's chart) and become more the Stalwart Enabler. Where there is a 72° quintile, often there can be a drive to portray one's identity to the world in a very creative light albeit with the same theme of consistent effort, but poised to present something new in the world. Such is the case with Samuel Hahnemann who was born into an impoverished family and indeed worked very hard during his early years, developing linguistic, scientific and research skills in many fields, culminating in his medical qualification. With Sun/Moon in Balsamic phase, thus carrying the potential for tapping into an unseen world, Hahnemann turned aside from his medical career after a while because, as a deeply dutiful man (Saturn/Moon Crescent with Saturn in its own sign in a solid earth house) he could not bring himself to treat people with the known medicines of the time which he frequently found caused them greater suffering. Instead he embarked on a career in writing and translating.

During the course of this, he came across a reference in a work he was translating to Peruvian Bark in treating malaria. From a totally 'unseen' source (so typical of the Balsamic energy) came the prompting to Hahnemann to test for himself (and indeed upon his own body) the effect of quinine, from which he eventually made his discovery that the symptoms produced were similar to those of diseased states it was used to cure. Thus he asserted the "law of similars" that diseases are cured by substances that produce their symptoms in the healthy. Over the next twenty years he worked solidly (and frequently in serious battle against the authorities) to build up his findings, including documentation of many other substances, researching toxicity, experimenting with dosage, solutions, potentizations etc. until in 1810 he published an exposition of all these labours in his *Organon der Rationellen Heilkunde*. Hahnemann's conscientious drive to bring a major task to light through testing, researching, discovering, never letting up (Crescent quintile) left the world with 'new seeds for the future' (Balsamic) through what he named Homoeopathy.

Saturn/Moon First Quarter Phase
Moon 90° – 135° ahead of Saturn

As this phase represents the meeting of a challenge, the pattern here is to project a clear-cut sense of identity, forcibly if necessary, to put oneself 'out there' and let others know who you are. In early life this person was probably encouraged (verbally or otherwise) to assert themselves and this continues to underpin how they go about creating and maintaining an identity. Sometimes standing up for the family as a whole can give rise to this pattern, e.g. "We are the BROWNS or the JONESES" or they are part of a heritage and history spanning several generations and standing for something in particular. Sometimes there is a past family structure where a longed-for ambition had to be foregone and this current individual is the one who is expected, even challenged, to pick it up and run with it in the present.

Whatever the actuality, these individuals do not usually have any qualms about self-assertion, nor the rightness of their way of dealing with things. They may even get into fights with others because they are continually trying to impress themselves on the world in an aggressive manner. This can be especially so nearer the square aspect where the energies can be strident and headstrong or the person seems always to be caught up in arguments in a bid to extricate themselves from something or someone they find hampering. On the other hand, I have often felt inspired by many clients who battled through harrowing circumstances of life with this aspect, on the basis of the modern maxim 'when the going gets tough, the tough get going'. The underlying belief system is something like 'Life is a battlefield – you have to take it on' and as the phase opens out more towards the trine aspect, there can be more of an ability to push oneself forward just as definitely but with more style and eloquence, often manifesting as practical competence in building one's life.

The need to assert might also be related to early experience of conflict within the environment, perhaps between the parents or other family members, as a consequence of which the person feels compelled to live it out as they grow, either in an endeavour to identify with and constantly replay it, or indeed to throw it off. The latter is preferable at this stage since the phase calls for a turning from the past and the forging of a road which enables the individual to do their own thing. Sometimes this may mean breaking a few rules which have been instilled along the way, or simply moving on to find an avenue out from long-held traditions and outlooks. One such avenue may be through creative work and this thread can be traced in the life of D.H. Lawrence whose early environment was one of conflict between his parents (later to be reflected in particular in *Sons and Lovers*).

Lawrence's father was a lowly, struggling coal-miner, either down the pit or down the pub. His mother, on the other hand, was a more cultivated woman with a set of socially superior standards which included a desperation that her son should follow an educated avenue in life. Within the context of this phase, Mars sits at the midpoint of his Saturn and a Leo Midheaven, squaring a more refined Moon/Venus conjunction in Libra (Venus being the first planet met by the Moon after birth). Deeply bonded to his mother, and indeed following the pathway she fervently wanted for him, Lawrence nevertheless found himself increasingly torn between a distaste for his father's more brutish way of life yet also with an admiration for the rugged comradeship that existed between the men of his father's time and their capacity to enjoy a rough yet vital sense of being. Within this he also became critical of the moulding of the young men of his era by succumbing to their mothers' dreams and unfulfilled desires. Similarly, a conflict existed for Lawrence in the environment itself, on the one hand expressing exquisite appreciation of its beauty, yet on the other needing to wrench himself free, also vividly captured in his novels as well as various essays and letters.[4]

While this type can get into conflict with others because of the need to imprint themselves concretely upon their environment, this is not in itself a negativity and may underpin a thrust to considerable achievement in the outer world. However, if it is developed with some kind of loaded aggression, then anything that appears to get in the way may be ruthlessly dispensed with. Here the person can display an arrogance, barging in ahead of others, believing they have the might and right to bypass normal observances of civilized behaviour. Should anyone question them, put them to proof of something or ask to see their credentials, they are apt to be treated with nimble disdain, furious argument, or both. Yet at the same time assertion in this phase can also be (at least to some extent) because the individual is making attempts at self-discovery by externalizing his or her views, opinions or ambitions *in order to get a reaction to them*. It is the reaction that eventually can enable them to make a shift one way or the other. Even though they may not always be very clear about what image or identity they are trying to establish, the important thing seems to be to put a lot of energy into it anyway. In other words, it can simply be that the person is not at all sure quite what is expected of them but is merely driven by the *strong sense that* **something** *is*.

At its most negative, there can be a tendency for this type to walk away and leave other people to pick up the pieces arising from their challenging actions. Fury and anger in this phase is a little like kicking your car when it gets stuck in a mud ditch on a dark and rainy night. Conversely, that very power can be utilized for positive reasons for the ferocity with which we kick the car is the same energy we could use to haul it out of the ditch and get it back on the road. More positively still, any history of breaking free from a troubled past which brought pain often forms a sturdy base for carving out a path forward, fuelled by the wisdom that the road to spiritual and psychological growth is so often strewn with obstacles to be overcome.

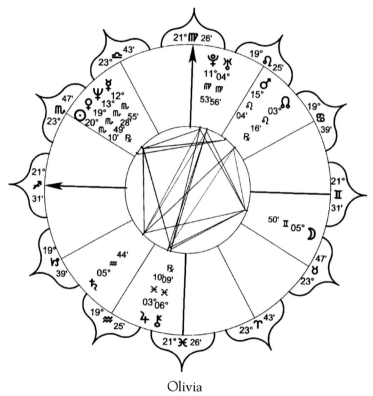

Olivia

Olivia came to see me having broken from an eleven-year partnership and feeling very lost, rejected and in need of redirection. A few further relationships had followed, all of which called forward issues in her life experience thus far and included discussion of the Saturn/Moon First Quarter phase with Saturn occupying the 2nd house conjunct South Node in Aquarius and in exact First Quarter trine to the Moon in 6th house Gemini. Our conversations veered for a while towards her work and pressing needs to work hard, do her best, achieve etc. – I was expecting to find something of the sturdy ability to rise to a challenge, but nothing seemed to matter to Olivia as much as the need to feel fulfilled in a relationship (Sun/Moon Full); thus it became the focus of my brief.

But then she met William and pretty soon had moved in with him. By now Olivia and I had got to know one another quite well and from time to time I would naturally ask how things were going in this new relationship. Her answers went from a flat-sounding "Fine", to "Oh… yes, oh… well, yes, fine really" to "…um… oh, I don't know… oh, OK I guess" and so on. Respectful of four planets in Scorpio I knew better than to push it or probe. But it was not long before she hesitatingly began to unfurl a deep discomfort, but one she simply could not put her finger on except that while things on the surface were "sort-of-ok", somehow she felt bothered that (in comparison to her other lovers) William was pretty "non-tactile". A little while later Olivia split up from William, needing time apart since the relationship did not seem to fit her needs.

A few weeks later still, Olivia heard that William had gone to stay with some mutual friends in the country for a long weekend. It was summertime, and the friends had set up tents in their garden for their children to play and sleepover. All was going well….. until a bombshell dropped. During the night, William abused a small girl child. When the news broke, the First Quarter Saturn/Moon Olivia – though shocked and deeply distressed – had no hesitation in rising to this dreadful challenge, speaking out and pouring all her energy into marshalling every resource known to her to help the parents contact the necessary authorities (which resulted in William's arrest) and also set in motion as many social welfare agencies as she could in support of both parents and child.

There followed of course many agonizing months for all concerned, but for Olivia personally the horror of what had happened touched a deep and very raw nerve, one that she had hitherto not spoken about. She had herself experienced abuse during childhood and through this current crisis she came to the thunderbolt realization that she wanted to turn her life completely and utterly around to address this devastating issue, speak out and make a difference. She re-entered University to study psychology and criminology, culminating in an MSc in Forensic Psychology. Nervous throughout, and especially whenever she had to hand in an important paper, I pitched my support of her directly at First Quarter threads of her emerging assertive identity, especially remembering her statement that she wanted to make a difference to societal wellbeing (Scorpio 11th and the Moon is first set to meet determined and committed Mars in the 8th in this chart). Olivia swept all before her in brilliant written theses, on at least one occasion earning high commendation and an award for her contribution to the field.

Thereafter she worked steadily over the next five years, often in volunteer programmes, with sexual offenders and their partners as well as carers directly involved with the protection of children and with government advisory Bodies. Today she continues to work in this most demanding of vocations largely through rehabilitation groupwork (11th) and she does so by being willing to go into Scorpionic depths using insight and communication skills (including published papers) in pursuit of her cause (Moon Gemini 6th, Uranus/Pluto 9th opposite Jupiter/Chiron 3rd) all within the context of having the guts to take on the battle in a monumental effort to help turn around and heal the lives of those who are so tragically caught up in this complex human predicament.

On some occasions I have found this energy used to keep intact (Saturn) some early dynamic which is being strenuously adhered to, the person often being rudely dismissive of anything that seems to threaten it. One example was a woman who idealized her dominant father to an exceedingly great height. It became clear that anyone who did not accept this version of events, and especially any man who presented himself as a lover to her but did not play the role of Strong Daddy Who Will Support Me Forever, would be sent packing without demur. Wanting a chart reading concerning her love-life, she told me she had visited many astrologers, all of whom (she insisted) were "no good". Eyeing the Saturn/Moon situation, I had the sneaking feeling that mine could be the next head to roll. And indeed, by whatever careful measure I felt I approached it, just the mere mention of gradually turning from a past and into creative self-assertion led to the consultation being curtailed and the entire subject of astrology summarily dismissed.

Barack Obama, who has indeed taken on the challenge of being the first black President of the United States, was born in this phase from Capricorn/12th to Gemini/4th. Brought up by his mother alone, he has reported that during his childhood she would encourage him to push himself forward through the development of his education (Moon Gemini square to Pluto in Virgo), waking him very early to give him lessons herself before he went to school. When (as any child would) he protested about having to get out of bed at such an hour she would say "Ain't no picnic for me neither buddy!" The phase contains Chiron in the 1st house opposing Pluto and squaring the Moon end of the phase, one representation of which may be viewed as the 'outsider' who takes up a position of power through the eloquence of his Geminian Moon.

Where there is an accepted breaking through of set conformities, there can indeed be much creativity in this phase. There is often an eloquent ability to communicate with the world around, in whatever form, to establish identity and push for achievement. We may cite Nelson Mandela's chart where the phase is close to the 90° aspect and contains Mercury in the 9th and Mars in the 11th (Aquarius house) sesquiquadrate Uranus in the 3rd – *The Long Road to Freedom* indeed. Such is also exemplified in the life of Henri Cartier-Bresson, pioneer in the field of photography and photo-journalism, who was expected to follow in the footsteps of his wealthy father in the textile industry. However, the idea of this appalled the young headstrong Henri and instead he turned to First Quarter drive to jump up and capture single fleeting yet defining moments of life through the lens of his Leica. Here, the Moon end of the phase is conjunct Venus and Neptune in opposition to Uranus rising in the first house (striking imagery). A man of great innovation, vision and style, the Sun/Moon phase is Last Quarter (reorientation to new roads ahead) which similarly contains the Venus/Neptune positions as well as a creative and enterprising Mars/Jupiter conjunction at the Sun end.

Perhaps more notable around the trine aspect there may have been encouragement in growing-up years always to be integrate, competent about one's being, regardless of whether this means battling against any alternative tides. Here we may those who speak out candidly, notwithstanding the risk of confrontation, in order to render something more effective. Olivia, earlier, is a case in point. There could also be experience of significant people from the past, such as parents, where one was consistently outgoing and assertive while the other remained more 'hidden' and quiet. There then becomes a choice in the growing child as to which is the preferential one to follow (if indeed either are followed) in building identity. Quite often there can be a rising above these two as a duality, instead an incorporation of them as a oneness from which to build the scaffolding of one's own being – for example, developing as a relatively quiet, and competent person yet with definite codes of behaviour for oneself and future development in life which, once hard won, are not yielded up.

Saturn/Moon Gibbous Phase
Moon 135° – 180° ahead of Saturn

The theme of focusing and deep consideration in this phase harnesses itself to the building of an identity. Consequently there is an emphasis in life on having to figure out pretty much for oneself what does, or does not, work in terms of how to take one's place in the adult world. This person will tend to pick their way very carefully through most things in life to ensure security and survival. The underlying basis for this is (more often than not) because few, if any, of the expectations collected up from earlier life are anything like an effective-enough guide for this individual as to how to build a concrete sense of self. In fact, many people of this phase can have felt somewhat 'out on a limb' in their growing up years, not really quite knowing how to be, who to be, what to do, when to do it, and no-one around ever seemed to make it clearer for them.

There are any number of reasons why this might have been so. Sometimes there was conflict going on in the background as a result of which no one paid much attention to the individual child, or s/he was one of very many children with few boundaries or specific patterns since everyone just 'mucked in' and got along somehow. Or this may have been a child who was caught up in the middle of turmoil not quite knowing who or where to turn to for direction. Robertson[5] suggested the parents may have been one-pointedly focused in building their material lives and being productive to the extent that they were alienated from the child who gleaned little except how to be machine-like, but there was not much in the way of human interaction. In other instances, people reported having to be very careful what they said in their early environment for fear of censure, or of course there may have been perilous situations in childhood or even birth itself, where survival was terrifyingly not guaranteed.

Some of this phase felt encouraged as children always to 'stay small'. J.M. Barrie, author of *Peter Pan*, was born with Saturn conjunct the IC and in Gibbous phase to Moon in Capricorn. Following the death of his brother David, who had been his mother's favourite, he tried to take his place by wearing his dead brother's clothes and generally acting in the way David had, all in a bid to comfort his mother, always to remain a child and never leave her. (Saturn is the Moon ruler and also squares Sun as ruler of the 3rd house of siblings). Generally, if and when this sort of dynamic occurs there can be arduous battles for Gibbous types in learning how to apply themselves later on to create platforms of responsibility, (responsibility being a key theme for Barrie in Sun, Saturn and Moon Capricorn threads of his chart). Whatever the circumstances, the underlying point at issue seems to be that this person has to consciously address, focus upon and work consistently at the building of identity both to adapt themselves to the outer world and to mobilize themselves to function properly within it (which, from another perspective of Sun as ruler of the 3rd house, Barrie was able to do as journalist, biographer, author and playwright).

The 'look before you leap' quality of this phase takes several roads. One is that, feeling somewhat displaced in terms of a strong core identity, when this person *does* find a way of being that seems to work, s/he may seize upon it vigorously to the exclusion of all else and be very reluctant to try anything new. Here we also have echoes of the Gibbous need to find a method to abide by. This is very understandable of course if early experiences have been those of bewilderment since whatever is discovered then comes to represent a solid life-raft one can cling to and say "Ah! This is Me". In the process, however, this person may sometimes appear 'wooden' or brusque. Caution and careful precision may be strong watchwords and can manifest on emotional, physical and material levels as a 'tightness'. More positively, the early environment may have been one of much learning, where the child felt the main road to tread was one of being studious, working well at school, passing exams *cum laude*... and this then becomes the primary avenue for their identity in the adult world. Indeed, many develop a meticulous concentration to master a skill and become experts in their field.

A further possible manifestation is that, since an identity is hard to develop without guidelines, there can be a tendency for this person to accept very readily the values and outlooks of their particular group or community. Even though they may be very versatile as individuals, following the herd can seem the safest thing to do. Alternatively, some may find a channel or pathway (such as a belief, faith, organization or career goal) and *that* becomes the vehicle by which they project themselves but always taking carefully controlled and planned steps. On the other hand there can be circumstances where the person may go completely to the other extreme, throwing aside inner uncertainty and instead embracing a hectic lifestyle by which they are always on the go, surrounded by a plethora of distractions, all in a rather jittery bid to avoid the vulnerability of walking on shifting sands rather than a firm foundation.

One woman traced that she made friends easily in her life, her natural warmth (Sun/Moon New) drawing people to her readily. Yet she was always aware that inwardly she took on a different identity according to whatever particular group of people she was with, simply hitching a ride on the prevailing view. This eventually became both unsettling and exhausting since she was continually having to 'look before she leapt' in order to ensure she could fit in, or otherwise feel a social failure. It emerged that her childhood consisted of seeing her father only rarely (he was a successful businessman who travelled a great deal) and she was thus left only with mother who led a very sheltered life, never worked nor moved out from the home much or socialised with neighbours; neither did the mother seem to demonstrate or discuss with her child normal skills of growing up (how to meet people, how to approach boys, how to eat in a restaurant, how to develop a skill etc.) ... out on a limb indeed. This client also brought to awareness how her husband (who, unsurprisingly, was a successful businessman who travelled a lot) was a man of very black-and-white opinions to which she readily conformed as she had built up no views of her own. When one day he returned from a trip abroad with a new lady in tow, announcing that he wanted a divorce, she felt utterly lost, devoid of any clue as to how to proceed with her life. Subsequent work involved helping her focus upon a skill or talent she could build upon, perhaps as a career and begin to form a more cohesive platform of identity in the world.

Having to figure things out for oneself can translate as being very *circumspect* – a key theme in any Gibbous Phase and often a wise decision on the part of the small developing child especially if it is growing up in an emotionally arid environment. Such was the case with a lawyer who certainly needed to be extremely attentive in his specialist area which was Criminal Law. He was able to identify that as a young boy at boarding school he was intensely aware of how all the others boys' parents seemed to turn up for Sports or Prizegiving Days; he alone had no one (his parents were caught up in a career abroad). Although he told them of such special events in letters, especially if he won a race or received a trophy, they would merely remark "Oh that's nice dear" and the matter would receive no further comment. No one to put an arm around and say "Well *done* son!" or spur him on to identify any measure of his ability and worthiness. Yet step by step he strove to figure it out and build a career life of focused insight, practicality, intelligence and success – for himself, by himself.

Consider also William Blake whose chart we met in Chapter 6 under Sun/Moon Full. One can only imagine how precarious a sense of identity was for the small growing child who, upon reporting a vision of God coming through his bedroom window or angels in the trees, collected a beating for it and was thereafter continually considered odd or mad. The Full Moon visionary Blake centred his being on his art and his mystic experiences, developing a mind and imagination that soared to timeless dimensions. But within this, he had to build an identity by which he could practically and carefully survive in his environment. He became apprenticed (again Gibbous) at the age of fifteen to an engraver through whom he developed a sound knowledge of copper line engraving which he studiously copied. Thus we have emphasis upon developing workable techniques (the aspect lies close to the biquintile) in the highly skilled craftsman community in which he was brought up. From one perspective, it seems out of keeping for this man of vision and originality to have to merely copy from elsewhere, yet Blake seems to have approached this not as a mindless task but as a fully reflective seeing-anew and beyond (Sun/Moon Full), such that works he did meticulously copy also came to be seen as works of originality and inventiveness. One such was based on a figure by Michaelangelo, faithfully reproduced and yet it became a figure (Joseph of Arimathea) on a seashore.[6]

Saturn/Moon Full Phase
Moon 180° – 135° behind Saturn

With the planets in opposing areas of the chart, the developing individual finds that the very basis upon which s/he needs to build an identity is one of some division, needing reflection. The task is to bring such division to awareness since early environmental experiences may not have presented a way of being or set of values upon which this person could rely, nor develop a pattern of conformities to which to adhere *with any consistency.*

What this individual feels is expected of them can be experienced as very confusing or even tormenting. If they feel totally divided inside they may frequently react to this by being very dramatic, even melodramatic, colourful and/or a little 'wild'; additionally they can then swing to the other extreme and be very withdrawn or aloof. One moment they are standing dominantly and defiantly before you, the next they 'disappear' or run silent; alternatively they may be sweetness-and-light for long periods but if the slightest thing goes wrong become vicious and attacking. More generally there can be a brooding temperament, analyzing and scrutinizing everything and everyone and *seeming* to reach out to others, yet never properly relating due to the inner doubt about the self. Much will depend on other threads in the chart, but inner uncertainties can arise where early experiences included not only conflict in the environment (which can have varied in its severity) but with an added climate of *unpredictablity* attached to it. Situations may have suddenly flared up due to overt hostility, accompanied by high emotional charge or destructive attitudes such that the developing child felt agonizingly caught up within it all and churned around inside. Some may have experienced bullying and blaming behaviours, whether or not directed personally at them and, while some can certainly feel burdened by this, others can indulge in erratic repetitions of these 'blowing hot and cold' dynamics as if they can see no other way of being.

In one way, the more overt these background difficulties were, the easier it may be for Saturn/Moon Full types to carry out a reconstruction job on themselves, for at least the fundamental dynamics can be readily seen, felt, touched, remembered, brought to light, spoken about and moved through. Some, however, may find that early divisions are harder to trace because the conflict was hidden – e.g. the parents may have been at war with one another but locked in silent mutual contempt, or strife was closeted under a façade of 'getting along' or 'staying together for the sake of the children'. As a less tangible version still, it may simply be that the parents were just two very different people and the developing child wavers in his/her identification with one or the other.

An inner sense of division may not pertain at all to any past significant people or trauma as such but can just as easily emerge as a divisional gulf between the codes of this person's upbringing and the surrounding culture or society in which they were located. For instance a person may be brought up by parents of one nationality (say, British) but in a geographical environment which contains entirely different norms (say, Africa); thus they may be schooled in British standards, expectations and ways of being but at the same time absorb the surrounding tribal life, customs and beliefs. The division may arise as the person grows and is expected to follow British cultural norms concerning education, profession, social values etc. yet on the other hand they are resonating inside to the ways of the tribe, invoking ancestral and spiritual energies from their *locus in quo* and needing to develop some kind of 'bridge' between these factors.

Such seems to have existed in the life of novelist William John Locke (1863-1930) who was born in British Guiana where his father worked in the colonial bank service. Educated both in Trinidad and at Cambridge, Locke was expected to enter a career as a teacher or architect (both of which he followed for a while). Yet his soul, suffused by the more enlivening, colourful nature of his birthplace and early years yearned for these opposite realms of expression. The birth time is unknown but Neptune conjoined a New Moon that day, with Saturn opposite in Full Phase. He is said to have studiously neglected his studies at Cambridge, turning up for only one lecture, yet ultimately he became rather better known for surrendering to the part of him that reverberated to the natives of Trinidad and holidays spent in Paris' Latin Quarter that made up the first 17 years of his life. From here he produced richly told and graceful stories, often revolving around the theme of a character functioning in one accepted context while called from within by something quite different, unusual and intriguing (best typified in *The Beloved Vagabond*, 1906).

Whatever the actuality, the upshot can be that this phase-type frequently feels confused about precisely what identity to project; some may even feel that the projection of *any* is so difficult that they barely bother at all, but coast through life albeit on very shakey foundations. Others still may direct these uncertain dynamics into interactions with others, but frequently feel that relationships are so highly emotionally-charged (as perhaps they were when this person was little) that they are potentially too destructive and so best avoided altogether. Alternatively their partnerships tend to be subject to intermittent 'storms' and the person goes from one painful relationship to another in a recapitulation of early images. We may also find the loner who is confused, terrified or angry deep down but may carry it under an identity banner of being, say, an outsider, a recluse, or a bit of a renegade. Some people of this phase also reported to me that they experienced a traditional early environment but one within which there was also an expectation from elsewhere (perhaps in the wider family) that they should break the mould in some way... and yet if they *did* break the mould, somehow they had to expect to be ousted. Damned if you do or don't!

Whatever the level at which opposing factors were originally experienced, there can be a feeling of being pulled between 'this' and 'that' in life, frequently dithering in the middle before deciding upon a road to take, or which part of the personality to portray upfront and what to 'sit on' within. These inner divisions can have the person feeling constantly toppled by life, both offending and denying the inner need for order and cohesion, so that they end up feeling that stability can only be achieved through non-participation. Alternatively, the need for cohesion, together with the inner certainty that it is not to be had, can be lived out through a certain rumbustiousness and unpredictability (again possibly as witnessed in early life) and as a way of replaying the one familiarity of 'identity' they were able to glean. One client said to me "I live a pretty reclusive life really – quite content, just me and my dog y'know. But every now and then I tend to kick up a rumpus one way or the other. Bit like my Dad I s'pose – he was a quiet loner type of guy but he'd kick off down the pub every Friday night". Prince Harry may experience some of these themes in his still as yet young life, his Saturn/Moon Full Phase reflecting the division between his parents so universally known, and his occasional 'kicking-off' round the nightclubs may be in part a way of working through whatever images he holds within and can move through to build his own sense of identity. His great-aunt, Princess Margaret, whose life included painful relationship experiences set amidst periods of loneliness, was born with the same phase containing Venus in the 7th opposing a rising Uranus and was generally regarded as a somewhat controversial, rebel princess. Another client with an illustrious ancestry wore a signet ring bearing the family crest and motto "Paratus Sum" – his way of kicking off was that he would swear blind to anyone who raised the question that it meant "I am a Parrot"!

Not knowing where one stands in the middle of inconsistency can also mean that Saturn/Moon Full types can feel very pulled between different viewpoints or choices presented. It takes them more time than most to go through a set of alternatives and their feelings about each, especially if they consist of disagreements or tensions. However, in tune with the 'full view' theme of the phase, these are not people who can or should adopt facades or sweep their feelings under any carpet. True, they may not *wish* to embroil themselves with anything which looks or feels tormenting or confusing, yet conversely they seem to stir these feelings up. They are usually helped more if they are able to verbalize their feelings steadily rather than repressing them, only for them to emerge again later in escalated form. One client, coming from a background of always feeling misunderstood, with people constantly at cross-purposes and never knowing what was going to happen next in a turbulent world said, "One part of me wants to lash out and scream and the other part wants to live in a cave".

Finding an equilibrium seems to be the main purpose for this phase. When they do take time to give validation to their experiences and feelings, there is often a marked ability to see both sides of a situation and find a middle road. This is be particularly so around the quincunx and biquintile points in this phase. It may take the form of some kind of therapeutic work in which they trace earlier antagonizing divisions by rising above and observing, rather than identifying with and getting stuck in, them. In adult life many of this phase type prove themselves to be of solid help and guidance to others going through the same kind of inner ruminations. Sometimes a turning point may arise through a change of career, or country (domicile) or name, but whatever the road taken they can then become adept at constructing a fuller, more meaningful identity that is all their own and that enables them to settle sturdily on a concrete road. It may be often found that from early experiences of deprivation and angst there are stalwart qualities within, an identity which harbours more enlightened ideas, even astuteness and brilliance. Thus they can engage with the illuminated awareness theme of this phase and construct for themselves a truer mission in life.

Johannes Kepler (Saturn in Scorpio 6th in full phase to Moon in Gemini 12th) spent an earlier life feeling very divided against himself, not only living through terrifying times and much ill-health but also believing himself to be unworthy, living in poverty and depression... yet he could also write of his delight at being inspired to discover and produce his ideas. Neptune is the first planet to be met by the Moon after birth and rules his Jupiter/Pluto 10th house conjunction sextiling Sun in Capricorn, which in turn conjoins Uranus (conjunct Mercury), while Saturn itself as ruler of these latter planets sits in insightful Scorpio. Weaving threads such as these he emerged as the man of exceptional mental brilliance as mathematician and astronomer, who gave us the laws of planetary motion. William Herschel originally travelled to England from his native Germany as a musician. It was by journeying by night to various places to perform and navigating himself by the stars that he became fascinated with astronomy. He brought his sister Caroline over to get her away from bullying parents – (the Full

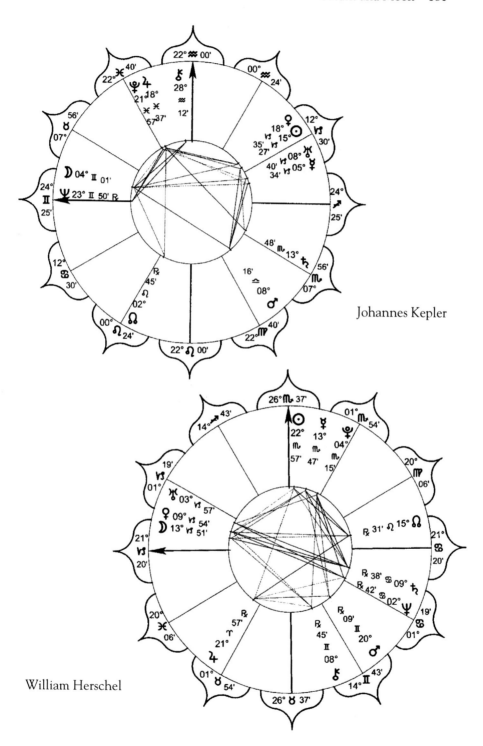

Johannes Kepler

William Herschel

Phase Saturn/Moon is across the Cancer/Capricorn axis) – and together they worked assiduously, building telescopes, writing papers and (again with inspirational Neptune and innovative Uranus focal, being conjunct and opposite Saturn respectively) Herschel discovered *inter alia* the 7th planet which initially bore his name but later became Uranus.

More contemporaneously, these themes are also reflected in the life of the eminent journalist Alistair Cooke, he of 'Letter from America' fame. He was born as Alfred Cooke (with Saturn in Aries in Full phase to Moon in Libra and containing a potent Pluto conjunct North Node in Gemini) into what appears to have been a fairly joyless and strict religious background in the north of England, He changed his name to Alistair at the age of twenty-two, went over to America a couple of years thereafter and at the time of his first Saturn return at twenty-nine entered into a regular broadcast arrangement with the BBC. This in turn led to his famous 'Letter' from 1946 right up until his death in 2004. From grim austerity to becoming a figure of legendary stature in broadcasting history speaks volumes for the profound capacity to build an identity of one's own out of divisive threads and the enduring stability that this phase can engender.

Saturn/Moon Disseminating Phase
Moon 135° – 90° behind Saturn

The essential purpose underlying this planetary phase is to communicate what you have learned, been told or has been held up to you as a standard to which you should adhere. There is an overall sense that doing what is expected of you is built upon some kind of 'protocol' or etiquette. It may simply amount to not only conducting oneself politely and doing 'the right and proper thing', but also developing an identity as someone who can be *relied* upon to do so.

The various conditionings we gleaned in our early years may never have been actually verbalized; they may also not have been personal. Many of the identifications we make are those which are implied or generally sensed. They may also not have been from significant *people* as such, but be taken from a wider arena – the extended family as a whole, the 'class' we are born into, our social environment, culture, ancestry; even a geographical region can carry its own 'character of the people'. Bearing all these possible threads in mind, it is usually to be found that there is a fairly clear set of guidelines in existence as to how this person should carry themselves in the world – and it usually has to do with remaining loyal to a set of definite principles. It is also usual to find that the person, no matter what the actual details or events of early life, readily attaches importance to these expectations as they seem designed to serve him or her well, thus there is no resistance to them. This mirrors the energy of this phase also, which is that of 'easy flow'. Whether or not they always *live up* to the standards implied is another matter, but this does not erase them from the deep recess of an inner conditioned belief.

There are some similarities between this phase and Saturn/Moon in New Phase, in that the identification with and submission to one's early belief systems is very strong, even automatic. In this Disseminating Phase, the person has the same kind of inner assurance of being right as the New Phase type, but usually without as much charisma and power. A major element here is for the person to go about life by 'putting up a good front' and making a favourable impression on others. Again, there may have been general spoken or unspoken standards to this effect – "always carry yourself well", "show good manners", "know your place", "don't give the neighbours anything to talk about", "hold your knife and fork properly" etc. But, whatever the details, this type is primarily concerned with having their act together so as not to be vulnerable to criticism. There may also be an emphasis on pleasing other people (which may or may not be conscious). This is rarely devious but it can present problems. Since this person attaches great importance to integrity, decency, etc. they often develop a kind of open honesty which is frequently endearing but can leave them open to being exploited and manipulated by more opportunist individuals. They have taken these principles on board comfortably in their early development and live them out automatically, so they tend to assume that the rest of the world abides by the same rules… then they are hurt and even shocked when they find that it does not.

I would reiterate that these themes appear to be present regardless of whatever other conditions, positive or negative, may be present. Some people are very happy in their growing up years; others may suffer hardships and cruelties. Yet beyond these, the call to convey oneself as a person of 'bearing' remains. Sometimes it may mean making a mark upon the world by holding your head up high even through duress and suffering. One client who was habitually cruelly treated by his father during childhood reported that he would then have to take himself to school, eyes red with crying and desperately trying to cover his bruises "so that no one would know".

This is the classic position of the abused child who displays loyalty to the abusive parent, never once telling his teachers of his suffering nor what was happening at home. When I asked "Did you feel afraid of what might happen to your Dad if someone knew?" he answered "No, not really – I just felt it wasn't the done thing, there was no dignity in telling… and anyway boys don't cry".

I recall a time early in my own therapy when I was trying to get to grips with factors of my early life in relation to handling arduous situations. It all felt rather intangible in its complexity but I vaguely sensed it was something to do with always expecting hardship and never feeling I had a right to ask for help. (I expect I just spent the session doing a 'woe-is-me' number and whining a bit). But my therapist began asking about my initial Hebridean upbringing and what it meant to me. Geographically the western isles of Scotland endure mostly cold weather, persistently pouring rain and the inhabitants of my particular island have to endure the icy blast from the Atlantic in their faces each time they step out of the door. As we talked I realized how this Highland race, its way of life and its geography unquestionably calls for any of its natives to be hardy and, in the immortal words of one Mr. Churchill (or it might have been my Great Uncle Angus!), just to "keep buggering on"!

In the same way that the Disseminating Sun/Moon needs interaction with others, so too does Saturn/Moon in this phase. Building an identity is often through developing communication with others in some form (writing, teaching, speaking) yet the nature of Moon and Saturn in relationship may inject something of a 'boulder in the river', obstacles of some kind to be overcome as part and parcel of the process. In tracing this particular thread in people's lives, I have very frequently found that somewhere along the line it calls forward their need to follow the right and proper thing even though it may alienate them from others who do not subscribe to the same internal edicts. In many instances, this took the form of resigning, say, from a job on a point of principle or daring to vote against a party line because allegiance to inner convictions and moralities would not allow for anything else. Some clients reported that they 'jumped ship' mid-career when they inwardly realized that what they were doing for a living did not truly feed their spirit of integrity nor mirror an inner creed of probity. In bringing the latter to awareness and tracing how it became developed, many clients told me it helped to recall (or imagine) how each of their parents would finish the sentence "Now always remember, don't ever *ever…*" (or "Whatever else you do, always *always…*"). Again the parent may never have actually said it, but the implication resides strongly within.

There can also be a loyal holding on to past familial/cultural patterns which seem to say 'it's the way we do things around here', even if those things are, conversely, dishonest and therefore to the world at large not at all the right and proper thing. One woman had been brought up by a single father who survived by doing all kinds of odd jobs here and there and was something of a charming trickster, always on the make and expecting something for nothing. She found herself following this pattern at her workplace where she was constantly pilfering things – pens, paper clips, stationery, fiddling a few expenses here and there etc. "Nothing that would really hurt anybody", she explained, but nevertheless it was what had passed for 'the done thing' in her childhood and was recalled by her with an air of loyalty of the 'honour-amongst-thieves' variety. Another client, with a Sun/Mars conjunction contained within the phase in square to Pluto, was constantly in combat with others; he had come from a background where the strong message seemed to be "punch the other fella on the nose first, ask questions later" – it was how they got through and survived, a duty and cause expected to be espoused.

A very clear aspect of the Disseminating Saturn/Moon phase can be seen in those whose lives necessarily follow obvious patterns of principle, where they are required to carry themselves with a decided measure of decorum (or a stiff upper lip). Some I met came from 'upstairs-downstairs' backgrounds – a class division of a bygone era where the gentry occupied the upper part of the house and the servants knew their place below stairs. International diplomats, lawyers, private secretaries, for example, are also often found in this phase, as indeed are those who occupy positions in high echelons such as butlers, footmen, ladies-in-waiting. Higher up the ladder still, the Queen and Prince Charles each have this phase in their charts, as does the next in line to the throne, Prince William. We witness the marked protocol in walking-with-hands-clasped-behind-back, coupled with "And what do *you* do…?" should they stop and talk to anyone. 'Tis the way they do things in the Royal Family.

Most often, this Saturn/Moon type will work hard to get to where it wants to be. While some among them may not always be pillars of piety and rectitude in any strict sense, there is usually a shred of plain human decency which can be traced within them and, indeed, appealed to. A sense of duty often prevails where they can persist with something not necessarily because they want to, but because it is a moral imperative – usually in relation to considering others around them. Building an identity through collaboration with their surroundings (people, causes, groups) is important to them, as are situations where there is a call for everyone to pull together, learn together, share together and contribute to the ongoing flow of solid practicalities being carried out in life.

Saturn/Moon Last Quarter Phase
Moon 90° – 45° behind Saturn

The pressure for this person to reorientate themselves along a different pathway emanates from an inner sense that what seems to be expected of them is totally at odds with what they feel to be their own true purpose. One way or another, there is a sense that there is an individual inside who 'wants out'. Astronomically and psychologically this is the opposite of the First Quarter phase which sought its identity as a self-assertive being, breaking out to meet a challenge. Here, there is a preliminary reticence to take a different road, a giving way to the status quo before taking any action.

Initially it can be experienced as a sense of inner dissatisfaction with oneself, ranging all the way from mild to chronic (depending on the actuality of the life circumstances). There may have been little or nothing 'wrong' with the early environment, nor the people in it, yet nevertheless this person always seems to have known from quite early on that they would need to turn from it in some way… they just always seemed to have a different 'take' on things compared to the rest of the family. Depending also on the level of awareness, this phase can emerge as either an ability to make that major conscious transformation in order to put oneself in line with a mature purpose, or as a kind of continuous and tormented kicking-against one's circumstances in a destructive, perhaps blaming, way.

At the end of the day, this person is rarely someone who can, or should, be ultimately moulded into what the world around expects them to be. However, it may be especially in the first half of life – and sometimes with a sense of inner ferment – that there is this giving in to outer pressures while silently gnashing one's teeth and possibly feeling (even appearing) ineffective or 'distant' and perhaps moody. Then at some point (when the pressure has built up enough) there is the taking of outer action in order to align with one's own real goals and purpose and strike out on a diversionary road taking them to the mature identity they are truly endeavouring to build. Young Reg Dwight completed his schooling and was urged by both his headmaster and his dad to start work in a bank. "But it was never gonna happen" said Reg, "inside me I always knew I wanted to do something with music – in fact at that time I thought I might work in the local record shop". Well, thank goodness Reg (better known as Sir Elton John of course) went rather further than either of those initial options and we have for decades enjoyed the unique output of this world superstar. The Last Quarter Saturn/Moon contains the North Node and Uranus in the 10th house where the call is to push the door open and emerge very notably into the outside world. As first factors to be met by the Moon after birth, they denote the prime direction for his life, in Gemini moreover where the accent is on communicating (of which musical performance is a key avenue... or perhaps I should say a *keyboard* avenue!)

In some circumstances, the phase may demand a great deal of courage in confronting and being willing to move on from early conditioned ways of being and, until that courage is in place, there may be a good deal of dithering-about not quite knowing how to make the turnaround, sometimes even preferring to stay with a devil one knows rather than meet the unknown one. Pressurized feelings can also lead to the individual (initially at any rate) doubting himself or herself. If they are constantly surrounded by people and situations which call for them to 'do it this way' or 'be like this, not that', again the ensuing self-doubt can make them give in to the pressure rather than risk being themselves and maturing into a purpose of their own... until the pressure pops, a change is made, a new route taken. In the process, we learn that many negatives in life (such as pressure) have their purpose too. If the environment is perceived as coercing this person to a high degree to fit in with its needs, the pressure serves to bring to consciousness the fact that these are simply unfitting. If others seem hell bent on making them what they just cannot be then – as we have seen – there is another identity inside all this ferment that wants to breathe freely. Of central importance is that this individual *needs to develop that identity of their own choosing*; then it must be gradually forged in the fire of a new direction, however uncomfortable it may feel to those around.

Sometimes, however, it may even be delightfully discovered that the environment is accepting of it and thus it is one's own *expectation* of dissent that may have been why the change was not made sooner. I recall Clive, a young man back in the late 1970s/early 1980s, who had been brought up in the north of England in a coal-mining area. His father and grandfather before him had been miners and his mother, along with many of the womenfolk, worked in the textile industry. But Clive yearned to leave this background and make a life for himself in London. Since this was the era of closure of the coal mines and deterioration of the textile and steel industries of the north, Clive had initially taken a menial clerical job with the local Council, where he sat behind a desk day by day grinding his teeth in bored frustration.

When the pressure had built up enough, it brought him to an interest in psychology and the newer therapies of what was then known as the Growth Movement, including the then emergent counselling astrology. He earnestly wanted to move to London and take up an initial four-year psychotherapy training programme. His father had died a year previously and now he was additionally tortured by guilt about his goals since it would leave his mother all alone. I asked him if he had talked to his mother about it at all, and the answer was 'no' as he did not want to upset her. She was a loving and caring mother and he could not face the prospect of her distress; besides she wouldn't understand his goals, he said. "Are you sure?" I asked him, after a short pause. The rather longer pause which followed that question, accompanied by Clive's direct eye contact beneath a fiercely quizzical brow, led me to feel we were millimetres away from the stirrings of a Last Quarter turnaround. The following weekend Clive went to visit his mother for Sunday lunch, after which Mum sat knitting by the fireside… and Clive tentatively and agonizingly unfurled his dream. When he had finished, the clicking needles fell silent, Mum sat with her hands neatly folded in her lap, and said, "You go fer it, son… can't spend the rest o' yer life linin' up paper clips along a desk".

Speaking of coal mines and closures (!), Margaret Thatcher was born not only with Sun/Moon in Last Quarter but Saturn/Moon in this phase too. Just as the Sun/Moon phase contains a mighty Sun/Mars/Jupiter/Pluto T-square, so too does this Saturn/Moon phase. The purpose was strong for her to become what she did at the level of her own being (Sun/Moon), but so too at the level of her conditioned self (Saturn/Moon) which could not rest within the confines of being a Lincolnshire grocer's daughter but sought a much more indomitable identity in the world. Both Moon and Saturn are angular in her chart in Leo and Scorpio respectively, giving added weight to the context of leadership and power within which she unfurled her life. Incidentally, the New Moon before birth (on 18th September 1925) fell on 25° Virgo. Rudhyar speaks of gaining "social immortality" and finding a place in history[7] while Marc Edmund Jones' keyword is 'Respect'.[8] That is what the Symbol says. Please don't shoot the messenger.

In other situations, there may have been background issues of tangible conflict (especially if there is a square aspect here) such as parental differences and a pressurized need to free oneself from that. Or the family background may have been more vocally adamant that this person should follow a particular avenue in life ... but they simply cannot find it within themselves to do it. Whatever the spur and however it arises, the need is to make a springboard leap into being true to their own inner nature and vision and *build it up through sustained dedication*. In many cases, I have seen this phase in the charts of those who sought to serve others in some way to help resolve perceived earlier conflicts in life and reach inner understanding, such as analysts, therapists, the helping professions generally (as we saw with Clive above). Again here there may be changes of name, or location, outlooks and interests which become the vehicles enabling this process of transformation to occur. What was a reality that the individual felt initially caught up in becomes replaced with a vision of what s/he truly feels inside, that s/he stands for and – importantly in Last Quarter – *must announce and take out into the world*, seeking to shape that world from their own clarity of perspective.

Saturn/Moon Balsamic Phase
Moon 45° – 0° behind Saturn

The same gap between what this person feels is expected of them and what they feel to be their true purpose (which we saw in the previous phase) is intensified here. In fact it is more of a *clash*, with the added difficulty that it can be something of a problem for the Balsamic type to see this clearly. We are moving back down into the 'dark' of the phase cycle here, where perception and understanding is more inward. Therefore, depending on the level of awareness, the clash may remain held at deeply unconscious levels, even for quite a while.

As a result, at least initially in life, this type may frequently succumb to the pressures of their environment to a degree that true individuality is almost completely stifled. Together with Saturn/Moon New Phase types, these can be the most unwitting purveyors of what they witnessed and learnt from the early life. As this occurs, they become immersed in the orthodoxy of their surroundings to the extent that they barely glimpse any conscious knowing of Balsamic seeds of purpose they have come in to life to sow. The clash is between that purpose on the one hand and the conformist identity, presented to them as scaffolding to be built upon, on the other. However, if they do not have a conscious awareness of this disparity there can be instead a high degree of idealism about living out the orthodox requirements. Generally they can be seen simply and limply to bumble along with what everybody else is doing unaware of the purpose they are carrying and must move toward in life and so possibly never ever defining or reaching it. Within this there can be resignation, a 'going-nowhere' type of daydreaming that says "if only I could…" or "one day I'll…" which is a but distorted version of the inner purpose.

In some situations, it is almost as if, in terms of reincarnation, they have brought into this current life a set of responses which are completely inappropriate to, or have no precedent within, the parameters of their society, culture or family. On the one hand it could be that this person finds themselves in an early environment which may be perfectly fine, deliriously happy even, yet somehow (reminiscent of Last Quarter) s/he does not quite fit in and *therefore* is moved to carve out a purpose of their own. It may, however, be more stark than this – they could simply not be understood by those around but instead considered odd, 'too different' or even outrageous and shocking if they display their individuality. This may also be a person who has come into the world to live out a specific talent or skill but their environment contains little or no recognition of anything to do with their field of interest. The person is fired with a purpose, but faces an arid desert. That desert instead consists of other values and drives which are as meaningless to the Saturn/Moon Balsamic person as 'the desert' (environment) finds theirs.

It is possible for this person to carry within them much in the way of insight, innovation, talent and vision, be indeed completely aware of this and even be poised on a brink of living them… and yet *still* be distorted by the pressures of society, culture, conditioning. Upon these latter constructs, they then build a whole set of beliefs, concepts and ideologies by which they live, but which do not truly fit their own inner values. It is as if they shuffle themselves off into an ante-room in which they feel they must stay as a fabricated identity of some kind. From here they fulfil a conformist way of being which is more satisfying and appropriate to their parents or society (who may indeed have taught this person to develop many useful qualities such as competence and erudition) but it is a mould (or even a straitjacket) into which they have been poured rather than a true expression of themselves. We saw a glimpse of this in the talented writer under the Sun/Moon coverage of this phase, who very nearly got wafted off into a mechanized, diminished approach to writing rather than portraying her own unique gifts. Alternatively still, one may enter the world ready to unfold a skill, which is accepted in essence, but it becomes diverted off onto a different path of the environment's choosing. For instance, someone may have a seriously profound mathematical skill couple with a spirit of invention and inspiration, but is born into a culture/environment where the accent is upon immediate practical application only, to which s/he acquiesces and ends up working in a computer shop. The skill will not go amiss, but neither has it quite hit its true mark, so there may be a nagging sense of diminishment that the person can't... quite... put... their finger on...

Since the demand upon the Balsamic Saturn/Moon is for *a total release of all concretized patterns of conformity* if they are to function as their true selves, this person needs at some point in their lives to let go of the scaffolding clung to from the past and instead forge an identity which is *uniquely* his or hers. Whether this means getting out from under a negative conditioned-environment or indeed one which was perfectly fine, this is the way that goals can be reached and put into the world so that the person can feel 'real'. If this is not achieved, or indeed refused, again the person may well spend a great deal of life allowing their own individuality to be sidelined, succumbing only to the pressures to conform, thus innovation again becomes suffocated or at least a little 'dulled'. What motivates other people is not necessarily what moves and calls this person – in fact it may even be completely unworkable for them. If, however, their inner vision can be clarified, then a much clearer 'no' to other orthodoxies can be achieved and lead to creative renewal (the Balsamic conjunction). This then would be the person who yields up its toughened seeds to endure into the future whether or not they fit any prior established conformity. Sometimes society's conformities become the very building bricks upon which this creativity can unfold, such as in the case of Charles Dickens whose early environment was of being a young impoverished boy roaming the streets, a background scaffolding he worked assiduously to rise above rather than be personally stifled by. The Saturn/Moon Balsamic (with Moon conjunct Neptune and Saturn in the 4th house) depicts the experience of deprivation (an 'arid desert') clearly. Yet, at the same time, it is that very scaffolding and those very themes of scarcity and suffering that underpin his profuse writings.

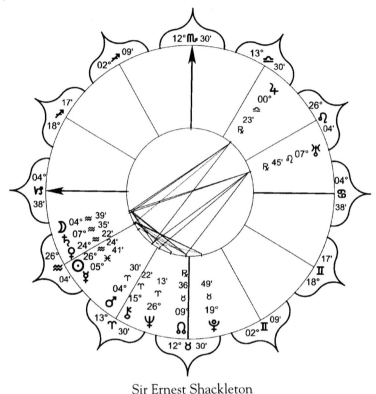

Sir Ernest Shackleton

The family of Antarctic explorer Sir Ernest Shackleton originally came from Ireland, his father being a landowner and doctor. Not much given to schoolwork or study, from an early age Ernest *longed* for the sea, but there was no precedent for this in his familial environment, indeed no notion of him doing anything other than following his father into medicine (which his father dearly wanted). But Ernest, with amazing clarity of purpose in one so young, rejected this scaffolding... and set out to sea at the age of sixteen.

Both the Sun/Moon and Saturn/Moon phases are Balsamic, thus a double emphasis on entering the still space deep within from which to unfold life purposes and yield up true insights and skills. His longing for the sea is reflected via Mercury in Pisces plus 3rd house Neptune/Jupiter 8th Gibbous phase (ocean, exploration), the Mars/Jupiter enterprising and explorative opposition, plus the Sun squares Pluto (ruler of the Midheaven) in the 4th (exploration of the depths – and you can't get much deeper than southern Antarctica). The Saturn/Moon Balsamic phase opposes Uranus, ruler of his four planets in Aquarius, reflecting his restlessness, determination and innovation, and the Sun/Moon phase contains Saturn/Venus suggesting hardiness and endurance, also assisted by Capricorn rising. Indeed his ship taking him into those icy regions was *The Endurance* (by which the 1914 expedition was as a whole known). Shackleton placed an advertisement in a London newspaper in 1912 which read, "Men wanted for hazardous journey. Low wages, bitter cold, long hours of complete darkness. Safe return doubtful. Honour and recognition in event of success. Apply…" This elicited nearly 5,000 replies! So as well as living out his own individuality, perhaps he was also answering a collective pioneering Aries/Neptune call to go beyond the limits! It puts me in a mind of certain gentleman born in November of the same year (with Saturn just 2° ahead in Aquarius) who would issue another call (this time to arms, in which we would "never surrender") and promised us nothing but "blood, toil, sweat and tears…"!

Mozart's musical genius, while not having any precedent, did of course have an accepting environment and yet he is also an example of how the Balsamic energy can be straitjacketed into an established conformity. His seriously ambitious violinist father, Leopold, took control of his son's talents (Sun and Saturn are conjunct in the 5th) as a means of achieving a higher status and prosperity in what was otherwise a lowly position for musicians. Earning sufficient money to exist was a constant problem, circumscribed as it was by the constant need to find commissions from high patronage. His gifts were also to unfold within the context of much physical debility and he died at the early age of thirty-five. The Moon falls behind the Sun by some 50° – thus within 50 months (4 years 2 months) of meeting the Sun. At that tender age he was able to play minuets and had started composing little pieces for harpsichord. From that age, too, he was to undertake with his father tour after tour, playing before many European crowned heads, the gruelling severity taking its toll on the brilliant young child's health. Both the Sun/Moon (Last Quarter) and Saturn/Moon (Balsamic) phases contain Chiron in Capricorn in 4th and it was his father who would administer to him to pull him through the severe vulnerabilities of illness in his young childhood.

And so we see the inspired child (Sun 5th opposite Neptune) who would write music as if taking dictation from the gods themselves, yet hauled upon the scaffolding of the cultural Saturn/Moon Balsamic norms of securing an existence and fulfilling ambitions, pulled this way and that by Leopold, successive archbishops and emperors, his survival set also against the growing dismay or jealousies of other composers of less inspiration or ability. Yet, more than once, his Aquarian/Uranian spirit saw him turn aside from existing norms (Sun/Moon Last Quarter) to follow his own path wherever he could, led only by his gifts from within (Balsamic). Mozart is reputed to have told a young man, who questioned him about how to compose, that he was too young to be thinking of such a serious occupation. When the young man pointed out to him that he himself was but a small child when *he* first began, Mozart replied "That is true, but then you see I did not ask anybody how to compose".[9] Gifts to be lived from an unseen realm indeed.

8: Jupiter and Mercury

Following Mars in the solar system, whereby we *first* have impact upon our outer environment, Jupiter is the means by which we go beyond that. We reach out, relate to, assimilate and co-operate with that environment, which of course includes other people. In seeking to achieve an expanded sense of self, any frame of reference may be taken, be it our family, a group or organization, or the world at large, but the heart of the matter is to experience ourselves as 'more' or even 'more properly' who intrinsically we feel ourselves to be.

Although frequently written about as if it were a ubiquitous Santa Claus arriving with armfuls of goodies, the function of Jupiter is not always manifested in happy, jolly ways. Since it requires assimilation and co-operation then, the human condition being what it is, there can easily be negatives. When working with the phases and the actuality of people's lives, we may come across assimilation being stressed at the expense of co-operation, others being prized only in relation to their usefulness; or a person may co-operate with others initially, only thereafter to seek a continual expansion of the self by an interminable striving to hog the limelight. The opposite extreme is also possible where an individual may devote much energy to being co-operative with others, but overdoes the helping of them to the extent that their *own* needs are not met and assimilated. This may well meet with social approval in certain cultures, but from the point of view of achieving balance in the psyche it can be just as pathological. A truer expression of Jupiter's drive is the ability to get along with others, contributing to the well-being of one's group/society, including oneself – this encompasses an element of protection and preservation and finds itself expressed in the more traditional associations of this planet in financial and legal matters. Jupiter is also equated with optimism and hope, both expressions of 'expansion'. This includes aspirations, expectations, 'faith' – notions that what we are reaching for could be secured. These elements are seen in the traditional association of Jupiter with religious and spiritual/ philosophical matters. But while hope and optimism may reign on the one hand, a never-ending stretching of them can emerge as continual restlessness for new horizons, agonized longings or even despair (as markedly depicted in George Frederic Watts' painting of Hope who sits forlornly plucking a harpstring).

Through Mercury's perception we collect information. It is, however, worth noting a deeper aspect to this planet – one that is little spoken of – its capacity for control and power. Initial perception of something in itself renders us a little more in control and powerful, but there are further aspects of Mercury which seem essential in the functioning of the human mind: *categorization, comparison and communication*. Communication speaks for itself (if you will forgive the simply dreadful pun) and in order to empower our perception we question, read up on matters and discuss with knowledgeable others. The power of comparison emerges when our interest is sufficiently aroused by something. Since we cannot learn much about, say, trees or animals by examining just one oak tree or a solitary pussycat, we search out other examples in order to perceive similarities and differences. As to categorization, we are not usually content merely to observe and experience something, for almost immediately we wish to give it a name. Indeed we are taught to do so from a young age – a little child in a garden stands entranced before an object which flutters in a magical conglomeration of black and yellow. "Yes darling it's a blackbird" says Mummy/Daddy. The experience is nailed to the floor into a category and reduced to the learning of a label. In fact, if we are unable to name something pretty immediately it tends to hold an unusually high energy charge and we may even experience stress before we are able to classify it. This may be minor irritation as we check out an unfamiliar word in a dictionary or temporarily forget the name of something though it perches precariously on the tip of our tongue; on the other hand it can be high-stress tension that might well be aroused by a totally unexpected perception... such as someone ringing your doorbell at three o'clock in the morning! Mercury is as much involved with physical mobility and skill (thus again a form of control and power) as it is with mental exercise. 'Learning' and 'doing' combine in different kinds of emphasis at different times. Right now my 'doing' consists of writing about what I have experienced (a lot of doing and a lot of learning) but this evening I might sink into an armchair in front of the TV (absolutely no doing and I'm not holding my breath about the learning!)

When Jupiter is combined with Mercury, that which we collected up as information is expanded into knowledge; we enter a wider territory, a fuller range and breadth, leading to further exploration. Tracing them through the phases enables us to identify how we utilize these abilities to convey ourselves through straightforward communication (including non-verbal means) or through performance and movement. Communication may take on a particular colouration and serve a key pathway – such as may exist for linguists, researchers, writers, teachers etc. – while through mobility (e.g. dance, sports) we convey ourselves as people responding to and expressing rhythm, co-ordination and precision. The pairing also reflects our capacity to be *stretched* in order to progress – to extend ourselves into wider possibilities, questioning, reaching out for fresh perspectives rather than be drawn into, and blindly follow, consensus thinking. In this sense Jupiter/Mercury helps us *navigate* our way in life and discover pathways to greater understanding.

When working with these planets through the phases, we need to be aware that there can also be many resistances since the human mind, with its interminable reasonings, analyses and justifcations, can take over, even submerge the drive for expanded awareness. We are then apt to become a collection of notions, ideas, interpretations and rationalizations; especially when faced with a stark reality or truth, we will use evasion, distortion, sublimation or even downright lying to in order to circumnavigate a clear experience of ourselves. Or we find a 'cause' for it, upon which we can then satisfyingly lay blame. We would do anything rather than look at an actuality and allow it to be there. And yet, when we do, the release and freedom contained within Mercury and Jupiter accompanies a fullness of realization, allowing something 'more' to arise which is of a wisdom that cannot be anticipated, predicted nor even necessarily described in words. Only experienced, absorbed and through which we can breathe more freely.

In keeping with the nature of these two planets, we can now expand our initial understanding of their pairing touched upon in Chapter 5. Their phase describes how we reach out and communicate via the spoken/unspoken or written word and through different forms of movement/co-ordination. It has much to say concerning our thinking patterns, the resources of our minds and how we come across in everyday interaction, as well as how we cultivate outlooks, ideas, philosophies and form an intelligent relationship with both our inner and outer worlds.

Jupiter/Mercury New Phase

While sometimes starting out in life as quiet and shy, this person nevertheless carries a strong inner ability to engage with others, instantly and effectively.

This means they can also gauge another person, or an audience, accurately and the real potential in this phase is to develop a way of communicating such as to *inspire* others.

This person needs to trust their instincts to provide the right thing to say and the right way to say it rather than attempt to formulate it mechanically ahead of time. If this is a public speaker or writer, then careful contriving, drafting and redrafting, or endless rehearsals of what one is going to say, will seldom work well, even though they may need to do so to a certain extent in order to feel adequately prepared. But, more than anything, they need to be flexible and willing to move away from a set script because they cannot know what *feeling-experiences* will accompany the eventual communication. A lecture may be prepared and due for delivery but there is as yet something missing which can never be anticipated. It is not so much the *content* – the words or phrases themselves – to which people will respond but the deeper quality *which comes through the spontaneity of delivery and the essential nature of the speaker*. There may be a gentle charisma with which they speak, or a strong capacity to hold sway over an audience by a depth, truth or clarity which shines through. Clearly these cannot be manufactured beforehand but only emerge on their own terms, in the moment.

Conversely, if a sense of commitment is lacking, or if the material itself is trite or superficial, then it can be very difficult for this person to be heard, make any real lasting impact or be taken seriously because the deep inner connection so redolent of New Phase is impaired. Similarly, too much consideration of the self, moving away from the essence of communicating to worry instead about what other people will say or think, can dull the shine of true spontaneity. I have also met those who have a decided flair for writing or speaking, but prefer to remain cocooned within themselves, perhaps taking easy routes out. A talented aspiring novelist may merely write short stories for weekly magazines or sells out to the superficial populist/pick-it-up-at-the-airport paperback. Or the actor who has everything within him to play Hamlet instead remains only on the sidelines treading the boards as a bit-player.

More positively, this phase may be found in the charts of powerfully inspiring speakers or writers especially where there are attendant outer-planetary threads. The written word may be from the pen of those who chronicle events (such as a diarist) with a profundity and vision that can speak volumes to many and perhaps over a long period of time. Chief among these of course is Anne Frank.

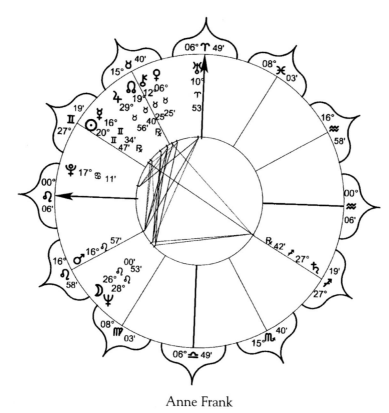

Anne Frank

Always busily writing, young Anne was given a diary on her thirteenth birthday and thus began the most famous chronicling of a young life in an era of horror and terror. Hiding from the Nazis in the upper rooms of her father's office in Amsterdam, Anne was to record her thoughts, dreams and ideals up until August 1944 when the family's hiding place was discovered and they were sent to concentration camps. Anne died in early March 1945 and her diary was eventually published[1] by her father who alone among the family survived. Her writing is full of hope and insight, a spiritual maturity beyond her years, kindness, courage and despair interwoven with clarity, compassion and acute observation.

The Jupiter/Mercury phase in the 11th house directs the theme of communication into wider society and is transformational (an Aquarian/Uranian house). Mercury is in quintile to Moon/Neptune and rules the 3rd and 12th houses, which picks up the theme of enhanced inspirational writing through, and living on from, death. Mercury also conjuncts the Sun which in turn picks up an opposition to the singleton Saturn in the 6th. Her unique gifts as a writer of course gave rise to the Foundation and Museum through which her story and her name are established for evermore.[2]

The Jupiter end of the phase squares the Moon/Neptune and her diary passages portray tapestry threads of optimism, compassion and suffering so redolent in her young life. Yet, engagingly, she also exudes an Aquarian/11th house/Mercurial unique quality of intellect and spirit when, with vivid honesty and Geminian chattiness, she examines her dual nature of good/ naughty, shy/mischievous and other 'contradictions'. Born with Saturn/ Moon in Disseminating Phase, Anne conveyed herself with an internal moral code of integrity, while the Sun/Moon phase is at the sextile point in Crescent Phase (reaching out to communicate within the context of struggle). This latter phase contains both Pluto and Mars, already collected up by the Moon at birth, to be taken on to the first planet (Neptune) and met as a major purpose in life – thus the brutality of war and the suffering of this poignant yet inspirational spirit.

In New Phase, the power is one of resonating what is, in essence, as yet without much form and substance, yet fully prepared to enter the epic task of growth whereby it ultimately reveals itself. Ideas, realizations, insights which awaken and illuminate this person may need moments of stillness and inner preparedness for their arrival so that they can be ultimately clothed in words and brought to life, connecting them to others. The power of the seed in nature also serves to remind us of how the energy is capable of flourishing notwithstanding the quality and condition of its surroundings. Even in poor soil (attendant difficulties) its purpose is to spring into life – as truly exemplified by the young Anne Frank.

With its capacity to speak and inspire, one might expect a goodly number of those in the political arena to be natives of this phase. Indeed the most oratorical of them all, Winston Churchill, can be found under this heading within the communicative context of Sun/Moon Disseminating. Jupiter, his Sun ruler, opposes Neptune (and he spoke to inspire the people while only able to offer them suffering, "blood, sweat, toil" etc). It also conjuncts Mars in cardinal 1st house ("we will never surrender") while the Mercury part of the phase squares Uranus in the 11th house (again speaking to inspire, indeed awaken and stir, the people). The spontaneity of the phase can mean these people are able to express in a few aptly chosen words that which others might take several sentences to do. Often they come up with something that completely hits a nail on the head, have lightning-quick wit, are eminently quotable (Churchill again) or able to deliver pithy one-liners. We may find them in the media displaying great resoluteness and 'taking things on the wing'. Straight-talking Nigel Farage of the UK Independence Party has the phase powerfully occupying a seat of outspoken power (at the 9th house cusp), again within a context of Disseminating Sun/Moon (communication and with Saturn/Moon in Last Quarter, the taking of a road away from those previously laid down and initially followed). Farage, formerly a commodity broker in the City of London, is a dedicated advocate of freedom of speech and beliefs "not subject to approval by a transitory authority. It is absolute or it is nothing. Such was and remains my conviction. And oh, it has got me into some delicious trouble".[3] The first planet to be met by Mercury is Venus in the 9th in an iconoclastic T-square with Saturn and Uranus; this within the context of Pluto on the Ascendant and ruling his 3rd house. Given that the phase sits astride the 9th cusp from Aries to Taurus, his autobiography *Fighting Bull* is supremely and aptly titled. Yet, although one is never in any doubt about his fearless outspokenness, he carries this energy within an engaging warmth and sensitivity.

Other examples include Albert Einstein whose chart contains this phase again within the context of Sun/Moon Disseminating. He did not speak until he was three years old as he felt disinclined to utter words until he felt quite sure inside himself that could put an entire sentence together. The Mercury end of the phase occupies Aries and is conjunct Saturn (speaking out with concrete completeness). This also reflects his need to communicate structures and underlying patterns. The Jupiter part of the phase, in Aquarius 9th, opposes the brilliance of Uranus in Virgo 3rd house, square to Pluto, transforming the human being's view of space and time. The late British astrologer, Roy Alexander had this phase containing yet another New Phase (Sun/Moon) – a powerful combination of two New Phases enveloping one another. The Moon is conjunct (and first meets) Mercury in Virgo in the 12th house. Roy was an astrologer of rare calibre, supremely able to stand at that giant crossroads where science, mysticism, psychology and philosophy all meet, imbuing it with his own deeply observant insights and cogent writings, again within the context of a warm disposition.

In terms of performance, again this will follow the lines of instinctive unfoldment of movement rather than strenuous effort. We may find those engaged in communicative healing work and/or who use movement (such as in psychodrama or again through dance) to bring to light awarenesses which may not always lend themselves to words. The work of musicians and/or composers here often carries a soft, melodic charm, rhythm and style, such as Burt Bacharach in whose chart the phase contains Sun and Venus in Taurus and who gave us the gentle delight of *Raindrops Keep Fallin' On My Head*.[4] Impromptu performers of all kinds may also be included, from s/he who would complete your evening with a Chopin étude, to the spontaneous mime artist, to the busker in the subway who cheers up your journey to work.

Jupiter/Mercury Crescent Phase

The way in which this person communicates is related to a quality of effort, tenacity and resilience. If the experience is one of negative struggle, they may find it hard to reach out and say what they want. It could be something of a burden to get their ideas across and make any sort of impression and so they may opt for being somewhat reticent. However, if the experience is one of strong tenacity, conversely they can 'over-cook the goose'. The tendency then becomes to talk too emphatically or dramatically, pushing for one's voice to be heard, being blunt and brusque and generally lacking sensitivity to what may upset other people. Things become blurted out, all sense of appropriateness lost and an entire wagonload of cats comes tumbling out of the proverbial bag.

On the other hand the struggle may be one of actual physical or intellectual difficulty, such as a speech impediment, or strain in being able to understand links or categorisations, such as may be seen in dyslexia. There may be the loss of a limb, or difficulties in sight, hearing, sensation. Whatever the struggle (and in echo of the 45° alert-point which opens this phase) there is often something which is pushing its way through the difficulty in terms of needed outward expression to the world. Stevie Wonder, blind from birth, presents as a man of charisma and benevolence as well as possessing formidable rhythmic skill as a musician and singer. Such was very clear at the beginning of his career in the early 1960s (in itself an era of music which struggled to break through from former societal restrictions). His career has been sustained ever since in true Crescent style, i.e. notwithstanding struggles, stresses or rigours. He suffered a car accident at the age of twenty-three which left him in a coma for several days, after which he discovered he had lost his sense of smell. The phase contains the sensitivity of both Venus and Moon opposing Neptune on the

Ascendant. The Venusian theme is accentuated by Sun in Taurus (conjunct the Mercury end of the phase) and Libra rising, while Jupiter is in the 5th house of creative performance. The phase value is 79° so Mercury, in pulling away from Jupiter, had already collected up the sextile and quintile points by the time he was born, all of these factors emphasizing his easy ability to reach out to his audiences and the enhanced creativity with which he does so.

In similar vein, minus the music, I once did a chart for a young woman whose mother had been given thalidomide while she was in the womb. She was born with no arms to speak of, merely two stumps with a few ill-formed digits on each. As she approached me after a lecture asking if she could make an appointment, I was fascinated by her ability to fumble in a handbag for her diary to write down the date we fixed. I was even more in awe when she came for the consultation and I discovered she was a journalist working in a busy top-of-the-hour newsroom in which (her words) "you have to be on your toes!" Here was a unique ability to use brave humour in struggle and affliction... since toes were something this remarkable person also had few of.

The human capacity to stretch and adapt in order to bring one's communicative gifts to light despite struggle is truly extraordinary, as these last two examples show. On the other hand, if this type remains inert to the need for *application* in life, they can often exhibit a self-consciousness about putting themselves across. Sometimes this might be due to experiences of humiliation in the background life, such that they feel little in the way of a *right* to speak up. Conversely, the *push* of this phase means they can go in the opposite direction and overdo things, even being seen as 'putting on an act'. One lady in a series of astrological workshops was very large, tall and statuesque, and always wore impressive flowing clothing for dramatic effect. The Crescent Phase was within the context of a chart containing a T-square of Moon/Pluto/Venus focused down on to the IC. She always occupied a seat at the back of the room and whenever she wanted to ask a question, she would stand up importantly, enunciating slowly and clearly every well-chosen word to the entire breadth of the room and the ceiling in particular. Her comments were indeed insightful, but after a few weeks of feeling I was witnessing a triumphal address to the United Nations, I realized the Jupiter/Mercury struggle within her and began, as imperceptibly as possible, to make a point of *asking* her for comments before she chose to make them and involving her more naturally in each factor we were covering. Gradually over the weeks she moved from the back of the room and took up a chair further into the middle, among everyone else, and became altogether less of an imposing steamroller. It seemed she simply needed to feel a sense of belonging and confirmation that she was valued.

Much more positively in this phase, effort is expanded in an *earnestness* to be articulate no matter how painstaking this may be. There is a strong onward purpose and a shoulder to the wheel when it comes to speaking, writing, exchanging ideas or putting something together. Bill Gates is reputed to be a seriously hard worker. This phase in his chart contains both Mars and Pluto, thus a focused ability to fine-tune down into the mechanics of how things work (also a feature of his Sun/Moon Gibbous phase). Microsoft was founded after Gates and Paul Allen worked day and night in his room at Harvard – the relentless, earnest, applied mind within the context of finding out/discovery. The Mercury end of the phase is conjunct Mars opposite Moon in Aries conjunct MC, adding the necessary drive and ambition, while the Jupiter end of the phase is powerfully conjunct Pluto in the 2nd house of resources, which needs no further comment, save that it also squares a Venus/Saturn conjunction and Gates is known for an acute awareness that wealth brings responsibility, exemplified in his philanthropic Foundation work.[5]

Sometimes the emphasis is on prior exhaustive preparation and research, such as those who undertake written biographies or historical tomes; also those who are educators in specialized fields and generally in people who show consistent, hard-won application. A fine example of this is Jon Savage, a well-known British writer and journalist whose background includes working as a researcher in television and being a frequent contributor to the mainstream press on matters of literary and artistic criticism. His award-winning book *England's Dreaming* is an exhaustive tracing of the rise of the Punk Era, focusing on the story of the Sex Pistols and set against the backdrop of societal turbulence and explosions of new music and fashions of 1970s' England. His first book was a biography of the group, *The Kinks*, his most recent is *Teenage, the Creation of Youth* which traces the emergence of differing teenage cultures, taking us through a detailed, comprehensive and wide-ranging sweep through history from 1875 to 1945.[6] Here lies the earnestness of the phase at its creative best, indeed the potential for which is highlighted by a quintile aspect. With exquisite sensitivity (Moon is conjunct Cancer IC in the chart) and meticulous attention to detail (Sun/

Mercury conjunct in Virgo 6th) Savage is able to weave an organizational skill through his material, bringing it to a wholly new, indeed unique, outlook on his subject matter. It is also telling that his Sun/Moon is at the sextile aspect in Last Quarter phase where one's ideas, knowledge and philosophies must be organized and poured out into the world.

But then there are times in astrology when something may not be immediately clear, or we are faced with chart factors that do not seem to square up with what we know of a person. Tracing the meaning of phases is no exception and we may need to probe a little more closely beneath the surface to uncover the threads of actual manifestation. The chart below is a case in point.

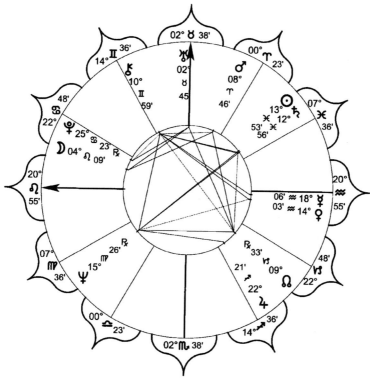

This young man was born and brought up on a family farm largely given over to the rearing of pedigree sheep. Here he always felt at his most comfortable and happy; he was known for being an outstandingly pleasant, integrate, unassuming and a somewhat shy person, also indecisive. He was privately educated and loved playing cricket. He is also described as not particularly technically proficient.

Now, unless there is something about the practice of sheep-farming which I have not quite grasped yet, a mere glance at this chart hardly puts me in mind of one who pursues such an occupation. Neither does it particularly evoke a destined lack of technicality. Granted, there is a Neptunian T-square, which may well account for it and suggest a more vague or poetic way of being. However, the sheer dynamism of Moon/Pluto square Uranus conjunct MC, Mars in Aries 9th, Jupiter in the 5th squaring the Sun (chart ruler) conjunct Saturn, an angular Mercury in Aquarius bolstering the Uranus/MC and conjunct the MC ruler (and all this before we even reach any of the phases) plays quite a different tune to my astrological ear.

When we come to the phases, Sun/Moon and Saturn/Moon are both Gibbous so there is a very distinct accent upon focused analysis, the potential for an incisive mind capable of finding out how things work, with the additional capacity for method, technique, high degree of skill. With Saturn/Moon Gibbous there is a context within which his early conditioning may not have provided sufficient for him to latch onto in order to build a strong sense of identity, such that the need is to mobilize oneself very deliberately and figure things out for oneself. But when we come to Jupiter/Mercury and find these two in Crescent phase – certainly capable of putting effort into the development of technique and skill, especially since the two are in orb of sextile, Mercury is angular and in Aquarius moreover – and I am told this man showed <u>no</u> outward signs of being technically proficient?... well I begin to mutter into my beard (or I would if I had one).

Jupiter occupies its own sign in the 5th, which speaks to me *inter alia* of opportunism and risk-taking. Mercury, as we have seen is on the Aquarian Descendant (swift movement) and conjunct Venus, as also noted earlier the ruler of the Midheaven which in turn is conjunct Uranus (more potential risk-taking, dynamism, innovation). And when I also see that the Uranus squares Moon in Leo (widely conjunct Pluto) yielding even further dynamic and individual power, I begin to get a sense of some kind of stunning, breathtaking, at least notable, ability which needs to be lived out. Jupiter's T-square is to Neptune on the one hand and Sun/Saturn on the other, the latter conjunction being the first planets met by Mercury in its pull away from Jupiter. Sun/Saturn/Neptune may yield positive themes of strong ambition, willingness to stretch oneself beyond limits, or more negatively over-reaching oneself through idealism, or indeed insecurity and shy withdrawal (which people describe of him). From an event-oriented point of view, Mercury meeting the 8th house Sun/Saturn as a focal theme in this life may point us to a solid completion/achievement or indeed an ending, perhaps demise, especially if the element of risk (Jupiter 5th) or over-optimism (Jupiter/Neptune) is added.

This is, in fact, the chart of Jim Clark, much-mourned World Champion British racing driver who was killed on the Hockenheim circuit at the age of 32. His early years on the family's rolling acres of farmland, while indeed a place of happiness, also afforded him the opportunity and space (Jupiter) to drive the family cars and tractors and become mightily adept behind a wheel. At the age of seventeen he started entering local car rallies, but on winning them became embarrassed by the attention (his shyness) which added to early feelings of guilt since his family were opposed to his racing (the Crescent theme of a struggle to be moved through and Saturn/Moon Gibbous experience of few guidelines being offered). His friends on the other hand (the angular Mercury rules 11th) goaded him to the point where his reluctance was put aside and instead he demonstrated his amazing natural talent. Through the 1960s Clark notched up a total of 25 victories in world motor racing, seldom making a mistake and suffering very few accidents.

He was indeed *not* technically-minded, *but found a 'brother'* (Mercury-sibling) in his partner (conjunct Descendant) and close friend (Gemini on 11th) in Lotus-founder Colin Chapman *who was*. We learn much from Brian Clark's excellent book concerning the inner search for the sibling-other, with or through whom we feel we can more fully develop our being.[7] It was Chapman who oversaw Jim Clark's career and translated his insights into technical engineering prowess. As a supreme champion, he always shunned the limelight or kept a low profile in public appearances, behind the scenes showing nervous indecisiveness and chewing his fingernails. Yet, *in a car*, Jim Clark was the epitome of calm, focused, controlled, dynamic aggression. He died on another Sun/Saturn conjunction,[8] this time within a few degrees of a 20° Aries Midheaven, conjunct his natal Mars/Uranus midpoint. Given the sudden, forceful impact of this latter planetary combination it is poignant that even on the morning of his death he was reverberating his inner resilient, technical understanding when he said to a team member "Don't get too close behind me when you come up to lap me, because my car is cutting out intermittently..."

Finally, in terms of movement and performance, we can see this phase lived out in those who go through long sustained effort (perhaps hardship).

The striving may be through endless rehearsals (such as in choreographed stage shows/musicals), or any situation where dedicated practice and perhaps fulfilment of technique is a hallmark. Rudolph Nureyev was born with Jupiter/Mercury right at the end of New Phase (charisma, presence) and just about to enter Crescent (technique, dedication, disciplined movement) in respect of which Mercury is also conjuncted by Venus and Saturn denoting solid artistic work. Plus, of course, his emergence as a world-renowned ballet principal was initially through the Crescent Phase struggle of defection to the west from his native Russia.

Jupiter/Mercury First Quarter Phase

The threads to be woven in this phase need to be along the lines of communicating very decisively and vigorously. This may mean being powerful or perhaps evangelistic in conveying a message, but it may also mean being outrageous, shocking, full of provocation. The way this person moves and approaches other people is often intense and driven, 'hot' with some issue they are bursting to deliver.

The emphasis is primarily *on the destruction of existing patterns of thought or belief, more than on the creation of any new ones.* Principally this person wants to speak out usually to attack the faults of something or challenge an ideology to which they are opposed. They are great believers in laying things on the line, calling a spade a spade and rarely tactful. These themes may appear ordinarily in day-to-day life as a genuine ability to speak up (perhaps so as not to be imprisoned by what other people think) or more negatively as a liking to hear one's own voice. However, they are also capable of being some kind of spokesperson or activist who will provoke argument and dissent at a social order. Either way, the fundamental drive is to stir people into action. This is an energy capable of being seriously brusque and impatient with other people's objections one a clear-cut course of action is seen.

Being able to say very clearly what they want, think and feel, this person will not usually follow a herd-mentality nor let any doubts or fears get in the way of speaking out *because the inner felt challenge is to effect a change.* Sometimes they may find themselves in (or create) circumstances in which tensions become so great that they feel they *absolutely must* speak out, whether it is wise or appropriate to do so. In some situations this may be foolhardiness, in others it may show great bravery. Sometimes it is 'the whistleblower'.

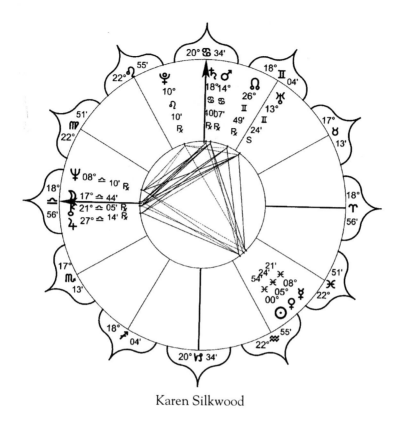

Karen Silkwood

Karen Silkwood was born with Sun/Moon Disseminating, therefore with an inner purpose of communicating what she knows and understands. Her Saturn/Moon is at the commencement of First Quarter with its emphasis (from the preceding Crescent) of being a worker who will fight hard to get through by asserting herself in a challenging manner. And now here, with Jupiter/Mercury, we have another First Quarter emphasis on the capacity to speak out whether or not it is wise or safe.

Having been hired as a laboratory technician grinding plutonium pellets for nuclear reactor fuel rods, Karen became an active Union member, particularly focusing on health and safety issues. At the chemical plant where she worked she apparently found serious violations along these lines, with several workers (including herself) becoming exposed to contamination through spillages and leaks of plutonium. She provided testimony to this effect to an official Investigative Commission and further alleged that quality control of fuel rods had been compromised. In November

1974 she made an appointment to meet with a Union representative and an investigative newspaper journalist, at which meeting she intended to provide documentation to justify her claims of negligence against her employer. Karen never reached that meeting for, on the way there, her car crashed off the road and she was killed. Much speculation and mystery surrounds the crash although Highway Patrol concluded it was caused by driver-drowsiness and blood tests showed a high quantity of drugs which might induce such, as well as radiation. Fresh dents and traces of rubber reportedly found to the back of her car led to speculation that she had been deliberately run off the road. The documents she took with her to hand over were never found.

It is very possible that Karen, given the strength of the Sun/Moon, Saturn/Moon and Jupiter/Mercury phases in her chart, did not give much thought to the consequences of what she was doing. As we saw earlier, whether this is dedicated bravery or unthought-out foolish bravado, First Quarter energy has a capacity *for going forward, no matter* what to speak out. In addition, the Sun/Moon phase contains Jupiter, ruler of her 3rd house and co-ruler of her Piscean planets. It is in the 1st house suggesting an open, confident ability to stride forward into her world, also conjunct Chiron lending further colouration to the sense of a healing mission. The Saturn/Moon phase is strong by dint of Saturn's conjunction to Mars, conjunct also a cardinal Midheaven and squaring the equally cardinal Moon on the Ascendant. One gets the feeling Karen would take on anything. That phase also contains Pluto in the 10th (the power and might of an employer/career – plutonium) and Neptune in the 12th, ruler of her Pisces planets, reflecting mystery/a 'veil' over her death.

The Jupiter/Mercury First Quarter itself contains the 5th house Sun and Venus – people with planets in the 5th can certainly feel that they need to concern themselves with Major Important Issues, sometimes the bigger the better. What she found herself caught up in was certainly 'big stuff' but by the same token what she did and intended to do may also have been a matter of *honour* for Karen (Sun-ruled house). The first planet to be met by Mercury as it pulled away from Jupiter is Uranus in the 8th, one reflection of which lies in the suddenness of her death, on a road (Gemini). Karen's father subsequently filed a lawsuit against her employers, who settled out of court without admitting any liability for her demise. Her life, her struggles to speak out and the mystery of her death were brought to world attention through the Hollywood film *Silkwood*[9] (films/cinema again reflecting the Pisces/Neptune/5th house themes of her chart).

In terms of physical movement and self-expression, we may see exceptional power, stamina, prowess and/or intensity with this phase. The genius Nijinsky, brilliant for his phenomenal ability to perform breathtakingly high leaps, is a key example. Here was a Balsamic Sun/Moon with intense beauty of expression (Pisces 4th house with Venus angular on the IC). The Jupiter/ Mercury First Quarter is the exact square and contains that Venus, with the Jupiter end powerfully opposite Pluto in Gemini (mobility) and Neptune (ruler of the Pisces planets). The Mercury end conjuncts the Moon as it approaches the end of the cycle to meet up with the Sun (Balsamic) to leave a legacy for the future. Alas Nijinsky's potential capacity to speak out forcefully was not sufficient to match his physical stamina nor withstand the power of those around him, in particular his powerful mentor, Diaghilev.

Taking ourselves to the opposite end of the spectrum, many rock musicians have this phase – hot, raw, exciting, pulsating sounds blasting to every corner of the venue, again conveying the challenging energy of the phase. So too we may find political debaters, such as David Lloyd George, known for the power of his leadership during World War I (the phase falls into the orbit of a T-square with a 3rd house Mars/Pluto conjunction). Although born in England Lloyd-George was of Welsh descent and *held out* for spoken Welsh as his first language. Where this phase is within orb of the 120° trine, there may still be the rather 'loaded' quality of speaking out, yet there is more fluency and the energy may be channelled into (say) musical composition or art. Vincent Van Gogh was as vigorous and expressive a writer as he was a painter. His letters to his younger brother, Theo, range in energy from calm expression (or despair) to wild excitement. But more potently the Jupiter/Mercury First Quarter trine in Fire (Sagittarius-Aries) reflects the vibrant energy of his brush strokes and use of colour. Helen Keller has the phase containing Saturn, Neptune, Chiron, Pluto, Venus and Sun. Through the help of her dedicated teacher, Anne Sullivan, she fought to overcome her deafness and blindness to write, translate books, lecture extensively and travel the world as an ambassador for the blind, inspiring an entire world in the process.

Jupiter/Mercury Gibbous Phase

Finding out what works means that there is a sense in which life is seen as a kind of jigsaw puzzle, with this person deeply immersed in finding all the bits and trying to fit them together. Communicating and conveying oneself is often a process of trial and error; this type will constantly think about what to say, how to say it, how best to get across to people… and how to pick up the pieces if it all goes wrong.

One effect of all this is that there is usually an enormous appetite for information. They will ask a lot of questions, either overtly or simply by delving in forensic scrutiny of any avenues which might provide answers. Many of the associations or friendships they make can arise out of developing a sheer curiosity about others' lives. Some may be drawn into debate/discussion, while others take the route of private, inner rumination. Here they take time to ponder over things, which can be very irritating to those who prefer alacrity, but the Gibbous energy is one of method and precision. They will often go to interminable lengths to research something, ask eleventy-four million questions, read lengthy tomes or camp out for six weeks in the British Library before feeling anywhere *near* able to make a clear statement of their findings. Alternatively we may find them being very careful, formal and particular in how they communicate, often with a quiet, confiding quality, or a more probing and profound intensity in their bid to discover information. Some have an eye for detail such that they zoom in and swoop like a hawk on minutiae. Then again, they may just be 'nosey-parkers'!

While this type may indeed be fluent and coherent, there can also exist an impression of being rather arid and impersonal. The analytical quality of the phase may be developed solely along intellectual lines which, taken on its own, may of course be applied very effectively in any number ways. However, on a more social level it can appear a little chilly. It is as if they can put the actual bits of the jigsaw together but a feeling-relationship with the overall picture escapes them. Indeed they may not even be interested in an overall picture, instead preferring to spend hours working away at one corner only, worryingly bent over the bits and pieces. Thus their capacity for conceptual analysis is extremely well placed where all that is required is, say, categorization or statistical research, but be found a little wanting in terms of a fuller emotional comprehension. The potential aridity of communication here could also mean that little is actually conveyed by the flow of their words. This may be because they have got stuck on a particular method or technique for communicating, one that they have found to work for them in the past but which has now become mechanical. There are one or two politicians around the globe who might fit this description! Shopworn phrases are trundled out such as "the green shoots of recovery" or "lessons will be learned" or they devise a whole new genre of 'business-speak' containing highly-practised jargonised phrases. In short it is a Gibbous-type invention to play for time while they try to figure out the bits and pieces racing through their minds.

In terms of relating to people through curiosity, some may place themselves in situations where finding out about others' lives is a legitimate function – biographers, interviewers, psychoanalysts, astrologers, investigative journalists, pathologists, detectives who must solve the riddle of 'whodunnit'. The theme of *method* in this phase may also be developed through such avenues as speech therapy, being a student or teacher of languages, the development of technique in movement, such as in gymnastics, synchronized swimming, or even sales people with a set 'patter'. In acting, this Gibbous energy can be very useful in learning lines and endless rehearsal, although the delivery may not be as free-flowing and alive as one might wish (unless there are other factors which would help this along). Others may be involved in typically Gibbous activities which require deep mental focus such as inventions, technology, archaeology, translations requiring exactitude, delving into mathematical equations, research of all kinds, or just people who like to fiddle around with gadgets… if only tinkering with that old bicycle in the garden shed.

Elias Howe was the inventor of the first patented lockstitch sewing machine in 1846. A man who experienced long periods of ill-health, Howe would lay bed-ridden watching his wife sew. For years, and like many others at the time, he had endeavoured to invent a machine to do what many thousands in factories were having to do by hand, often suffering failing eyesight as a result. Yet he could not quite make his ideas work and time was running out as he was being pressed for money by his creditors. But then he had a dream.

In the dream he was being chased and captured by a savage tribe waving spears who tied him to a stake and danced wildly around their prey, getting closer and closer as they moved in for the kill. Just as they were on the point of killing him, he noticed that their spears *all had an eye hole near the point.* Here, through dream metaphor, was the inspiration sought and he awoke with a start. Howe realized that for the sewing machine, the eye of the needle had to be on the opposite end to a hand-held needle. Although we do not have a birth time for Howe the Sun/Moon phase is Full and here was a 'solution' riding up into consciousness and brought into being; not by reason with which in his waking life he was grappling, but emanating from a perception and illuminated awareness beyond our everyday senses, yet which would bring his Jupiter/Mercury Gibbous to a conclusion. He had previously trained as a machinist's apprentice in a textile mill and had gone through years of working with looms, bobbins and cloth. Mars in Taurus trines the Jupiter end of the phase, while Saturn trines the Mercury end and is close to the Mars/Jupiter midpoint. So the unrelenting focus of Gibbous also meant he *stuck at it.* Besides, his increasing poverty, and being the father of six children, made for necessity... and Necessity, as they say, is the Mother of Invention.

Around the beginning of the phase and perhaps particularly nearer the biquintile, there may be more of a creative capacity to assemble or compose something, prompted perhaps only by some inner sense that it might work. This may be an artistic endeavour, a business, perhaps even an empire ...

Sir Richard Branson was born with Sun/Moon in New Phase, Saturn/Moon Balsamic, and Jupiter/Mercury Gibbous. Taking these three in turn, the New Moon phase had reached 36°, therefore an inner felt-sense awareness of a burgeoning purpose to be lived and a thrust to give much into the world. Contained within this phase are elements of perception, discovery, maybe chewing over things endlessly inside himself while he delves into their possibilities (Mercury lies in the 12th) plus a dominant need to feel a sense of personal creative power (Pluto/Leo/1st house conjunct Ascendant).

The Saturn/Moon Balsamic phase suggests that his conditioned self, from early life, may not have afforded him a clear set path for how to put this into operation. The background career pattern in his family was in Law, but Richard was not a particularly bright scholar in the ordinary academic sense. Thus, rather than trying to conform to set ways of building an identity, he had to figure one out for himself. What a good job, then, that he incarnated with Jupiter/Mercury Gibbous since figuring it out for oneself is precisely one of the things this phase is so very good at. It is also interesting that the Jupiter end of this phase is within opposition of the Moon/Saturn midpoint: largely through his mother he encountered themes of self-sufficiency and self-preservation (Saturn in the 2nd house is the first planet to be met by the Moon after birth). He has spoken in several interviews of how his mother once left him out in the countryside as a small boy and told him to find his own way home, a distance of quite some miles. These themes are echoed also through the Moon and Saturn in an Earth sign as well as the 2nd house, adding endurance and practicality in applying oneself to work it all out and create stability. Mars and Neptune are conjunct in the 3rd yielding additional themes of something larger than life, widespread and inspirational in the pursuit of experiences to galvanize the mind and provide constant activity (such as the building of an empire and making it work). Tellingly, this conjunction forms creative threads of enhanced incentive through a biquintile to the Jupiter end of this phase and quintile to Mercury, augmenting the entrepreneurial quality of this chart as a whole.

Jupiter/Mercury Full Phase

There is very high ability to reach out to others and communicate with clarity. However, unlike the New Phase where this was spontaneous, crucial to the success or failure of a writer or speaker here is the development of *reflective, considered thought*. If this person does not consciously develop a measure of self-awareness in what s/he is conveying, there is a converse tendency to overdo things and plunge into muddle, indiscretion, overstatement or to dramatize everything to the hilt. Others may simply be over-loquacious, words tumbling from their mouth or onto paper with all the power of a cascading waterfall, but generally they do all have the capacity to think for themselves and look at things in stark clarity.

In general social interaction, this can be the type who, again from a negative perspective, seems to find catharsis by constantly talking about their own personal interests, but it can be very self-defeating if it is done from a position of unconsciousness because of the tendency to bore or otherwise alienate the listener. There may have been an early life experience of difficulties in being heard and this can lead to the development of a compensatory emphatic, even 'bossy' way of speaking. Yet, positively, clarity of communication may emerge from being exposed to a background in which the constructs of language were respected and developed in, say, fields such as classic acting, linguistics, the judiciary, authorship – or, better still, through being *included* as a child in family discussion and given validation for their contributions. I have also met those who found it was *through* earlier anxieties that their ability to communicate ultimately declared itself. One man (a best-selling writer) told me that his elder brother had always been the favourite with his parents. From a very early age, anything he said to his brother was automatically reported to his parents but not before being completely twisted around, embellished and embroidered to give it an ultimately negative 'spin'. After being repeatedly admonished – no protests ever being heard about being so unfairly represented – my client learned that he must reflect very carefully before saying anything. In adult life his words and sentences are of very measured clarity which has largely underpinned his literary success.

Also positively, when one is more open to the potential for illumination in this phase, there can be a striking ability to know not only what to say and how to say it, but also to display an appropriateness as to *when* to say it and who to say it *to*! There is an attendant consideration of others, a willingness to see the world through their eyes, to allow that person space to be heard. Carl Rogers, founder of the client-centred approach to counselling, alerted us to this simple yet vitally important ingredient in our interactions. And it is one which becomes increasingly important in a world which would imprison you in who you *should* be and what you *should* think, or fills every available space with endless chatter and information. In general, this phase type needs to be more open to allowing something to develop organically rather than following any line of quick wit or instantaneous decision. It may be called 'sitting with it for a while' but in the long run is both wiser and often more creative – for had it been communicated precipitatively one might have missed deeper realizations still to expand from it (Jupiter). This capacity is often seen in those who introduce innovative ideas and it may also arise in music (composition) or in those who have a deep curiosity and need for exploration in life which bids them read extensively, travel widely, learn from every quarter. At a deeper level still, it may certainly arise in religious and spiritual pathways, in the development of consciousness through metaphysical thought and deeper philosophies.

In the chart of His Holiness the Dalai Lama the phase contains all the personal planets, plus Pluto and Neptune – vast purposes for Mercury to collect up and 'take home' to Jupiter at their next conjunction. Unsurprisingly for one who was to be supreme spiritual leader of the Tibetan people in exile, the Sun rises as the first of these planets, then Pluto (conjunct the nodal axis), both in Cancer (nurturing, protectiveness) squaring a 4th house Mars. Through the qualities of leadership and self-mastery he leads the battle for his homeland and people with determination and focused perception. Mercury is in the 12th house forming an exact semi-sextile to rising Pluto – this is the Balsamic Pluto/Mercury revealing seeds ready to be yielded for a powerful and creative renewal of purpose. He is the reincarnational chosen Leader. Jupiter forms part of a Kite formation in the chart, so often found in those whose intention is to be of meaningful service in the world. It sextiles a Moon/Neptune conjunction in Virgo (compassion, service) which forms the apex of the Kite while Uranus in the 11th gives voice to the need for freedom, especially in spiritual terms (Aquarius on the 9th). Jupiter in the 5th house seems to fit his engaging, avuncular-type laughter, his enthusiasm and charisma emanating from a combination of impressiveness and joyful ease of relating.

I have also found in this phase those who are able to reflect with clarity upon that which yields coherence to the range of human experience over a particular period of time. This may again be a writer (such as Charles Dickens), a philosopher, or artist such as Pablo Picasso.

The phase is across the 10th/4th houses and Picasso's work carries strong threads of awareness in, and commentary upon, social movement (10th) and inner experience (4th). At each stage of his work we can see cultural temperament articulated within the underlying experience of people of the time. With the Sun/Moon in New Phase (containing Mercury) his work stands as a powerful *language* describing shifting world themes. He does so not only with great power (Jupiter conjunct Pluto) and vividness (trine to Uranus) but with an accompanying ability also to shift and transform (Mercury/Scorpio opposite Jupiter/Pluto) his artistic approach according to that which he perceives or is illuminated by. For example, early Picassos show figures bathing by the sea (in the 1920s just after the First World War) but these then gave way to more metallic and impersonal shapes (representing the more mechanized and robotic development of humankind in the 1930s), compounded by the mighty *Guernica* which depicts the stark outrage and suffering of a despairing, fragmented humanity. Here there is no colour and indeed, as the 1930s led into the 1940s, this remains the case with the pictures becoming numbered not named, yet a further portrayal of the greying dejectedness of the human condition. Here, as in all true

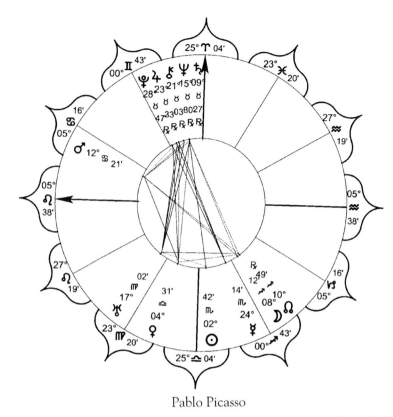

Pablo Picasso

creative artists, we see the intertwining of the person with that which he encounters in full illuminated consciousness.

By the same token, writers, commentators or journalists, especially those who involve themselves bravely in fields of confrontation or strife, are able to convey to others with great clarity an unfolding dynamic and to do so movingly. In this connection, we have a set of astrological twins, ushered in on the 1939 summer/autumn T-square of Mars/Saturn/Pluto which saw a world steel itself to the outbreak of war. The first is John Pilger, world famous journalist, author and documentary film-maker who has won numerous journalistic and human rights awards. Seemingly fearless and ultra-determined, he shines a searching light (Full Phase) on world affairs, reporting cogently and insightfully upon that which tends to be hidden behind facades. A former front line war reporter in Vietnam, he is primarily a critic and campaigner upon issues few other journalists appear to have the courage to look at and bring into the open. Harold Pinter remarked of him that he "unearths, with steely attention, the facts, the filthy truth, and tells it as it is". The time of birth is unknown but we can see that all the planets are already on board in the phase, leaving only Mars to be collected up by Mercury in its return journey back to Jupiter. And there we have the heart of the matter – for the aforementioned T-square picks up the nodal axis, is conjoined by Mercury and also the Sun-ruler, Venus. 'Steely' is indeed apt – the tough, sleuthing Grand Cross which sums up the grit and purpose of this man's capacity for measured, enlightened, polemic communication.

Pilger shares his birth date with another award-winning writer, journalist, and campaigner for human rights, the late James McClure. McClure was notable for his use of the crime novel as a vehicle by which to highlight and speak out against apartheid in his native South Africa. Subsequent works included factual and authoritative portraits of front-line police divisions both in Britain and America, the research for which necessitated many months of McClure working alongside (and thus *fully exposed* to the same dangers as) the officers he was examining and reporting upon.[10] Here again we see the theme of making encounter with that which needs to be revealed and communicated, so that others might be aware… and again with the same consummate bravery as his astrological twin.

Jupiter/Mercury Disseminating Phase

Following on from learning the lessons of awareness and reflection at Full Phase, this phase denotes the capacity to be highly aware of what one is communicating and the effect that is being created. The ability to judge an audience (or simply another person) and modify words and phrases accordingly makes this type a very plausible and persuasive person. As in the Gibbous phase (minus the intensity) there is often an additional confiding quality as though the person they happen to be talking to were the only one in the world. This is a person who can not only take an idea and convey it vividly, but also imbue it with a sense of style, perhaps a 'savoir-faire', that makes you warm to them without once stopping to question it.

The epitome of sartorial elegance, Alan Whicker is known internationally for his journalistic skills as a social commentator and award-winning television programme and documentary-maker. With exquisite subtlety, ease and gentle cultivation of a relaxed and courteous style, he has been able to enter the world of people in very particular and privileged settings – from film stars to billionaires, world leaders to the rich ladies of Palm Springs. With all the sophistication of an English gentleman immaculate

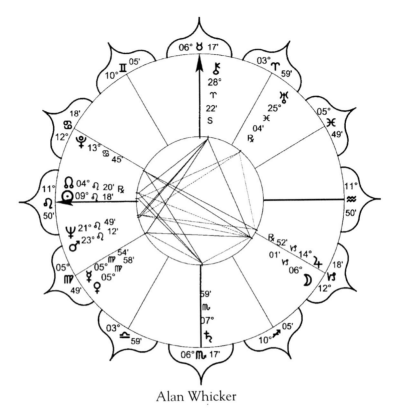

Alan Whicker

in blazer and tie, an air of bespectacled erudition and suave moustache, Whicker's vocal tone is that which lulls people into a comfortable niche from which they are automatically persuaded that he is indeed a trustworthy friend to whom they can impart anything at all. But this is not with any ingratiating sentiment and honeyed words; his style of questioning is barely discernible as potent, direct, critical probing – yet that is precisely what it is, as befits his overall Sun/Moon Gibbous. Moving imperceptibly but with a dignified respect from person to person he has been able to conduct exclusive interviews with the reclusive John Paul Getty, the Sultan of Brunei, Haiti's dictator 'Papa Doc' Duvalier and countless others whose lives revolved in and through luxurious palaces, lavish cocktail parties, fabulously wealthy health spas and clubs – in other words the rarely observed and ultra private worlds of the seriously rich and famous.

As noted, the Sun/Moon phase is Gibbous, with its accent on ferreting out detail, developing method and workable techniques. The Saturn/Moon phase is Crescent, at the sextile aspect. Here we have the conscientious worker (with Moon in Capricorn) applying himself to bring a major task to fruition, developing stamina and effort and using interconnectedness (the sextile) to establish a road ahead; moreover bringing something to light in thoroughness and capable professionalism. The Sun is in Leo in the 12th house – Whicker probes the unseen, hidden, private worlds of those whose lives we rarely get to see and does so with style and flair. The Capricorn Moon in the 5th house adds the creative competence and professionalism for which he is so known, as well as merging with those of 'high born' status. Saturn is in Scorpio at the IC – again probing, dissecting, sometimes concentrating on one particular powerful individual and deftly unveiling the mystery and depth surrounding them. The angularity of the Saturn would give him a 'handle' for all these skills to be applied purposefully and of course opposes a Taurus Midheaven (wealth) whose ruler is conjunct the Mercury end of the phase in the 2nd house, the very stuff of his communicative life. This Mercury/Venus conjunction in Virgo again reflects the charm, the courtesy, the ability to concentrate upon detail, single it out and communicate it with skill and resourceful ingenuity. Jupiter occupies 6th house Capricorn – the heightened sense of professionalism, the focused exploration – and opposes Pluto in the 12th – power, supremacy, those of immense influence whose lives are hidden, yet the urbane Mr. Whicker is able to introduce us to this world without any hint of invasion or inappropriateness.

With Jupiter forming a biquintile to the rising Mars/Neptune conjunction (an enhanced application and arrangement of subtle creative skill), Whicker's technique is worth studying, yet at the same time is so sublime it is often difficult to grasp and put into words. This is because it is not applied mechanically but is a natural outpouring of his own decorum and insight. He will often walk directly to the camera as if speaking to you and you alone, thus including you personally in the setting and with the person he is interviewing. Sometimes he will ask a direct question or be critical/praising, but more often he affords his viewers the privilege of coming to their own conclusions rather than being told what to think or feel. Whole legions of people have tried to impersonate him over the years, each endeavouring to cultivate the slightly nasal drawl, the soft confiding tone, the raised eyebrow in place of a direct question, the diffident 'aside'. Whicker himself heard of such an impersonation contest taking place in America and anonymously phoned the show to enter. (He came third!).

Although, positively, this is the communicator *par excellence*, if they have been discouraged in life from speaking up they may not superficially present an image of a confident speaker. Nevertheless, however habitually taciturn they may be, when they *do* say something it will usually have a convincing ring of authority to it. A key danger, however, is that of intolerance, or 'preachiness', where nobody else's views are given credence. Nearer the 135° point, this person may be a provocative communicator, but this is not necessarily a negativity for their purpose is often to stir others up (this is an alert point) in such a way that they awaken to something that clearly needs to be seen. Nearer the 120° trine, there is often a particular ease or grace in the way this person talks and moves, perhaps with an attendant need to show how adept they are at something. The phase can produce some excellent speakers, writers, teachers and performers, but it is crucial for them to develop a specific field and/or material of their own in which to develop these skills. If not, or if they simply 'follow a herd', then they have a tendency just to go on conveying with great conviction that which they were taught, trotting out the same thoughts as a mere extrapolation of everything that everybody else has ever said or thought before them. Positively this may proffer a 'comfy quaintness' but negatively it can be simply outdated, therefore less believable and perhaps even yawningly boring.

Earlier under Sun/Moon Disseminating, we looked at the chart of Prince Harry and found that the same phase applied to his Jupiter/Mercury. I have to say it would be hard to conceive of a person born with *both* these phases Disseminating who was *not* a naturally gifted communicator, thus I would reiterate my expectation that this is a dynamic Harry can develop more and more as his life progresses. He may have rather more work to do than is ordinarily the case since the 'job' of Mercury (as it is positioned and before it returns to Jupiter) looks quite loaded – it has to collect up first the Sun, then Venus, Pluto, Saturn, South Node, Uranus, Mars and Neptune. Well, one aspect of Mercury in Virgo is that it likes to be kept busy! But it does again make for a sense of Harry having many paths to tread in order to discover that particular and specific field for which he is best fitted as a communicator. The quintile from Mercury to the Midheaven (an enhanced ability to speak out for new ways forward) may point us in the general direction of his purpose; an additional quintile (between Venus and Neptune) and biquintile (Moon and Neptune) may point more specifically to a spiritually-based compassion and understanding (perhaps for children

– Moon 4th, Chiron 5th) and he does already, of course, commit himself to charities serving this purpose[11] as well as an experience of a strong feminine role model from his mother during early life.

Jupiter/Mercury Last Quarter Phase

The task for people of this phase is to communicate their own perceptions, values and ideologies in order to contribute to new, different roads for the future of their society. We may find them as reformers of some kind, speaking out and championing causes that give scope to new opportunities, particularly concerning anything or anyone that seems to need release. However, the individual's willingness to step out from the past into a maturity and embrace this turning point is crucial to its effectiveness. This is usually experienced only after sufficient pressure has built up, that very pressure of course propelling them into it. If this is resisted there may be a constantly re-enactment of the past rather than creating and following a road of one's own.

There is a tension in communicating in this phase and it can be quite considerable. It may go hand in hand with the pressure but it is often composed of a mixture of needing to reach out to people on the one hand, coupled with a feeling of dissatisfaction about the ability to do so on the other. This may lie at very subtle levels within the psyche, but it can nevertheless be a source of great irritation to them. Frequently they feel misunderstood, or carry an *expectation* of being misunderstood. Nevertheless, many who are spurred to become a spokesperson for reform in society may well go forward and do so in spite of this. The phase contains both quintile and sextile aspects and thus offers scope for the development of enhanced creative courage notwithstanding inner misgivings, plus the ability to reorganize their lives to stand behind that which they speak out for. In terms of promulgating specific causes, several of the well known people we have already met are examples of this – Martin Luther King, Prince Charles, Baba Ram Dass, Margaret Thatcher. We might add the striking Aung San Suu Kyi, recently (November 2010) released from house arrest in Burma, to this list. All of these people in their separate ways have addressed their world intent on a particular endeavour, moral view, innovation and/or emancipation of something, in order to transform the direction in which their environment is heading. The themes raised in Prince Charles' chart (of insight and progressive social concern) are again highlighted by the two planets having already formed a quintile and sextile prior to his birth, and Mercury had last touched the sensitive and insightful Venus/Neptune conjunction at the IC/ Libra/Air. It first meets the Sun after birth and then Mars before returning to Jupiter. The Sun in Scorpio squaring Pluto in the first house again points to his ability to convey his convictions but the tension and pressure of the phase is clearly seen and felt when you hear Charles speak and can also be traced through the amount of criticisms, distortions or oppositions he seems to attract. In Mrs Thatcher's chart, the phase contains the dominant Saturn conjunct Scorpio Ascendant; it is one of three Last Quarter phases (alongside Sun/Moon and Saturn/Moon), thus the unmistakeable drive to transform society through unshakeable conviction, speaking out and taking a different road, again in the face of opposing pressures.

Some Jupiter/Mercury Last Quarters may have lived the earlier part of their lives in an environment which actively supported the notion of conveying an important new idea (e.g. educational, journalistic or religious backgrounds). Others had no such example but it simply arose as a path onto which Life itself seemed to point them. But it is ultimately of very little consequence in this phase since the true purpose of it is to create a specific platform *of one's own* from which to articulate progressive ways forward. And even if one does have an established background pattern, one cannot merely regurgitate and copy it – with this phase it must be moved on from and positioned contemporaneously.

Oliver Cromwell, for example, was happily farming away in rural Huntingdonshire. "God knows" he said "I would have been glad to have lived under my woodside and to have kept a flock of sheep, rather than have undertaken this government".[12] Yet this was the man who was to take the head of a hapless and ill-advised King and reconvene a whole nation on to a diversionary path. The phase is at the sextile – the drive to champion a cause and reorganize that which you have reformed. He was also born under Sun/Moon First Quarter (the answering of a challenge). Mars, Pluto and Uranus rise in Aries 1st house which rather fits his troops (Ironsides) specifically picked for their strength, bravery and zeal. Cromwell's tension and pressure, apart from having to turn from his farming, was that he was not a particularly good speaker, but as a religious man he had a penetrating and earnest fervour which led to flashes of oratory. The phase contains Venus solidly sitting in its own sign and house, squaring his ruling planet, Neptune in the 6th (determination and service to a cause aligned to the religious faith in which he had been schooled from early years).

On more ordinary levels, the individual may seek to introduce some kind of crusading quality to the way they go about their world. Some do so vociferously since it can be the case that the expectation of being misunderstood becomes something this individual is constantly defending against, therefore an accompanying tendency to *provoke* it. Contention follows, often with too great a readiness to invade the space of others and stir up further irritation through attention-seeking or ill-mannered behaviours. Italian Prime Minister, Signor Berlusconi (born with the phase from Jupiter in the 3rd to a rising Mercury conjunct Sun) famously got himself ticked off by the Queen at Buckingham Palace when he punctured the sedate gathering of Heads of State. "Why does he have to shout?!" asked HM, thereby opening us all to an awareness of a culture in which very many harbour a fear of not being properly heard or given enough attention and thus we create a compensatory irascibility.

Overall his type does need consciously to address the issue of how they convey themselves and go about their world if there are to get the best out of relating and their contacts with others. If not, they may unwittingly build a presentation of themselves as being very irritating, purposely dramatizing things or stirring up contention in a wholly unnecessary way. When this type has a pet theory – or indeed a pet grievance – they can go completely overboard about it and thus invite the very lack of understanding or condemnation from others they so fear. And in the process the *real* path they need to turn, and contribute, to recedes more and more into the distance. But from a more positive vantage point, they can draw upon the more feisty elements of their nature to haul themselves out of any ruts they are stuck in. Turning their minds to a specific field of endeavour, they can bring it to vivid life and move it forward.

Jupiter/Mercury Balsamic Phase

Even more so than in the previous phase, the pattern of communication in the Balsamic type needs to be based on establishing new ways of seeing things. The main shift as we move into this phase is that there is a more definite inclination *to go against the grain and speak out for things that are not generally accepted*, but which this individual nevertheless feels need to be known and attended to for the future. This is a person who may be considered as ahead of their time, or indeed a black sheep/maverick, out of kilter with what are considered normal or usual corridors of thought and outlook. To this person's way of thinking 'only dead fish swim with the current' and what is conveyed may seem decidedly odd, shocking or outrageous… or it may be ground-breaking and awakening. Either way, it is at least noticeable, often arresting.

Here too there is tension. In Last Quarter this consisted of feeling, or expecting to be, misunderstood; here there are concerns of being misquoted or running the risk of distortion and ridicule by others. If they feel unable to withstand this, they may simply clam up and allow themselves to deteriorate (the 'wilting' plant) into conversing only by trite and superficial pathways. However, the tension can also act as an inner spur to arouse, electrify, urge, shake up or jolt others into an awareness of something that this type sees all too readily and feels s/he must alert people to if a future road is to be trodden successfully. Some may be steady of demeanour and reasonably pleasant in their manner of speech, while others can be outspoken to the point of anarchy, caring not a fig whether they are getting along with their fellow human beings or not. It can be noted that the phase commences with the 'irksome' semi-square whose purpose is to stir something into realization. Whatever the actuality, the overall tenor is of someone who is not backwards in coming forwards when something needs to be said. In the process they may well run the gauntlet of derision or be discredited, attacked and labelled a scurrilous person for having such outlandish ideas or ways of being.

David Icke is a former English footballer and sports journalist who, in 1990, experienced a deep personal interior transformation. He emerged as a prophetic speaker and conspiracy-theory writer on hidden global agendas, networked societies, the nature of perceptual reality and changing states of consciousness. On the one hand he has collected a degree of public humiliation that would crush a person of less determination to stand his ground and on the other increasing vindication for his pronouncements. An articulate man, in his chart Mercury and Jupiter rule the 9th and 3rd houses emphasizing communication skills as well as the 11th/5th axis emphasizing the need to develop personal and social creativity in order to apply his insights. The Mercury part of the phase is particularly strong by dint of its link into the Grand Cross formation involving a crusading Moon/Uranus conjunction in the 9th (speaking out one's own insights and philosophies) in opposition to Chiron, in the 3rd (battling against the odds to get himself across and be heard) squaring Saturn and Neptune in the 12th Libra Air

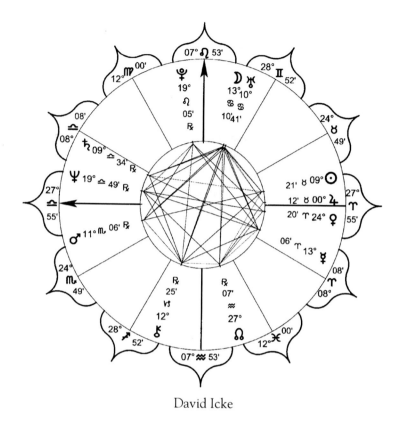

David Icke

(uncovering the unseen and concretizing it through insight/communication arising from depths which may be seen as strange or unusual). This overall pattern carries a sense of clarity to be fought for and indeed a radical audacity to speak out for a liberation of that which he perceives as limited, boxed-in, held down.

The phase also contains Venus, his ruling planet, which opposes Neptune in the 12th and trines Pluto in the 10th house. Much of his work centres around the theme of lifting the veil of mystery and secrecy to access and expose hidden power structures which he perceives as mass propaganda hypnosis and, on a psychospiritual level, the uplifting of human consciousness from myopic levels to encompass a higher perspective of unitary Love. These factors are set against a backdrop context of Sun/Moon in Crescent Phase (the sextile) and the Moon had already absorbed Uranus in the few months just prior to his birth, leaving the first planet next to be met – Pluto in the 10th. Part of his struggle (Crescent) has not only involved radical changes in his career life and battling his way defiantly through colossal humiliation, but also physical suffering (rheumatoid arthritis), also reminiscent of the Chironian input to the Grand Cross. A Saturn/Moon in Last Quarter, moreover, will not endlessly toe any line it sees as restrictive or stifling to his true nature and purpose. Thus Icke's life reveals a thread woven whereby he has raised his head above a parapet to forge a single-minded identity of his own, in the process confronting societal conditionings on a monumental level and speaking out for that which he feels the world needs to know.

Clearly this phase can be the 'alternative vision' person, who seems to have both a present and a futuristic glimpse into how things are and how they *could* be, *need* to be or even *should* be. As such they can often have a hard time living in the ordinary mechanized, mundane '9 to 5' existence of society. Should they be caught up in such a lifestyle, they will usually seek some way (however small) of creating a tributary river along which they can periodically row their own boat, announce a viewpoint which goes against the tide or blaze some new kind of trail into a different way of being. If they do not, then they are apt to sit at home as a kind of armchair-revolutionary, grumbling away about the state of the world and protesting "why the hell doesn't anybody listen to me?" There may be prophetic glimpses into the pattern of things, perhaps particularly once the 30° semi-sextile has been reached, an ability to see the intricacies of how things are fitting together and where they may be heading, and to use this foresight to speak out for a better future, or even to clarify things in the present so that they will lead to that better future. At the very least they will raise pertinent questions – even if they are not immediately answered, this type will leave them hanging in the air for all to see anyway, for this is not a phase inclined to brush things under a carpet.

Overall the need to identify and proclaim a clear alternative direction may lead to societal changes in their lifetime for which they have opened up a road and facilitated. Alternatively, it may be one that eventually emerges after their lifetime but (at least partly) as a result of what they had hitherto contributed (often a feature of Balsamic energies). D.H. Lawrence completed his controversial and sexually-explicit *Lady Chatterley's Lover* (which he originally wanted to call *Tenderness*) in 1928. Lawrence's chart contains the Balsamic Jupiter/Mercury in Virgo, with Mercury squaring an 8th house Pluto and Jupiter conjunct the Sun (ruler of his Leo Midheaven). With prophetic awareness he wrote to a friend in 1927 that he felt in a quandary about the book. "It's what the world would call very improper", he said, then continued "But you know it's not really improper – I always labour at the same thing, to make the sex relation valid and precious, instead of shameful. And this novel is the furthest I've gone. To me it is beautiful and tender and frail as the naked self is, and I shrink very much even from having it typed. Probably the typist would want to interfere".[13] Some 32 years later (and indeed 30 years after Lawrence's death) it was more than a typist that would seek to intervene. Upon its publication by Penguin Books, in 1963 they were to be tried at the Old Bailey under the Obscene Publications Act.[14] The degree to which Lawrence's work was puncturing the established social norms was famously highlighted when Counsel for the prosecution addressed the jury, inviting them to consider whether it was the kind of book "you would wish your wife or servants to read". The literary merit of the work prevailed and thus Lawrence's last novel was available to the public.

Within the overall need to speak out for an alternative view, there are two distinct threads which might further colour or distort the process, sometimes one running into the other. First there may be a (perhaps Neptunian) bid for escape from the mundane, to seek a more idealistic existence. Here one may find the Bohemian drop-out or the dreamer who either complains of being a suffering martyr because no one listens to them or has wonderful visions of being the saviour of the world when that world *does* listen to them! Alternatively one may find a type who, perhaps unsure of their own ability to communicate an individual point of view and stand behind it, will attach themselves to some kind of 'cult thinking'. They may appear very eloquent about this since they are simply repeating that with which they have been indoctrinated. However, such types may be acting out a rebellion against conventional values but without a clear sense of an alternative purpose.

Finally, the chart of Germaine Greer portrays someone who, with typical Sun/Moon First Quarter ability to meet a challenge, has very much forged her own road in life. There is a strong Uranian theme in the chart since the Sun rises in Aquarius and is in First Quarter phase to the Moon conjunct Uranus itself. The Saturn/Moon phase is New, suggesting someone with a sense of identity very powerfully shaped by experiences of the original environment, which again may have been Uranian (rebellious, broken, different, at odds with one's personal needs). In this connection too the

Moon/Uranus conjunction in the 4th house of home/family/roots lies on the nodal axis suggesting an additional emotional vulnerability/insecurity and a need to extricate oneself in order to develop a degree of self-mastery and powerful purpose (North Node, 10th, Scorpio).

When it comes to the Jupiter/Mercury phase against the backdrop of these fundamental threads, we similarly find the capacity to embrace that which is alternative, defying conventions and/or containing a prophetic awareness of changing precepts. The phase contains the strong rising Sun position in Aquarius (in wide opposition to Pluto as well as the contact to Moon/Uranus) leading us also to suppose a powerful need and ability to break through established patterns and bring to light alternative and transformative outlooks. The ground swell of shifting socio-cultural outlooks of the 1960s brought within its wake a further wave of feminist activity, previously arising in the earlier part of the century, more popularly referred to as the Women's Liberation Movement and among the several publications emerging came *The Female Eunuch*.

Professor Greer's early background in Australia was deeply unhappy, those around her seemingly unable to respond positively to her vital, individual and headstrong temperament. Having experienced cold distance and lack of affection from her father and a regime of corporal punishment from her mother, she left home at eighteen, eventually making her way to the opposite side of the world to continue her academic studies in England. Her book, published in 1970, not only helped blaze a growing trail in feminist writing (*inter alia* Betty Friedan's *The Feminine Mystique* had appeared in 1963) but also rapidly established her as a writer, broadcaster and academic, for which she remains in the forefront today. With a reputation for dismissiveness, confrontation and even vitriolic attack in her interactions with others, nevertheless she also has a rapier wit, humour and does not flinch from speaking out on burning, alternative issues that she feels need to be thrust into an arena.

9: Mars and Venus

Like the other planets with a double rulership, Mars has two faces: direct, spontaneous action is associated with Aries/1st house while delayed action, borne of subtle planning and nurturing a desire until it is ready to move out, is more the province of Scorpio/8th house. Mythologically, it is akin to the difference between the Roman Mars and the Greek Ares, but whether we look at this planet from one or other of these perspectives, the objective is the same: to energize the will in order to achieve what is required.

It sounds simple enough but of course we can run into difficulties since what we desire is not always the same as what is valued and Mars may just as frequently *not* go after what Venus wants. This is clearer to us if we consider that the traditional meaning of Mars is of a physical, sexual drive to fulfilment and that of Venus is emotional love. We may want (Venus) a loving, stable relationship, yet our Mars drive could involve us in a series of torrid affairs, thus detrimental to what is wanted. (Or it could be the other way around of course). Furthermore, we need to bear in mind that while the emphasis with Venus is on *personal* pleasure (or at least avoidance of pain) it can also operate to draw us to that which may not be *socially* approved and could thus constellate *displeasure*. And since it is concerned with avoiding pain it may also manifest as dislike, disgust, even hate. All these factors can be a major source of conflict in our lives, often reflected in the Mars/Venus phase.

We learn the three R's from early in life and grow with the ability to read, write and do our sums as second-nature. But there are two further R's which can be every bit as complex, at least to begin with, and sometimes throughout our lives – Rapport and Relating. Our willingness to be open to interaction with our fellow beings, together with the ways we approach this, is similarly crucial to our development and well-being. There are, of course, all kinds of relationships and they take place in all kinds of settings and over varying duration. Rapport is the ingredient that can turn any relationship into a positive experience for, as we learn to build it, all parties feel a movement forward in shared exchange, a sense of meaning and purpose.

When it comes to romantic love, one of the difficulties human beings experience is of not being quite sure what it actually is. There are many *assumptions* about it (including the assumption that it is understandable!) and most of these run along the lines of equating love to supreme happiness, if only it could be found. If and when we *do* find it, either it is a sustained and transformative experience or we inhabit Cloud Nine for a while until our preconceptions of love become confronted with the realities of who we are in relation to who the loved person is. For many of course the whole matter may settle down into a comfortable and workable, rapport-building, ongoing relationship which may even last the rest of their lives. For others, however, there can be an idealistic craving for love which is hard to relinquish in spite of the suffering which tends to go with it. Indeed its appeal is perpetuated in the name of 'romance', so much so that an entire music industry of popular songs (as well as much classic literature and opera) is built on its premise of yearning, searching, hurting. Songs of sadness and loss (with their can't-live-without-you/please-don't-go type lyrics) form the larger percentage of popularity rather than the joy and fulfilment we tend to equate with 'Love' and are hoping to find. In other words our experience of love, while craved and sought on the one hand, is frequently a chronicle of disillusionment on the other.

The Mars/Venus phase can provide a clear context for the way we approach this whole situation. It has been said that we never really meet another person and see them as *they* are; instead we see them as *we* are, yet imposing our value-judgments upon them which gets in the way of seeing their larger meaning and purpose. While Mars and Venus may not always be in alignment/agreement within us, if we take them as a pairing and submit them to our previous analogy of a Control Tower (Mars) and aeroplane sent out on a flight (Venus), then – and in the same way we saw with the Moon in Chapter 3 – very often the first planet to be met by Venus can point us to the essence of what, or who, we are striving to meet. If we are working with synastry, each individual chart should be considered before submitting them to cross-comparison, but the Mars/Venus phases in each chart can also be evaluated (preferably also in the light of at least Sun/Moon and Saturn/Moon as main background phases) as well as any other planets contained within the phase.

Mars and Venus do not function solely in the province of our relationships but also have much to say about our interior equilibrium, sense of worthiness

(Venus/Libra/Taurus) and physical abilities in individual, inspiring and committed ways (Mars/Aries/Scorpio). Thus this pairing also reflects our creative endeavours – whether these are acts of joy, challenge, obligation, duty or conscience – things we do, or are, if for no other reason than we feel we owe it to ourselves and others. Much of our personal pleasure comes through social interaction and Venus is the part of us which seeks to be compromising and pleasing, whether we have direct contact with others or not. Pleasing others can be achieved indirectly by producing something that gives delight – a musical score, a flower arrangement, an oil painting... These may be undertaken solely for oneself also, and here we are reminded that pleasing self and pleasing others conveys that other Venusian quality: that of balance, which is often a fine and fluctuating one. When Venus is operating with a concern for mutual ease and balanced interactions, it reflects the needs of Libra/7th, whereas when functioning from self-pleasure, experiencing enjoyment and valuing one's own sense of aliveness it is more synonymous with Taurus/2nd house.

Overall, Mars/Venus is the inner drive to express ourselves as creative, loving, sharing and sexual beings. Our approaches to relating, accommodating and creating rapport are reflected by their phase, but so too are our urges to bring into the world that which we feel expresses our unique resources and sensitivities.

Mars/Venus New Phase

Love and creativity are spontaneous here, even a little impatient. Not that impatience is necessarily a feature of this Phase but, given the planets involved, their immediacy can feel pulled into manifesting in this way. This is not the type of person who sits down and *thinks* about what or who they love, or what they want to create; they just feel it and move on it. Being in love, and indeed physical love, is extremely important to them. While for most of us it makes us feel 'special', that we stand out and all our energies are heightened, for this phase often the sheer intensity of the desire nature is enough to attract relationships into their lives without them necessarily having to take any contrived action to find them. It can also be very *easy* for them to fall in love since there is a wholly subjective idealism operative and this can including falling 'head over heels', being in love with love, carrying an endless 'torch' for someone and/or love at first sight.

The closer to the conjunction, the more there is a need simply to let the inner desire energy have its way, for this takes them where (and to whom) they instinctively feel drawn. Their warmth and charisma can operate as pure animal charm, attracting people powerfully. Once their feelings are aroused they are usually very good at taking initiatives, often being the one who essentially stirs the relationship into life. When the phase nears the 30° semi-sextile, they often feel 'so full' with love they have enough to serve the entire world, or they are *bursting* with much they want to give and create. If these two planets are occupying sober or quiet positions in the overall chart, then there may simply be resonance to an inner sense of rightness about a relationship (or indeed an equally sure sense of wrongness about it). Either way, they act upon their instincts.

Planets contained within the New Phase, as well as the first planet to be met by Venus as it pulls away from Mars, can provide further clarification. One woman had been invited to a family gathering because a distant cousin from Australia was visiting. A couple of days later she was asked by a friend to go to a local art exhibition – but she turned that down because it would clash with the family party. On the day itself, she drove to her relatives' house (or so she thought) – half an hour later she 'came to' and found herself … outside the art gallery! She had no idea how she had got there, it was as if some kind of automatic pilot had driven the car, she said. She glanced at her watch and figured she had time to at least have a quick look at the exhibition, maybe stay ten minutes or so and then go on to the family party. She went through the swing doors, only to collide slap-bang with a man coming out. Profuse apologies emerged from both as they picked themselves up and checked for injuries – and looked at one another… (*cue violins*) – well, that was fifteen-odd years ago and they are very happily married with a couple of children. Pure instinctual Mars/Venus New Phase. And in her chart, the first planet out from Venus is Uranus, in the 5th. She met (nay, collided with) him at an art gallery… suddenly!

Sometimes this phase-type may feel it is not always easy to be faithful to a partner since they seem to need the excitement of pursuit and new relationships (although please note this is by no means a 'given' in this phase). This, in turn, can stem from a need to experience the power of their own physical and sexual attractiveness, perhaps to feel a constant sense of *aliveness*. But there can also be accompanying vulnerabilities and frustrations such as may arise in any relationship but which New Phase finds hard to tolerate, such as humiliations or lack of emotional support. Often there is an instinctual impulse for both finding and giving unconditional love. I asked one client who was going through a divorce (and at the point where they were 'dividing up the spoils', i.e. furniture, possessions etc.) "What's the most important thing for you in all this?" Straight away she said "My dog! I mean, he just loves me no matter what – doesn't matter what I look like, how much I earn, whether my lipstick's on straight, or if I've remembered to clean the kitchen floor… whatever – that dog just plain loves me. *And I don't have that anywhere else in my life*". Here in simple words was the innermost need for instinctual connection – something animals are far closer to than humans and we have much to learn from them.

Similarly in creative endeavours, the same kind of passion and spontaneity can be seen. Whether one is creative in the sense of being an artist or otherwise developing a life in which something new is being brought into existence as ideas or turning points, it will usually be found that these do not have any prior planning attached to them but arise from an unspoken dimension and are responded to instinctively, often with vivid, spectacular outcome. Pedro Linares was a Mexican artist, born in 1906, who in the 1950s became extremely ill and was close to death. Happily he recovered, but he began to tell his family that he *had* in fact died. More than this, he reported that on his way through to the afterlife he became aware of the uncanny presence of very strange figures emerging from wooded hillsides around him. Some were part-bird, part-snake, others fantastical dragons or spiders, some winged creatures, others with scales and plumes, each constantly changing from one shape to another and crying out "*Alebrije, Alebrije*" (a word which has no meaning in the Mexican language).

Don Pedro was part of the densely-populated *Mercado de Sonora* district of Mexico City, known for its herbs, witchdoctors, magic potions, and the colourful world of *cartoneros* – artists with a folk tradition of handicrafts and papier-mâché objects, skills handed down from one generation to another and evolved largely through religious festivals. Continuing to speak of the figures he had seen in his 'delirium', gradually his family encouraged him to depict these creatures through his artwork. At first he made fairly plain looking figures, but then added more colour and flair, evolving through his own imagination, ingenuity and craftsmanship methods of reproducing these "*Alebrijes*" (as they are now known).[1]

We do not have a birth time for Pedro Linares, but Mars/Venus are in

New Phase containing Mercury. The Mars end of the phase is powerfully conjunct Neptune and the Sun, in Cancer. Here was an artist working in the family environment where, in the Mexican tradition, skills are handed down from father to child and all the family are involved in the process. The triple conjunction of Sun/Neptune/Mars is opposed by Uranus (illumination and transformational experience) in Capricorn (the traditional family environment and customs) – and (possibly) in square to the Moon, ruled by Venus.[2] Here moreover is the instinctive artist who, from his own inner perception (Mercury), created a whole new *genre* from symbolism arising out of a profound, unprompted and unsought transformational experience. In doing so he formed a new bridge between folk art and fine art which, in turn, has given rise to exhibitions in world-renowned museums and specialist collections.[3]

As well as an outpouring of talents and skills, we may also see goodwill and generosity of spirit. The rivetting Josephine Baker, she of the spectacular Banana Skirt dance, was born with the phase from the end of Gemini to early Cancer, with Neptune contained between the two, opposing Uranus in the creative 5th house. From an early life living on the slum-streets of Missouri, she became world-renowned for her dancing, singing and acting, always exciting, dramatic, magnificent in her self-presentation. She adopted many orphaned children from different ethnic backgrounds and France as her home country, assisting the French Resistance during the Second World War, for which she was decorated, as well as the Civil Rights movement in America.

Monumental in his philanthropic activities, Andrew Carnegie started life as a cotton mill bobbin boy and went on to become the world-renowned steel magnate and industrialist who bestowed his vast fortune upon British, European and American organizations as well as donating numerous personal gifts through various trusts. The phase occurs in Sagittarius, possibly straddling the 2nd house cusp (which would be particularly apt) but since the birth time is uncertain this cannot be relied upon. Nevertheless the theme of New Phase generosity of spirit, creativity and spontaneity in relating is seen in his legacy of free public libraries throughout the world so that all might benefit from self-education. Carnegie was adamant in his assertion that a wealthy person should indeed supply the needs of their own family but beyond that it should be utilized and spread among the community for the benefit of all.

Mars/Venus Crescent Phase

Synonymous with the underground seed moving out from its casing and extending first roots into the soil, Mars/Venus in this phase brings to relating/creativity an inner approach of struggle, yet determination. Often this person feels unsure about love, sexuality, relating and creating and patterns from the past may not support them in the encounters they make. Consequently they go forward in a bid to transcend these, willingly but with some trepidation. A frequent manifestation is they may have great doubts about a relationship but enter into it anyway, convincing themselves it really *is* what they want or that it will 'work out in the end somehow or other' but it often proves to be arduous. Others will bring to relating a more dour caution, uncertain of whether they can or cannot take the plunge. And yet others still, riding over their inner misgivings and acting seemingly 'out of phase', will present themselves as passionate and sensual, even strident, in asserting their sexuality, but much of this may turn out to be a lot of 'noise' to obfuscate the fact that they are not as sure in their approach to this area of life as they would like to be.

Generally, it can take time for this phase type to move beyond hesitancy, establish their 'roots' carefully and go forward with a true evaluation of their own desires rather than any those around may impose or wish for them. In some instances, this may be a person who relates to and perhaps marries someone not 'acceptable' to their family/friends and, if their feelings about this person are sure and true, the struggle and effort then comes through maintaining their position on the basis of those principles. Similarly, there may be situations where there are religious or racial differences, or where one's sexual orientation may be seen as a threat or 'disgrace' to traditional outlooks. Still another variation on the thread is that the person may have come from a background which contained only very negative experiences in relating and therefore there is a built-up belief that love is a hard road, does not really work in the long term, and so one might as well not hold out much in the way of hopes about it anyway.

More positively the hesitancy and caution may have a quite simple basis. For example, Mars in Capricorn in Crescent Phase to Venus in Pisces might have a fundamental drive for stability and longevity of relationship (Capricorn) and the 'mission' of Venus is to tread carefully (Crescent) in finding a person of sensitivity and compassion (Pisces) to help fulfil this need. Similarly the patient capacity to build something up and keep working at it, so characteristic of this phase, can be seen in the person who goes about relating with a determination that is hard to resist. In meeting someone they feel drawn to, they may doggedly pursue that person with all the persistence of a terrier-dog with a new bone… even in the face of repeated refusals and brush-offs! Conversely, if they are on the receiving end of another person's attentions, but feel unsure or cannot return the feelings, then they will dig their heels in and be unwilling to take the risk.

This is a person who needs to develop their own values, but not be hassled in any way. Small children with this phase, for example, do not always excitedly join in the party-games, balloons and ice-cream scenarios. I recall an aunt of mine arriving to take me out for the day when I was six. Since she was a very kind and warm person, and I rarely saw her, I was eager to go. However, she decided that a visit to the local fairground was just the thing. (I have Mars/Venus right at the end of New Phase and beginning of Crescent). I *hated* it. Cried all day. All that noise, people flying through the air in dangerous-looking contraptions, sad little goldfish being despatched into plastic bags for onward transmission to God knows what fate, and I powerless to save them from their plight. No, no and thrice no. Not even my aunt's kind purchase of a stick of pink candy floss would cut any ice with me. The point is that, however well-intentioned, one simply cannot force Mars/Venus Crescent (nor any phase) to relate out of synch with its inner nature. This one in particular takes time to emerge – it is not First Quarter which would be only too ready to boogie all night or go to fairgrounds. Crescent needs to find its own way of *anchoring* in order to develop 'inner-rooted-ness'.

In developing creativity, here too there is a sense of applied and consistent effort but if this is not met they can get stuck in feelings of inadequacy, perhaps settling for second-best or experiencing general constraint and hardship in unfolding their skills. Others still, in recognition of the need for applied effort, work hard to summon up the courage to reach out for what they know they can do, and do it to the highest of their ability. Often they spend time working quietly in the background, even with toil and struggle, yet the creative work carries resilience, stamina and resoluteness as foundational qualities. The chart of George Harrison is a case in point.

Known as 'the quiet one' of The Beatles, Harrison was also noted for being the least smiling of the four on stage due to profound concentration on his guitar work. The phase conspicuously contains Mercury at the IC in opposition to Pluto/MC denoting intense focus. Writer, broadcaster and friend of The Beatles, Hunter Davies, noted that "as with everything he has always taken up, he does it almost with a fanaticism. He sometimes plays the sitar all day long".[4]

It had been ever thus for George. Born also with Sun/Moon Disseminating (fluidity of expression) and Saturn/Moon Gibbous (again, as with Mercury/Pluto, deep focus and concentrated effort), he taught himself the guitar, practising *endlessly* sometimes until his fingers bled, so determined was he to master the instrument. The same applied as he progressed into Indian music after a meeting with Ravi Shankar in 1965 where again he found "it's murder on your fingers".[5] Together with yoga exercises, he learnt how to hold a sitar which took a great deal of practice due not only to its awkward shape and size, but also because it necessitated the gourd on the bottom of the instrument resting in the ball of the left foot. But George was nothing if not persistent, even driven, in his quest to develop his skills. Derek Taylor, Press Officer for the group, speaks of him as always endeavouring to be first class, rejecting the sloppy standards of others who were not in pursuit of excellence.[6] Less prolific a songwriter than Lennon and/or McCartney, George Harrison's early contributions were either dismissed or relegated, but later compositions such as *Something*[7] and *My Sweet Lord*[8] set him apart. That *Something* was the only Beatles' song ever covered by Frank Sinatra speaks volumes for the excellence of the song... and indeed its composer.

Like his contemporary and colleague Henri Cartier-Bresson, Robert Capa was a photo-journalist. The birth time is unknown but the Moon's passage for the day was from 16°–29° Cancer. As in Cartier-Bresson's chart, we can discern in-phase links with the creation of visual images, particularly via the Moon/Neptune conjunction picking up on Uranus opposite (striking images). But the phase itself, being Crescent, suggests not only persistence but also has the enhanced incentive of the quintile aspect moving towards the 90° square. Here we see the photographer in a 'blood 'n' guts' struggle and Capa was a photo-journalist *par excellence* on many war fronts, most notably the Spanish Civil War and World War II.

Born in Hungary, he left home at 19 after a political anti-government skirmish, and sought work in Germany and France, taking on whatever he could find in freelance journalism. Here is the Crescent theme of leaving a homeland (a past) to stretch out 'roots' into a new future, in furtherance of a creative drive. Over and over, he risked his life on five different war fronts, in particular with the allied troops during in June 1944 for the famous D-Day landing on Omaha Beach. His definitive images of the Normandy invasion have become classics. With the Venus end of the phase trine to Uranus and squaring Pluto, it was the capturing of pungent, dramatic moments that was of most importance to Capa. Mars in Cancer, which can certainly exude a tenacity second to none, is in enterprising opposition to Jupiter in Capricorn which carries its own signature of dogged persistence and tough work. Capa's sustained courage and images of soldiers in many settings, fighting for their country and their lives, underpins his fame as the world's greatest combat photographer.

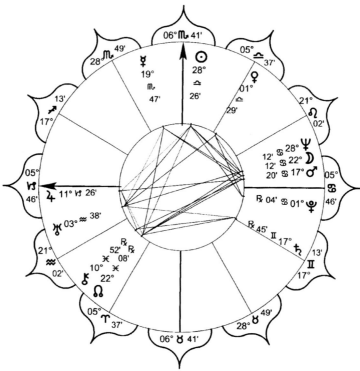

Robert Capa (Noon chart)

In his relating life, Capa is reputed to have suffered much in the way of loneliness and insecurity, especially after the loss of his first love who was killed during the Spanish Civil War (the Mars end of the phase again possibly containing Moon, linking to Neptune, while Venus squares Pluto). A subsequent lover eventually married somebody else, after which he is thought to have had a love affair with Ingrid Bergman. This might have led to marriage but the relationship had its struggles and moreover he did not want to live in America. In the event he never married and sadly his life came to an end at the age of forty when he stepped on a land mine during the 1954 Indochina War.

Mars/Venus First Quarter Phase

Here too there can be an underlying sense that the whole area of relating or creativity is fraught with difficulty. The difference here is that there is usually more conscious awareness of this and the frustrations can be correspondingly greater; but then so can the drive to overcome them. This type will usually act very assertively in relating, seeing it as a challenge to be met. Even if they do not do so overtly themselves, they tend to attract people who either act assertively towards them or are of such personality that it draws from them an impulsive fighting quality. This phase always likes to keep things moving and there could correspondingly be a tendency to live a somewhat hassled relating life, even one where fights and arguments hold sway.

They can be particularly inclined to think in terms of making conquests and a distinct danger for them is to look upon their partner as conquered territory that must be held. Hence they can be especially prone to jealousies or fears about a partner's loyalty. Related to this, I have sometimes found that there is a tendency for them to think in terms of the personal gains to be had from a relationship, rather than the quality of the relationship itself. Similarly, there can be an inclination to chase after what or who is wanted, right there and then, without giving it any consideration and probably burning the candle at both ends. Several relationships (or creative ventures) may be kept juggled in the air at the same time, but certainly the drive is for action, 'grab it (him/her) while you can' or forever wanting to hasten a relationship along to an end goal (and possibly a self-indulgent one). In short, it can all be quite 'heady', exciting and stimulating, but often with a sense of overkill, but which they will probably see as a deep commitment to the loved one.

While usually taking a managerial lead in an established relationship, when the phase reaches further towards the trine aspect the capacity for being quite so upfront eases. They may indeed be the boss in the relationship but it is not so stark and demanding, perhaps more cajoling and encouraging. Or it may be the person who actually instigates the relationship, calls all the shots ... but it does not appear that way. It reminds me of an old song from the 1950s about a man chasing a girl but it's she who catches him![9]

The challenging quality may also manifest as rebellion against a past pattern (as in Crescent phase) although here it is much more overt since we have reached the first Turning Point of the 90° square which has a bust-out-of-jail quality to it. This may be the person who can be decidedly out of step with what their background might wish for them or consider the norm. They may chase after (and fight hard for) relationships wholly unacceptable to those around or generally adopt a social life somehow not quite in keeping with what is expected of them. We can see this in the life of Princess Margaret, born with the phase from Mars in Gemini in the 3rd house to Venus in Libra 7th. With Mars as the Control Tower, squaring Mercury and thus calling for plenty of activity, Venus forms a rebellious and/or freedom-loving opposition to Uranus rising and square to Jupiter. Living such a set of dynamics within the confines of royal life might have been well nigh impossible, were it not for the T-square formation between Venus, Jupiter and Saturn conjunct a Capricorn Midheaven which adds a sense of duty to her overall personality. Margaret was the party-loving princess whose love affair with Group Captain Peter Townsend in the 1950s certainly flew in the face of royal protocol and, under pressure from Crown and Government, she renounced the possibility of marrying him. Her later marriage to Anthony Armstrong Jones ended in divorce and thereafter she was continually associated with a succession of (sometimes controversial) admirers, in what was variably perceived as a colourful, or scandalous, relating life.

In terms of developing creativity, this type can have outstandingly high impact. They may be found in music, theatre, literature... any platform where they can put a decided stamp on their environment. The creative ability to answer a challenge carries tremendous improvisation and it is rare (unless other attendant threads show otherwise) for them to remain unnoticed. George Gershwin has the phase within the easy-flow orb of the trine while Frank Sinatra has it right at the end of the phase, having already picked up the trine and Mars is in Leo 10th (the showman). Elvis Presley is another 10th house Mars with Venus also in Capricorn, but with the phase closer to the 90° turning point, thus with a more arresting, dramatic presentation (think white sequinned catsuit, much bejewelled hip belt). This is augmented by the 5th house (personal display) rulership of Mars, with Uranus in the 5th forming a very powerful and dynamic T-square with Venus in the 2nd opposite Pluto in the 8th – *All Shook Up...* indeed.[10]

Sometimes the ability to push through and have impact in a creative life dovetails with the ability to assert oneself in relating. Such a thread can be traced in the life of Mary Ann Evans, better known as 19th century novelist George Eliot.

Born with Sun/Moon in Crescent Phase at the sextile, she wove threads of moving out from the past with persistent determination to establish her own path. The Saturn/Moon phase is Last Quarter, where the building of one's identity comes eventually not from what one has been brought up in, even though one may go along with this for a while, but through

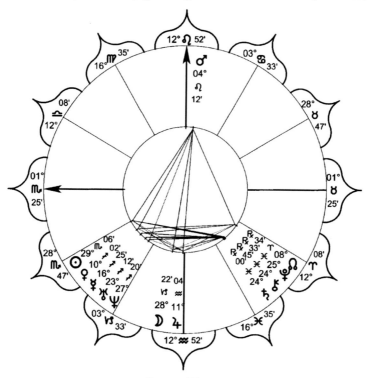

George Eliot

realigning oneself on a different road. The Jupiter/Mercury phase is similarly Last Quarter and again this involves a diversionary path to effect a new presentation of the self, standing for one's own perceptions, morals, values and progressive ideas.

Mary Ann's mother died when she was sixteen; her father was a land agent and a very religious man, to whom she was very close. In these early years she began to weave all three of the main threads outlined above: first she sought out and made new influential friends (Crescent Phase sextile seeking connection and anchoring); secondly, she began submitting articles to a local newspaper – unusual for a young lady of the Victorian era, but this was a girl with Crescent Phase 'guts' as well as Last Quarter drive to communicate her own perceptions. Thirdly, she began questioning the religion in which she had been brought up, refusing to attend church and this distressed her father greatly. For a while she went along with his needs for her to go to services, but inwardly Mary Ann always remained single-minded about her own views (Saturn/Moon Last Quarter), the Mars/Venus phase adding assertion of her own felt values.

After the death of her father, Mary Ann became Marian Evans and moved to London to earn her living. Here was the start for the Mars/Venus thread to break through in terms of both her creative abilities and her relating life. She had had one or two relationships, but with men who could not return her feelings... until she met George Henry Lewes. He was tied into an unhappy marriage, but did return her love and so they began to live together – scandalous behaviour for those times! Again a 'rebellious' thread where, like Princess Margaret, the pattern of relating does not meet with the acceptance of one's personal or collective environment. But through Lewes' support for her, Marian began to develop her gift for fiction writing which Lewes, (himself a writer) submitted to publishers on her behalf under the pen name of George Eliot. This, in order to protect her work from any association with scandal and because male writers attracted more respect. Her first novel, *Adam Bede*, was published in 1859 and, by the time *The Mill on the Floss* was ready for publication, her 'cover' was blown and her pen-name status revealed to the literary circles of London. The Mars/Venus phase stands at 126° therefore already imbued with the flow of the trine. In spite of her controversial personal life, the quality and stature of her works made them a success, to be followed later by her masterpiece, *Middlemarch*. George Eliot died in 1880 and although she merited burial alongside other great literary figures in Westminster Abbey, her denial of the Christian faith prevented this. She is, however, commemorated at Poet's Corner in the Abbey, her works forming an enduring part of British literary heritage.

Mars/Venus Gibbous Phase

With its capacity for analysis, one main thread occurring in this phase can be an over-intellectualized approach to love and relating, often obsessively so. A great deal of time is spent pondering and talking about love, endlessly trying to figure out what it is and how it all works. As a result, they may either be people who have great insight into their relating dynamics or, more usually, get into interminable discussions of their own and others' motives and desires, often to the point of tedium. They mull over every single thing seeking explanations, rationalizations, rehashing incidents and finding a multiplicity of justifications for their own behaviours and attitudes.

One woman consulted me when her marriage was beginning to feel "a little shakey". She had strong suspicions that her husband was seeing somebody else, but when (bearing in mind the "little shakey" wording) I asked her what she was actually feeling, she recited a huge litany of all the steps she had taken that had led to her suspicions – going through all kinds of bits of paper from his desk, the pockets of his suits, emails on his computer, cigarette ends in the ashtray of his car when he was a non-smoker, traces of perfume... all interspersed with "and then he said to me two Fridays ago... and then I said to him... and he said to me... and then there was the time he was rude to my mother..." and so on. And when I asked what it was she wanted to happen with this marriage, she replied with some irritation, "Well I don't know do I?!" and just ploughed on with the barrage of information as to who said what to whom and all the incriminating bits of evidence she had discovered.

This session clarified two things for me about this phase: first, when its sense of stability is threatened this type can indeed race around fanatically analyzing the situation till the cows come home and I was reminded that it can indeed be a painful experience. We want to rant and rage, grieve and even retaliate; only then may we be ready to turn to the deeper core of what is occurring and access a turning point. That in turn led to the realization that people of this phase *need* to go through the meticulous picking over every tiny morsel in their emotional lives *in order to* put them in touch with what they *do* actually feel in the here-and-now. What may seem to an onlooker as just a tiresome, self-justifying exercise can, if we suspend judgment, become the very prelude by which they eventually reach down into what is truly important for them on a feeling level. This can be especially so around the biquintile and quincunx aspects where insight as to what needs to be sorted out and rearranged can form additional threads of meaning.

Sometimes the relating life may be highly experimental, the person forever trying to figure things out as if engaged in a game of chess. "If I do this… will he/she still love me…? Or maybe if I… he/she might then…? Or perhaps if I threaten to leave then he/she will…" and so on. Again it is an intellectual, rather than a feeling, exercise and there may be an attendant pattern of reaching out to relate to someone just because it seems a good idea. But it frequently cannot be sustained because it is a strategy, based on 'relating from the head', that cannot withstand the test of either time or true feeling. A second thread is that this experimental theme can sometimes mean that the person will experience different *types* of relating, e.g. marriage or co-habitation, or explorations of sexual/gender diversity, until they reach a clarity as to who they are and what lies within them that they can bring to a relationship. But if this type is not able to come out of the analysis of everything they can become stuck in problems and prone to bitterness or holding grudges. If this becomes a repetitive pattern for the Gibbous type, it can be reflected in a tendency for them to get involved with partners who treat them badly or to whom they feel compelled to behave badly. More positively, however, they can respond to an appeal to see how their inner values (Venus) about love might be out of synch with the actions they take (Mars). Focusing upon such inner misalignment raises the awareness to the point where the relationships they build become a truer reflection of their inner feelings. Indeed I have worked with several professional relationship therapists with this phase, mirroring their ability to give deep consideration and understanding of the dynamics between two people.

The creativity of the phase also emerges through scrutiny, arranging, devising, putting things together. We find this in people who are able swiftly to see what is needed and how things fit; often they may be in the fields of design, architecture, engineering, even the construction of new legislation, or research processes. Artistically and creatively there is often a capacity for inventive and exquisite attention to detail. Here we may consider again William Blake whose 'Illuminated Books' are a supreme example of this creativity in action. In them he produced his own technique of producing illustrations and text without the need for separate plates and typesetting. Instead he devised a format for etching in relief using a copper engraving plate and impervious medium, then printing from the raised surface rather than incised lines. The technique involved protecting the text and illustration while etching away with acid the surface parts that did not print. Mars/Venus focused ingenuity in this phase enabled Blake both to devise and implement this demanding and laborious process, reflected in the fixity and staying power of Mars in Leo in the 2nd combined with steady, hardworking Venus in Capricorn in the 6th. His first successful use of the technique came in *Songs of Innocence* (1789) and *Songs of Experience* (1794), the prelude to a remarkable series of illuminated printing which was to occupy Blake to some degree for the remainder of his life.[11]

In this phase also the creative life may spring vividly from, or be allied to, painful or circuitous routes in exploring and expressing feelings with honesty.

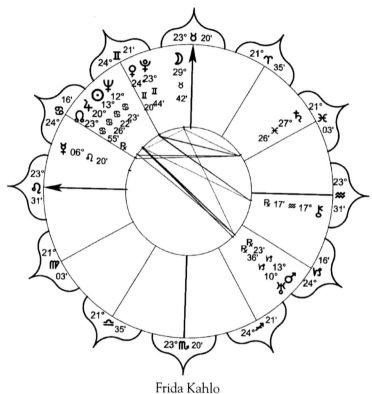

Frida Kahlo

One of the few Latin American artists to have achieved global reputation, Frida Kahlo's creativity and emotional relationships were inextricably interwoven. A road accident in her early adult life put her in hospital with a smashed spinal column and fractured pelvis, injuries from which she was to suffer all her life. At the same time it was to be the gateway to her life as an artist. Unable to move from her bed, her parents brought paints and brushes to her side, together with a mirror in which she could see herself. Thus began her series of formal self-portraits, all of them expressing the sense of burden, loss, pain and sorrow deeply focused (Gibbous) on the truth of what she saw and felt. A very striking looking woman (of German/Mexican/Indian extraction) she painted herself *in veritas*, making no attempt to prettify the dark eyebrows which met in the centre of her forehead or the moustached upper lip – one may say even a *defiant* adherence to the truth and detail of reality.

At the age of 21 she married the celebrated mural artist Diego Rivera. Her paintings continued to reflect her burden and pain as well as deep sadness at not being able to have children. The relationship with Diego was tumultuous, insatiable, impassioned and tormented. Diego was a philanderer, although Frida too reputedly had occasional affairs (allegedly with both sexes) prompting more grief and melancholy, plus there was much loneliness and homesickness for Frida when they travelled abroad, for she longed to feel 'rooted' (Scorpio on IC, Pluto conjunct Venus square Saturn in the 8th, and Moon in 10th house Taurus). All this weighed heavily upon her soul. The Mars/Venus Gibbous phase draws the eye at once into arresting dynamics of her chart as a whole, just as her paintings strike at us as symbolic portrayals of her inner emotional turmoil. Mars is dramatically conjunct Uranus in the creative 5th while Venus conjuncts Pluto in the 10th squaring an 8th house Saturn in Pisces, adding a sense of deep vulnerability and tragedy, but also an unwavering survival instinct. The first planet to be met by Venus is Neptune which conjuncts the Sun, adding to the signature of artistry as well as vulnerability and loss. This especially as the conjunction opposes the Mars/Uranus conjunction (again sudden catastrophe and impassioned drama). Moreover Sun and Uranus are chart ruler and ruler of the 7th respectively, which draws us to her personal development through relating being a main avenue through which all these threads would be woven.

From the point of view of the Gibbous propensity to become obsessively entwined with detail, Frido Kahlo could be said to be consumed not only by her relationship with her husband but also with Mexico itself. For Frida it was something of a higher truth that she and Mexico were inextricably linked, born as she was just prior to its revolution in 1910, a beloved homeland with which she constantly identified herself, as a child to a parent. Diego, on the other hand, was *her* 'child', over whom she loved to worryingly fuss (also Gibbous), but his infidelities were a constant source of anguish. Here, the lover (Mars/Uranus 5th) and child (a real child being a heartbreaking impossibility for her) become as one in her emotional turmoil. One self-portrait contains an image of a youthful Diego seated at the centre of her dark uni-eyebrow signifying her constant and obsessional thoughts about him. At the same time, the skilful, sharp and insightful elements of Gibbous Phase are equally traceable in her honesty. This, not only in relation to the absence of feminine vanity in her artistic self-portrayal, but also the open declaration of her sensuous passion and her avoidance of pretensions throughout life itself. Having been turned down by a previous lover (because of her physical disabilities) she wrote telling him that he deserved the very best in life "because you are one of the few people in this lousy world who are honest to themselves, and that is the only thing that really counts".[12]

Mars/Venus Full Phase

As this phase is directly opposite to New Phase, the need here is to learn to be reflective rather than spontaneous or impulse-driven, since the inner values/feelings and the desire nature can be, at least initially in life, decidedly at odds. In relationships, reflection comes from learning (often through hurtful experience) that it is important to be clear within oneself what is, or is not, truly wanted and sought. If this is not properly considered, or merely wafted over, there can be a tendency – even a *compulsion* – to chase after something (or someone) *other* than what is really wanted or needed. This may or may not be conscious, but it can put one on something of a collision course when it emerges that what they are really after does not square either with the choices they make or indeed how they present themselves. This major theme may be repeated several times before the person becomes aware of how prone s/he is to running this pattern.

Alan was a gregarious and interesting person with a distinct ease of communication. Mars was in Full Phase to Venus in the 3rd from Capricorn in the 9th house. He enjoyed the company of women and felt he had much to offer in terms of a long-term relationship, yet somehow could never seem to get past sustaining any beyond the first few dates. Gradually, we began to shine a light on the potential clash between the needs of his Venus and the drives and desires of his Mars. It took a while since it meant trawling through what precisely had occurred that resulted in the ending of each relationship. As we talked I began to realize that most of what Alan said revolved around his own interests – "I took her to watch me rowing on the Thames" or "We went to dinner with an old school chum of mine and his wife" or "we went on holiday together to Mexico as I've always wanted to go there". Barely any mention of what had interested each lady personally. Choosing the moment carefully and focusing on one woman he had been particularly sad to lose, I asked "What did you and Sarah mostly talk about when you were together?" The answer which came served to open up the phase. Alan said "Oh God...er...well, *me* mostly... oh God...no...ach!..all of the time!" So here was Venus needing to experience plenty of activity, communication, friends, interests, good social life – yet in a disparity with Mars in Capricorn in the 9th which harbours a drive to set itself upon a definite and dominant platform and retain freedom to, call all the shots, set and answer all the challenges in its own way. While undoubtedly well able to go out and 'get the girl', when it came down to brass tacks it was 'All About *Alan*'!

In a compulsion to chase after something or someone deemed to be necessary, yet contrary to their real needs, some people of this phase can generate an *inordinate* amount of drama in so doing. The romantic poet, Lord Byron, is a classic example, his very name lending itself to the dynamic that so pervaded his life, surging from self-obsessed scornful melancholia on the one hand to inflationary flights of passion and turmoil on the other.

In Byron's chart the phase is nearing the last degrees and at the doorway of Disseminating, thus the capacity to convey his varying emotional states through the written word. The Sun/Moon phase is also Full which so often accompanies a profound need for relationship such that one cannot conceive of life without it. Saturn/Moon phase is Gibbous, with few guidelines from which to build a sense of identity and therefore stepping into life feeling somewhat out on a limb and a tendency to latch on to whatever template for development he may have before him as being the safest thing to do.

In this latter connection there was a familial pattern where obsessions or capriciousness can be traced and so perhaps were merely repeated. Byron's father was something of a philanderer who had been married once before, squandered his first wife's fortune, then married Byron's mother, squandered her fortune too and then went off to live in France where he died. On Byron's mother's side, not only had there been the loss of her fortune (and inherited property), but her own father had committed suicide thus adding themes of much emotional turmoil and disarray into the mix. Moreover, she was a woman who related to her son with excessive and immoderate fondness but then was prone to take flight into paroxysms of violent rage.

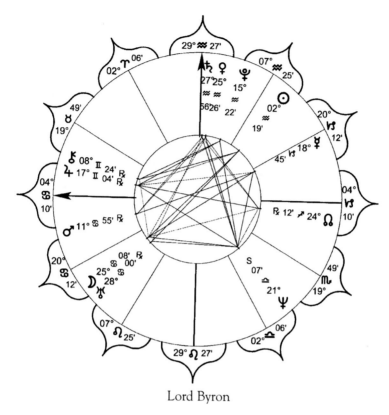

Lord Byron

We can therefore begin to see the outline of Full Phase context of division, if not instability. Mars rising in Cancer suggests a distinct drive to find a sense of emotional containment, yet the ruling Moon is conjunct Uranus and in a T-square with Mercury and Neptune, the ramifications of which were experienced as described in his relationship to his mother (above). The Venusian feeling-values of the phase are dominantly latched on to that planet's conjunction to Saturn at the (soon to move into Pisces) Midheaven, forming a grand trine with the inflationary Jupiter and Neptune (rulers of MC) and quincunx the Moon. The need to be extremely reflective in relating were flooded and submerged by these highly charged, self-indulgent dynamics which made for a life full of stormy passions, lofty vanity and brooding heartache, with the result that his moral compass pointed him every which way in his complex series of love and marriage experiences.

As an extremely handsome young man, the world was Byron's oyster in terms of his position and his skills, yet not much peace of mind with one inflamed passion after another taking him to soaring heights followed by fluttering down into displays of an aching, despairing, sorrowful heart. Such contradictions were also echoed in his response to his mother's death as well as the demise of his marriage. He had little affection for his mother during her life but upon her death he claimed that he had had only one friend in all the world "and now she is gone". And, having clearly given his wife the impression that he would die of a broken heart if she did not marry him, she succumbed – whereupon he treated her with harshness and eccentricity and finally threw her out. Once she was safely back home with her own family (together with their child), Byron pined for reconciliation with her, professing great love for his child... but then went to live in Italy and embarked upon a whole new life of decadence.

Key questions for those of this phase can be "Do I *really* want what initially excites me?", or "Does including this person in my life really align itself to my values about relating?" or even "Can I handle this? Can I sustain it?"... and perhaps ending up with "What is the fulfilment I am truly looking for in this person (or situation, event, action)?" At the end of the day there is much potential for the coming together of desires and inner values within the self through the seeking of higher realms of awareness which transcend the sense of separateness between who we are and what we strive or yearn for. It often takes most of us much of our lives to tread painfully through the seeking of outer fulfilment via another person, situation or activity, together with all the blamings, disappointments and negativities, only to find that we return again and again to what composes our inner being. The 'seeking' quality of Full Phase Mars/Venus can lead us to realizations as to the synchronicity of what arises outwardly in our lives as being an integral reflection of what lies within. Like the garden, it takes some digging, continued maintenance, a bit of uprooting or replanting here and there, but since we cannot change another person (however irksome we may perceive them to be) it is ultimately – to paraphrase T.S. Eliot – "at the still point of the turning world... there the dance is".[13] This awareness dynamic is one of the potential gifts of Full Phase when we allow ourselves to stand openly at its doorway.

Mars/Venus Disseminating Phase

Rather like the Gibbous type, those with Mars/Venus here have very definite ideas about what they want from a relationship and how to go about getting it. The main difference is that Gibbous will use its incisive mind to adopt a strategy that fits a specific situation, whereas Disseminating has more of a general *idealized* picture about what a relationship should be. There can be some tendency to stage-manage their relationships by subtly casting others into roles which fit this prescribed image. Sometimes their ideas can be so definite and their capacity for putting them into action so fluent that they can create problems for themselves by being too dogmatically certain that their way is the only right one.

This person can be absolutely charming in the way s/he moves ahead into relationships with reassuring confidence. However, much can depend on how well their basic notions about love actually square with the reality of the other person and the situation generally. As long as they interact with, and especially fall in love with, people whose basic views fit their own idealized picture, love will run smoothly. But if they come up against someone whose assumptions, approaches and experiences are different, they can be completely thrown off-balance. The results can be many and varied, from whimpering in hurt and vulnerability, to ending the relationship quickly then finding another and running exactly the same pattern, to creating great stormy arguments and heading for the divorce courts armed with an outraged sense of being exploited, to petty or seething blame and/or spite. One only has to consider that this phase appears in the chart of King Henry VIII to see how thrown off-balance one can be when one's cherished notions are not upheld in reality by a partner!

This type will do anything to hold on to basic beliefs about love and in the process fail to recognize that other people operate under different patterns which they feel have equal validity. A frequent manifestation is that this person will always believe it is the partner that has to change when things go wrong. An experience of several relationships of this type and slowly, slowly we are led to the realization that we need to look inside and review the contents of own attitudes. Running parallel to this, there may also be a tendency to model one's approach to love on some romantic notion or that it should follow the lines of a great sweeping romance from history, literature or the movie-screen. Perhaps more specifically in today's world it might be to match it to those of the tabloid celebrities, emulating these assiduously in the belief that this is how love and marriage should be. A key danger is one of 'shallowness', a light dusting of geniality in social situations where little tokens of pleasantness are used to great aplomb, but which are really serving some idealized picture. It can be the person who greets you across a room with "Darling! How *wonderful* to see you!" while looking over your shoulder with shining eyes to see if anybody more interesting might be coming into the room. The essence of this is not a sneakiness so much as it is a need for this person to relate in the way they have pictured life, preferably flowing smoothly like a gentle river. In the process, they will report what they think they *should* feel (i.e. is 'nice', 'acceptable') rather than what they *do* actually feel.

Geoffrey, with Sun/Moon First Quarter from Aquarius to Taurus, Saturn/Moon New from Aries to Taurus and Mars/Venus Disseminating from Gemini to Aquarius, consulted me in 1992 complaining about his wife. He was fed up with her and wanted a divorce – "I want *out* of this marriage!" he announced vociferously, striding up and down the room. Taking things one step at a time, I asked if he had talked things over with his wife, what were her feelings etc. But it emerged that Geoffrey had very, very idealized and solid views – Man is King in His Own Castle, Master of his Own Home, Man Calls the Shots, woman is submissive, a servant... etc. My personal thoughts were that there was little chance of such a notion surviving in today's world, yet he had managed to attract to him and marry two wives previously. The charm and ease of the phase became clear as he recounted these relationships, how he had lavished all manner of things upon each lady, pursuing one of them to the opposite side of the world to win her fair hand. Both of these wives he had divorced when they failed to meet the criteria. When I repeated my query as to whether he had talked things over with his current wife, he said, "Oh she just won't listen – she just goes into one of her damned long silences and she's so manipulative and controlling, I tell you she even *threatens* me sometimes".

CR – "How does she threaten you, what does she threaten you with?"

Geoffrey – "She threatens to **leave me**!"

CR – "But isn't that what you want? You came here saying you wanted your marriage to end."

The features of Geoffrey's face rearranged themselves to display a distinct level of dark scorn and frustration – hugely understandable when you consider that his treasured notions of what a relationship should be were being confronted and challenged. But only then could we start a proper conversation about the situation and how it might be fitting or unfitting to the true nature of either of them. The current wife was born

with Mars/Venus in First Quarter Phase and her chart contained strong
Saturnian and Plutonic aspect patterns to the personal planets, so it seemed
she too was unlikely to be a submissive kitten who would purr and roll
over to accommodate his dogmatic ideology. This proved to be so as he
continued to unfurl the story, ending with the roar "she *continually* usurps
my authority!". I must admit I shot a quick glance at the calendar on my
wall to make quite sure I really was living in the twentieth century, but more
than anything it became clear that Geoffrey's difficulties in relating were
unlikely to abate unless there could be some dismantling of the cherished
certainties he held about the rightness of his point of view.

Princess Diana also had very definite ideas about relating – people should
be hugged, a husband should love his wife and she should not have to make
appointments to see him even if he is the Prince of Wales, children should
be brought up in a happy, emotionally-secure environment rather than stiff
formality, and so on. The Disseminating Phase in her chart involved the 5th
house Venus position and included her Cancerian Sun, hence the warmth
and caring for which she was known and indeed remembered. Had she
married into a situation more freely able to match these values within her,
all might have been very well but they came right up against the pungent
severity of royal life and the inner pattern of her husband who likewise was
contending with emotional vicissitudes within the same powerfully difficult
context. (The Mars/Venus Phase in Prince Charles' chart is Last Quarter
which we shall examine next).

The question of authenticity can arise in terms of both relating and
creativity. These people can be remarkable in their flair for developing any
creative line – be they painters, writers, or administrators of some kind.
Whatever they do, they often have a knack of getting things to flow well
together, to be streamlined and vibrant all at the same time; yet sometimes
they may need to be aware that they could be limiting themselves if they are
merely perpetuating what they have learnt from others rather than devising
something new out of it or remaining only on superficial levels. In this
connection the person may be engaged in a career, sport, or other pursuit,
but find difficulty in following it to the heights and successes they may *truly*
wish for themselves because they are coming from *a set of ideas* about it
rather than the actual inner felt experience of doing them.

Authenticity in relating can also reveal a tendency to repress deeper
feelings. As touched upon earlier, love then becomes expressed more as a

sentimentality, held at surface level and surrounded with fluffy pink hearts and teddy bears. Such a person may again be full of charm and ease but it tends to be placatory, oozing sweetness and an ability to 'say all the right things'. Where grief, despair or anger are expressed to this person they may offer only soft consolatory attempts to dissuade someone from such emotions and look on the bright side instead. Fear of conflict may underpin this person only presenting themselves as Mr. Nice Guy or Miss Sweetness-and-Light. The Jungian psychologist Marie-Louise von Franz identified this dynamic as a dilemma of western culture where fully-embodied passionate feeling is robbed of its visceral energy.[14] Instead we have whole swathes of people wandering around in what Mark Barrett in turn called a 'soppy niceness' with each other.[15] Moreover, von Franz alluded to Eros being confined to a cellar, awaiting an opportunity to break out. The more the energy expresses itself merely as sentimentalized feeling, the darker and more angry, even brutal, may be the shadow behind it. We saw a little of this with Geoffrey – a very personable man who sweet-talked his way through three wives promising them the Moon but when the jig was up and they did not follow the set ideal he espoused, he became a veritable Vesuvius. But I suppose it could have been worse... could've been Henry VIII!

Mars/Venus Last Quarter

This person is usually very well aware of his or her potential for entering into and maintaining a satisfying relationship, or developing their creative gifts; yet there is frequently difficulty (at least earlier in the life) in being able to manifest even a small part of this potential. As a result s/he may spend quite a lot of time experiencing a great amount of friction in these areas of life, even chronic dissatisfaction. The phase is synonymous with the point where a plant must now be harvested and it is usual to find that the individual lives a life where one set of experiences is gone through until a turning point of one kind or another becomes clear to them. If they look below the surface manifestations of their lives, they will see that their past has served to bring them to this juncture... although whether the path is taken or not is a moot point.

Difficulties may well form part of the younger emotional life but eventually, through them, the individual is propelled into turning to that which is truer to their nature as a whole. There may be heartache, loss, strife, 'wrong choices', challenges, and amongst it all often a compulsion to chase after what is not wanted, rather than what is. This is similar to Full Phase, but whereas, there, the inner purpose was to drive the person into being more reflective, here at Last Quarter it is as if they are trying to prove to themselves that all they have ever been led, from the past, to believe about love can no longer be adhered to and needs definite transformation. Their task is to lift out and move on from them. Before any of this becomes conscious, however, and in pursuing someone they do *not* really want they may tell themselves that at least it is something new and different, at least it might lead to a sense of adventure, or perhaps it is for no other reason than it seems a good idea at the time, there is no-one else around, so why not marry him or her?

There may also be a need to fulfil a sense of duty, keep the peace and appease a familial/societal expectation, yet an inability ultimately to sustain it for a far deeper loving self begins to claim recognition and expression instead. Here we may meet those who feel compelled to enter into relationships which are expedient, the 'marriage of convenience' orchestrated for personal gain or to protect wealth, family title, inheritance or property, or even forge empires, but with little or no consideration for their truer personal capacity for love. The 'mistake' then serves the purpose of awakening that individual to the turnaround where who s/he really is, as a loving person ready to commit at a soul level, can emerge. Still others may soldier on with first choices but go through a convoluted questioning, even agonizing, as to what love really is, especially if the earth is not moving and the heart is not singing as one has been led to believe they should. It is through experiencing the pain of their choice that they begin to see that on some level they needed to have it that way, i.e. *so that* they can prove to themselves that all their prior conditioned beliefs about relating do not work. Therefore, and at last, they turn to their own true path. Some may not of course, but exhibit yet more hesitancy, even greater stress, or choose merely to succumb to 'their lot' due to fear that ending the relationship might upset too many applecarts, so they make statements such as "I have made my bed, now I must lie on it".

Most, if not all, of these themes can be seen in the life of Prince Charles. The Last Quarter in his chart is at the reorganizational, reformulating sextile and involves a poignant interior emotional longing held within the Venus/Neptune conjunction at the IC. From the context of his background it was without question that he was expected to marry an aristocrat at the very least and preferably an heir should be produced. Apart from that, well there were always affairs .... Princes of Wales throughout history have had them, *n'est-ce-pas*? At any rate since he was designated King he could not divorce. I may not of course have it precise but the 'template' would appear to have been something of that order. But this did not allow for any consciousness of how it might fit the inner reality and potential for Charles *personally* to create, develop and express a happy love relationship from his own inner self. Hence he met this reorientation point. He could have shied from the fence and carried on (as some Last Quarters do) and forever been immersed in deep emotional dissatisfaction and longings for fulfilment. But in Last Quarter if one is trying to maintain a *status quo* when the inner life is clamouring for you to be more who you truly are, eventual reorientation of some kind arises from the pressure. Foregoing both Diana's and a nation's hoped for romanticized notion of love, Charles instead turned from that in which he had been schooled and submitted to a rehabilitation of his emotional self. Given the Plutonic overtones of his Scorpio Sun (square Pluto) sitting at the gateway to 5th house and contained within this phase, this was bound to take him through many depths (turmoils). The tragic events which followed constellated an irrevocable diversionary road indeed, precipitating him into a redirection of his life along the lines of his own inner self, which are now (in his words) "not negotiable".

Sometimes a realization dawns that the 'relationship' sought in life is not perhaps with *a person* at all, but more with a cause which clamours for direction. We can trace this theme in the life of Thomas Paine, one of the founding fathers of the United States. Born in England, Paine originally went down several roads in a bid to develop his life, working as a corset-manufacturer, a schoolteacher, an excise officer, even endeavouring to become ordained in the Church of England, marrying twice in the process and moving from his native Norfolk, to Kent, to Sussex, to London. All the while and along the way he had constantly to find inventive ways to keep one step ahead of his constantly mounting debts and identify a sense of purpose. His first wife died during childbirth and it was through his second marriage (which did not survive the difficulties of his lack of success) that he was introduced to political discussion via his father-in-law. The Mars end of the phase is in Taurus exactly squaring Sun in Aquarius which reflects his persistent yet restless drive for innovation and independence. Campaigning first for better pay and working conditions, Paine then moved to London after separation from his wife, where he met his turning point in the form of Benjamin Franklin who advised him to cross the Atlantic. The rest, as they say, is history, Paine becoming at one with those who were thirsting for independence from their colonial ties to Britain. His chart also carries a Jupiter/Mercury Balsamic Phase in revolutionary Aquarius – the ability to speak out clearly for that which most are merely murmuring about; also Sun/Moon Balsamic Phase which seeks to leave something of its life contributions for posterity.[16] Paine's short pamphlet published in 1776, entitled *Common Sense*, led to his becoming known as Father of the Revolution, influenced both Washington and Jefferson among many others and was followed by *The Rights of Man* in 1787.

Last Quarter threads are also entwined in the life of Jane Austen who never married since such opportunities as were presented to her could not be followed through either because they did not fit the respective families' social/pecuniary needs, or they did… but kindled nothing within her heart. Instead she developed her writing skills, her novels revolving around the vicissitudes of love. The phase contains the position of Sun in opposition to Jupiter in Gemini in the 9th house and Mercury in the 3rd house (writing/publishing). Moreover it is within orb of the enhanced release of talent of the Last Quarter quintile. The exhilarating Leonard Bernstein, with Mars in Scorpio in Last Quarter square to Venus conjunct Neptune in Leo, was musical composer of *West Side Story*, a contemporary version of Shakespeare's *Romeo and Juliet* where a first love endeavours to flourish against the backdrop of warring ethnic-cultural backgrounds. Bernstein's own romantic life veered between homosexual relationships, to a heterosexual marriage and children, back to homosexual love affairs again, then returning to his wife but suffering much depression after her death. The phase contains the Sun conjunct MC opposing Uranus – flamboyant, vital and passionate, Bernstein spoke of his relationship with music as "a total embrace".

Mars/Venus Balsamic Phase

Largely due to the visionary quality of the phase, this person can be somewhat disillusioned with the obvious and superficial pleasures of love and sexuality. S/he may have very strong feelings, but an additional underlying sense that a relationship is not an end in itself but rather a means to personal growth. To those who operate on more immediate levels of fun, joy and exhilaration ('the thrill of the chase') this type can appear to be very irrational, perhaps even hard to reach and understand. This is because they are capable of becoming involved in relationships (of any kind) for abstract reasons rather than because of the prospect of personal satisfaction. Indeed many new spiritual realizations and psychological awarenesses may occur through their relating and creativity.

On the other hand sometimes the disillusionment can mean that they fall into being rather cynical about the whole business of relating and, in compensation, completely flip to the other side and become inveterate flirts, wanting to find enchantment in every new person and around every corner. The inspiring pianist, Arthur Rubinstein, known as something of a 'ladies' man', fell for one such seated opposite him at a formal banquet. "My foot found hers during the fish…" he later thrillingly recounted to a friend. Either that, or they feel constantly martyred by love, or seek relationships where they can be either the 'saviour' or the 'saved'. And then there is the enticingly-painful pull of Unrequited Love – one client, after an agonizing session talking over her experiences of such, sent me a card of Tiepolo's pen-and-brown ink depiction of *Apollo and Daphne*, upon which she wrote "How very sad it is that love always struggles for expression".

Most often this is a person who is attracted to another for the *potential* held within that 'other'. They see something in that person that perhaps they themselves do not yet clearly know, yet the Balsamic type is able to assist them in identifying and bringing it out. Alternatively, there may be qualities (abilities, skills, characteristics, potential) within that person that they *do* know but for one reason or another do not readily show to the world – and again the Balsamic seems able to reach into this and act as a catalyst for manifestation. Therefore they are able to encourage others to function at an increased level of their being, and progress in life. One example of relationship here might be that of benefactor and protégé, such as exemplified in Lerner and Loewe's *My Fair Lady* (based on George Bernard Shaw's *Pygmalion*), i.e. between Professor Higgins and Eliza. Indeed in the creative world, this person may be a patron of the arts, or one who mentors a student or apprentice in a particular skill. The phase also appeared in the chart of a CEO of a group of companies flourishing on a wide scale who ensured that one large room in their headquarters was given over to being a library (which he personally funded). Here his employees could retire if they so wished, during lunch, tea or coffee breaks, to 'lift out' from the demands of their work and enter into whatsoever would inspire or please them, be it novels, travelogues, biographical books or indeed those along the lines of personal and psychological development. And yes, last time I was there a steady trickle of astrological literature was evident!

However, this dynamic can have its negative manifestations also. In harbouring a clear vision of what a relationship could be, this type may also feel driven (though they may say 'inspired') to do all in their power to *mould* that relationship (and the other person) into what s/he would personally see as its greatest possibility. But this may take on a hue of coercion rather than simple loving encouragement. Here we may discern overtones of the Mars/Pluto Scorpionic rulership of this phase and the person may come across more darkly as a Svengali than a Professor Higgins. The person on the receiving-end can then feel 'cornered', worried that they are required to be a puppet on Balsamic's strings and subject to a 'make-over'. The upshot might be that they balk at this, raising serious remonstrations against Balsamic's apparent motives and thus the flow of relating may reach an imbalance.

I was first consulted by Susannah, an accomplished artist and designer. Wholly pleasant and gentle to meet, she also contains powerful reservoirs of strength and determination to have impact upon her world and succeed. (Sun/Moon First Quarter containing Uranus at the Midheaven, with the Moon conjunct Saturn and next to meet Pluto after birth). Like many of this Balsamic phase, creatively there was much love, zest and passion poured into her work which stands indisputably as a legacy for the future. None of this presents any special problem to Susannah, but falling in love with Michael was "a conundrum" she said. Michael is also very talented as a writer, also enjoying success in his career for which he has worked hard (Sun/Moon and Saturn/Moon both Crescent). In terms of their careers they are not in competition or trying to keep up with each other; each is 'happy in their own skin' and the love between them was very palpable.

But while all this provided a strong bulwark for the relationship to flourish, it was the actuality of day-to-day relating that caused a few ructions. In the way of all things astrological, it took a little dismantling and examining, questioning, proposing and supposing, until we looked at the Mars/Venus phases. Susannah's is in Pisces in the 7th. Michael has the phase in First Quarter Phase from Aries in the 2nd to the 7th house cusp. While Susannah's Balsamic was indeed inspiring to Michael, and she lovingly bestowed validation upon him for his talents, it emerged that in daily life Michael felt coerced into being and becoming what felt like

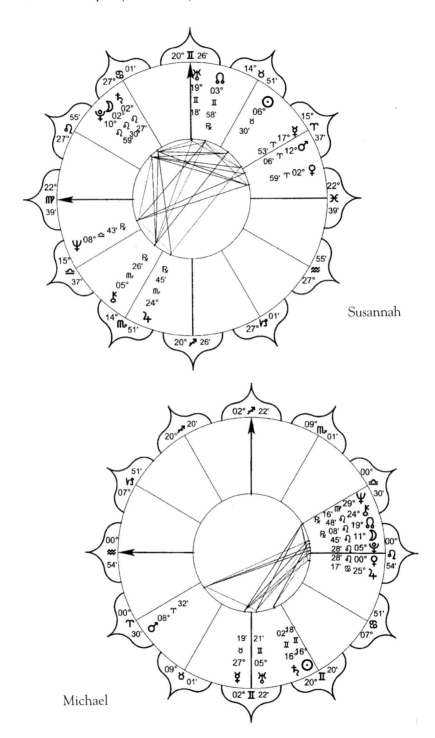

Susannah

Michael

more Susannah's *ideal* of how he *could be* (the visionary quality of Balsamic, perhaps compounded by her 1st house Neptune in Libra, ruling the 7th house). Susannah, meanwhile, loved Michael's assertion in his creative life (First Quarter), readily following up brilliant ideas and setting them on a definite platform via his collected works (the phase contains Mercury, Uranus conjunct Gemini IC, Saturn/Sun conjunction and Jupiter in the 6th, ruler of MC). But he seemed always to break away from her when she required something of him or offered her viewpoints. It became clearer how the Balsamic relating energy of one and the First Quarter relating energy of the other were somewhat out of kilter and perhaps might underlie the "conundrum".

As we talked it through, notably at one point Michael said, "It's just that I don't want someone calling the shots at me night and day, telling me how things should be done". And, equally notably, Susannah said, "Oh I just want everything to be perfect for him, I suppose because I don't want anything to hurt him or for him to be found 'wanting'". The clarity of each of the Mars/Venus phases being spoken in this way enabled the three of us to open up the other phases in the hope of a little more illumination. Alongside her First Quarter Sun/Moon which was readily evident in the way she had developed her life, Susannah was astounded by the automatic identity she had taken on from her Saturn/Moon New Phase. It emerged she had experienced her parents as being exceptionally controlling, although in a loving way because they wanted the best for her. She added that she always felt she must get everything "properly right" and work hard to ensure that nothing was ever out of place ("found wanting"). The Jupiter/Mercury phase is Gibbous and at the biquintile where the need to focus and arrange is a strong drive. Virgo rises with an 8th house Mercury which can manifest as a compulsion to leave nothing undone, everything in order and perfect.

Michael's creative struggle and persistence in life (Sun/Moon, Saturn/Moon both Crescent) was borne of a background where there were very many siblings and consequent difficulties in developing individuality. His parents' way of handling their large family was to wield a sturdy rod of 'what we say goes' although, like Susannah, this was within a loving context. However, he was particularly aware of experiencing his parents being great 'reformers', their discussions revolving around 'how the world should be and what the government should do' and this also spilled over into their interaction with Michael "don't do it *that* way, do it *this* way it's much better", with no prospect of Michael's own insights being given a platform, thus he had built up an expectation of having to fight for them.

With great emotional intelligence these two people came to work with their respective inner dynamics of Balsamic (Susannah's ideal visionary outlook) and First Quarter (Michael's need to fight through apparent challenges to his creativity). Alongside they identified how they had also constructed their world partly around recreating something of their earlier conditioned patterns and grafting these onto the present relationship. Subsequent therapeutic work enabled them to focus more definitively on these dynamics and extract the more valid elements of their separate gifts without encroaching upon each other, while at the same time maintaining the undoubted mutual love that underpinned their life.

The truer purpose of the Balsamic Phase is to yield new seeds for the future; at its most positive, therefore, its qualities can provide exactly the inner substance from which a better life can be envisioned, not only for the individual but for many. Dame Vera Lynn, born with the phase in Pisces, in turn contained within a Sun/Moon Balsamic Phase, galvanized an entire nation and especially its fighting troops during the Second World War, her strong clear singing voice holding them with the promise of meeting again and seeing bluebirds over the *White Cliffs of Dover*.[17]

10: Saturn and Jupiter

This planetary pairing does not have quite the same personal meaning as those previously covered since their cycle spans 20 years, thus in the same relative position for a great number of people and occupying a phase for some 2½ years. On a collective level it shows economic and working practices in society, therefore conditions which existed as we were developing in our early years. In turn such trends are operating within broader contexts of transformation across the globe, more especially reflected in the three outer planets of Uranus, Neptune and Pluto.

Those who specialize in mundane and business astrology are very cognizant of the Jupiter/Saturn cycle and their work is valuable not only for those who wish to pursue a special interest in these fields, but also from the point of view of enabling us to have some acquaintance at least with those broader trends occurring during the time we were born. Whether we arrive on this planet during a time of 'boom' or 'bust' can have great bearing on the conditions of our personal environment and significant people within it. A growing child will clearly infer different kinds of meaning if its development takes place set against a backdrop of unemployment and struggle or, conversely, stability in a land of plenty. Similarly, whether our birth culture in relation to other nations was in a state of alignment and goodwill or the intensity of cold (or indeed even hot) war. In short, we cannot examine a person's birth moment without taking into account the condition and temperament of the social environment in which it took place.

On a personal level Jupiter represents the drive within us to grow through interaction and the pursuit of goals. We relate to others by adding our own endeavours in what we call 'co-operation'. Our personal experience is thus expanded into one of being a socialized individual, belonging to a larger whole which then empowers us further through its containment and support – being part of a community and a wider world. Saturn is where we give concrete form to this experience by *defining* our sense of 'place' (and permanence within that place) through some kind of structured function, which we call 'goals', 'work', 'ambition', 'career' – with its concomitant themes of duty, responsibility, formality and attainment of position.

In looking at these two as a pairing, Saturn 'sends out' Jupiter to seek and bring back all that is required to fulfil and stabilize our lives. Considerations as to tenacity, endurance, inner confidence and willingness (or otherwise) for industry, as well as the clarity (or otherwise) of our objectives, will all come under scrutiny. It can also define our inner moral compass as well as philosophical, spiritual and/or religious reflections when it comes to establishing ourselves in the world. Here we may clarify the 'shoulds' and 'oughts', 'musts' or 'must-nots' we carry within, some of which we may have taken on wholesale from our cultural and familial patterns. Perhaps particularly in the current world-situation we become aware that while the human race may amass a huge amount of industrial and technological progress through acquisition, knowledge and exploration – consuming more, striving for and demanding yet more and more and more – underneath we need also to develop a solidified wisdom in what we are doing, why and how we are doing it.

The first planet to be met by Jupiter as it pulls away from or returns to Saturn can yield additional insight into career approaches and goals to be striven for, as can planets contained within the phase. The Great Conjunction of Jupiter and Saturn which took place prior to birth can also be examined as a 'marker' for the meaning of the cycle as a whole into which the individual has incarnated to take his/her place. As always, along with conventional chart insights, this phase should be considered carefully against the backdrop of the more personal inner-planet pairings (especially Sun/Moon and Saturn/Moon).

Overall, we may say that not only does this planetary pairing reflect the background collective level of social, economic and working trends but, on a personal level, highlights the individual's potential for career development and success, their approach to and capacity for financial and other forms of achievement, together with the general lines along which they will most tend to focus these considerations in their lives.[1]

Saturn/Jupiter New Phase

This person has an instinctive sense of how to build life in practical ways, earn a living and ensure they can get along in the world. They may not always be able to put this into words but, deep down, things always work out better for them when they follow their intuitive judgment rather than being guided by any outer reasoning or logic. There is often a matter-of-fact quality within them when it comes to looking at the question of work; making money and following a career are not especially conscious 'issues' since they know these are things that have to be done and so they simply go ahead and do them.

How *well* they do them might be a different matter and much will depend on the inner sense of self-worth. One manifestation can be that the person automatically accepts the prevailing values and economic patterns of their socio-cultural/familial group and so their way of 'making it' in the world is basically to repeat the general lines of what they were shown in the past, or that they instinctively feel would meet with parental favour. This is not usually contrived or premeditated, just the following of an automatic sense-perception. It may also be a person who follows a career which is a more particular *given*, i.e. one into which s/he was expected to step because it maintains a continuity. So there may be an entire ancestral line of, say, lawyers and, while there may emerge space for some differentiation, anything other than a career somewhere in the legal field merits little or no consideration. And then there are situations where choices are minimal or non-existent and a line must be followed absolutely; it may even carry a certain weight and formality.

Prince William was born with Saturn and Jupiter 15° apart in New Phase, containing Pluto – a function and role allied to power and following a set path. Jupiter is strong as the chart ruler, conjunct the Midheaven and trine the Sun. This alongside his Sun/Moon New Phase which is also powerful by dint of it having been an eclipse.[2] Occurring as this did on the morning of his birth at 29° 47' Gemini, it highlights the Ascendant-Descendant axis conjoined with Neptune and evokes William's situation of being a person taken into the hearts of the people (Cancer 7th) as the admired ideal (Neptune) yet also containing a deeper powerful purpose (the solar eclipse which, in Rudhyar's terms, represents a powerful absorption of the past brought into a present glorification) as future King. The Great Conjunction of Saturn and Jupiter prior to his birth occurred on 31st December 1980 on 9° 29' Libra (the eventual birth position of Mars in the 9th which is nothing if not open to a challenge) in square to the Sun in that chart on 10° 22' Capricorn. This, in turn conjuncts the Sun and MC/IC axis in both the chart for England (1066) and that for the United Kingdom (1801).[3] Here we have a glimmer, if not a heralding, of a concretization of special position and authority as a thread to be woven in this life. The Sabian Symbol (for

10 Libra) is given by Rudhyar as *Having passed safely through narrow rapids, a canoe reaches calm waters*[4] reflecting experience of emotionally choppy waters before reaching the stability of one's destination. While the tradition is to round up the position of a conjunction to the upper degree, it is also worth noting that the symbol for 9 Libra, is *Three "Old Masters" hanging on the wall of a special room in an art gallery*[5] and here Rudhyar speaks of the continuity of a new seed from the past entering into a tradition of *succession*. Such additional threads seem very apt for a person born automatically to succeed to the throne after his father and whose life has indeed already, like the throne itself, encompassed emotional turbulence. The phase as whole marries well with the Saturn/Moon Phase (Disseminating) with its accent on standards, principles and propriety.

The closer to the conjunction the more there is a pull toward Jupiter displaying an automatically absorbed pattern. It has only just left the 'embrace' of Saturn and thus is imbued with the need for construct and operating within defined boundaries. Sometimes this includes the need for building a stalwart career and achieving *longevity* of position. Some may additionally feel they always need an 'authority' behind them in their working lives to tell them what to do and generally act as a voice of conscience. Others may gravitate towards situations where they are tethered, like a goat in a field only allowed a certain radius within which to graze, unable (perhaps unwilling) to separate from restraint. However, where the phase widens towards the semi-sextile and beyond, there can be more leeway for individual fulfilment to peek through. Planets positioned between Saturn and Jupiter indicate requirements to be incorporated into outer world achievement, yet still with an instinctive sense of standing as a 'new seed' to flourish concretely and preferably long-term. We can see this in the following chart which is of a man born to a middle-class suburban schoolteacher father and hairdresser mother who was raised automatically to follow in his father's career footsteps.

However, the phase is almost at its extremity (at 44°), thus about to enter the 'prod-alert' of the semisquare and the Crescent Phase need to break out and forge new avenues by which to anchor himself. Moreover, since pulling away from its conjunction to Saturn prior to birth, Jupiter has already taken the Sun in Leo on board and remains in conjunction with the Sun for potential creative success in communicating with the environment (3rd). Post-birth it is set to race toward the potential for even more powerful

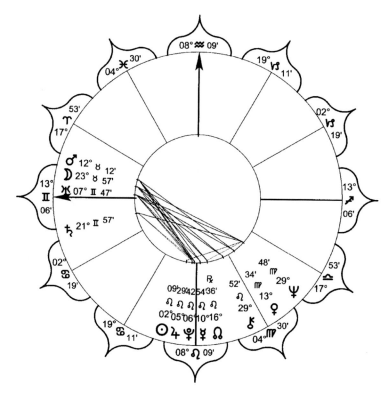

communication via Pluto and Mercury in Leo opposite an Aquarian Midheaven whose rulers are Saturn on the one hand (the 'control' for this phase) and Uranus on the other, the latter rising and sextiling Mercury the chart ruler. It's a heady mix but we begin to get an arresting sense of a person really quite *driven* to establish a decided sense of standing with a *frisson* of exciting, innovative, alternative, even unbridled energies waiting at this gateway to be unfurled.

The contextual backdrop of Sun/Moon Last Quarter Phase (just past the quintile) echoes the need to take a diversionary road, both creating and communicating from a platform of one's own and possibly incorporating a specific talent (quintile). The Saturn/Moon phase is Balsamic, reflecting an experience of a conditioned environment that perhaps held no template for the innovation and vision (Uranus contained within Saturn/Moon) which awaits externalization. This person may well have faced a choice either to be stifled by a conformity or to weave a pattern of his own and become a truer self, the overall phase-threads being weighted in favour of the latter. The Jupiter/Mercury phase is New (communicating to inspire) and contains Pluto (again power, possibly disruption and even mayhem given the connection to MC and Uranus). Mars/Venus is in First Quarter phase, even further adding to the sense of high impact and all-round creative *bezazz*. A suburban school teacher? Well, er… not even close. More like *Jumpin' Jack Flash*. This is the chart of Mick Jagger of The Rolling Stones who has sustained a megastar career for over fifty years.

More generally speaking there may be a pattern from the past where economic and career choices were more fluctuating – now experiencing success and plenty here, now having to tighten belts there. This then becomes the automatic expectation and underpins the construction and pursuit of the working life. In turn it may manifest as an instinctual sense for going so far and no further in the pursuit of goals, a knack perhaps of knowing just how far they can push their luck or instinctively knowing what is practical and viable and what is not. More negatively it can arise as prevarication about a career or how they perform in it, which others may experience as 'dithering'. On the whole, I have found this phase to be good at taking the lead or instigating new avenues in their work, the ultimate career choice also often being imbued with a strong sense of inner purpose usually carried out with a quiet self-reliance. In addition they can be very practical about money, although they also have something of an 'easy come easy go' attitude and can be extravagant. Sometimes there may be a strong tendency to equate money and possessions with a personal sense of inner validity but much can depend on early life conditions and how the person saw the parents deal with monetary considerations, as well as the wider collective financial climate that prevailed.

Saturn/Jupiter Cresecent Phase

Capable of great achievements in career development, nevertheless the effort of this phase can mean that this type feels obliged to do things the hard way. Therefore they often feel unable to *enjoy* their achievements either in the process of working towards them or, indeed, after their completion. Depending on the cultural background and era, there may also be something of the 'Protestant Work Ethic' within the overall nature, such that the struggle for economic survival can be burdensome for this person who may again, if only imperceptibly, make a rod for their own back.

At heart, this is a person who may prefer to be dependent on someone else for their material survival. Again this might be because their socio-cultural and personal background may not have shown them anything other than a belief that earning a living is an exceedingly difficult and arduous road. Adherence to such a pattern will not ultimately work for this type and one of their major life tasks could be to be willing to examine and re-evaluate those beliefs. Often it feels to them that emerging into the world of work is like steering a ship across an ocean in the dark with no charts, compass or radio-contact. The big temptation is not to get involved in such a dangerous enterprise but to stay with what is safe and known. Therefore, and again while perfectly capable of achievement, this type may limit their goals and capacity for success by staying in the 'safe' job or performing menial tasks, often for little reward or choosing endlessly repetitive work that requires no particular prowess or knowledge and there are no particular pressures (the tedium of it all being pressure enough). There may also be a tendency to take what is a straightforward-enough task but turn it into a monumental burden that weighs heavily upon them. Yet the 'alert' of the semi-square opening the phase forever prods them to go just that bit further – surely there is more that can be achieved, surely it could be a little more enjoyable? Yes there is and yes it could, once the conditioned approach with its limiting or negating values can be brought into the light of day. Indeed it is often that 'prod' which brings the person to the astrologer with a request to review the chart for issues of work and career.

The real need here is to develop Crescent energies by listening carefully to one's own intuitions and acting on them with circumspection until they have proved their practical value. This is not a phase where one could, or should, plunge in to some great enterprise, wafted on the wings of a hoped-for Big Achievement/Major Success. That is not to say that big achievements and major success are beyond their capability – merely that the path to them is one of step-by-step, prudent yet heartfelt persistence. More often than not, that which is of true worth to this person (both in material and inner psychological terms) comes through drawing on qualities of steadfastness and the willingness to build creative structures for their career life, neither being pulled by past patterns nor spiralling off into future hopes, but concentrating on present-awareness in terms of what they are personally bringing to the job in hand.

Where this individual occupies a position in which there is a steady, safe pattern of work, perhaps followed by a secured pension at the end of it, they may well decide (if they are solidly wedded to notions of wearisome plodding effort) that this is sufficient for them. The consistent wage, month in month out, enables such a person to continue living by caution as a watchword, feeling more secure when they follow general prevailing trends. As such they may be stalwart professionals, building a solid body of work even though there can be attendant feelings of being 'boxed in'; on the other hand they may again deplete into 'pen-pushing' with all its accompanying dreariness. Those who are aware of this may, however, also cultivate other interests in life (outside of their work) which call forward a greater feeling of inner fulfilment. More positively, the willingness to perform repetitive tasks can also be seen in the person who (either in a work situation or more generally in life) is both happy and well able to deal with what others might regard only groaningly as 'chores', thereby providing a reliability for holding things together cohesively.

Some of this phase may, however, feel caught between their steady job on the one hand and wishing that they could really have a career in whatever is the 'outside interest'. Or, out of sheer boredom they dream of being self-employed or doing something much more enlivening but they are curtailed by their choice of menial situation but which 'at least is consistent'. Such a person may find themselves in financial difficulties, perhaps several times over, before coming to a conclusion that by being wedded to the 'menial' means wedded to a negative struggle. The pattern is then either to remain as they are, or awaken to generating some new roads out. If the latter, whatever is chosen will not be ready-beaten nor necessarily 'safe', but it will call forward this person's ability to anchor themselves through courage and persistence even if set-backs and obstacles appear. It is a pathway of earnest, creative struggle and durability, reminiscent of the hero in myth and fairy tales who must navigate a way through ogres, dragons, seemingly-impossible tasks and conundrums… before finally reaching the princess in the tower or discovering the treasure. The effort of the journey, though daunting, need not restrain or halt this Crescent type, unless s/he staunchly believes otherwise.

At the sextile there is often an ability to strike out in the world with a flowing productivity or display of skills, yet still through consistent effort and input. Alan Whicker (see also Chapter 8) was born with this pairing at 66°, containing the Moon in Capricorn in the 5th house harbouring a natural inner response to solid creative work. Jupiter first meets Uranus after birth, ruler of his 7th house, reflecting his unique television presentations of the lives of others in rare quarters of society. Where the phase reaches the quintile, there is often a marked sense of a purpose to be fulfilled (which almost certainly will have nothing to do with past patterns) but will carry an inspirational quality giving incentive to this person to strive forward. As the phase approaches the perimeter fence of the first 90° square, the quest for achievement may well go up a notch or three, the person wanting a career of higher impact where s/he is ready to make a mark and there are solid tangible goals in sight. Entrepreneur and property tycoon, Donald Trump, has the phase at 84° with Venus (ruler of Taurus Midheaven) conjunct the Saturn end of the phase (development of concrete resources/real estate) and Jupiter in Libra (also ruled by Venus) ruling his 5th house (entrepreneurial) Moon in Sagittarius (Jupiter's own sign) in opposition to a high impact triple conjunction of Uranus, North Node, Sun.

We saw earlier under Saturn/Moon First Quarter how D.H. Lawrence's background was that of the Nottinghamshire coal-mining industry and his personal struggles with the patterns of each of his parents' outlooks. He was of course fervently manoeuvred away from the working man's pattern extant at the time by his mother's close relationship to, and hopes for, him. He was first a teacher before flourishing as a writer, but Lawrence never made much money, was often dependent on other people to provide a roof over his head, his more cultivated qualities often finding themselves somewhat at variance with the reality of his situation. Reflecting the context of Crescent struggle, Saturn is in the 9th ruling the 3rd (writing, publishing) and Jupiter in the 11th due to first meet the Sun after birth; this also reflects not only his ultimate success but, in Virgo, his more cultured and refined bearing. In a letter to a friend who was to put one of his manuscripts before a publisher, he implored him not to ask for an advance on royalties. "Do not present me as a beggar. Do not tell him I am poor... let me be presented... as a respectable person"[6] he wrote. Yet, this man of literary genius was also a person who, in day-to-day life, was pragmatic and not above the performance of lowly tasks in the pursuit of cohesion and stability. Aldous Huxley reports that he could cook, sew, scrub the kitchen floor, chop wood to light the fire and even milk a cow.[7] Nothing was too humble a chore for him, but he also knew how to sit still with himself, seemingly 'doing nothing', but absorbed in every present moment. This underpinned his feeling-relationship to Virgoan detail, a prevalent feature of his literary works. The phase value of Saturn/Jupiter in his chart is 69°, therefore approaching the enhanced creativity of the quintile.

Saturn/Jupiter First Quarter

Given that this phase energy requires a break from the past and the meeting of a challenge, one would expect this type to be very assertive when it comes to the question of getting along in the world and rendering their lives economically stable. And indeed it is so. In fact, it may well be that this person experiences constant battles in the bid for material security, the whole question of money and success being something of a Major Issue in their lives.

One aspect of this can be that they can feel so goaded by this need that, while acting very strenuously in pursuit of it, they also inwardly generate a great deal of tension for themselves about it. A fear of poverty (which they may equate with helplessness) may be a background theme for this person, yet could well have been coupled with turning points in their past whereby endeavours were made by significant people to haul out of it (the 90° square) and establish a path of wellbeing. Such a pattern can certainly underpin this person's way of approaching work and earning in the present and, whether or not they are wealthy or at least comfortable, they can be very demanding, if not all-out aggressive, where material acquisition is concerned. In some instances I have seen this dynamic operating in those who see a lack of money as being the sole restricting force in their life and who believe that, if they had more money, they would have all the other virtues in life as well. If the material life becomes Major Top Priority to the exclusion of all else, there can sometimes be a pattern of creating a rollercoaster ride of one exhausting battle after another, from solvency and success, to over-reaching, to plunging into difficulties, then battling to get back on top again. Less intensely, this phase type may simply be 'a good hustler' for money or a career position. They know what they want and they go all out, whatever it takes, to ensure they get that wad of cash in their pocket, the bank account is never overdrawn or they are first in line to climb up that next rung of the success-ladder. It may even be something of a game for them, a challenge to be met into which they dive quite happily, using all their skills of improvisation and alertness to recognize opportunistic avenues. Planets contained in the phase can offer further threads of insight as to how this is done or the direction in which it is taken.

Where this person has emerged from a background of 'plenty' there may again have been a longer history of their ancestry fighting for and building up a stability that continues to serve the individual in the present day, or of which s/he is the custodian (such as in inherited wealth, land, property, titles). I have come across it in the charts of those who live in stately family homes but who, in today's world, have constantly to find and develop ingenious ways of funding their upkeep. In true First Quarter style, an extraordinary amount of intense work goes into these situations, such people often providing innovative changes for the environment as a whole, e.g. by the creation of gardens, exhibitions, musical events etc. In other situations where there is a past history of sustained stability, the drive for monetary acquisition may not present in obvious terms, nor be allied to fears of impecuniosity. Instead, we may see it more directed into worthy causes or sponsoring those with a specific goal they wish to achieve, to whom it would make a big difference if they do not personally have the means to fund it. Prince Charles has the phase from Saturn in the 2nd house of resources to Jupiter in the 5th house of creativity and young people, reflecting his investment in the youth of the country getting their careers off the ground via The Prince's Trust which he set up in 1976 with his severance pay (of £7k) from the Navy.

Both leaders of the UK coalition government, formed in May 2010, came from affluent backgrounds and have the same First Quarter Phase having been born only a few months apart. (Due to retrograde/direct motions of these planets during October 1966 – January 1967, the zodiacal positions are identical in their charts, with a phase value of 127°).

David Cameron and Nick Clegg were born upon the heels of the 1965 Great Conjunction of Pluto/Uranus in Virgo opposing Saturn which heralded the onset of an era which would contain many turning points in social/economic reform and technological advances. Now in their adult lives they are poised in leadership positions to meet the tumultuous First Quarter Phase of that Pluto/Uranus cycle to which the world has now turned – and steer a country through it. Meeting the challenge of material cohesion is much to the forefront of their political alliance given that they are presiding over a nation facing a massive economic deficit, with all the attendant 'what-to-do's' surrounding it. Additionally there are global shifts of evolutionary/revolutionary bids for freedom from tyrannical patterns. Both men display a keen alacrity to puncture such situations as quickly and effectively as possible, while others in the general political arena call for a more graduated approach. Their shared 'first-quarterness' reflects the outreaching cardinality of their charts – Libra/Air in Cameron's case (where the four angles also align with the cardinal points), and Capricorn/ Earth in Clegg's chart. Cardinal energies generate 'power', the ability to take action. Cardinal Air does so by making connections between what it perceives, assessing the relationship between different factors and making value judgments based on comparison and categorisation, while Cardinal Earth acts through strong awareness of what is actually happening, grasping immediate factors and dealing with them in pragmatic ways. While this is (necessarily for present purposes) an over-simplification of the elements' functions,[8] it serves to augment the underlying threads of meaning in these two charts in terms of the First Quarter energy. Cameron has two further First Quarter phases – Saturn/Moon and Jupiter/Mercury – while Clegg has Mars/Venus in this phase. In both men there are threads to be woven, albeit in different ways, of standing up and speaking out as well as cutting through what they see as deficient circumstances to create change. As with all First Quarter energies where challenge exists, the need for anyone in this phase is to develop steady circumspection alongside, so that action taken is not merely to feed a gung-ho 'Boys Own' (or even Girls Own) sense of adventure. It needs to be clear-cut with intelligent discernment as to an end result.

For the most part I have found this phase type usually dedicated to the pursuit of having *impact* which will release them from any negative past patterns of work/career; thus you will not find many Saturn/Jupiter First Quarters starving in a proverbial garret. This type wants to bring home the bacon, make sure the mortgage is paid and live another day as Captain of a Ship sailing the seas of ongoing battle for practical survival in a material world.

Saturn/Jupiter Gibbous Phase

When it comes to the business of setting up life on practical, secure grounds, fundamentally this type needs to go about it by taking a very considered approach. There can be intense focus (even fastidious control) concerning the pursuit of goals and overall they fare better if they are prepared to be highly organized since relying on instinct and intuition alone do not work so well for this type. They need a solid, proven way of doing things that they can learn from their own experience.

One of the problems can be that gaining such experience on their own is likely to be a little hazardous, if not disastrous, since the phase theme is essentially one of finding out through trial-and-error. Formal learning may not always appeal to them, or may provide only a theoretical understanding of the job-in-hand but not the grounded application of a skill. So along the way they often need a helping hand. This may be by way of a mentor, or one to whom they are apprenticed – someone who will introduce them to their chosen career bit by bit, show them the ropes, provide a structure for arranging it, help them sort and classify, raise their awareness of pitfalls to be met and perhaps hold their hand while they take their first steps. This might simply be a solid family member or friend with sufficient life-experience, or indeed a person already established and experienced in the field, but the crux of the matter is to feel guided while finding their feet. Once this phase type is making great strides forward, such a helper may take more of a back seat in their life, or be dispensed with altogether… perhaps unless and until something goes a little 'wobbly' and they need back-up again. Something of this dynamic may have been part of Gordon Brown's strategy for his ailing government in 2008-09 when he drafted back into it previous members of the former Blair government to take up parliamentary positions, albeit without a mandate. (Brown was born with Sun/Moon as well as Saturn/Jupiter in Gibbous phase). On the other hand, should the intensity of this phase (and/or the wider chart factors) also contain strong threads of dominance, the need for a mentor as such may not exist, the individual using their own power and control to establish their position in the material world.

In terms of handling the practicalities of finance, the desire to save money and the desire to spend it are often in an irritating and disruptive conflict and a conscious balance may need to be struck. One man was efficiency-itself in keeping detailed records of his investments, following the world markets in the financial press, making astute decisions as to the potential for greater yields – yet on the other hand would suddenly 'blow' quite a few thousand pounds on a classic car which he neither needed nor could use (since he was not a driver)… simply because he "felt like it"! It would then sit in a garage until he could sell it, usually in order to prop up some other investment – which had now plunged since he had temporarily taken his eye off it while being entranced with the car. Here, Saturn was in the 3rd house of steady, concentrated thought while the Jupiter end of the phase was conjunct Venus and square to Neptune (flights of idealism). Often this phase may be found where the person (especially in their younger adult life) would benefit from assistance and advice on matters of investment, tax, savings plans etc. – generally cultivating a sound and realistic approach to these matters so that the likelihood of financial idealism and muddle (which may be fuelled by inner anxieties or impatience) is lessened in later life.

The theme of 'sorting things out' in this phase can also mean that the person dithers between wanting to follow a conventional career path on the one hand, yet drawn to taking a risk with something exceptional on the other. This might mean wondering whether to plump for the relative safety of being an employee with a steady pay cheque or make a leap off the beaten track to go for a self-employed venture. Often, there is a pattern of starting out on one of these bases and then switching to the other. One young woman came to me at her first Saturn Return; she had been working steadily and successfully in a large company but felt it did not stretch her abilities as far as she would like. She wanted to know whether, if she gave up her job, she could be successful in putting herself 'out there' to take up more of an entrepreneurial role. Here was the 'I need to look before I leap' theme so often prevalent in Gibbous phase. She was a Sun/Moon Disseminating type (good communication skills), with Saturn/Moon in First Quarter (ability to assert herself and forge a sure identity); Taurus was on the MC with Venus well aspected (a need for ample and tangible security) and a 3rd house Mercury in Scorpio which was adept at thinking on her feet and going straight to a point, all within a Sun/Saturn aspect structure needing solidity. "So, what do you reckon?" I asked when all this was before us, "what are the options and avenues that you know of, out there in the world, that might truly provide a viable foothold for what you're seeking to do or be?" Here I was appealing to the Gibbous need and ability to scrutinize, look carefully and deeply at actualities and details. She eventually came up with several identified paths/people where she was certain her skills were known and she had established a concrete reputation. She took the plunge, handed in her notice to her employer and was immediately head-hunted by three such identified areas clamouring for her services. She has never been out of work since and today runs her own successful business development company.

Like that client, Saturn/Jupiter Gibbous people are often skilful and sharp in their field of work. Opening at the 'alert' of the sesquiquadrate, this heralds the fact that something needs to be intently cultivated to ensure it will come to completion. Much needs to be assembled, arranged and made thoroughly viable. Their job may reflect this, e.g. requiring focused precision (such as working with tools or mathematics) or they may be extremely adept at profound analysis, concentration and cohesion (often around the quincunx) or where they can keep a steady eye on a ball (sometimes literally! – e.g. sports, athletics). I have also met several astrologers who started off in another career but then felt pulled by their respect for the deep meaning, order and rhythm that astrology calls forward, thus left their beaten track of employment and became consultants, counsellors, researchers in the field. This theme may be prevalent around the biquintile where the inner urge to arrange and develop strategies to bring something to meaningful life is highlighted. Frequently the career choices may involve the need to feel both anchored and in a position of communicating (reflecting the Taurus/ Gemini element of this phase).

There may be a background theme in the life whereby the family environment was in the process of taking stock of its financial wellbeing or otherwise when this person was born, or a parent changed jobs in order to cater to a growing family. Alternatively great importance may have been accorded to the type of education this person should receive, often with an eye on a future formal career path. Whatever the actual focus was in the past it can be utilized in the present by this person developing know-how, insight and conscientiousness so as to reach for the accomplishments they are undoubtedly capable of achieving. In turn, they too may become mentors or solid supporters for others who follow.

Saturn/Jupiter Full Phase

The basic context within which this phase type operates is one of meeting conflicting drives within themselves, from which they gradually build a sense of reflective awareness of how to take their place in the world. They frequently feel very unsure about how to get along or even a mite defeated by the whole process, even if to all intents and purposes they appear to be doing so reasonably competently. The issue deep down is often a strong desire on the one hand to plunge into a working role, but on the other an equally strong reluctance to do so. They might be found occupying a perfectly conventional and responsible position, yet there is a feeling within them that they are merely going through the motions. At heart, there may be deeper feelings of guilt or anxiety about the business of earning a living, making money, even a (perhaps unexamined) sense that somehow it is rather a sordid, grubby or unworthy thing to have to do.

One client was brought up in a family where the parents were materially comfortable by sole virtue of their respective family trusts. But as time went by and their child (my client) was grown, the world had also moved on and while the parents still had adequate means for their own continued survival, my client of course had to develop a career. When I met her she was a struggling opera singer and having quite a hard time of it. This was not an easy profession at the best of times but she felt extremely worn down by it all and asked me to look at her chart. At first I thought that her tiredness was due to the enormous effort one has to put into establishing such a career – endless auditions, vocal coaching, chasing up every avenue to land a role, the travelling... But it quickly emerged that it was in fact simply the very *thought* of these things that she found too tiresome to bother with in the first place! Not only did she have no role models from the past which showed her how to step into the world and search for work, but it also transpired that she lived in a small apartment in a very smart part of London, the rental for which she could barely afford but she had filled it with impressive furniture, rugs and paintings from her original family home, as if trying to live in that style, trying to fit that niche.

This phase requires that we reflect consciously on what is truly meaningful to us. This has to be done before we can put the business of earning a living into a context that is workable, rather than constantly trying to live out of a context that is not. Most often I have found that the basic need for this phase-type is to find some *larger issue*, something above and beyond merely surviving financially, that they can commit to in life. Being practical, making money, being productive and successful – all of these things have very little inherent power in themselves for this person (which is one reason why they react so wearily to them). Nevertheless, they have to survive in order to be able to do the things that *do* have meaning. Once making money is put into a broader, purposeful framework, this type can indeed be very successful in life. The opera singer began to speak of her commitment to music as being part of a more visionary sense of wanting to participate in an organizational arena, among other people (Full Phase) where she could combine a willingness to work with artistry and her own talents. When I last heard from her she was teaming up with others from some then-emerging improvisational touring groups, similar in style to *Commedia dell'Arte*, to present opera around the country and abroad for special events… and doing so extremely competently.

In other instances, the phase may exemplify a context in which conditions of struggle and deprivation on the one hand meet with a thrust toward competency and success on the other. Along the way, much in the way of creative skill may be hewn from a determination to emerge from a hard existence or searing vulnerability, to win through. Yet even though one may soar to great heights of personal and material satisfaction, there is still meaning to be sought beyond that. Such a thread may be traced in the life-tapestry of the world's foremost exponent of television talkshows, Oprah Winfrey.

The theme of communication is immediately recognizable in the Disseminating Phase Jupiter/Mercury, at the trine aspect. This holds a natural ability for fluidity of discussion, conversation, debate, even crusading and is augmented by Jupiter, as chart ruler, occupying the 6th house of work in Mercury's sign of Gemini. Oprah Winfrey's rise from a poverty-stricken, emotionally deprived and abusive childhood is well-known and, from a phase-perspective, is reflected in Saturn (Scorpio) in New Phase to Moon, containing Mars also in Scorpio. It is difficult to find a better positive expression of these placements than the granite determination to survive and secure oneself in the outer world (Saturn 10th, Mars 11th). This is further enhanced by the square from Saturn to the Sun/Venus conjunction in the 2nd, all within the Saturn/Jupiter Full context of a see-saw between deprivation on the one hand and the enhanced realization of one's truer capabilities on the other (the waning biquintile).

With Sun/Moon phase in Last Quarter, clearly she was always set to take her earlier experiences and use them as a springboard to turn her life around on to a path of greater self-authenticity. It is also a phase in which communication of one's own outlooks and philosophies needs to be given a clear platform. As she has been called "the world's most influential woman", I daresay one cannot create a clearer platform than that! This latter description also aptly reflects the Jupiter 6th/Neptune 10th and Pisces on 3rd house expansive reaching out and her global fame. The waning sextile relationship of Sun and Moon also points to a capacity for organization, in such a way that the contributions being made in the outer world need also to be focused upon continuing into the future and those who follow after.

Mars/Venus are in Crescent Phase and have passed the quintile point. Here is a creative drive which intends to reach out to people at large (Mars in 11th Aquarian house sending out Venus, in Aquarius itself) whose first task is to meet the Sun in the second house and thus generate material resources from her efforts. Just as a plant's first roots find nutrients from the

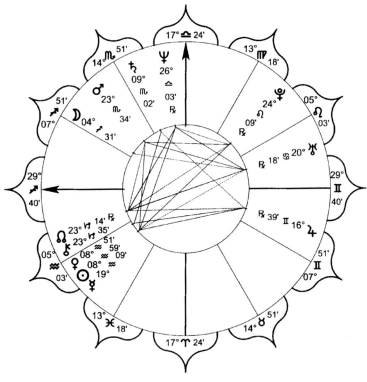

Oprah Winfrey

soil to further its growth, Oprah has forged her career path in such a way that people have responded to her communicative skills, her laser-beam insight (Mercury/Pluto) and the Sun/Venusian empathy/concern she brings to each situation. From all of this, the quest for *meaning* in the rugged outer-world structures cradled within Saturn/Jupiter can be seen in her investment in many charities for helping the underprivileged around the world, notably her establishment of the South African school for impoverished children to which she has referred as "the fulfilment of my work on earth".[9]

Saturn/Jupiter Disseminating Phase

This type will usually go ahead with the confidence that their social attitudes and assumptions about life will work for them when it comes to establishing themselves in a career. One of their main assets is the ability to see the practical value of an idea and communicate it successfully. In fact, this type is *best* fitted to earning a living by communicating in some way, rather than (for instance) in the production of tangible goods. This may involve an element of demonstration, publicity, teaching, training or performance as well as straightforward speaking, writing or salesmanship. Some forge a career where they utilize communicative skills for and on behalf of others, e.g. speech writers, ghostwriters, negotiators of all kinds. Where the trine exists, communication may take on an easy flow although, given the nature of this planetary combination, that does not necessarily mean it is not hard worked for. Industrialist Andrew Carnegie, while establishing the steel industry in America, was of course also known for his extensive philanthropy, spreading (Disseminating) his vast fortune to establish free public libraries, schools and universities in the English-speaking world and also devoting his life after retirement to writing.

For any communicator, their skills will often stand the test of time such as in the case of Winston Churchill whose abilities in this respect we traced via the Disseminating Sun/Moon and Jupiter/Mercury New. His Saturn/Jupiter phase contains Sun and Venus in the 3rd as well as Mercury in Scorpio opposing Pluto, again pointing to his powerful oratory. Similarly, Jon Savage, who we met in Chapter 8 as an example of organized and detailed communication borne of steady and earnest effort (Jupiter/Mercury Crescent) has this phase with Jupiter in Gemini 3rd (writing) as the last planet touched by the Moon prior to birth, while Saturn has just set on the Descendant with Neptune imbuing the phase with inspirational creativity and the capacity for sustained work (6th). The whole phase contains *all* the other planets in his chart, thus further underlining his flair consistently to present himself in journalistic or literary form to the wider world. The placement of Leo and Virgo in the chart can also often portray further lines along which these abilities can be developed. Here there may be emphasis upon flowing performance of some kind (Sinatra is again an example) or they may take a lead position as teacher, perhaps even a chief exponent of something that has fluidity and they feel called to develop and share. Such can be seen in C.G. Jung's chart where the phase is between Saturn in the 1st house in Aquarius to Jupiter in Libra, forming a trine (free-flow of energy, in intellectual Air). While Jupiter occupies the 8th, Saturn rules the 12th, both houses concerned with depth and exploration. Jung drew upon reservoirs of psychological, mythological, oriental, historical and spiritual thought in the formulation of his ideas. Jupiter rules the 11th house of social innovation, where we find Mars in Sagittarius (the philosopher) sextiling both ends of the phase. Not only is Mars the one planet contained within the phase (which makes it a very important energy for Jupiter to be 'bringing home' to Saturn) but we also have both sextiles in the 360° cycle – one of reaching out to the environment (the waxing Jupiter/Mars) and the other of organizing one's contribution to society (the waning Saturn/Mars). Jung reached out with his innovative ideas and organized them into a coherent theory and practice of analytical psychology which continues to be *disseminated* far and wide. That his Jupiter/Mercury phase is also Disseminating adds to the overall thread of proliferation.

These people can also be natural organizers, not only because of their grasp of the principles involved but also *because of their ability to persuade others of the value of their work and recruit their support and help.* They would fare well in any situation where they can interact with others, perhaps through formulating strategic solutions for the management of any undertaking. It may be the entrepreneur with practical skills and monetary intelligence, or the public relations specialist who knows how to negotiate, network and speak out on behalf of others. One client was a civil engineer contemplating early retirement, but very unsure whether he was *quite* ready to give up work altogether. He told me of the many projects he had headed-up, including major undertakings such as new town-building. At first the only point of identification I could make with Saturn/Jupiter Disseminating was when he spoke of mediating between architects on the one hand, planning authorities on the other, and further still the building workforce itself. But there was to be a double-underlining of the phase when he said, "Y'know, you asked me what I would miss about my job if I were to retire now, and to be honest it's … well I just get a kick out of devising the whole infrastructure around these towns – y'know the roads, the networks, the rail links, figuring how people are to get in and out… the tributary layouts y'know. And just being part of a vast structure of skills and know-how that will help open things up, and flow". Pure Disseminating-speak.

A similar thread of connecting and uniting (building a communicative route) might be seen woven through a body of work which stands for something of *educative* value, such as in the life of Elias Ashmole. A man of great learning and many skills, including astrology, he particularly set his heart upon collecting. He was much taken with the work of John Tradescant, pioneering herbalist and botanist who, by 1630, had built up a hugely impressive collection of seeds, bulbs, rare plants and general curiosities of natural history. (The plant *tradescantia* carries his name). In order to feed his natural curiosity (Sun/Moon New Phase with Mercury contained between them), Ashmole catalogued this collection and became intensely, even ferociously, determined to acquire it. Saturn is conjunct Pluto in need-to-have Taurus, and in Crescent (persistent, determined) phase to the Moon in acquisitive 2nd house Cancer. Historian and astrologer Annabella Kitson also noted[10] a combination within him of an informed sense of the past plus the will to conserve it for the future and this too points to the Disseminating movement of something flowing from one point to be demonstrated and spread for its educational value (Jupiter 9th) among others. Eventually Ashmole inherited the Tradescant collection, ultimately donating it to Oxford University.

Saturn/Jupiter Last Quarter Phase

The essential theme of Last Quarter is that of reaching turning points which, if taken, place the person in a situation of more self-authenticity, usually with some specific purpose to be developed and contributed to the outer world. In terms of practical self-sustainment, a frequent pattern is for the individual to launch themselves into a working role early on in adult life, possibly even one that seems just right for them, yet it becomes boring and meaningless at a fairly early stage. It is also common for a person to report that they feel like 'outcasts' in the prevailing culture's work and career considerations. They increasingly cannot connect with them and seem to be casting around as if looking for a place where they might 'fit'. Superficially it may look as if just sheer bad luck or general social circumstances have placed this person in difficulties, but at a deeper level it has arisen from an inner pressure within this individual to challenge the accepted ways of being in the world by 'proving' that they do not work. Nevertheless they may swim around in this sea of apparent meaninglessness for a while until the pressure from within mounts to the extent that they feel compelled to turn to an alternative path, one that *does* have a purpose.

It is also possible that this phase manifests as the person who follows a career which seems to suit them very well, they enjoy it and would be happy for it to continue forever. But somewhere along the way, they get *ousted* from it for whatever reason and find it very hard to get back in. They may balk at this situation, the frustration sometimes turning to anger and blaming and much energy can be expended in trying endlessly to get back on track. But they may be endeavouring to maintain an old pattern in their lives which, though comfortable, is one which the soul is seeking in this life to *move beyond* in order to express itself in more mature terms. Others try to shunt such a person into a different direction altogether, but this is resisted. Or it may be tried, but fails to work out because the heart and mind are not truly in it. They just want their old job back. But this would be like a plant that wanted to just bloom forever when it should be turning to its harvesting. The frustration and sense of loss are of course hugely understandable, but their purpose often becomes meaningful when, manifesting as an agonizing crisis of no job, no money, no outlook, the individual lets go of the insistence upon that from which they have been ousted, and at last turns to a different road.

Some natives of this phase may not follow what society might call a conventional career – or they start off that way, but then become deflected off on to a nonconformist road but which more properly fits who they are. Others may try for a career which they are feel is acceptable in the eyes of society or their personal background and may even fit their own true inner preferences... but then find that the pathway to that goal is very convoluted. They may even end up working at something which looks as if it has absolutely nothing at all to do with their true goal, but which turns out to place them in a situation, at a time or with a set of people who ultimately are *catalysts* for the road they were searching for all along. A case in point was Peter, who wanted to be a barrister. He saw himself as a leading Queen's Counsel, addressing the Judge in High Court, holding forth with all the ingenuity, aplomb and communicative flair of a high-flying lawyer complete with flowing black gown and much bewigged. Better still, he envisaged his life as culminating in becoming a High Court Judge himself. His father was a solicitor in a provincial town and Peter was encouraged to go to law school and had graduated. When I met him he was endeavouring to place himself in Chambers (seeking pupillage under the auspices of an experienced QC) but could not find a placement. This went on and on interminably and became very painful for Peter. Money was short, his father was running out of patience saying he should be standing on his own two feet by now, he wanted to marry his girlfriend but could not afford to... and so on. Eventually the financial pressures became such that he had to take whatever work he could find. Signing on at the Job Centre, he was given a job.... as a bricklayer.

For nearly three years Peter laboured on building sites, comforting himself with the thought that he could at least pay his bills. Until one day, on site where apartments were being constructed, a new owner arrived to inspect progress. The foreman called Peter and a few others over to join in the conversation which went along the lines of how soon such-and-such a wall, staircase or doorway would be *in situ* – until eventually the new owner said "Well, I have to go now – I'm due in court in twenty minutes". Peter was rooted to the spot and held the man a minute or two further in conversation. It turned out that he was a QC – *and there was a space in his Chambers for a new pupil! Nunc Gloria in Excelsis...!* All that was over twenty five years ago. Instead of trying to control life, Peter was prepared to listen to it and follow whatever path opened up before him. That path had suddenly turned into 'The Road'. Today he is a leading QC specializing in corporate law. And guess which division of *that* world has over the years most sought out Peter for his counsel, his ability to thoroughly understand their position and represent them in court cases? Yes – the construction industry.

One of the key assets within this person is the ability to generate new ways of doing things and display an innovative flair in their field of endeavour. From an early and exacting academic education, Microsoft boss, Bill Gates, first intended to be a lawyer but then took the road off into computers. In his chart, this phase contains another – the Jupiter/Mercury Crescent which we touched upon in Chapter 8 – as well as the inspiration and originality of a Sun/Neptune conjunction square Uranus, plus the Mars and Pluto positions for drive and power. Saturn/Jupiter Last Quarter, which saw his turning point from law to computers, also contains all the other planets bar Moon and Uranus (innovation) which stand in a Disseminating (communications) trine from the 10th (Moon conjunct Aries MC) to the 1st. However, if a person does *not* find such a road, it may be that part of the problem is that their insights seem impractical or even destructive to those around (who may be following a more conventional pathway). They may see this person as 'out of step' or a 'rebel' or just plain awkward. But, as we have seen, they are looking for *meaning* in their world of work and if there is sufficient clarity about this, then the rumblings and grumblings of those around who may have a problem with the radical or innovative are less likely to be given credence, or even heard. On the other hand, if the individual finds no road open but keeps insisting that there *should* be one, they may need to resist trying to control life by foisting themselves upon it to go down precisely the avenues they personally want, when they want it. Instead they may need to simply surrender to whatever *does* arise, even though they may deem it alien or undesirable, but which (as for Peter) can eventually emerge as the route to what was sought all along.

Saturn/Jupiter Balsamic Phase

As a phase which calls for a depletion from the past and a concentration upon the future, it gives rise to a prescient sense of an alternative purpose to be developed, one which this person feels powerfully drawn to bring into being and even totally preoccupied by. If this is unrecognized, or refuted, conversely there can be a sort of world-weariness as a result of which (in Saturn/Jupiter terms) this person will seem disconnected from the goals and material trends prevailing in their society. They may be aware of them, peripherally, but still function in such a way that they appear to be oblivious to, or a victim of, them. Alternatively they will endeavour to embrace them, even successfully, but at the same time balk at them petulantly or in strident outrage.

To examine these possibilities more fully, if the level of practical ability within this person is low and/or they have not experienced any pattern from the past by which to organize their resources and skills into a workable role, then they may descend into feelings of helplessness (which again may appear as obliviousness or even indifference) and meet one failure after another. People around them may say they simply do not know how to handle the practicalities of money and successful career-building and describe them as "out of touch", "hopeless", or dreaming of a Utopia. Alternatively, they may work at something quite low key and appear not to be bothered at all about whether they have any money, or can contribute to society, perhaps even living hand-to-mouth from week to week. Some may be Heath Robinsons reaching high to build up a functioning economic life but from an idealized vision not sustained by any concrete viability. Others may live an ascetic life entirely; still others merely disorganized, impractical, dependent.

If this person (consciously or no) resents having to go out into the world and work at all, then urges from others for them to get a grip and get a job may be met with an air of obsessive indignation underpinned by a light (or heavy) layer of hostility. Sometimes this is not openly expressed (and, again, may be unconscious) but manifests as being unreliable, losing things, abusing their credit cards, getting in financial muddles and having to be bailed out. All in all there may be an inability to grasp their own inner platform of responsibility and instead they may blame the world at large for their plight. At some level, unless this type is very self-aware, s/he will often have an image of themselves as being a victim of society. The whole matter is one where they may feel put-upon by a world which would have them fit its material conformities, requiring something from them when all the time they are a wilting, dying plant (Balsamic). Ah yes, but – there those are seeds to be dispersed, a legacy of some kind to be left. This can often lead us to a clue as to what this individual has within them when it comes to taking their place in the world. Even if they cannot wholly identify with the clamours of the market place, there may well be the beat of a different drummer inside that wishes to develop and convey something of lasting value. That 'something' *may* have been shown to them by their past, but I have more often found it is a road of their own making, or one that few have trodden before. Either way, there is something this person wishes to inject with their own brand of purposeful vision, to enable it to stand the test of time. More positively still, and especially if they are open to deciphering what is truly meaningful to them, the urge from others to "get up and get out there" may well provide the spur they need to bring this into being. This can mean that they can inspire both themselves and those around them in devising opportunities to provide a workable means of sustaining themselves. They may or may not receive any back-up or support, but if their vision is clear enough this in itself can provide all the motivational force they need to galvanize them in their quest.

If there are residues of the past still being clung to, this person may harbour (or evoke in others) a sense of outrage or resentment, although not always able clearly to state what this is about. There may be patterns from the past they are unable to throw off where painful struggles were experienced and they saw no other way of developing; or there was a lack of tangible direction and support for their career goals from their family or wider environment, about which they are still smarting. However, there are also individuals under this phase who are very set upon their vision of where they want to head and are indeed successful in terms of material/

goal acquisition, yet still we may find there is another layer (of helplessness, weariness, petulance or outrage) which diverts their full attention. Such a thread can be traced in the life of John McEnroe who pitched up at Wimbledon many years ago as a brilliant young tennis player but whose preoccupation was to balk relentlessly against the authority of Wimbledon itself and especially one or two of its hapless umpires! Yet the seeds dispersed by this man were ultimately to lead him to a concretized sense of standing and prestige.

There are no planets between Jupiter and Saturn, thus nothing more for Jupiter to pick up before returning home to Saturn. This makes Saturn

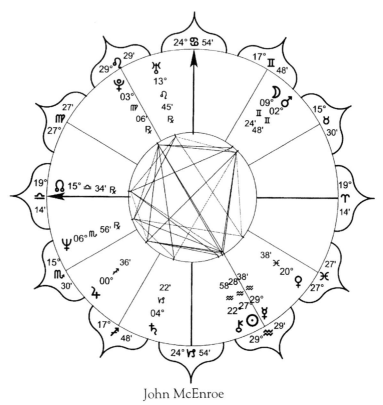

John McEnroe

a crucial point in McEnroe's overall purpose and sooner or later he was going to need to turn to and embrace its position in 3rd house Capricorn as opposed to retaliating angrily (quincunx an intense Moon/Mars 8th house conjunction). His route to doing so was indeed through being notable and rebellious: Uranus is the first planet to be met by Moon after birth and its

10th house position can, negatively, reflect a somewhat dominant need to impose oneself unnecessarily upon everything and everybody around. More positively in this chart, however, it calls for a creative uniqueness when seen in the light of the 5th house cusp Aquarian Sun/Mercury conjunction, as does the powerful Pluto in opposition. Having started out being labelled "a brat" McEnroe has over the years mellowed into a truer expression of Saturn/Jupiter themes as a consummate professional, today held in high gentlemanly esteem as a tournament commentator/broadcaster (3rd house) of well-merited authority and ability (Capricorn/Saturn). (The reader may also consider Sun/Moon and Jupiter/Mercury, both First Quarter, in relation to these themes in McEnroe's chart).

Another key theme for this phase-type is that they can feel very confused or disoriented by the discrepancy between what they witness around them in the concrete world and what they sense at some deep level. At their clearest, they are able both to see and articulate different (perhaps more compassionate) ways of contributing to their society other than entering the competitive rigours of a workplace. Such a person will focus upon (for example) a starving population in a third world strife-torn country while in the west we throw away millions of tons of edible food every year. Although most of us share this concern, it is the Balsamic who can particularly feel bowed by, and indignant about, it. Whether they are able to contribute a practicality which would enable compassionate and swifter action to take place, will be dependent on the condition generally in the chart of both of these planets (and Saturn in particular given its correlation with structure). Others will make stronger attempts to utilize their imaginative and inventive qualities to speak out for how things could function better, whatever profession they follow. We may find spokespeople for inspirational ideologies which are not based on hard currency, some crying out for a world where money does not exist on the basis that if we dispense with it altogether we would also do away with the foundation for many other types of hostility on our planet. Again they may meet with ridicule or be dismissed as over-idealistic but at a deeper level they are motivated by a profound felt sense that the way in which we human beings have gone about building our world contains many painful failures and is in sore need of a more humane approach. This thread of sensitivity and urge for amelioration may be expressed in whatever work they *do* contribute, such as charity or care workers. Or they show a particular concern for children and young people seeing them as emblems of a better future and supporting them to that end.

Creative writers, poets, artists, actors, musicians, whose work so often is reflective of changing cultural climates and collective feeling-values, may also be found under this phase, as can other kinds of world leader who speak out generally for benevolence (freedom, peace, love, unity). Two key examples are Nelson Mandela and Michael Jackson.

While it must be noted that the birth times of both these men are uncertain, in both charts the Saturn/Jupiter phase contains Neptune. In Jackson's case, it rules the Pisces Moon reflecting the fluid, childlike vulnerability of his personality as well as the deep interior emotional pain of his life (opposite Sun/Pluto). He frequently evoked in others either a sense of outrage concerning what they deemed as disconnections with prevailing conformities or indeed a compassionate understanding and admiration. The same may be said of Mandela's chart where the containment-in-phase of Neptune is accompanied by the powerful cardinal energies of Sun and Pluto in Cancer, the latter planet being conjunct Jupiter which, in Cancer, is noted for its caring concern. Pluto rules the Moon (in First Quarter square to Saturn), thus the entire phase leads us to several threads of his powerful emergence from strife and imprisonment to speak out for that which lies beyond cultural conformities to past patterns, asserting instead his vision of a new compassionate purpose in our world.

Part III

Further Dimensions

and Progressions

11: Further Dimensions for Planetary Pairs

The five core planetary pairs we have covered are sufficient to provide a deeper contextual understanding for our personal individual development. When we go beyond the boundary of Saturn we meet that which is unconditioned and we are called upon to be open to a greater dimension than we consciously know of ourselves. At the Saturn/Jupiter level we saw how the need was to establish goals and reach out to bring them to a workable conclusion in the practical world, both to underpin ourselves and establish our place in the society of which we are a part (reflecting Capricorn and Sagittarius). We could also see this pairing through the rulership lens of the successive signs of Aquarius and Pisces as we go beyond to the outer planets and build greater awareness that we are also part of a larger body of mankind and 'of our times'; thus our experience of ourselves moves from a personal, to a social, to universal level.

Speaking of the three outer planets with precision (especially in condensed form) means to attempt something which is contradictory since it means using personal functions (mainly Mercury and Mars) to express transpersonal states, beyond the personal drives that make up our conscious identity and often beyond words, yet they will seek to manifest and come into expression in the individual life whenever and wherever possible. If we are firmly entrenched in our Saturnian boundaries we may not be at all aware of Uranian flashes of heightened perception striking at the walls; neither can we incorporate Neptunian glimpses of unity beyond what we already feel, value or know, nor Plutonian depth-charges of shattering transformation so that something new can emerge and be born. Nevertheless when accessing these planets in the birthchart (including phase relationships) then, as with the personal planets, we need to acknowledge and allow their dimensions within us, not from a mentally-constructed viewpoint but as living functions permeating deep layers of the psyche as a whole, thus also serving our unfolding purpose through all its changes, complexities, transitions.

Pairing up an outer planet with any of the personal planets (including Sun and Moon) follows the same root idea of the phase cycle as a whole, where their relationship as a duo traces its eightfold themes. The principles of each planet need to be considered separately prior to their combination as a pair and there are similarly many levels through which we can trace and explore their outworkings. As the central unitary force of our existence, the Sun is not under the dominion of any planet and therefore takes precedence in being written as a pairing. Charles Harvey, for example, traced the *Sun/Neptune* dance through the cycle where, from a starting point of 'Individual Unity' (Sun) and 'Collective Unity' (Neptune) he wove a thread through the various facets of their combination (dissolving of the individual self, confusion, chaos... to enchantment, mystique, illusions, idealisms etc) through physical, familial, emotional, intellectual and spiritual levels and unfoldment of the will.[1] Similarly we may wish to examine our capacity for awakening and releasing from established patterns, questioning, discovering, developing innovation, insight, rebelliousness, breaking through to or away from, encountering the transformative – and for this we can look at *Sun/Uranus* which Virginia Ewbank and Joanne Wickenburg (writing as 'Jinni & Joanne') traced in *The Spiral of Life*.[2] Through such pairings we can similarly link natural polarities (such as Leo/Aquarius, 5th/11th in relation to Sun/Uranus), while other pairings in that same vein also yield deeper significance to chart understanding, such as *Neptune/Mercury* linking Pisces, Virgo, 12th and 6th houses and *Pluto/Venus* linking Scorpio, Taurus, 8th and 2nd.

The astrologer can also take a pairing that seems most to fit a specific area of life under consideration and submit *this* to the phase-cycle (again, whether the planets concerned are in aspect or not). For example a client may want to explore their capacity for developing life in consolidated ways that call forward stamina, self-discipline and cohesion (Saturn/Mars) or there may be a need for pioneering action, enterprise and improvement (Jupiter/Mars) or stability of love and relatedness (Saturn/Venus) ... and so on. While previous literature on planetary phases is not plentiful and much may be rather abstract, I would suggest that astrologers can 'play with' these wordings for themselves – and build upon their own understanding of the planetary energies to produce new insights on their combined role. Stephen Arroyo displays a very fine command of this ability in his *Chart Interpretation Handbook*.[3] Additionally, Alexander Ruperti, in *Cycles of Becoming*[4] covered many planetary patterns of growth through generic cycles of the hemispheres and quadrants as well as personal and collective unfoldment.

The Outer Planets

Uranus

When working with Uranus in planetary pairings we look to new perceptions breaking into awareness, challenging old patterns of being. We awaken to a way of seeing things beyond our socially-conditioned earthbound self alone (Saturn). It is perhaps most clearly identifiable as a flash of recognition that there is meaning in the Universe, one that goes against the grain of how we experienced things before; suddenly we see a road through a situation or state of being that, had it remained intact, might well have stifled us. Its energy is frequently experienced as lightning striking at the boundaries of where we had previously been 'boxed in', as though an electrical charge had built up and found sudden outlet. The result may indeed be illumination but along the way there can be unpredictable actions, feelings or events which feel disruptive yet can ultimately take us there. At other times, Uranus within us may emerge more continuously and operate through the personality in ways in which we are being anything from mildly 'unusual', to 'original' or altogether out-of-step with those alongside us. If we are completely shaped by the prevailing conformity of our cultural values we may have difficulty in relating to this planet and display no individuality at all, in which case the Uranian energies, needing release, may express themselves as high tension, nervousness, accident-proneness, catastrophic disruptions etc., not as any external fate striking at us from On High but reflective of our inner need to break free of matter and embrace a changed perspective.

Neptune

In order to reconcile the 'pieces thrown up into the air' by our experience of Uranus and give value to its heightened perceptions, Neptune is synonymous with an all-embracing feeling of unity within a formless state. If we have difficulty in taking an entirely open attitude to Uranus, this is even more true of Neptune, for the states of consciousness described by the mystics as feelings of universal love, bliss and ecstasy in the presence of wholeness are an expression of this planet. These are fairly rare states, even for mystics, and perhaps the nearest most human individuals come to absorb and express them is through momentary feelings of uplift and serenity evoked through great works of art, poetry, music, prayer etc. Some may experience a more particular state of surrender to, and envelopment by, the totality of everything as One – where there is no separateness and the logical (or any other kind of) mind has no place. A more usual expression of Neptune manifesting in the average human being is romanticism – a vague glimpse of beauty beyond the concerns of everyday life. Neptune requires the sacrifice of personal values and if this is responded to willingly an evolutionary spiritual step ahead can take place. Most often we become aware of such inner dynamics in a wordless way and over a period of time through a deep immersion in something dissolving from our lives. Neptune can also function as discontent, or the need for fusion and oneness can emerge as a regressive longing for a return to what is perceived as an ideal or perfection. Neptune is further linked with illusion, disappointment, deception and loss; all these ideas are valid when we view them from the standpoint of our personal lives and our usual 'success-or-failure framework'. But the needs of the total psyche may well be different from what we merely see as personally desirable. Hence we may stumble blindly through disappointments or losses in the totality of our lives so that inner fixed concepts of ourselves (planets up to Saturn) can be revealed and submitted to revelation and dissolution, as if slowly drawing aside a curtain covering a doorway.

Pluto

In today's evolutionary consciousness, significant numbers of people are learning to embrace the principles of Uranus on a personal individual level without too much distortion, if only for short periods; attaining a similarly undistorted expression/inclusion of Neptune and Pluto is taking a little longer but it would seem that a fuller incorporation of these outer planets is the next leap for us to assimilate as we go further into this millennium.

Pluto represents the transpersonal drive for a total shattering of the Saturn-bound personality so that a complete rebirth can emerge. But what does this actually mean for the individual? One example of it in operation was perhaps the experience of St. Paul on the Road to Damascus. Whatever its actual nature, it is clear he went through some kind of explosive and traumatic transformation beyond his personal power to control, which resulted in the death of his old identity and the birth of a new one. While we live on Earth, we need to operate within some kind of form and it is the familiarity and structure of this form that is submitted to the Plutonian upheaval. What the average human individual may expect of Pluto is perhaps a transformation of small parts of the personality, or rather the roots that underlie a part of the personality, such that after the experience of

Pluto one may remain much the same outwardly, yet inwardly something is significantly and irrevocably changed. Others around us may not be aware of the huge shift which has occurred, but within the totality of our individual experience there is no question. This kind of inner upheaval can occur through any pathway, but through it deep-rooted decisions about ourselves are exposed to the light. While we may be able to continue functioning in our lives on a day-to-day level (or in some instances we may need assistance and understanding to help us move through the process), nevertheless our being as a whole will be permeated with an entirely new quality. Pluto within us can be very subtle (the mythological Pluto wore a helmet which rendered him invisible to earthly men) hence our experience of this planet can be difficult to detect and define with immediacy. One side of Pluto may be the rare, dramatic conversion of a St. Paul, while another, perhaps more common, manifestation is the slow, inexorable, yet deeply fundamental emotional changes accompanying the shedding (or indeed 'shredding') of protective layers in an individual's life. If we remain totally unaware of the process, Pluto (if it is to manifest at all) will probably appear as obsessiveness or needs for pungent control.

Chiron

Chiron is situated between the orbits of Saturn and Uranus and since its discovery in 1977 much fascinating work has been done[5] to bring its meanings to the forefront of astrological understanding. It symbolizes both the dark and the light: the submission to the darkness of carrying a wound in our lives and the subsequent reaching toward the light of recovery and renewal. Conversely, embracing a suffering may be supplanted by circumnavigating it, thus the individual continually recreating and experiencing the wound in one form or another.

Much of the work on understanding Chiron has come from studying the mythical figure of half-man, half-horse, wounded by a poisonous arrow piercing his lower body and from which he could not heal. His subsequent training led to his running a school for heroes-in-the-making from which he passed on his skills in warfare, medicine, music and much else besides. This marks his courage and audacity in *going through* in spite of the carried wounds. His healing/teaching qualities have been focused upon in Barbara Hand Clow's work[6] and also in Eve Jackson's researches,[7] while Dennis Elwell has written vividly of the maverick who cannot be encapsulated into any fixed category, and follow a conformity.[8] Many times people with Chiron prominent cannot 'belong to the club' because to do so would be to sacrifice the step they know they must take to go through transitional wounds to find a greater and deeper truth about their inner selves. It takes considerable mettle (or a little bit of 'spunk') to step up to the plate and follow such a path and Chiron's role in phase-relationships can often reflect this. Dr. Martin Luther King wrote of being a "transformed nonconformist"[9] in a world where the pressures of the crowd bid us to follow its prevailing opinions and beliefs; notably he was born with Chiron rising in Last Quarter (need for proclamation) square to Mercury in independent (maverick) Aquarius in the 10th house.

Tracing this planet within the phases, we may elucidate much about not only our woundedness but also the threads of perseverance to meet the challenge of its meaning, to which the phase itself will also be a guide. In so doing we find that the experience is not only personal to us but simultaneously takes us to our connectedness among others where we give recognition to the wound as a collective archetypal process. For a consummate coverage of Chiron's astrological, psychological and spiritual connections, I would particularly refer the reader to Melanie Reinhart's work, *Chiron and the Healing Journey*[10] which provides many pathways for discovery, borne of the author's profound research and direct inner experience.

Collective Cycles and Phases

It is similarly instructive to look at world trends set against the backdrop of the eight-fold cycle of phases. As an example, in the early 1940s, then again in the late 1980s, there was a conjunction of *Uranus with Saturn* (the cycle from one conjunction to another being c.45 years). Thus a fusion of 'the old' with 'the new' and a generational turning point which can commence with great tension and irritability, out from which springs a breaking with established traditions in order to introduce newer, progressive outlooks. Robertson[11] offered a cyclic tracing of this pairing where at New Phase that which is seeking liberation is automatically expressed through the unfolding lives of individuals born during it. As the cycle progresses to Crescent (roughly six years later) those born at that time will put more obvious striving into individuality rather than clinging to a past; on to First Quarter where we find activists, fighters, warriors demanding change, into Gibbous whereby a workable way forward can be found for the changes that have occurred, on to Full Phase (where we are at the time of writing, 2010-11) and where the meaning of the earlier conjunction (1988) comes into full realization. Whatever arose twenty-two years earlier at the conjunction has to be brought into awareness and a balance struck between being an individual person on the one hand and a social being on the other (the opposition point). Indeed some of the emerging current dissents against curtailment of freedom are but one expression of this and as we progress through this cycle from now until the next conjunction (in 2032) people will be born who will come to reflect the remaining phases of Disseminating, Last Quarter and Balsamic where, consecutively, awarenesses can be shared and communicated more openly, then emerge into more matured expressions and finally submitted to deeper transitions to pave the way for the next conjunction where the old and the new must meet again to build yet another evolutionary cycle.[12]

Still wider and deeper expressions of our collective turning points and transitions can be explored from planetary pairings such as *Pluto/Uranus* (a long cycle of c.127 years where the conjunction last occurred in 1965 in mid-Virgo and we have now (2011) entered the First Quarter square). The fusion of these two planets represents truths, principles and progressive ideas forcing themselves out from darknesses under which they have long been held. The need for release from constraint is accompanied by a plunge into fragmentary unrest, dissension, escalations of a revolutionary nature and catastrophic events in nature. These we see heralding, indeed already accompanying, many changes across the globe today, rocking foundations and toppling repressive power structures (Pluto, which is also now travelling through Capricorn moreover), shaking free to find a more liberated spectrum within which to function. That planetary cycle in turn accompanies a New Phase Uranus/Jupiter (2010-11) denoting an impulse for radical change, creating new openings and expansion to new horizons. In addition Jupiter commenced a New Phase cycle with Neptune at the end of 2009 and Neptune entered its own sign of Pisces in 2011-12. This latter cycle suggests a more expanded and encompassing spiritual quest, the advent of which many are now also feeling, in which we are more and more turning not only to examining the exterior conditions but also the interior meaning of our lives, the one reflective of the other. As we move further into these cycles it is indeed to be hoped that we can do so with integrity and compassion for ourselves and each other, as well as for those who will come after us.

The very many possibilities for exploration of these and other cycles throughout human history require careful and deep scrutiny in the understanding of our evolutionary growth, the prior conjunction to any planetary pair always providing the essential touchstone for what is endeavouring to unfold. For a profound exploration and coverage of planetary cycles in magnificent detail, the work of philosopher and cultural historian Richard Tarnas in *Cosmos and Psyche* is not surpassed.[13]

12: The Progressed Lunation Cycle

The progressed cycle traces the movement of *progressed* Sun and *progressed* Moon (not progressed to natal) following the day-for-a-year technique of secondary progressions. It reflects the overall growth of the person in terms of moving through each of the different phases depicting the ongoing cyclic *relationship* between the two Lights.

Progressed-to-natal calculations show us positional changes. The progressed Sun alighting upon the natal Moon would highlight the essential meaning of the Moon (according to its sign, house, aspects etc.) and, from that part of us, for a while we may shine further or deplete. The natal Moon, however, does not impact upon the progressed Sun, hence they are for a while in a positional interaction rather than a shared cyclic relationship. These progressions (whether between Sun and Moon or any other progressed to natal planet) refer to our subjective growth and are largely used in terms of tracing events or other correspondences along the lines of the planets involved. The progressed-to-progressed calculations, on the other hand, put us in touch with a more transpersonal perspective of interior purpose developing from who we intrinsically are. Here there is less attachment to identification with outcomes in concrete terms, more a detached observation of an overall meaning unfolding. Within this, however, the quickly progressing Moon can also help us clarify more tangible correspondences bringing this meaning into actuality. Just as the synodic period between two successive New Moons is approximately 30 days, so too the progressed Lunation Cycle corresponds to roughly 30 years. Therefore if we live to the age of 90 years or more we can experience three such cycles, each reflecting a significant characterization to the 30-year period unfolding. Correspondingly, each hemisphere will cover some 15 years of life, each quadrant approximately 7½ years and therefore each of the eight phases some 3½ years.

The fact that we were born during a particular phase of the Lunation Cycle means that we will experience the progressed phases at different junctures of our lives, but our natal Sun/Moon phase will underpin the way we approach them. In terms of the two main points dividing the waxing and waning hemispheres (progressed New and Full Moons) these mark important beginning-and-ending transitions. If we are born in the waxing part of the cycle we will first meet a progressed Full Moon and then, about 15 years later, a progressed New Moon – whereas if we are born in the waning hemisphere we will first meet a progressed New Moon and then 15 years later a progressed Full Moon. Psychologically the difference is an important one in the light of the essential two hemispheric meanings which we met in Chapter 1. If we are born in any of the phases of the waxing hemisphere we will develop our lives inwardly from a context *of building and developing out from a past* until the progressed Full Moon is reached. From that point we are the waning hemisphere and can start to relate outwardly to the environment, based on what we have been able to form in the waxing hemisphere. Conversely, if we are born in the waning hemisphere we will first express an innate interaction with our surroundings *dispersing our energies outward into a future*, until the progressed New Moon is reached where we will start a cycle of building up our inner development along the lines of a new set of circumstances. However, while the New and Full Moons and the way we move through them are crucial in meaning, we are not of course just dealing with two hemispheres, but eight phases in all.

The movement from one phase to another begins in childhood where, objectively, there is limited capacity consciously to act. A person may be born with Sun/Moon in Balsamic Phase and meet a progressed New Moon at, say, 1½-2 years old. In terms of tangible input there is nothing the little child can personally do to start a new individual way of life, yet within the entire experience something new will be 'born' which constellates a turning point in the psyche of that child. As an existential experience, it becomes an important inner motivational energy given that it is occurring at a young age when conditioning is developing. The fact that s/he is not actually capable of personal individual action concerning it may even become part of a frustration in his/her overall consciousness. Some 30 years later s/he will meet a second progressed New Moon when there is of course more ability to meet the transition in greater awareness (and even relate it to the original young babyhood experience if such is known).

Tracing progressed phases during your earlier life by recalling (or hearing of) important transitions, can provide much illumination for witnessing your unfolding self-actualization from birth as well as tracking the cycle onwards after the age of 30. One man was born with Sun/Moon towards the end of Full Phase, shortly to enter Disseminating. Always a very outgoing child, he readily adapted himself to all that his world had to offer in terms of learning, activity, relating etc. By the time he reached the age of 5, it was clear that he was an exceptionally bright child, especially when it came to music and more especially playing violin and piano. By progression, he had reached the Last Quarter Phase (diverting to a different road) and his parents began murmuring about whether they should seek specialized tuition. As that phase progressed and he headed towards 8-9 years, he was indeed increasingly seen as a 'child prodigy' and by the time he entered his progressed Balsamic Phase he was enrolled in a specialist musical school (there to disperse the seeds of his innate talent to live on into the future). Some 30 years later when he met another progressed Last Quarter moving into Balsamic he was prominent as a soloist on all major concert platforms and immersed in long-term recording contracts.

The following diagrams show (a) the generic themes of the two hemispheres/four quarters of the progressed cycle and (b) the eightfold cycle

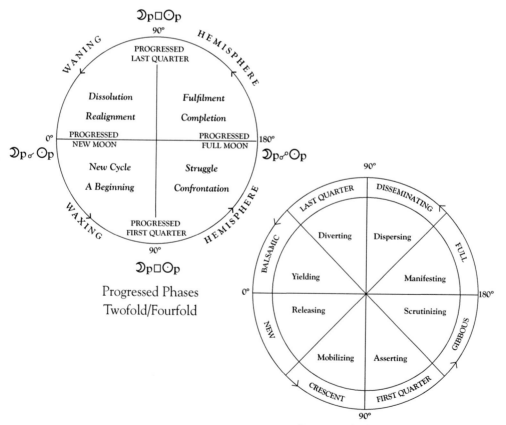

Progressed Phases
Twofold/Fourfold

Progressed Phases Eight-fold

with more specific intrinsic processes, each stage unfolding as a continuity in the cycle. Scanning over significant turning points alongside the progressed phase movements enables us to assimilate the pattern of meaning that lies behind what may be only our usual concentration on what is occurring in the foreground of our lives. Demetra George offers a helpful 'workbook' for this purpose in *Finding Our Way Through the Dark* (Chapter 2).

The Progressed New Moon

Meeting a progressed New Moon is always an important turning point. Wherever it falls and whatever its condition then, as with the other progressed phases, it will always be experienced through the lens of your natal Sun/Moon phase since this is the intrinsic 'way of you' throughout your life. We will look more closely at its meaning in terms of actual life experience in the next section, but for the moment there are some fundamental points to be borne in mind when approaching this point:

- There is a sense in which whatever has gone before in your life, particularly over the last 15 years or so, begins to mean less and less – you want to go in a different direction even though it is not immediately clear. In fact there is an inner *impulse* to do so which you also only gradually become aware of, yet deep inside you know you want to follow it. There may be a sense of 'coming home to' yourself. How you go about this will depend on your natal Sun/Moon – if you are a First Quarter you will absorb it as a challenge to be met; if Gibbous, then you will scrutinize it carefully for its meaning … and so on.

- The world around you may or may not recognize, understand or accept this new cycle of life arising, especially since you may not have it too clearly defined within yourself anyway. But as it grows, it takes consciousness, courage and staying power, particularly if there are no support systems; the exercise of the will (its strength or otherwise) is a fundamental factor to focus upon and bring to light.

- The planet last met by the Moon prior to this its new conjunction with the Sun is an important indicator of the issues and needs now to be addressed. It also symbolizes the function, drive, or quality within you which you will most need (indeed want) to draw upon; it may also describe a key area of life which is being accentuated, as will any planet accompanying the conjunction or in strong aspect to it.

- The Sabian Symbol for the degree of the progressed New Moon (rounded up to the next full degree) may offer further food for thought on the nature of the new cycle. [Symbols for the opposing degree or rising and culminating degrees of the progressed chart itself may also apply].

- There is no requirement for haste! You have a whole 15 years or so in which to develop this new cycle and bring it to a fulfilment, plus another 15 after that to release its full meaning and potential into your world/life as a whole.

- The 3 years or so preceding your progressed New Moon are useful to survey because whatever you experienced then (inner and outer) will show glimpses of how you were in fact preparing for this new start. You might have let go of certain things, retreated into other pathways, tried out this and that to see what works and what doesn't. Planting 'seeds' in fact (the preceding Balsamic Phase)… all the while something within you knowing that the real moment to start anew is when the New Moon is here.

It is important to set up the chart for the progressed New Moon using the location at which you were when it occurred (astronomically), which will usually be the birth place. If you are examining the progressed chart for your 35th year of life, you would be looking at 35 days after your birth, but if in the first days of your life your family moved with you to another place then *that* is the location to take. The Progressed New Moon Chart is the priority chart for examining the now-unfolding life, representing as it does the new 30-year cycle being embarked on, but charts for each of the progressed phases can also be calculated as additional guides to what needs to unfold as you progress.

In terms of *when* things occur, we may track the quickly-progressing Moon by the approximation of 1° per month or of course by its exact calculation; while the two may not always dovetail, they will not be far apart and a generality of timing may be taken. In this connection the universe is not waiting for a man-made clock or calendar to register an absolute timing but moves in its totality unfolding each small (or large) spiral of growth to be woven in a way that includes the person's readiness to absorb and experience it. Therefore a precision of mathematically-calculated planetary movement, which befits other applications of astrology, needs to be approached with a more variable outlook when it comes to human expression. The gardening book may tell us that daffodils will appear in March, but nature shows us they will appear in their own context of time… not far off March, but when they are ready.

Finally, it cannot be ignored that the duration of the progressed lunation cycle approximates to the Saturn transit cycle of approximately 29 years. Whereas in the relationship between the luminaries (Sun/Moon) we are developing our intrinsic sense of being, Saturn is a *planet* whose function correlates to developing in the world of form where we devise structure and identity. Its cycle enables us to trace this development from baby to adult with all the intervening seven-year stages in-between. As with the progressed Moon and the Lunation Cycle, it is possible to go through three Saturn cycles in a lifetime and its movement can be correlated with our ability to identify the concrete ways in which we live out the progressed phases. As the progressed Moon moves through the zodiac primarily suffused with the purpose of the Sun which she gathered in at their conjunction, the attendant Saturn transit can define how we seek to make this a settled part of our development, the areas of life in which it can be grounded, given a sense of containment from which to flourish.

Sun/Moon Progressed New Phase
Progressed Moon 0° – 45° ahead of progressed Sun

> "… at new moons the people shall bow before the Lord at the
> entrance to the gate"   [*Ezekiel 46 v.3*]

Many people expect the progressed New Moon to coincide with a spectacular set of events, or at least one, heralding a new beginning. But momentous though this turning point is since it opens out to a whole new 30-year cycle of experience, it may not emerge with banners waving or trumpets sounding. Usually it is far less perceptible, emerging in still silence or with a whimper, groan or soft sigh. We *might* have felt ripples of it during the preceding year but, even so, it is likely to have been experienced deep down in a vale of wordlessness. Standing at the threshold of we may not know precisely what, the momentum is one of new possibilities emerging from the dark of an old cycle ending. We are twirled up into a new impulse which takes us to where and how we need to be, learning and adapting as we go. Outcomes are not the point here – indeed too much focus on what might occur can even halt the progress of what is inwardly unfolding:

"A cloud does not know why it moves in just such a direction and at such a speed. It feels an impulsion... this is the place to go now. But the sky knows the reasons and patterns behind all clouds, and you will know too when you lift yourself high enough to see beyond horizons"[1]

If we reflect back over the 3 years or so prior to a New Moon, we become aware of having gradually cast much aside from what went before. Perhaps some 'unwanted baggage' has been jettisoned leading to a sense of release on the one hand, yet perhaps also perplexity as to way forward on the other. Mostly the initial stages of the cycle call forward a need to be receptive rather than active so it is a time when we can act on our hunches and go with whatever we intuitively feel is right for us but there is no necessity to *push* for things since life has its own momentum now and we react instinctively to the emergent pathway. It may help to consult the Sabian Symbol for the degree of the exact progressed conjunction, although again it may not make immediate sense because objective, intellectual appraisal is inappropriate at this time given that any new phase is wholly subjective and we are thus undifferentiated from its essence.

During the coming 3½ years, at first we feel preoccupied with new possibilities, maybe even feeling a mite lost if they remain vague or only a dim outline on the horizon. As the phase unfolds, however, we begin to get inner promptings of where we seem to be heading. Even if these too seem imprecise, they can hold a gentle fascination, enticing us to follow until gradually it dawns on us that we are, in fact, developing in a new direction. There may well be new roads to be travelled or we find ourselves taking the lead in something (which in itself may seem to come from nowhere). We are the dance which this new cycle of life is now performing and, as it unfolds, the energies portrayed by its particular choreography become clearer so that we join in the steps with more awareness. Studying the chart for the progressed New Moon alongside our natal chart can further help us identify the gateway we are now standing at and bowing before.

As the phase moves towards the 30° semi-sextile, a new point of focus is reached and we feel prompted to enter into greater creativity. Even if we are still largely in the dark about it, at the same time there is a fuller feeling inside of something being 'on the move'. As we near the end of the phase there is a more obvious input to what this new cycle is about and our own striving is enhanced, especially as we advance towards Crescent which will require our persistence. Much has already been left behind over the past 7 years (since the progressed Last Quarter of the old cycle) and now we can allow ourselves to reflect upon re-anchoring our lives by finding a comfortable, workable place within from which we can enable the new beginning to emerge.

Sir Winston Churchill had a progressed New Moon in March 1943, the chart for which shows the 'new seed' in the 12th house powerfully conjunct Saturn (also the last planet to have been met by the Moon before conjoining the Sun). By this time he had been Prime Minister for some three years and here, at the height of the war, we have a sense of a new cycle needing to be established through an indomitable spirit, to create structure (Saturn) through chaos and fragmentation (12th opposition Uranus).

This New Moon on the 18th degree of Aquarius would provide a 4th 'arm' to the T-square of Mercury/Pluto/Uranus in the natal chart. It also falls on Churchill's natal Sun/Neptune midpoint and within orb of his Mercury/Pluto midpoint. All these factors give a picture of the inspiring orator in the middle of a theatre of war, stirring the people into strength of purpose and never yielding, while at the same time negotiating his way through destruction and dereliction. He would certainly have needed to trust his instincts (New) and tread warily (Saturn 12th). Just prior to this period but post-victory at El Alamein, Churchill had made a speech in which he said "Now this is not the end. It is not even the beginning of the end. But it is perhaps the end of the beginning". Perhaps he was endeavouring to verbalize an inner sense of this impending progressed New Moon but the chart for it shows three main threads to be woven: the building of alliances, endurance on all levels and strategic planning. Taking these in order:

The first planet for the progressed Moon to meet is Mercury (communicating/negotiating) the dispositors of which are Jupiter and Neptune, in opposition and each aspecting Venus on the cusp of the 11th house (allies, friends). This Venus position also falls on Churchill's natal Capricorn IC suggesting an added need for diplomacy, sensitivity, feeling his way through cautiously. Mercury itself is in wide square to Mars in the 9th (the god of war across the channel) opposite Pluto. Instinctively he worked tirelessly and taking a long-term view, not just of victory against the German forces but also wanting to avoid a post-war communist threat in Europe as a whole and for this he needed to build and maintain relations with others, notably Roosevelt and Stalin. Yet these were often agonizingly difficult since there were many matters on which they were in disagreement

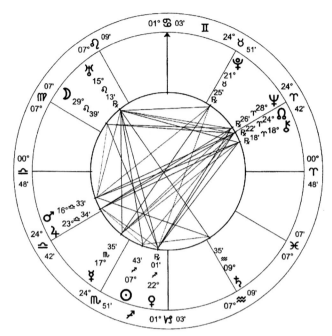

Winston Churchill: Natal

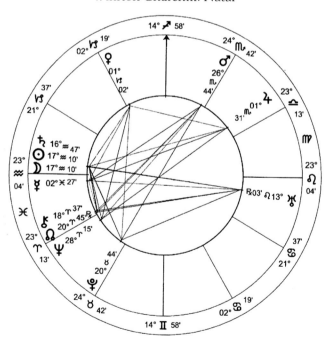

Churchill: Progressed New Moon: 6 February 1875 (equates to March 1943)

– in itself often an anathema to Libra rising who can find it stressful to have its own views countered by opposing thought.

During 1943 and 1944 in particular Churchill suffered a great deal of ill-health (the New Moon opposes the chart ruler in the 6th house of the progressed phase chart) mostly through pneumonia but (and especially as an elderly man approaching 70 by this time) severe stomach ailments through having to sit through long official banquets, sometimes lasting four or five hours, with Stalin. Coupled with stress from the previous few years which saw appalling loss of life on both sides of the conflict, he also bore the need to hold back and trust his instincts. Especially given the arduous meetings with other leaders who did not always share his view, plus many visits to the front including the D-Day landings in 1944, the call upon endurance for the New Seed conjunct Saturn at age 70 would have been *enormous*. Yet at the same time, things were beginning to take a turn for the better for the allied armies with success in North Africa and Sicily and the liberation of Paris. (Co-incidentally, as Churchill entered his progressed New Phase, Hitler entered a Full Moon Phase (completions/endings) with the Sun and Moon across 22° Gemini/Sagittarius – his natal Sun/Saturn midpoint).

Insofar as strategic planning is concerned, Mercury in Pisces plus the 12th house emphasis in the progressed phase chart suggests hidden goals, secrecy of planning – again, with Saturn involved, to ensure stability of purpose. The Sabian Symbol for 18 Aquarius is given as 'A man's secret motives are being publicly unmasked' and Rudhyar speaks of difficulty in keeping things secret.[2] Indeed, at this time Churchill was having to keep an awful lot under wraps in order to protect his methods and plans to ensure victory. This was the time when much work was taking place at the secret codebreaking centre and Intelligence HQ at Bletchley Park to break the German Navy's signals, followed by scrambling devices built to maintain secrecy of conversations between Roosevelt and Churchill. This has been said by historians to have shortened the duration of the war by two years.

The Moon's first mission in meeting up with Mercury (within 15° = c.15 months) takes us to June 1944 when the famous allied D-Day landings took place on the beaches (Pisces). By the time Victory in Europe was secured (May 1945) the Moon had reached 17° Pisces which is the midpoint between the Sun/Moon/Saturn triple conjunction and Chiron in the progressed phase chart (the healing through arduous process); moreover it marks the 30° semi-sextile 'burgeoning' point for New Phase at which realization begins to filter through that one is living and being the manifestation of a new beginning. By September 1945 and final end of the war the Moon had reached 22° Pisces which opposes the Jupiter/Uranus midpoint of the progressed chart (release) and also squares Venus (peace) in Churchill's natal chart, which is also the chart ruler and dispositor of his first house cardinal Mars/Jupiter (leadership, action, accomplishment in major undertakings) and a new era could begin. The spirit of this Progressed New Moon, in Aquarius, conjunct Saturn and opposition Uranus, speaks loudly of a dogged determination to break through and prevail. It is further preserved in emblematic form by the statue in London's Parliament Square – the heavy-overcoated, bulldog-chinned, indomitable stance with sturdy stick.

Prince Charles entered a New Moon progressed phase in May 1994. It is conjunct Jupiter in Capricorn in the 11th house of that chart (a royal head of state in the public eye) forming a First Quarter trine with Saturn in the 7th. This is accentuated by the last planet met by the Moon, which was Venus (squaring Saturn). His marriage to Princess Diana was of course over, their separation having been announced in 1992.

On an event level, tracking the Moon's movement at approximately 1° per month, it would meet Jupiter which rules the MC in this chart in 2° and two months later in July 1994 Charles appeared on television admitting his adultery. By the time Moon reached Mercury in March 1995, Camilla Parker Bowles had ended her own marriage. Upon reaching Mars by November 1995 Diana appeared in a television documentary and the war of the Waleses was at its height. By late summer/early autumn of 1996 when the Moon reached the Aquarian Ascendant, their decree nisi was announced. And by the time Moon reached 16° Aquarius and therefore in opposition to the 7th house Pluto, it was August 1997 and Diana was tragically killed.

Lifting into the level of meaning we can also see that the 9th degree of Capricorn for this New Moon also conjuncts the MC/IC axis of both the United Kingdom and England charts, so whatever was to emerge would impact upon the nation as a whole. The Moon's subsequent movement through Aquarius, crossed the Ascendant/Descendant of the progressed chart which is a reversal of this axis in Charles' natal chart, thereafter to meet in opposition with Pluto, the natal Sun ruler and in powerful square to the Sun (which in turn is the chart ruler). So we are led to a theme of irrevocable upheaval and transformation needing to emerge from the core

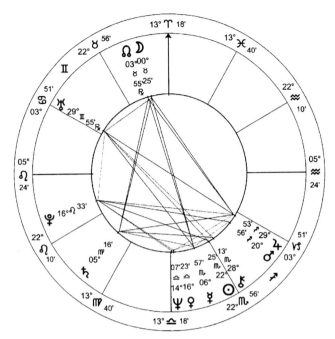

Prince Charles: Natal

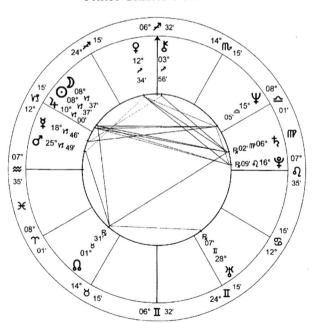

Prince Charles: Progressed New Moon
30 December 1948 (equates to May 1994)

of this new cycle powerfully focused on Charles' personal status and his relating life. Even more crucially, Pluto squares the midpoint of Charles' Mars/Venus Last Quarter Phase, the subject of our discussion in Chapter 9. Thus this period was to 'detonate' all of the issues of that phase through some kind of shattering in terms of his emotional development in order to lead him to a new threshold.

Sun/Moon Progressed Crescent Phase
Progressed Moon 45° – 90° ahead of progressed Sun

> "The Crescent at evening still startles the soul with its delicate flashing"
> [D.H. Lawrence]

It is not unknown for people to enter this progressed phase feeling irritated, put upon and perceiving life as tedious since it opens with the first 'alert' point in the cycle, the 45° semi-square wake-up call. Much will depend on the natal Sun/Moon phase as to how it is approached but fundamentally there is a distinct need to get going and keep going. There is much to be done and built up. It may be that during the preceding year or so (since the 30° semi-sextile of New Phase) there have been rumblings from below the surface that call our attention to just what it is we have to do. Now, it becomes more decidedly on-the-move. We know that we must put one foot firmly in front of the other in pure, solid endeavour to *anchor* ourselves in some way.

Each inching forward becomes a little more elongated than the last yet we know there is no turning back. Sometimes we find ourselves examining our insecurities here, but even if each step seems shot-through with withering effort, there is a deeper person inside who knows we can do it. Sometimes the obstacles may be illnesses or catastrophes which seem overwhelming in some people's lives, yet we see them responded to through incredible portrayals of human endeavour. As the phase progresses to the sextile, then quintile and certainly once we begin to feel more the pull towards the 90° First Quarter square, we attract assistance from those around us and the pace quickens.

The tedium and misgivings arise from the expectation of obstacles to overcome, some small but persistently irritating, some gigantic and forbidding. Where I live in England, there is a great deal of underground stone, often great hunks of the stuff to be dug out and there seems no end to the task. Yet it is constantly amazing how a new seedling will push its way around such obstacles and come up trumps in settling itself in the first bit of free-flowing soil it can find. Likewise, there are trials and tribulations for the human individual but it is in the gradual easing forward that we reach a clarity of intent and strength of purpose. However, part of the struggle also stems from an inner realization that we are leaving behind an established pattern that we had been attached to. Whether positive or negative it provided us with a comfort simply because of its familiarity, but then comes the 'other knowing', that we will be stifled if we continue with it. Modern-day speak calls this 'coming out of your comfort-zone'. Some people worry in case they fall at the first fence, but we can take some wisdom here from the small baby (somewhere around ten to eleven months old) who entertains no such mind-notions but, notwithstanding a few tumbles in the process, stretches and hauls itself up into a standing and soon-to-be-walking person.

In short it is a time of developing resources (both outer and inner) to ensure ongoing survival. Toward the 60° sextile, any feelings of stuckness and/or exertion can gradually peter out and a more sure-footed deliberation set in train. People, places, events somehow seem to dovetail more readily our needs and we can open doors on to a new sense of thriving. As we near the quintile, there is a heightened awareness (perhaps reflected in an outer set of events) of adjusting to a future turning point to which we are keenly attuned, even taking first steps to 'call it in'. There may be something specific to organize here or skills to be displayed in the service of rendering life secure. Conscientiousness and persistence are key themes at the core of this phase, adding strength to the new cycle we began in the previous few years.

Samuel Hahnemann (who we met in Chapter 7 under Saturn/Moon Crescent) was in a progressed Crescent Phase when he started translating William Cullen's *Materia Medica* into German and was thus prompted to notice what later became known as "the law of similars". The chart for this progressed phase shows the Sun in Taurus, harnessed in earth through a Grand Trine with an angular Saturn and the North Node, the latter notably in the 3rd house where the task is to develop a capacity to find out, search, study, learn from what is around you. Saturn is notably in the 6th of applied hard work, so redolent of his Saturn/Moon Crescent natal phase. Jupiter in Virgo is at the cusp of the 3rd, co-ruler of the 9th and still in its natal opposition to Uranus, here in the 9th – an assiduous, explorative, probing,

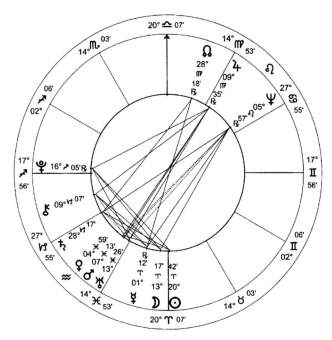

Samuel Hahnemann: Natal

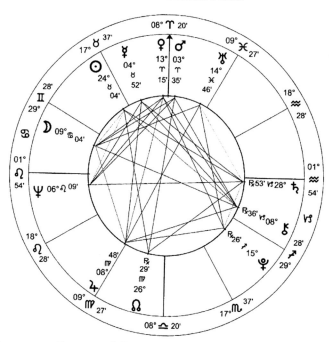

Samuel Hahnemann: Progressed Crescent 15 May 1755 (equates to Sept. 1789)

search which would lead to a discovery. The Moon end of the phase opposes Chiron in the 6th house of health/healing and trines the 9th house Uranus. Hahnemann first published his new principle in 1796, by which time the Moon would have progressed its way from the 12th, collected up Neptune (saving/healing and ruler of the 9th house of innovation) and gone on to conjunct the Jupiter in Virgo in the 3rd house position opposite Uranus, a signature of innovative publication. Although he would of course continue further to advance his doctrine over the years, this initial period provided the alert of Crescent Phase to work upon and develop his initial findings.

Quite often it is important to consider what it is we are being alerted *to* in this progressed phase. Sometimes it is the road we are about to travel, but sometimes it can be something within us that needs attention. Meeting a difficulty or disaster can frequently enable something within us, which might have remained dormant, to awaken and, through the alert, weave a thread that stands us solidly on our feet as a more stalwart person than before. This is something I learned from several clients along life's way, most recently via Tom:

In the early Spring of 2009 Tom decided, during a brief lull in his career as a television presenter, that this would be a good time to undertake major renovations on his home. A warm and engaging New Moon type, he approached the whole matter trustingly, placing the reconstruction and planning in the hands of a builder who had been recommended. Some money changed hands... much money – in fact many thousands of pounds, but on a mere handshake and with no contractual paperwork to underpin it. (Aaieee!) The (perhaps) inevitable happened and Tom found himself with a half-built extension in a now uninhabitable property, much dust and debris, the job abandoned, the builder having 'done a bunk' along with the money. Moreover no proper planning authority had been obtained.

By the time I got to hear of this (August 2009) Tom had passed the sextile aspect in this phase and had been helped and supported in this disaster by family and friends rallying around. However, something about it nudged at Tom a little deeper such that he phoned me to talk it over. He was now at the quintile enhanced prompt point in the phase where, as we saw earlier, there is a awakened prompting to the oncoming First Quarter square. Looking at this progressed Crescent Phase in conjunction with the previous progressed New Moon Phase (which had occurred during 2003-2007), my eye was drawn to the latter as its MC/IC axis directly focused on

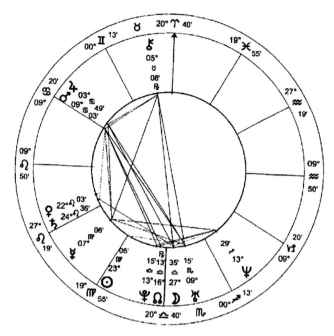

Tom: Natal Chart

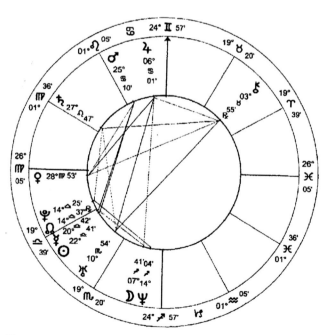

Tom: Progressed Crescent: (Equates to November 2007)

his natal Venus/Saturn conjunction, indeed with Saturn itself at the IC. A need for anchoring, grounding, realism perhaps, and here was the next stage of the cycle (Crescent = struggle) which might be calling that forward? Was the 'lull' pointing to a wider or longer period of less public exposure than might immediately be obvious?

The progressed Crescent chart shows the Moon first meeting Neptune (= loss). Well, yes, quite. In considering whether this was in fact alerting qualities of resilience and practicality to be brought into play in his life, I looked at his natal chart and recalled what I knew of him from previous conversations. Sun/Moon New Phase had come from a very happy and secure family background. Neptune 5th plus Mars conjunct Jupiter trine Uranus has great zest and enthusiasm for life. These gifts are lived out in 3rd house Sun and Neptune 5th creative avenues – he is a successful TV presenter and film-maker. Saturn/Moon Crescent calls for him to apply himself and indeed he puts great endeavour into all he undertakes. However, with Venus conjunct Saturn I wondered how he felt about steadying down to make value judgments and meet less active and outgoing periods... after all, it may not be easy to switch from a larger-than-life Neptune in the 5th, Mars, Jupiter, Uranus life of action, excitement, bright lights and TV cameras... into a boring old Saturnian need to check the practicalities and follow a more sombre road. Did Tom perhaps (even unconsciously) feel it was easier just to 'go with the idealistic flow of things, hope for the best'? And did this Crescent Phase call forward the need to mobilize himself more cohesively now? Indeed his natal Sun/Moon New Phase contains Pluto in the 3rd house conjunct North Node – was there perhaps a need for taking more focused control into his own hands rather than leaving things to 'happy chance'? Since I had also been told that this whole building programme had started during the rare triple conjunction of Jupiter/Neptune/Chiron on 27° Aquarius (opposite his natal 2nd house Venus/Saturn) again I felt this inner need to anchor his choices and decisions in solid reality rather than idealism, was perhaps the crux of the matter. And if so, had it just been waiting to emerge in a situation of struggle and material loss?

Just as I was pondering all of this Tom phoned, announcing in a very calm, sturdy voice, that he had taken matters in hand, liaising with the Local Planning Authority and setting legal proceedings in motion, as well as arranging for the building work to continue in other, surer, professional hands... plus solid paperwork. "I should have focused more" he said, "...that

Internal Supervisor we talked about" (Venus/Saturn) ...and his workload was changing from on-screen appearances more towards behind-the-scenes preparation of creative ideas. Here was a man sounding clear, forthright and resolute. With this experience of discovering, through struggle, the more grounded and concrete part of him, Tom has a greater chance of advancing toward his progressed First Quarter Phase, still flying free with all the aplomb of Neptune Mars, Jupiter, Uranus *et al*, but also keeping one foot sturdily and securely on the ground through his own hard-won willingness to be open to awarenesses of all that he holds within him.

Sun/Moon Progressed First Quarter
Progressed Moon 90° – 135° ahead of Progressed Sun

"There are risks and costs to a program of action, but they are
far less than the long-range risks and costs of comfortable inaction".
                                                                    [*John F. Kennedy*]

This is a distinct turning point with an upward gear-change. A challenge is to be met, and a breakthrough made. At the very least energy needs to be expended to set something in train that would turn life into a new direction. It is also a more distinct departure from the past, where we 'break cover' and emerge in a new light.

We are now drawn to a future that requires something to be taken to a full completion (the Moon is being drawn towards the opposition). As we look back over the last 7 years or so, life has consisted of finding our way perhaps somewhat gropingly, struggling to decipher next steps. Now we can begin to seek new involvements, perhaps with those who might help put this turning point into action. It is equally possible, however, that others have less influence in our lives now, the 'breaking out' theme arising as a literal one – repudiating past situations, people, places, events, perhaps decisively and finally. So too we begin to relinquish old fears, attitudes, worries, beliefs... and in their place comes a dedication to a new cause.

Much will depend on the level of clarity about the turning point itself. It may be starkly apparent but equally it may still be only half-intuited. Quite often we identify one turnaround here, only to find a little further down the line that it is something else altogether that is pulling us on to its path. Life is different to the mental expectations we had placed upon it. Nevertheless, we begin to feel we have some kind of 'mandate' and, if the way forward is obvious, then the energy is usually assertive and courageous, although this can translate as being headstrong and impatient. Remembering the Aries rulership of this phase, some people will try to do too much, too quickly, often charging out like a battering ram. It is true that we feel committed to this road, but we may be directing our energies with an intensity that demands everything should fall into place at once. If it does not (which is likely) then matters can become haphazard and disruptive. Turning to a new future requires steady action over the next three years or so, rather than a rushed bravado which just leaves us (and perhaps others around) rather frayed at the edges. There *is* a great ability to take risks but they need to emanate from steady determination rather than fraught desperation.

The first year or so of the phase may need to be given over to a developing awareness of what is actually being broken free *from*. It can mark a time psychologically when there is a shifting out from old decisions, established patterns of behaviour, or assumptions unconsciously built up to which we are still attached and may be eating away at us. We may feel caught in the grip of old negativities until they become escalated to a pressurized point; then the need to break free becomes acutely necessary. Remembering the need at this stage for 'de-cision' we can also cut through a lot of our old familiar 'mind-games' – those endless justifications and rationalizations we human beings come up with for defending our behaviours. Identifying them through an accepting observance can do much to silence the judgmental mind which would berate us for having them or indeed even ramp them up!

It is also not unusual to find that whereas we needed to reach out for help and support while making our way through the progressed Crescent Phase, here at First Quarter we may well find there are not so many hands to hold. This may be because they are not actually needed (although at the early stage of the phase it is part of human nature to believe that they are). Secondly, as we keep on reaching out for support and keep on finding nothing there, we at last awaken and are more ready to turn to the requirement of this phase which is the *individual* and *independent* acceptance of a challenge. Moreover, those around may find it difficult to assist since *we* have now moved to a different plateau, an identity shift has occurred. Maybe they cannot reach us even if they wanted to, and we feel misunderstood or alienated; but these too may be mentally-constructed *interpretations* that can halt the growth process that is more truly in operation here. That which we are seeking to underpin us in our quest actually lies within us, and possibly has done all along. So on the one hand it can feel lonely and frightening to break away from a pattern in life and face a challenge – on the other it is a comfort that instead of constantly striving for something that is absent or weak, or based on an old history, we have our own reservoir of courage waiting to be lived. Self-doubt is both understandable and a necessary spur to our development here, since compassion for ourselves as we embody change enables steps forward to be made.

Gradually our attention is drawn a little more to what we are turning *to* but we are as yet unsure what the long-term outcome might be. It is frequently important not to become too hung up on looking for definite outcomes in this phase. These are usually pictures set in stone by the mind and its preferences but (and especially as the phase moves out towards the trine aspect) there is instead a kind of inevitability about the way life is unfolding. We may indeed make crucial decisions, but still not know entirely where they will lead us, nor what *ultimate* purpose they may contain. Consider for example being at progressed First Quarter, fed up with your job and you decide to answer an advertisement for another position. You are selected for interview, pass it with flying colours and now you are on an entirely different road in a brand new career. That may satisfy us at one level of understanding the progression and we would say that the change of job *is* the concrete breakthrough. However, two floors below you in the same building is another person working in a different department. You meet in the elevator, you chat, you date, you fall in love, eventually marry and have children. Forty years later you are the grandparents. Three new little people in the world are playing at your feet. The decision to find another job way back then has led to an outcome which constitutes far more than you could consciously have known. This turning to meet a challenge and say 'yes' is a process akin to what a spiritual/religious orientation may call 'submitting to the Will of God' – a deeper purpose emerging from the more transcendent Self.

Sir Ernest Shackleton entered his progressed First Quarter Phase in November 1911 and began his plans for exploring Antarctica. It was during the following year that he issued his famous advertisement (see Chapter 7) in preparation for the expedition which was to take place in 1914.

In the progressed First Quarter chart the Sun is in the creative 5th house on the 5th degree of pioneering Aries, conjunct his natal exploratory Mars opposition Jupiter. The Sabian Symbol gives "A Triangle with Wings –

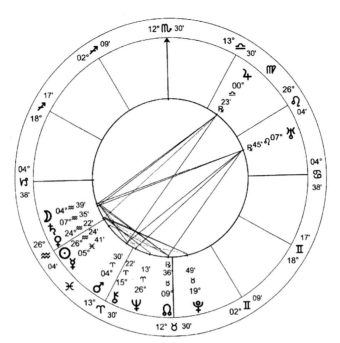

Sir Ernest Shackleton: Natal

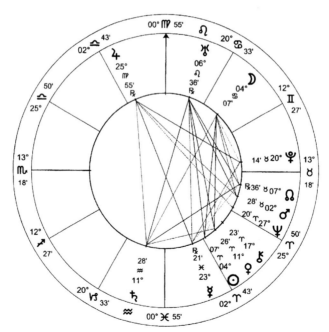

Shackleton: Progressed First Quarter
24 March 1874 (equates to November 1911)

reaching for higher levels of aspiration". The Moon is positioned in the 8th (hidden depths) her first task being to meet Uranus in 9th (exploration, discovery, long journey). By the time the Moon had progressed to 4° Leo (the progressed First Quarter trine) in June 1914 Shackleton had everything in place and two months later when it progressed on to Uranus, *Endurance* left British waters (on 8th August 1914). Notably, Uranus in this chart opposes Saturn in the 3rd – the long arduous journey of discovery.

Sometimes there are creative gifts long held within a person that now arise again to yield 'new fruit'. Donald was a successful civil engineer but had led an emotionally very arduous and lonely life (*inter alia* Saturn in the 4th opposing Pluto) and was now nearing retirement. He felt weary and tired of it all, harbouring no thoughts other than being able to put his feet up and just continue on his lonely way. But suddenly he was approached with a massive assignment for a project in the north of England for which he would have overall responsibility and would probably extend over some four years before completion (a progressed phase period!). From one perspective it was the culmination of his prowess in his professional field for which he had worked hard all his life to become a person of known supremacy (Pluto in the 10th). But from another, it would mean postponing retirement. Memories of tough, gruelling effort through a difficult life rose achingly within him and he almost collapsed at the sheer weight of the project looming. Yet, as he talked he began to realize that it was this very tough and steely resilience that was precisely what was required for the success of this project. He saw that his expression of Saturn opposition Pluto was through arduous aloneness focused powerfully upon a goal. In short, he began to validate these qualities and the purposes to which he had directed them, rather than seeing them only as a cross to bear leading to weariness. He answered with a very firm and immediate "Yes" when I asked if he was indeed the man to pull this job off; thereafter his whole demeanour became one of feeling compelled by it rather than fearful of its overload. Donald did not in fact retire for another seven years, not only overseeing the major task that initially terrified him, but two smaller key projects alongside, in the process being honoured (at progressed Full Phase) with a prestigious award for services to industry.

Sun/Moon Progressed Gibbous Phase
Moon progressed 135° – 180° ahead of progressed Sun

"Knowledge dwells in heads replete with thoughts of other men;
Wisdom in minds attentive to their own." [*William Cowper*]

By now we have come through a little over three years in which we made at least one turnaround in life. Maybe many things have changed and been achieved, while others have been despatched as unnecessary for the continuance of our life's purpose. The way things are going, we need to be very focused now because we are more and more pulled toward the Full Moon completion point.

The phase commences with the second interim 'alert' in the waxing hemisphere, the 135° sesquiquadrate which marks a need to pay attention to details. Therefore, and perhaps in marked contrast to the last few years, here we need to quieten down and become more circumspect. We start inwardly to question and go through a bit of self-assessment. We particularly look at whether there is anything we now need to correct or improve about our lives. If we are looking back in time, maybe things have not quite worked out the way we wanted them to, or thought they would, and perhaps there is a coming to terms with that. But as we enter the doorway of this progressed phase it is as if while one part of us is looking back, Janus-like the other part *is looking forward*. It could well be that part of the 'correcting' or 'improving' and paying attention is because we are now aware that something needs to be *properly* in order if we are to meet the next bit of the journey successfully. Inherent in this theme is a great sense of responsibility as well as focused insight.

A friend of mine who has run her own flourishing business for over twenty-five years is halfway through this progressed phase and looking ahead to the next eighteen months at which point she expects to retire. Before she does so, she is intent on ensuring that her business is in ship-shape condition, with all the accounts up-to-date, fully audited and that the order book continues to fill so that when the right time comes she will be in a healthy position to sell. Since several prospective buyers are on the horizon she is dotting every 'i' and crossing every 't' before nearing fulfilment (the coming Full Moon). Some people find themselves surveying long-term relationships or friendships, maybe looking back over past/present frustrations, arguments, blamings that now need to be put right since the future will be better if these can be cleared. Still others have reported that they know something has to come to an end soon – a way of life, a set of beliefs, an habitual outlook or a situation they have been in for a while which is less than ideal. Whatever it is, there is an awareness that one is on the last lap towards a completion, whether it be of attainment and ongoing effectiveness, or a failure which enables us to turn to something else.

There can also be an emphasis on searching out information or acquiring fresh knowledge that might open up avenues to a goal. It is not unknown for people to embark upon a learning programme of some kind that will provide them with workable skills and qualifications (particularly around the biquintile and quincunx stages). Sometimes an event can arise which calls this forward, such as one man whose wife became suddenly ill with what turned out to be a rare ailment. Many long months were spent working with medical specialists to research and understand the symptoms and find underlying causes, looking into dietary, medicinal and alternative approaches. The wife was eventually restored to health but in this Gibbous progressed process they met up with several others who emerged suffering with the same symptoms, both helping in their recovery and opening up the condition to more public scrutiny so that it could be more widely known and researched.

Inner doubts, anxieties and worries also may come under scrutiny, particularly if we are persevering very hard with something. Many of these feelings may revolve around whether we have been productive enough, 'done all we could'. Synonymous with the part-Geminian rulership of this phase, it can be helpful to keep open and flexible for there may be new realities to adjust to, or compromises to be made as life becomes reformulated. It could also be that there is a new inner value-system being built up, coupled with a strong need to eliminate anything which does not seem to contribute to this. People will often present for counselling or astrological consultation (or to any other means of help) at this time in order to help them sort out what their goals and values are for the immediate future, especially if doubts or fears of failure are also crowding in as these need to be heard and openly addressed.

Sometimes there is a sense of *waiting*. Waiting for what? It could be anything – an appropriate time, the right person, place or thing… inspiration maybe. Countless numbers of clients with this progression have said "It's all a bit in limbo at the moment… I've got everything on hold *pro tem* … it's not the right time…". The sense is that they will know when it is here. It can be worth gently checking that they are not waiting for perfection, however, since the process of waiting may turn into procrastination if one is looking for the absolute ideal rather than the workable. If, conversely, one enters this phase wanting to dash into things haphazardly, usually I have found that there are underlying fears (or panics) that provoke such potentially fragmented actions. There *is* a point – more towards the end of the phase and approaching the progressed Full Moon – where energy becomes escalated into rollercoaster activity, but in the initial stages it helps to approach matters as if you were about to create a beautiful landscape painting – it takes steady time and care to make the most of blending colours together, whereas recklessness can mean we mix and match our paints in a muddy way that does nothing to depict the beauty we had intended.

The real relevance of this phase is to know very clearly inside you that, yes, you are striving toward something, but right now is a time for carefully ensuring that all is in place and nothing has been left out. It is perhaps a little like being a host/hostess for an important dinner party, an occasion upon which much may ride. Have you checked every place setting properly? Are the glasses and cutlery correctly positioned? Have you ordered the right wines?... etc. The quickening of energy and escalation of output as we move toward the latter stages of progressed Gibbous is synonymous with the buds of a plant now being fully in place and almost ready to open into full-flowering. For our VIP dinner-party host/hostess above, this might be the last-minute dash upstairs to check hairdo, lipstick, is-my-tie-on-straight, before serenely opening the front door to first arrivals.

The escalation of energy heralds a closure, a completion, the cementing of one set of circumstances to turn to a new beginning. Musician, singer/songwriter, Buddy Holly, was approaching the final degrees of progressed Gibbous at the time of his death at the early age of 23. Poignantly reminiscent of the 'quickening' theme are the lyrics to his enduring song *Everyday*.[3]

Buddy Holly died on 2nd March 1959. The exact progressed Gibbous Phase had commenced some three years earlier in 1956 with Sun progressed on 5° Libra and progressed Moon 135° ahead on 20° Aquarius. This progressed Sun was conjunct his natal Venus in the 9th (conjunct Mercury) while the progressed Moon position opposed his natal 8th house Mars (he was killed in a plane crash). The birth chart certainly points us to inner themes of a life lived through perhaps disillusionment and loss but also persistent determination and the capacity for inspiration, with its Grand Cross of Sun/Neptune opposite Saturn squaring onto Jupiter opposite Chiron. These also point up his religious (southern Baptist) background as well as early musical

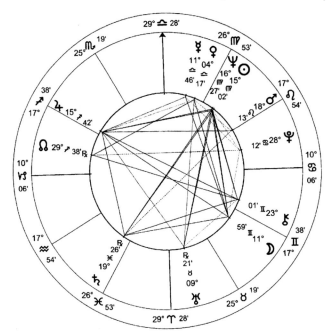

Buddy Holly: Natal

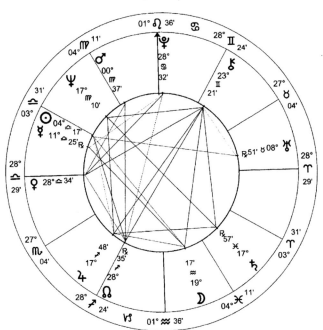

Buddy Holly: Progressed Gibbous
27 September 1936 (equates to June 1956)

inspiration. But more specifically from the perspective of our examination of the progressed Gibbous Phase, the Sun and Moon in that chart occupy the 12th and 4th houses respectively, both houses being reflections of end of life. The Moon was poised first to meet the Saturn arm of the Grand Cross in the 5th house of creatively-inspired drive. Holly certainly seemed from 1956 onward to be putting things gradually into place, as it were, like buds arranging their formation to full flowering, prior to his progressed Full Moon which was due in September 1959. During this three-year period he had become signed to various record labels, had hits with *That'll Be the Day* and *Peggy Sue*, then went through a flurry of activity from late 1957/early 1958 touring Australia and the UK plus releasing *Rave On* and *True Love Ways*, the latter on the occasion of his marriage. By this time, the progressed Moon on 18° Pisces would reach Saturn's position and all was in place for him to become established as one of the word's greatest artists, moreover inspiring many, many more around him and for a very long time to come.

The oncoming progressed Full Phase chart for Buddy Holly had the Sun/Moon opposition across 8° Aries/Libra – his natal Sun conjunct Neptune/MC midpoint. So often in encountering the astrological we are directed toward deep experiences via the paradoxical through which we can, in turn, access a settled sense of meaning. With Neptune, it is often that in surrendering to loss and grief we gain entry to the gift of inspiration contained within it, which is then released and permeates our entire being. At the time of his death the progressed Moon had reached the end of Pisces and was about to move into Aries, thus moving from the realms of inspiration and artistry into a new beginning. Had he lived he may well have experienced an even further magnificent blooming in whatever ways he was perhaps envisaging these; instead the world mourned his loss. But his Neptunian thread of enduring inspiration had been woven into the Whole and Buddy Holly did indeed achieve full-flowering of his talents and shines on in his purpose as a profound, creative influence in the history of popular music.

Sun/Moon Progressed Full Phase
Progressed Moon 180° – 135° behind Sun

> "Behold the flowers are diverse in stature, in quality, and colour, and smell and virtue, and some are better than others; also, where the gardener hath set them, there they stand, and quarrel not with one another."
>
> [*John Bunyan - The Pilgrim's Progress*]

With our arrival into Full Phase, we have reached the end of the developmental hemisphere of the phase-cycle. There is no further 'building up' to be done and whatever we have made of our lives in the preceding 14-15 years now stands. When we reach this culmination point, for good or ill, brilliant and wonderful or we think maybe not quite right, nevertheless there it is. No more can be put into it and now it must be related to the outside world.

This is a place of endings and beginnings before which we need to stand in awareness. Particularly over the past 7 years or so since First Quarter, we have been developing some cherished goals, succeeding or failing, battling/ flourishing, wishing/hoping, maybe ducking 'n' diving. If the arrival at this point is accompanied by endings which we deem negative, it is here that we can most be aware of the three-fold process of creation, preservation and dissolution. A negativity here can see us protesting and endeavouring to fix and resist it – a relationship may end but, oh, how we want that person to stay; work redundancy may be placed before us, shaking us to our roots and we try everything to stave off the loss and insecurity; a long hoped-for goal may fail or be wrested from our grip and we seek antidotes to the heartache. Such things take a hard toll and it can be exceedingly difficult for us to stare daringly at and accept them as they are. Yet in doing so (which may take gracious time as we allow our painful feelings to be expressed) we also come to see that they take us naturally into a process of dissolution of one cycle and the meaningful beginning of another in the never-ending creative spiral of life. A positive completion here may see us blooming beautifully but it is also the culmination of all we *can* reach at this time and so we can reflect upon it not only as a crowning point but also a gateway into new meaning. If we avoid this awareness we can over-reach ourselves, wanting to bloom forever and ever, perhaps blowing things up out of proportion. Overall, what we have developed and come to see about ourselves thus far is now fully illuminated, whether glaringly, brilliantly, blindingly, painfully, thankfully – but it needs to be *consciously*.

Sometimes people meet the completion of something their whole life may have been devoted to, or they come to a realization that there is a creativity from the past perhaps barely started but now coming to life. *Striving* for success is not the point here for if success is to be it will arise just as the petals of a new bloom naturally unfurl in the summer sun. Viktor Frankl reminded us of how deliberate aiming at success in life may mean we miss it:

"for success, like happiness, cannot be pursued; it must ensue… as the unintended side-effect of one's personal dedication to a cause greater than oneself…" [4]

Freedom after strife may be an additional theme, perhaps now leading us to an opportunity for something to emerge because a restraint has been removed. And sometimes what we thought we were embarking on as a new beginning following an ending can take us to unforeseen vistas of meaning and purpose. The astrologer, Alexander Ruperti, once recounted the story of his progressed Full Moon in the summer of 1939. He had finished his studies and decided to go to Switzerland for a little holiday before settling down to start his chosen career as a physiotherapist. He had also begun to have an interest in astrology and so he took some early Rudhyar books and writings with him plus his typewriter. *Fifty years later, he was still there!* What had happened of course was that the Second World War broke out in September of 1939, which broke everything else up and Alexander had to stay where he was as there was nowhere else he could get to. He could not practise as a physiotherapist because he was not a Swiss-national and therefore not permitted. Thankful that he had brought his typewriter and Rudhyar writings with him, he turned to astrology. *It was the end of his life as he had known it and the beginning of a new one.* As a Disseminating Sun/Moon type, he developed Rudhyar's ideas, after the war running workshops in Switzerland and France and thereafter spreading and sharing his understandings more widely. In the process he became known as a leading commentator on Rudhyar's work and contributed immeasurably to the development of our astrological understanding.

Sometimes the progressed Full Moon accompanies the end of physical life for this is a point of transformation. There are those whose passing holds us in its grip, such that we can remember where we were when we heard – JFK, Martin Luther King, Princess Diana… and we reflect (Full Phase) on their meaning, their purpose, that which they have left behind as a permanent legacy in a world of impermanence. John Lennon entered his progressed Full Phase in March 1977. The Sun and Moon in the chart for this show them positioned across 3rd/9th houses. By this time his home (Moon) was 'abroad' (9th), his application for residency in the United States having been granted in the previous year.

The Moon in the progressed phase chart is conjunct Uranus, ruler of the 5th house, the cusp of which is conjunct his natal Moon (opposition Chiron and Pluto in the natal 5th). For the bulk of this period Lennon stayed at

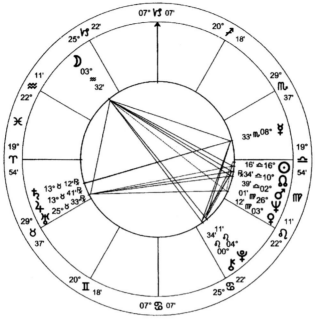

John Lennon: Natal

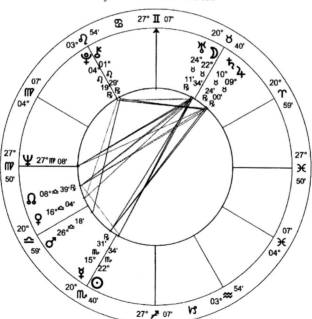

John Lennon: Progressed Full Moon
15 November 1940 (equates to March 1977)

home, simply caring for his young son, Sean, while Yoko Ono managed the business side of their lives. Given the natal lunar opposition perhaps we may surmise there might also have been an awareness (Full Phase) within him of now fulfilling that which he did not/could not do, or be, earlier with his firstborn son, Julian, by his former wife Cynthia. By the early months of 1980, the progressed Moon had moved to 27° Gemini, the position of the progressed chart MC, in square to Neptune rising. He resumed his song-writing, working notably on the *Double Fantasy* album (double – Gemini, fantasy – Neptune). Moreover it was a collaborative work with Yoko Ono (two of them – Gemini). This album would ultimately be released in the month prior to his death.[5]

In December 1980 when he was shot, the progressed Moon had moved on to 7° Cancer, which is conjunct the natal IC (end of life). The progressed Sun was on the 26th degree of Scorpio, approaching the 8th house (physical death) cusp of his natal chart; it also opposed Uranus, ruler of his natal 12th house (also end of life). Saturn had retrograded since birth back to 10° Taurus, thus within orb of a square to Pluto (which it did not form at birth), and occupies the 8th house of the progressed Full chart. Pluto in this chart is the ruler of the Sun in Scorpio and Saturn remains in conjunction with Jupiter (as it was at birth) but now, in the progressed chart, ruler of the IC (end of life again). One of the most memorable songs on this last album is *Watching the Wheels*[6] where the lyrics speak of letting go. Given that Full Phase carries much symbolism of an ending followed by a beginning, in the days that followed John Lennon's death the first track from the album, ((*Just Like) Starting Over)*[7] became a massive hit worldwide.

Karen Silkwood who we met in Chapter 8 under Jupiter/Mercury First Quarter, was also coming to the end of a progressed Full Moon Phase at the time of her death. The phase had started in October 1971 and by November 1974 the Moon had reached the biquintile stage (on 5° Scorpio to Sun progressed on 29° Pisces) suggesting an enhanced awareness that she possessed within her all that she needed, and by which she could distribute to her world (the next phase, Disseminating) that which she understood. She was on her way to deliver allegedly incriminating documents to the authorities.

The Sabian Symbol for 27° Pisces is 'The Harvest Moon illumines a clear autumnal sky' and speaks of fulfilment through work well done.[8] Since we know of her demise in the car crash of 13th November 1974, which came after her protracted difficulties in being a whistleblower, it is

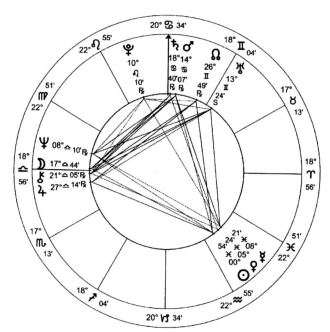

Karen Silkwood: Natal

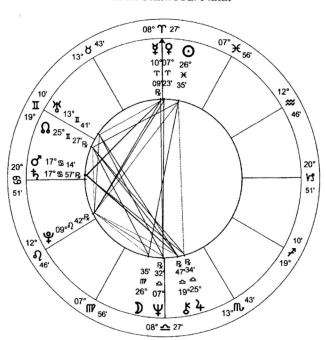

Karen Silkwood: Progressed Full phase
17 March 1946 (equates to October 1971)

again with poignancy, as in John Lennon's life, that we may surmise she had fulfilled that which she came into the world to do and be. The chart for the progressed phase also shows Neptune at the IC (again, end of life) opposing Venus and Mercury on an Aries Midheaven (a brave, outspoken, young woman) with Mars (ruler of the MC) conjunct Saturn in the 12th (end of life). The Ascendant conjuncts her own natal Mars/Saturn/MC conjunction which in turn squares Moon/Chiron rising. Mercury, ruler of short journeys, squares the Mars/Saturn – she died in a car smash on a road, suddenly. The progressed Full Moon squares Karen's nodal 9th/3rd axis and within orb of her natal Mars/Uranus midpoint (taking risks to speak out her own truth).

In this phase too, an awareness of our life hitherto enables us to understand what might now be relinquished. 'Relinquishing' can mean seeing clearly that, even though nothing may have gone wrong, something in which we have invested a great deal of time and energy must now be turned aside from; or we may feel disillusioned and sense the time is ripe to call a halt on something before it comes crashing down around us. Some people may initially feel the need to withdraw from the hurly-burly of life activities for a while (as we saw in John Lennon's life) so that clarity of vision and maturity of outlooks, or indeed fullness of being, can find their level within. In some circumstances, the completion theme of this phase may mean a defeat – something you hoped would 'bloom' in your life has failed to do so, or otherwise remains a possibility but elusive. Submitting to a different kind of new beginning can mean that whatever emerges from there turns out to be much better, or more meaningful, than what we thought we wanted (as in Alexander Ruperti's life).

Wanting to be alone or only with those who truly understand us is not unknown in this phase. At the same time a balance is being reached between, on the one hand, a need to think things through and feel your way steadily, and on the other reaching out to people around. There may be a special relationship in your life into which you pour more energy now, or there may be a new relationship beginning while others end, or a new *kind* of relating arises in an established partnership. Together with an awareness of *how* you relate to others, these themes can feature strongly to bring you to new realizations that will ultimately take you to the next progressed phase, where you will share and communicate what you have become, who you are, what you understand, more freely and widely. Indeed, as in the lives of both Silkwood and Lennon, this is so even after physical death.

Sun/Moon Prog. Disseminating Phase
Progressed Moon 135° – 90° behind progressed Sun

Good, the more communicated, more abundant grows.

[*Milton - Paradise Lost*, v. 1:17]

Particularly as we passed through the quincunx and biquintile stages of Full Phase, we became ever more aware of what we had learned and can now share. As we enter Disseminating we feel the need to communicate this understanding, by speaking, writing, publicizing, teaching, demonstrating or performing. Different people seem to come into our lives as a result of all this, but they also serve to open us up to fresh viewpoints or the reworking of old ones we held in the past. Perhaps there are some ideas running around in our minds here, but we are *not* in fact communicating them… yet aware that maybe we need to, ought to, should. Our voice may well need to be heard now for we may be able to speak out with a clarity that enables others to see a crucial meaning. Or perhaps we have the proverbial 'novel in the head' that could have been rumbling away for quite some time, but now the urge comes to put it down on paper and submit it to a publisher. As in the previous Gibbous Phase, we may also be drawn to learning courses, but in Disseminating it is so that we can exchange ideas with like-minded people.

If we met failure or defeat during our Full Phase we may also be licking a few wounds here, perhaps adopting a compensatory lifestyle to take our minds off things, or just fretting. At a deeper level what is occurring is an *adjustment* between what we hoped would happen and what in fact occurred (and needed to occur) although a continued seeking of reasons and justifications which would satisfy our mental constructs is an understandable human frailty and experience here. Again we may need to review old ideas taken for granted but never really given deeper thought. We also become aware that quite often our views are not the same as other people's and inwardly are invited to consider that their views are as meaningful to them as ours are to us.

A naturally communicative person will find themselves perhaps more consciously validating themselves for this ability during this phase and find a way of putting it to good use. Alternatively, an habitually quiet person may now take the risk and speak out. What they have to say could have real impact. If we are making decisions in this phase, especially those which involve other people, we need to be aware that we can also get carried away by our own opinions and believe we know what is best for everybody! Our world may expand socially as we go through this phase and we see that most of what (or who) comes into our arena has to do with what we are 'giving out' through our gifts of communication. This is directly synonymous with the plant attracting bees and other insects as an essential precursor to the continuance of life... which is what this and the next two phases are most intent upon.

Some people find they are asked to take their skills into 'foreign territory', treading a path not habitually known but which, in treading it, produces an element of learning and sharing information/know-how. I clearly recall my last Disseminating progression during which I was busy running astrology seminars and counselling training courses; at first I thought little of it since it was par for the course, although I was aware of an escalated demand which meant I had to schedule rather more than originally anticipated. But then I was interviewed by a Business Journal, which again I gave little thought to, until in the few weeks that followed I was astonished suddenly to find a whole host of corporate managers on the phone wanting an appointment. Within a short space of time I found myself on a learning curve, taking the astrological into boardrooms, human resources, recruitment potentials, partnerships, CEOs, MDs, and 'all stations north' in the corporate world.

Others may find they are written or spoken about more widely or publicly, such as Princess Diana, already in the public eye of course but whose life and marriage were chronicled in expanded-detail in a book by journalist Andrew Morton[9] during her Disseminating progressed period, which began in 1991 and the chart for which contains a Sun/Jupiter/Neptune T-square (the glare of publicity) and a Moon/Mars/Venus T-square (the struggles in her emotional-relating life). For others it may be that works they put into train find a pathway to become more widely known. Notably, Anne Frank (see Chapter 8) began to write her famous diary as she was about to enter into progressed Disseminating Phase in July 1943.

During the early months of 1944 the Moon would have progressed to form oppositions with both Mars and Neptune symbolizing both the hiding place and the hope of evading capture as well as the potential for deception and mystery. It has never been firmly established and remains a mystery, just how the Gestapo knew they were there, although it has been said that far from being discovered by chance, the Frank family were betrayed by Nazi sympathizers. By August 1944, when they were captured, the Moon had

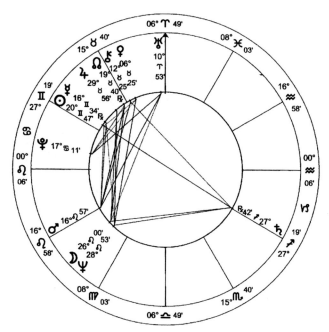

Anne Frank: Natal

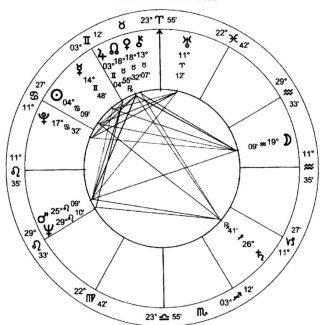

Anne Frank: Progressed Disseminating
26 June 1929 (equates to July 1943)

progressed to 3° Pisces, squaring the Jupiter in the progressed phase chart and also Anne's natal Venus/Saturn midpoint, symbolizing the curtailment of freedom. By the time of her death in 1945, and tragically near to liberation, it had moved to 10° Pisces, her natal Sun/Jupiter midpoint – a release and a flight into a different kind of freedom, we may say. The Moon would not reach Uranus of course until after Anne's death since the distance between them is some 52°, therefore equating to roughly 4½ years from the start of her Disseminating Phase (July 1943). Her diary was published in 1947.

Speaking, as we were just a little earlier, of 'learning curves', below is the chart of Helen together with her progressed Disseminating chart which equates to January 2004.

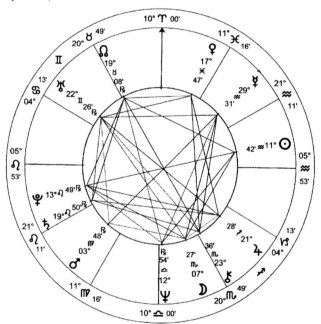

Helen: Birth chart

As a Deputy Head Teacher, in 2002/2003 Helen (then in progressed Full Phase) felt increasingly at a crossroads in her career. She decided to leave in order to become a government schools inspector instead. However, a short way down that road simply left her feeling dragged down into a negative spiral of formalized rules and regulations, constantly changing statistics-driven techniques and educational targets without, it appeared, any focus upon educating a child from the primary perspective of who that child inherently *is*.

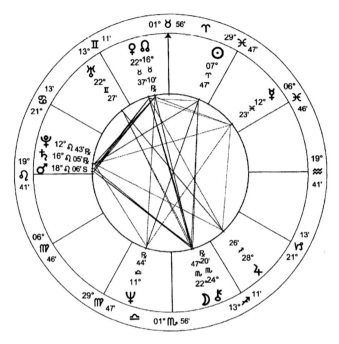

Helen: Progressed Disseminating (equates to January 2004)

Maybe many of us have a memory of an early teacher who, however momentarily, led us to a state of grace by giving consideration to our personal being. My old Latin teacher was one such and, in an overall unhappy childhood, she was a shining beacon whose classes I adored. Alas, one day she announced her impending retirement and after our last lesson we filed past to say our goodbyes. But as I went to leave the room, she softly tugged me back by the sleeve of my cardigan until the others had left. She told me she was going to live with her sister in a countryside village and, dipping into her pocket, she held out a little piece of paper on which was written a telephone number. This I was to use if I ever needed her, or felt sad and alone. Such little acts of unseen kindness have indelible impact on the growing psyche of a child. I had never spoken of my unhappiness, yet here she was addressing it lovingly, trustingly. I never did telephone this remarkable woman though, to this day, I still have that little scrap of paper in my possession. So when Helen began to speak to me of her increasing inability to identify with the educational changes being implemented in society, and how she felt compelled to focus upon the individuality of the child, something inside me resonated 'Ah yes, I do believe I have met this kind of true educator before'. She began to outline her felt sense of somehow needing to be a bridge between the methods of educational trends and parental ambitions on the one hand and their suitability in the child's intrinsic being on the other. Her natal Sun/Moon are in Disseminating Phase within orb of the waning square aspect; this, together with Saturn/Moon in Crescent Phase combine within Helen to produce a natural communicator and hard-working person who means what she says and simply cracks on with it.

As she entered the Disseminating Phase, and particularly as the Moon conjuncted Chiron in the 5th house of her natal chart by March 2004, she felt impelled to take the risk (the audacity of Chiron) and start looking into the possibility of developing her own private educational centre, working from her home. The Sun in the progressed phase chart occupies the 9th house (education) and the Moon is in the 4th (home). In respect of Chiron's position also, it is to be noted that this is the first planetary body to be met by Moon after Helen's birth, followed by Jupiter, both within roughly the first 3½ years of life. She had earlier described a childhood characterized by the joy of free creative self-expression. Early lunar meetings with planets reverberate each time this occurs during the life; thus, here was the progressed Moon touching off yet another round of this creative liberty and being presented as a drive to help today's children similarly to absorb this within them. Helen's aspiration (9th) was to focus on one-to-one tuition with the child (5th) while relating to the family as a whole (4th) but essentially teaching and liaising (Disseminating) "as a kind of 'ambassador' on behalf of the child" (her words). All of this would mean much preparation and work, not the least of which would be some skills retraining, *much* personal inner development (full, 'heavy-duty' Mars/Saturn/Pluto in the 12th house in T-square with Moon and Venus) as well as ensuring her standards, methods and never-ending paperwork met the necessary legislative requirements. It was a gruelling process but by the summer of 2005, the Moon had moved to 12° Sagittarius forming a trine aspect with both Mercury and Pluto in the progressed phase chart and about to enter the 5th house. Helen felt more confident that her goal was viable and purposeful.

As the Moon made trines to both Saturn and Mars conjunct Ascendant, Helen negotiated with her husband (who also ran *his* own business from home) as to alterations to accommodate a fully equipped classroom. With her natal Mars in Virgo opposite Mercury precision, together with a powerful sense of purpose suggested by the Sun/Moon/Pluto T-square and the natal Saturn/Moon in Crescent Phase, Helen briskly applied herself and soon had the whole thing in order. By April/May 2006, the Moon had progressed to 22° Sagittarius opposite Uranus, ruler of the Descendant (reaching out innovatively to others) and conjunct the natal Jupiter in the 5th (encouragement and education of children). Helen said "I suddenly feel completely *au fait* with what I'm doing – it feels like a great release". By the Autumn Term of that year her educational centre opened its doors to first pupils. By the time she entered 2007 the Sun had progressed to 10° Aries (conjunct her natal Midheaven) and the progressed Moon had entered Capricorn in trine to the Midheaven of the progressed Disseminating Phase chart, symbolic of the successful woman in the outer world. So too is the resourceful Venus conjunct North Node in Taurus/10th house of the progressed phase chart with which one frequently has to push doors open very definitely in order to take one's values into society – in Helen's case through her skill in sharing what she knows, understands and wishes to share with coming generations.

Sun/Moon Prog. Last Quarter Phase
Progressed Moon 90° – 45° behind progressed Sun

> "The Road goes ever on and on
> Down from the door where it began.
> Now far ahead the Road has gone,
> And I must follow, if I can"
>
> [J.R.R. Tolkien - *The Fellowship of the Ring*]

Having completed its blooming, the plant turns to the hardening up of its seeds and harvested crops are turned into produce to sustain ongoing life. Those left in the ground will host the arrival of insects looking for a place to live, especially those most accomplished of eight-legged weavers who will only too gladly hoist the first of their silken threads upon the now withering heads of the last blooms. The essential theme is of a turning point, which is one of maturation and letting-go.

From the perspective of maturity, since the inception of the cycle at the previous New Moon we have gone through a great deal. Now we stand at a bridge, captain of that collected up set of experiences which defines us.

We have to adjust to a platform whereby we express ourselves in our own right, with our own views, skills, ideas, standing on our own two feet. This reorientation may manifest as an obvious turning point – or there may be no outer event at all, merely an inner sense of knowing you need to 'tweak' your life around to go down a different avenue and something whispers in your ear "take a left here". We might, for instance, have built up a solid body of work in a particular field and perhaps find we now stand as a leading exponent of it. This needs to be released along a road where it can be utilized for the future good of all. One man who had travelled far and wide as an antiques collector, decided at Last Quarter that the time had come to retire and set down in an illustrated book all his knowledge of furniture and artefacts, east and west, through different historical eras. Others may take wholly different roads, maybe changing to an utterly different occupation or even emigrating.

From the perspective of letting go, for those who feel a great reluctance to release one way of life and adapt to another the fact of the matter is that one door has closed as another opens. Helen Keller once said that we often look so long at the closed door that we don't see the one that has opened up. If we are looking back in sad refrain we can be guided by the plant in nature which does not hanker after its days of blooming in the sun. It accepts the natural dismantling of what has been hitherto and turns to what its purpose is *now*. We often have to 'toughen up' (like the seeds) under Last Quarter, screwing our courage to a sticking post. Trusting the process is an implicit keynote in turning from once-sustaining anchors and striding out on to our own detour road. This may arise as a faith in the future or in the sustenance of the Universe itself and/or one's God.

Another client had enjoyed a lifestyle of much wealth and leisure, in the role of proud and vibrant hostess to her successful husband's many business contacts in their several homes in the city, the countryside and abroad. However, her husband suffered a heart attack within eight months of her entering progressed Last Quarter. Totally at a loss and of course in distress, she was at first unable to focus on the intrinsic meaning of the phase … until one day she phoned to say that she had come downstairs in their magnificent home that morning, wondering what on earth the palatial circumstances, the swimming pool and the exquisite gardens were actually all *for*, and idly turned on the radio. She caught the tail-end of a religious broadcast where the presenter was intoning "…and here shall thy proud ways be stayed". In that moment she *knew*. *This* was the letting-go and she immediately set off for the hospital to discuss with her recovering husband ways to take off all the pressures, perhaps sell up and dismantle the lifestyle. Nothing mattered more than that he should get well and their life together was precious whether they lived in a palace or a tin shack. When I last heard of them they had 'downsized' considerably and turned their resources towards a developing hospice movement.

If there is a whirl of activity in a person's life, it might be difficult at first to discern the underlying thread that is endeavouring to be woven here. Some may well try to resist it, while others report they want to take on something 'different' but find it doesn't quite work because (if they look at it more closely) they are in fact just trying to play a different tune on an old fiddle. But then one comes across those who Life itself seems to invite to step forward in a maturity of their being, hewn from the rock of their encounters, experiences, completions, joys and even sufferings thus far. Princess Diana entered a progressed Last Quarter Phase in March 1994.

The previous progressed Disseminating Phase had seen an escalation of publicity around the state of her marriage and this Last Quarter Phase continued the process of being hounded by the press. The chart for the phase shows the Sun in the 10th and Moon in the 7th, both forming a T-square to a rising Neptune (an aspect-pattern also carried over from her previous Disseminating period). From Diana's perspective the focus was upon her marriage (Moon in the 7th) and what she was up against in terms of her position and that of the Royal Family (Sun conjunct Leo in the 10th), with Neptune in the 1st mirroring the overwhelming publicity within which all this took place. Yet now in Last Quarter there were turning points and roads forward to be taken, initially manifested via her famous television interview in 1995 and, of course, the divorce from Prince Charles in 1996.

The Neptunian T-square not only suggests the maelstrom of publicity, but also the emotional suffering, loss and searching she was going through, and, still further, themes of sacrifice and transcendence. Viktor Frankl referred to 'self-transcendence' as the capacity to emerge reaching "beyond self concerns in order to fulfil a purpose and/or forge encounters with others in dedication to a cause".[10] In this connection one of the interesting factors is the *containment* of planets within the Sun/Moon, i.e. Venus and Mercury. Beneath all the obvious marital and emotional mayhem she was dealing with, there was a maturity of communication beginning to arise within her

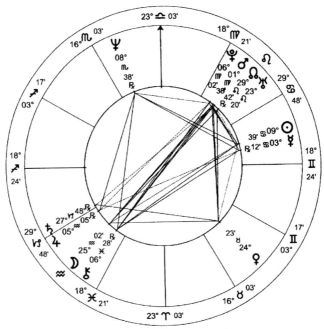

Princess Diana: Natal

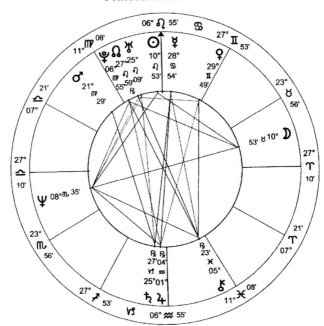

Princess Diana: Progressed Last Quarter (equates to March 1994)

and, as she was born with Sun/Moon on the cusp of Disseminating Phase (the natural communicator), this was indeed important. While, in the earlier days and still very young, there was not particularly a sense of someone who could command attention through the spoken word, by the time she had moved through the progressed Disseminating Phase and was now firmly in Last Quarter – and even though she once endearingly referred to herself as "thick as two planks" – here was a young woman who more and more was coming into her own as a spokesperson for the things that mattered to her in the world; she wanted to do something concrete to this end (both planets aspecting the Saturn/Jupiter 3rd house conjunction). Her campaign against landmines during this Last Quarter period emerged powerfully as a case in point.

Venus, as ruler of the progressed phase chart, sits at the 9th house cusp in Gemini – the young, beautiful woman speaking out her own philosophies. Mercury rules both that house and the 11th (society in general) as well as conjuncting the Midheaven, albeit widely. As we have seen, it also opposes the sturdy Saturn/Jupiter conjunction in the 3rd house of communication (tighter than at birth for Jupiter had retrograded by some 4°). Mercury had also progressed to an opposition to her natal Saturn in the 1st house – so often an area of self-doubt in earlier life, but which with maturity (such as a progressed Last Quarter calls forward) can emerge as a clear determination. So here she was, not only speaking out but wanting something to be done about it. She may well have displeased the powers-that-be with her campaigns (the opposition to the formality of Saturn/Jupiter and also a reflection of the triple conjunction of Uranus/Node/Pluto in the 10th). I somehow recall her being criticized as 'a loose cannon' but it did not deter her – Chiron opposes that triple conjunction and with considerable aplomb she carried on in spite of the wounding criticism.

Given she was due to remain in this life only a short time, that she initially felt shy and awkward and thereafter was carrying a monumental emotional load, Diana completed an important Last Quarter mission by going beyond herself (as Frankl pointed us to) and developing turning points through word and action. Had she lived, she might have gone on to develop these qualities to a still more resolute and purposeful degree (the Moon by progression would have gone on to meet Venus and Mercury in the 9th). Alas, at the time of her death the Moon had only reached 21/22° Gemini, having just crossed her natal Descendant where she was endeavouring to forge new relationships, but in square to the Mars position in the progressed phase chart and to her natal Uranus/Midheaven midpoint – and a tragedy unfolded.

At the progressed quintile and sextile aspects respectively in this phase, there is a prompting from within which enables us to turn to whatever new road we are now opening up, then an increased ability to rearrange life to accommodate the adjustments being incorporated and reorganize ourselves. For Princess Diana, the progressed quintile came as she gave her Panorama interview to a worldwide television audience and the progressed sextile came at the announcement of her divorce. Like a well-trained wolf cub we can 'sniff out' how to be and what to do at these stages, ever aware that our actions and orientations are being driven by our need to participate in our wider society, earnestly wanting to contribute to it as a result of who we have become.

In setting our cap at a different angle during this progressed phase we might at first do so only tentatively as we nurture and protect the changes arising. But the pressure of relinquishments to be made will gradually show us that something has run its course, our next progressed phase (Balsamic) leading us more clearly to what finally needs to be released from the past so that we can be at the helm of a new pattern to be woven at the oncoming progressed New Moon.

Sun/Moon Progressed Balsamic Phase
Progressed Moon 45° – 0° behind progressed Sun

"One may not reach the dawn save by the path of the night"
[*Khalil Gibran*]

Perhaps you can recall a time when you had been on a long, long… *long* journey – and then, finally, you were headed home. You were on the last lap, perhaps driving from the airport along the motorway, dog tired but there were only another ten miles or so to go. How you *ached* to get there. Visions of a hot shower, glass of wine maybe, your own bed at last and a good night's sleep, all danced at the back of your mind… alongside memories of what you had been through on this journey, the sights you saw, the people you met, the things you learned. And yet, being a steady focused driver, you were intent on just these last few miles and completing the journey.

At the Balsamic progressed phase we are nearing the end of the eight-fold cycle of experience. Like the last miles of the motorway, the going may be reasonably straightforward (late at night, not much traffic, clear weather) or more fraught (pouring with rain, only one windscreen wiper working, running out of petrol) but amongst it all we have a deep knowing that once we have reached our destination we will have completed something important and, after a rest, will soon be ready to start anew. The overall theme of this next 3½ year period is twofold: yielding the past on the one hand, preparation for a new cycle on the other. Our experience of it can hinge very much upon whether we approach these themes willingly or hesitatingly, consciously or with eyes tight shut. In the previous progressed phase there were already situations in which we diverted from past patterns and so here at Balsamic we are already attuned to the idea of releasing. The difference is that it is now much more apparent because there is a definite new road awaiting us, as yet unknown and unknowable, but powerfully impelling us forward.

Picking up the threads of our earlier analogies, the Moon is reaching the end of her 'shopping trip' and will soon empty the bag in which she has collected up all our development over the past 27 years or so, as she comes home to the Sun. An aeroplane coming in to land may have to jettison some fuel first (letting go of excess baggage) so that the landing can be made safely. The phase as a whole is one of healing through completion and transition and, as we enter it, there is an increased need for contemplation and inner questioning. Whatever the events and circumstances, and even though we may not always feel we have a grip on life, everything we think, do, plan, feel during the next three years or so present themselves as leading to a new purpose.

At the beginning of the phase, when the progressed Moon is still 45° – 30° behind the progressed Sun, there may still be remnants of the 60° sextile (reorganization – Last Quarter) theme we experienced some 15-18 months previously. Additionally there is growing awareness of the two levels of 'shedding' or 'yielding' – dumping baggage that would otherwise impede our 'landing' and dispersing 'seeds' as we turn to create a new future. Both levels are to be completed in this progressed phase for, as Rudhyar reminds us, "the potential (or seed) of the future is already operating at the core of the present".[11] If the turning points of the previous phase found us diverting off into unfamiliar territory, there can be a pull here at Balsamic to run back to what is known, particularly if that territory is not working out as well as we hoped. One man left his wife and two children for someone else... only for that someone else in turn to find someone else! Rather than face what he felt was an ever-stretching landscape of loneliness ahead of him, he went back to his wife and children… only for the marriage to fail as he approached the progressed New Moon! Others will surrender to such a vista as part of the process of Balsamic – releasing expectations and just going forward with what is unfolding even if it sometimes means going through stretches where nothing appears to be happening or we are stumbling around in the dark. In some agricultural communities farmers will leave a field fallow for a whole season. The purpose is to allow the ground to recuperate, be renewed. Since nothing is grown there, it looks (on the surface) as though nothing is happening, yet such a field is being freely accessed for an entire cycle by weather changes and bacteria to improve soil structure and build up fertility. Much unseen activity in preparation for the next period of growth.

There can be a preoccupation with (even necessity for) interior thoughts and feelings, wanting to retreat a little, turn down the volume on life. Often this may include *reflection* on past patterns and experiences, learning from them without necessarily having to run back into them. If, like me, you have shared your life with a much-loved cat or dog, you may well have experienced the phenomenon of that dear animal *just knowing* when you are due to arrive home. S/he takes up position and sits loyally by the garden gate at least fully five minutes before you arrive; day in, day out, never fails. The biologist Rupert Sheldrake wrote a fascinating book on the subject.[12] Similarly, we are *sensing* in this phase, keeping our whiskers attuned as to how life might unfold, yet we cannot necessarily communicate our outlooks coherently for they are not yet fully defined. But as we access pictures emerging from instinctive levels and become acquainted with deeper transformative feelings, soon, in the distance, we hear the rumblings or see the first outlines of the brand new start on the horizon.

People, places, activities and lifestyles once hugely important to us and in which we were thoroughly immersed are now not so necessary and may be relinquished. While there may be doubts, fears, confusions and hesitancies, we can at this stage embody inner qualities of vision, thus open ourselves to the capacity for illumination. Many possibilities can emerge from working through intangible avenues such as dreams, meditation, spiritual practices, rather than becoming entirely submerged by events in the outer world. Nevertheless some of those events may also serve to point us in the direction of unresolved dilemmas from the past which now seek to be brought into awareness and released (as we shall see shortly when revisiting Olivia's life). Many find it useful to talk things through with another person on the same wavelength but if no such person is around it may be indicative of the need to seek the prudence of our own inner listening, rather than trying to relate to others who might fail to understand the deeper levels to which we are now attuned. Our inner experiences are too important in this phase to be trivialized.

It is not unknown for feelings of disillusionment and disorientation to arise as we arrive at the end of a cycle, as many of our old assumptions taken for granted are dissipated. Sadness at this stage can see us wanting to bury our head in the sand rather than face a future before us which we feel we can do nothing about because it is as yet unknown. We may seek 'retreat' as escape and withdrawal in such a way that we lose connectedness with others who might otherwise help us get more of an all-round perspective. On the other hand of course, a person may legitimately want to just close-off if "hell is other people", as Jean-Paul Sartre once said, and the need is to be away from the hurts and complexities of the world. This may not, in fact, be as negative as it sounds, even if the accompanying feelings are of inertia since the deeper purpose can be to invite the person to examine and shed their social conditioning which leads to such feelings. Frequently in this phase we feel our hardships very keenly *often because we are about to liberate ourselves from them.* Like a prisoner in a cell coming to the end of a long sentence and due for release in the morning, the final night can feel never-ending. But it is a crucially important transition since we are no longer blindly accepting a narrow or limited situation but are about to metamorphose. Especially as one reaches the final 30° of the phase, there is a sense of being a chrysalis – in the dark, pending, awaiting – and we might remember Richard Bach's statement that "what a caterpillar calls the end of the world, the master calls a butterfly".[13]

If we do still cling to and repeat the remnants of a past cycle, we can get caught up in a warped knot of threads in the overall canvas. Pulled back to what has gone before, we remember our history, the positive and negatives, the wonders and terrors. But it is in becoming thoroughly circumscribed by and immersed in them that we allow our mental constructs to get in the way and then we are stuck again. Astrologers themselves can be particularly prone to this dynamic: we say "Oh, I've got Saturn coming up to square my Mars – last time I had that, XYZ happened, it was *dreadful!*" and then we hunker down in expectation of XYZ coming to 'get us' again. We have turned it into a *quod erat demonstrandum*, but this is a response to a mechanical, repetitive universe (it happened then, so it will happen again) rather than one which is alive, changing, evolving.

More positively in this progressed period comes our sense of vision as we allow for the dissolution of the past. Perhaps, like me, you can remember old school reports which said "could do better" or "must try harder" or "must learn not to gaze out of the window day-dreaming" (*mea culpa* to all of these!) The point is our culture/society has preferences to which it expects us to conform but which doesn't always allow for any individual 'gazing'. If our vision trails off into some great blue wistful yonder, we may only emerge as lacking in purpose, allowing ourselves to drift and become apathetic, interminably weary like a dying plant and perhaps expecting others to deal with practical needs. If, on the other hand, our energies are sufficiently strong and geared to following through on the 'gazing', this can take us beyond entreaties to be like everyone else and instead become an individual listening for the road ahead by which we can be *galvanized*, take our place and serve some future purpose. We can trace such threads in the lives of Jimmy Carter and Winston Churchill, both of whom took leadership positions during a progressed Balsamic Phase at crucial points in their respective nations' history and the causes being espoused: Carter negotiating the Camp David accords between Egypt and Israel, Churchill leading the British through the Second World War.

While going through her progressed Last Quarter Phase, Olivia (whose story unfolded in Chapter 7, pp 169-171) was working in a company that 'folded' and she had to change direction several times to follow alternative prospects, but mostly her priority was still to be happy emotionally. As she came to the end of that phase and about to approach Balsamic, she met William (October 2002). Her progressed Moon had just passed the natal Mercury/Neptune conjunction. Mercury rules her native 7th house and the relationship soon became one in which she could not precisely articulate what it was she felt was not quite right (the veil of Neptune). She entered the Balsamic Phase in December 2002 with its theme of yielding the past and preparing for a new cycle (the 'as yet unseen/unknown').

In the Balsamic Phase chart, The Sun/Moon contains Venus, thus highlighting the relating principle. Venus falls opposite the Chiron/Node midpoint, conjunct Uranus/Ascendant and square to Uranus/Node – all of

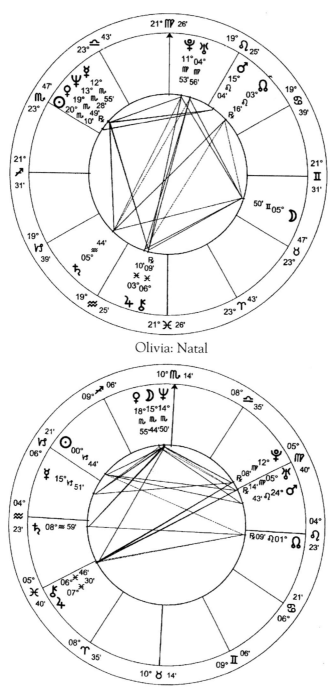

Olivia: Natal

Olivia: Progressed Balsamic (equates to December 2002)

these very appropriate to the break up and harrowing emotional pain (both past and present) this relationship was to bring to the surface, as well as the transformation to which it was leading. The Moon in this chart meets Venus in approximately 3° and three months after the start of Balsamic Olivia was beginning more frequently to voice her inner questionings and doubts (as described in the earlier chapter), vague though they were. At this time the progressed Moon had reached 19/20° Scorpio, her natal Sun/Venus position in that deeply insightful sign.

The abuse of the little child came four months later in July 2003 when Olivia's progressed Moon had reached 23° Scorpio, the cusp of her natal 12th house (descent into a darkness through the arousal of hurtful memories from her own personal past). This conjuncts the Pluto/Ascendant midpoint in the Balsamic chart, squares Mars in the 7th house and also the Jupiter/Saturn midpoint. The first two of these seem to convey the signature of the volcano of emotional distress that erupted, while Jupiter/Saturn reflects Olivia's responsible and dutiful handling of the situation. William's trial came in the autumn of the following year (2004), when the progressed Moon had reached 9° Sagittarius and crossed into the 11th house of the Balsamic chart (society's court of law). This Moon had also opposed Olivia's natal 6th house Moon (wanting to nurture, be of service) in the month or two leading up to the trial. Since the natal Moon squares Uranus/Pluto in the 9th opposite Jupiter/Chiron 3rd, this progression was triggering the transformational push from within which she then brought to me as a galvanizing decision to turn her career life around completely to that which she could feel fully committed. She threw up her job and re-entered university to begin her studies and training (3rd/9th) "to make a difference in society" (11th house Scorpio planets). By the time Olivia met her progressed New Moon in December 2006, she was already two years into her new studies.

The Sabian Symbol for the degree of the progressed New Moon (5° Capricorn) reads "Indians on the Warpath. While some men row a well-filled canoe, others in it perform a war dance".[14] Here there is a spirit of energy and fight (war) being aroused, perhaps through the original provocation (the abusive experiences which awakened Olivia's spirit to ameliorate her world). Here too we have Olivia devising, structuring, running therapeutic groupwork and becoming an authority (Capricorn) in her chosen field. It is additionally interesting to note that the progressed New Moon forms a disseminating trine to Uranus 9th Virgo (teaching, communicating) and first meets Mercury in the chart which is the dispositor of Uranus and rules the 6th house of work – again reflecting communication skills through training, teaching and applying what she understands. Overall in this excerpt from Olivia's life we see the thread of a wisdom being distilled from the past (bringing to light and resolution of past painful issues) into a form that would become the basis for that which was to emerge as a new road of transformational healing and service.

And for those who like an even happier ending, in the process of it all Olivia met Frank, a New Moon in Pisces man (conjunct Olivia's IC) who has contributed much love, sensitivity and care and with whom she has now enjoyed a committed relationship for the past five years – and continuing…

"We sleep, but the loom of life never stops
And the pattern which was weaving when the sun went down
Is weaving when it comes up in the morning"
[Henry Ward Beecher, 1813-1887]

Copyright Permissions

References

Introduction

1. John Keats, *Endymion*, Book III, l.144-146
2. In an exquisite and accomplished book by Jules Cashford, (*Moon, Myth and Image*, Cassell Illustrated/Octopus Publishing Group Limited, 2003), the author traces a vast array of mythical and historical discoveries, ancient rites, translations of ancient texts, tribal life and rituals, cultural shifts and their ongoing permeation of every aspect of our lives. Similarly, the phases are covered from a mythological/psychological perspective with particular reference to the final stage of the cycle where the Moon meets maximum obfuscation in *Mysteries of the Dark Moon: The Healing Power of the Dark Goddess*, by Demetra George, Harper Collins, 1992.
3. BBC News Channel, 1 September 2009, Pallab Ghosh, Science Correspondent http://news.bbc.co.uk/1/hi/sci/tech/8226735.stm. The proposed lunar clock is intended to be built on the River Thames and will be powered by its tides. It is to be made from three concentric rings of recycled glass and, as light shines through the glass in time with the lunar cycles, the largest ring will show the current phase.
4. David Rooney quoted in the BBC news item in 3 above.
5. J.C. Tefft, *The Christ is Not a Person: The Evolution of Consciousness and the Destiny of Man*, iUniverse, USA, 2008.
6. D.H. Lawrence, *Selected Literary Criticism*. Edited by Anthony Beal, Heinemann, London, 1956, p.155.
7. Mircea Eliade, *Patterns in Comparative Religion*, Sheed and Ward, 1958, p.180.
8. Ibid, p.181

PART I

Chapter 1

1. HH the XIV Dalai Lama, *Book of Awakening*, Element, 2002.
2. Bernice Prill Grebner, *Everything Has a Phase*, American Federation of Astrologers Inc., 1982.
3. Marilyn Busteed and Dorothy Wergin, *Phases of the Moon: A Guide to Evolving Human Nature*, American Federation of Astrologers, 1976.
4. Martin Goldsmith, *Moon Phases: A Symbolic Key*, Whitford Press, 1988.
5. Busteed and Wergin, *Phases of the Moon*, p.16.
6. Jinni and Joanne (Virginia Ewbank and Joanne Wickenberg), *The Spiral of Life*, The Digested Astrologer Vol.III, 1974, pp 34-35.
7. Demetra George, *Finding Our Way Through the Dark*, ACS Publications, 1994, pp 80-85.

Chapter 2

1. Idries Shah, *The Pleasantries of the Incredible Mulla Nasrudin*, Picador/Pan Books Ltd, 1975, Pan Macmillan Publishers.

2. Peter Tompkins/Christopher Bird, *The Secret Life of Plants*, Harper and Row, 1974, p.8.
3. Ibid, p.9.
4. Ibid, p.44.
5. Philip Ball, *Shapes: Nature's Patterns*, Oxford University Press, 2009.

Chapter 3

1. Judy Hall, *The Karmic Journey: The Birthchart, Karma and Reincarnation*, originally published by Penguin Arkana, updated as *Patterns of the Past* and *Karmic Connections*, The Wessex Astrologer, 2000 and 2001 respectively.
2. A.T. Mann, *Life*Time Astrology*, George Allen and Unwin, 1984.
3. Rodney Collin, *The Theory of Celestial Influence: Man, the Universe, and Cosmic Mystery*, London: Vincent Stuart, 1954; New York: Weiser, 1971; Boston: Shambhala, 1984, London and New York: Arkana, 1993.
4. Dane Rudhyar, *The Lunation Cycle*, Servire-Wassenaar, The Netherlands, 1967, p.138.
5. Marc Edmund Jones, *The Sabian Symbols in Astrology*, Shambhala Publications Inc., 1953.
6. Dane Rudhyar, *An Astrological Mandala*, Vintage Books, 1974, p.25 et seq.
7. Lynda Hill, *360 Degrees of Wisdom: Charting Your Destiny with the Sabian Oracle*, Plume/Penguin Books, 2004.

Chapter 4

1. Leyla Rael/Dane Rudhyar, *Astrological Aspects: A Process Oriented Approach*, Aurora Press, 1980, p.31.
2. Charles Harvey, *Essay adapted from paper given at L'ARCC Conference, Palais du Congres, Paris, 1995 to mark the 100th anniversary of the birth of Dane Rudhyar*, subsequently printed in *The Astrological Journal*, July/August 1995.
3. Bil Tierney, *Dynamics of Aspect Analysis*, CRCS Publications, 1983, p.2.
4. Charles E.O. Carter, *The Astrological Aspects*. L.N. Fowler and Co. Ltd, 1930, p.7.
5. John Addey, *Harmonics in Astrology*, L.N. Fowler, 1976.
6. David Hamblin, *Harmonic Charts*, The Aquarian Press, 1983 and *The Astrological Journal*, Winter 1983/84, p.14.
7. Roberto Assagioli, *Psychosynthesis*, Turnstone Books, 1975, p.40 et seq.
8. Jack Kornfield, *After the Ecstasy, the Laundry*, Bantam Books, 2000, p.197.
9. Rollo May, *The Courage to Create*, Bantam Books, 1975.
10. Hamblin, *Harmonic Charts*, p.48.
11. Dennis Elwell, *The Cosmic Loom*, The Urania Trust, 1999, reprinted Third Edition, The Wessex Astrologer, 2008 and *The Astrological Journal*, Autumn 1978, pp 167-8.
12. Elwell, *The Cosmic Loom*, p.48.
13. Michael Harding and Charles Harvey, *Working with Astrology*, Arkana, 1990, p.186.
14. Dane Rudhyar, *The Lunation Cycle*, Servire-Wassenaar, The Netherlands, 1967, p.40.
15. Leyla Rael/Dane Rudhyar, *Astrological Aspects: A Process Oriented Approach*, Aurora Press, 1980, pp 44-47.
16. Maritha Pottenger "Aspects of Life: Minor Aspects", www.ccrsdodona.org/m_dilemma/1982/pis/aspects.html

Chapter 5

1. Marc Robertson, *Cosmopsychology I: The Engine of Destiny*, American Federation of Astrologers, 1975.
2. Jinni and Joanne, *The Spiral of Life*, The Digested Astrologer Vol.III, 1974.
3. Dane Rudhyar, *The Practice of Astrology*, Penguin Books, NY, 1971, pp 63-64.
4. For further and much fuller coverage on the teachings of traditional astrology, there are very many scholars in various parts of the world, but an excellent starting point from which to access the subject is the website of Deborah Houlding at www.skyscript.co.uk
5. William Shakespeare, *As You Like It, Act II, Scene VII*: speech delivered by Jacques, attendant to the Duke Senior.

PART II

Chapter 6

1. Michael R. Meyer, *A Handbook for the Humanistic Astrologer*, Anchor Books, 1974, p.195.
2. Paul Coelho, *Manual of the Warrior of Light*, Harper Collins, 2002.
3. M. Scott Peck, *The Road Less Travelled*, Arrow Books, 1978.
4. Dane Rudhyar, *The Lunation Cycle*, Servire-Wassenaar, The Netherlands, 1967, p.64.
5. Sir David Attenborough, *The Private Life of Plants*, Princeton University Press, 1995, p.38.
6. For additional material on positioning within the family and general family dynamics, the reader is referred to Barbara Somers with Ian Gordon-Brown, *Journey in Depth: A Transpersonal Perspective*, Archive Publishing, 2002.
7. Howard Sasportas, *The Twelve Houses*, Aquarian Press, 1985, p.66.
8. Pema Chodron, *When Things Fall Apart: Heart Advice for Difficult Times*, Shambhala Publications, 1997.
9. Leyla Rael/Dane Rudhyar, *Astrological Aspects: A Process Oriented Approach*, Aurora Press, 1980.
10. Dane Rudhyar, *Person Centred Astrology*, ASI Publishers Inc., New York, 1976, p.43.
11. Beata Bishop, *A Time to Heal*, First Stone Publishing, 2005.
12. Charlotte Gerson with Beata Bishop, *Healing the Gerson Way: Defeating Cancer and Other Chronic Diseases*, Totality Books, 2007.
13. Frank Sinatra, *Come Fly With Me*, (Sammy Cahn and Jimmy Van Heusen, arranger Billy May), recorded October 1957, Capitol Record label.
14. Frank Sinatra, *None But the Lonely Heart*, (Tchaikovsky), recorded January 1945, CBS broadcast of The Frank Sinatra Show, Columbia Record label.
15. Roy Alexander, *Meet Your Planets*, Llewellyn Publications, 1997.
16. Frank Sinatra, *My Way*, (Claude Francois/ Jacques Revaux), lyrics by Paul Anka, recorded December 1968, Reprise Record label.
17. Dr. Arthur Janov, *Imprints: The Lifelong Effects of the Birth Experience*, Coward-McCann Inc., New York/General Publishing Company Ltd, Toronto, 1983, p.77.
18. Ibid, p.77.

19. Ingrid Seward, *Edward*, Century, 1995, from abridged extract reported in *The Daily Mail*, July 1995.
20. Richard Bach, *Illusions – The Adventures of a Reluctant Messiah*, Arrow Books, 1998, p.103.
21. Gilbert White's original manuscripts remain on view at his original home in Selborne, Hampshire, which is open to the public.
22. Leyla Rael/Dane Rudhyar, *Astrological Aspects: A Process Oriented Approach*, Aurora Press, 1980.
23. Anthony Storr, *The Art of Psychotherapy*, Martin Secker and Warburg, William Heinemann Medical Books Limited, 1979.
24. Jules Cashford, *The Moon: Myth and Image*, Cassell Illustrated/Octopus PublishingGroup Limited, 2003, p.19.
25. Eckhart Tolle, *"Stillness Amidst the World"*, Findhorn Retreat 2004, New World Library, 2006, p.11.
26. Virginia M. Axline, *Dibs: In Search of Self*, Penguin Books, 1964.
27. *William Blake, The Complete Illuminated Works, Jerusalem, Plate 10*, Thames and Hudson in association with The William Blake Trust and The Tate Gallery, text: David Bindman, 2000.
28. Marc Robertson, *Cosmopsychology I: The Engine of Destiny*, American Federation of Astrologers, 1975, p.65.
29. Leyla Rael/Dane Rudhyar, *Astrological Aspects: A Process Oriented Approach*, Aurora Press, 1980, p.100.
30. Ram Dass, *Be Here Now*, Lama Foundation/Hanuman Foundation, 1971.
_____ *Still Here*, Riverhead Books, 2000.
_____ *Fierce Grace*, Zeitgeist Video, 2003.
31. www.menuhin.org
32. www.sentebale.org
33. Demetra George, *Finding Our Way Through the Dark*, ACS Publications, San Diego, 1994.
34. Bob Dylan, *The Times They Are A-Changin'*, October 1963, Columbia Record label.
35. Elisabeth Kubler-Ross, *On Death and Dying*, Tavistock Publications Limited, 1969.
36. Eckhart Tolle, *A New Earth*, Dutton/Penguin Group (USA) Inc., 2005, pp 306-7.
37. Anthony Storr, *The Art of Psychotherapy*, Martin Secker and Warburg Limited, 1979, p.52.

Chapter 7

1. Dane Rudhyar, *An Astrological Mandala*, Vintage Books, 1974, p.284.
2. Plato, *The Republic X, The Myth of Er* (in which a Er having been killed in battle goes to the place where lots are cast by each soul to choose the lives they will next live, before drinking of the waters of *Lethe* [river of forgetfulness] which causes them not to remember that they have so chosen).
3. Charles Carter, *Zodiac and the Soul*, The Theosophical Publishing House Ltd, 1928, p.94.
_____ *Essays on the Foundations of Astrology*, The Theosophical Publishing House Ltd, 1947, p.161.
When I first came across this chart long ago on reading Charles Carter's above works I was touched by the author's obvious sympathies for "a helpless soul... defeated and

driven back from the material plane". Mr. Carter expressed dissatisfaction at being able to provide sufficient explanation from the chart as to Jane's demise. It is with respect to Mr. Carter and certainly without any claim to enlarge upon his findings that I would re-offer the chart from the perspective of our coverage of Saturn/Moon in New Phase.

I am additionally grateful to Surrey Heath Borough Council/Museum and The Bagshot Society for material concerning the life and death of Emily Jane Popejoy. R.I.P.

4. D.H. Lawrence, *Selected Letters*, Penguin Books Ltd, 1950 and Alan Sillitoe, D.H. Lawrence and His District, *D.H. Lawrence – Novelist, Prophet, Poet*, ed. Stephen Spender, Weidenfeld and Nicholson, London, 1973.
5. Marc Robertson, *Cosmopsychology: The Engine of Destiny*, Astrology Center of the Northwest, Seattle, 1976.
6. William Blake, *Joseph of Arimathea Among the Rocks of Albion*, Engraving c.1773, Fitzwilliam Museum, Cambridge.
7. Dane Rudhyar, *An Astrological Mandala*, Vintage Books, 1974, p.166.
8. Marc Edmund Jones, *The Sabian Symbols in Astrology*, Shambhala, Boulder and London, 1978, p.324.
9. Alfred Einstein, *Mozart, His Character – His Work*, Panther Arts, 1971 and Eric Blom, *Mozart*, J.M. Dent and Sons Ltd, London, 1935.

Chapter 8

1. *The Diary of Anne Frank*, first published by Contact Amsterdam, 1947; edition 1954, Pan Books Ltd.
2. Anne Frank House, Prinsengracht 267, Amsterdam.
   Anne Frank Foundation: www.annefrank.org/ www.humanityinaction.org
3. Nigel Farage, *Fighting Bull*, Biteback Publishing Limited, 2010.
4. B.J. Thomas, *Raindrops Keep Fallin' On My Head*, (Hal David/Burt Bacharach), October 1969, Scepter Records.
5. Bill and Melinda Gates Foundation: www.gatesfoundation.org
6. Jon Savage, *England's Dreaming*, Faber and Faber, 1991.
   —— *The Kinks: The Official Biography*, Faber and Faber, 1984.
   —— *Teenage: The Creation of Youth 1875-1945*, Chatto and Windus, 2007.
7. Brian Clark, *The Sibling Constellation: The Astrology and Psychology of Sisters and Brothers*, Penguin Arkana, 1999.
8. Jim Clark's death occurred on 7 April 1968, 12:39 hrs, Hockenheim, Germany.
9. *Silkwood*, directed by Mike Nichols, starring Meryl Streep, Kurt Russell and Cher; writers: Nora Ehron, Alice Arlen, 1983.
10. James McClure – author of the 'Kramer and Zondi' series of detective fiction, including *The Steam Pig* (1971) for which he won the Crime Writers' Association Gold Dagger Award.
    —— *Spike Island – Portrait of a Police Division*, Macmillan, London Limited, 1980.
    —— *Copworld – Policing the Streets of San Diego*, Macmillan, 1984.
11. www.Sentebale.org and www.wellchild.org.uk
12. Encyclopaedia Britannica, *Thomas Cromwell*, 14th Edition, Vol. 6, and *Cromwell and His Men*, British Encyclopaedia Volume 1, Educational Book Company London Limited, 1940.

13. D.H. Lawrence, *Selected Literary Criticism, Part II: Puritanism and the Arts*, edited by Anthony Beal, Heinemann, London, 1956, letter to Miss Pearn of 12 April 1927.
14. *Regina v. Penguin Books Limited*, Old Bailey, London, October-November 1960.

Chapter 9

1. Susan N. Masuoka, *En Calavera – The Papier-Mâché Art of the Linares Family*, UCLA Fowler Museum of Cultural History, 1994.
2. If birth had occurred very early in the morning the Moon would have been in the last degrees of Virgo and therefore not have picked up the square aspect to Sun, Neptune and Mars. It would, however, have formed a square to Jupiter/Pluto and become dispositor to Mercury (contained within the phase under discussion). In either event, Linares' artistry being externalized through instinctive application (New Phase Venus/Mars) and transformational experience (opposition to Uranus) remains.
3. Fowler Museum of Cultural History, UCLA, USA, the British Museum, London, the Pompidou Centre in Paris, and specialist exhibition at The Museum of Mankind, London, 1992.
4. Hunter Davies, *The Beatles: Authorized Biography*, Jonathan Cape, 1985, p.403.
5. George Harrison, *I Me Mine: Autobiography*, W.H. Allen, 1982, pp 55-56.
6. Ibid, pp 76-77. My thanks to Elizabeth Lewis for additional research material.
7. George Harrison, *Something*, 1969, produced by George Martin, recorded February 1969, Apple Record label.
8. George Harrison, *My Sweet Lord*, (Harrison/Phil Spector), January 1971, Apple Record label.
9. Irving Berlin, *A Man Chases a Girl (Until She Catches Him)*, from the film *There's No Business Like Show Business*, distributed by 20th Century Fox, 1954.
10. Elvis Presley, *All Shook Up*, (Otis Blackwell), January 1957, RCA Record label.
11. William Vaughan, *William Blake*, Tate Gallery Publishing Ltd, 1999, David Bindman (text)/William Blake Trust and The Tate Gallery, *William Blake: The Complete Illuminated Books*, Thames and Hudson, 2000.
12. The Arts Council of Great Britain, *Mexican Art*, 1953 Kahlo: *Self-Portrait as a Tehuana*, 1943; PBS: The Life and Times of Frida Kahlo/Amy Stechler.
13. T.S. Eliot, *Four Quartets, Burnt Norton II*, 1935, *Collected Poems*, Faber and Faber, 1936.
14. Marie-Louise von Franz, *Archetypal Dimensions of the Psyche*, Shambhala, 1999.
15. Mark Barrett, *Crossing: Reclaiming the Landscape of Our Lives*, Darton, Longman and Todd, 2001.
16. The birth time for Thomas Paine is uncertain, thus the house positions of the planets have not been taken into account in the commentary. This does not, however, alter the Mars/Venus phase as Last Quarter (nor the Jupiter/Mercury Balsamic Phase also mentioned in the text).
17. Vera Lynn, *We'll Meet Again* (Ross Parker/ Hughie Charles) and *White Cliffs of Dover* (Nat Burton/ Walter Kent) 1942, UK Decca/London HMV labels.

Chapter 10

1. For further material on career considerations, including material on the Lunation Cycle phases, the reader is referred to Joanne Wickenberg's *In Search of a Fulfilling Career*, American Federation of Astrologers, Inc. 1992.

2. Eclipses have traditionally carried a sense of great portent in astrology, although taken singly their 'effects' are in my view not always clearly marked in immediate terms. Given also that both solar and lunar eclipses are entwined with the Nodal axis, I am rather more inclined to take note of the cycle of eclipses occurring over a period of time, thus each one being part of a larger, holistic pattern. However, I have not made a specific study of the subject but would point the reader to Rudhyar's coverage in *The Astrology of Transformation*, Chapter 3, p.69 et seq; also Alexander Ruperti's *Cycles of Becoming*, p.66. From the perspective of predictive astrology, the reader is referred to Bernadette Brady's *Predictive Astrology: The Eagle and the Lark*, Weiser Books, 1999, (Chapter 5) in which the Saros cycle of eclipses is covered (and the author offers further commentary on the chart of Prince William).

3. See Data Section under 'England' and 'United Kingdom'.

4. Dane Rudhyar, *An Astrological Mandala*, Vintage Books, 1974, p.178.

5. Ibid, pp 177-8.

6. D.H. Lawrence, *Selected Letters*, selected by Richard Aldington, Penguin Books in association with William Heinemann Ltd, 1950.

7. Ibid, Introduction, pp 27-28.

8. For superior coverage of the subject, the reader is referred to Stephen Arroyo, *Astrology, Psychology and the Four Elements*, CRCS Publications, 1975.

9. *The Oprah Winfrey Leadership Academy for Girls*, Johannesburg, South Africa, opened in January 2007.

10. Annabella Kitson, *Carter Memorial Lecture*, Astrological Association Conference, University of Norwich, September 1994.

PART III

Chapter 11

1. Charles Harvey, *Essay adapted from paper given at L'ARCC Conference, Palais du Congres, Paris, 1995 to mark the 100th anniversary of the birth of Dane Rudhyar*, subsequently printed in *The Astrological Journal*, July/August 1995. This article can also be read courtesy of Deborah Houlding's website – www.skyscript.co.uk/sun_nep. html

2. Jinni and Joanne, *The Spiral of Life*, The Digested Astrologer Vol.III, 1974.

3. Stephen Arroyo, *Chart Interpretation Handbook*, CRCS Publications, 1989, pp 141 et seq.

4. Alexander Ruperti, *Cycles of Becoming*, CRCS Publications, 1978.

5. The late Al H. Morrison and also Zane Stein in the USA have contributed much preliminary work, referring to Chiron as 'an inconvenient benefic' or sometimes I heard this reported as 'a beneficent maverick', the latter also being used by Charles Kowal (who discovered this planet) to denote its unusual size and orbit.

6. Barbara Hand Clow, *Chiron: Rainbow Bridge Between the Inner and Outer Planets*, Llewellyn Publications, 1988.

7. Eve Jackson, 'The Wounded Healer', *Astrological Association of Great Britain Journal*, Winter-Spring 1984/85.

8. Dennis Elwell, 'Chiron's Heroes', *Pulsar: The Journal of the Scottish Astrological Association*, No. 5, Summer 1990; also Elwell, *Cosmic Loom*, The Urania Trust, 1999, pp 95-100.

9. Martin Luther King, *Strength to Love*, Fontana Books, 1969, Chapter 2.
10. Melanie Reinhart, *Chiron and the Healing Journey*, Penguin Arkana, 1989 and (3rd edition) Starwalker Press UK, April 2010.
11. Marc Robertson, *Cosmopsychology I: The Engine of Destiny*, American Federation of Astrologers, 1975.
12. For a useful listing of planetary conjunctions and their cycles, these appear in Appendix 4 to Bernadette Brady's *Predictive Astrology, The Eagle and the Lark*, Weiser Books, 1999.
13. Richard Tarnas, *Cosmos and Psyche*, Plume/Penguin Group, 2006.

Chapter 12
1. Richard Bach, *Illusions: The Adventures of a Reluctant Messiah*, Arrow Books, 1998.
2. Dane Rudhyar, *An Astrological Mandala*, Vintage Books, 1974, p.260.
3. Buddy Holly and The Crickets, *Everyday*, (B. Holly and Norman Petty), recorded May 1957, released as B-side to *Peggy Sue*, September 1957, Coral Records..
4. Viktor Frankl, *Man's Search for Meaning*, Beacon Press, 1959.
5. John Lennon/Yoko Ono, *Double Fantasy*, Lenono Music/Capitol Records Inc., 2000.
6. John Lennon, *Watching the Wheels*, Lenono Music/Capitol Records Inc., 2000.
7. John Lennon, *(Just Like) Starting Over*, Lenono Music/Capitol Records Inc.. 2000.
8. Rudhyar, *An Astrological Mandala*, p.286.
9. Andrew Morton, *Diana: Her True Story In Her Own Words*, New York, Pocket, 1992.
10. Frankl, *The Unheard Cry for Meaning*, Washington Square Press, 1978.
11. Dane Rudhyar, *An Astrological Mandala*, Vintage Books, 1974, p.257.
12. Rupert Sheldrake, *Dogs That Know When Their Owners Are Coming Home*, Arrow Books, 2000.
13. Bach, *Illusions*, p.134.
14. Rudhyar, *An Astrological Mandala*, p.232.

The following main sources for chart data have been gratefully used:

AA – The Astrological Association of Great Britain – gathered through the years from their Journal and database.

SF – Solar Fire 7 Gold program/chart database.

Clifford – Frank Clifford Chart Compendium/Solar Fire.

Astrodatabank – outstanding collection from the late Lois Rodden of the USA, now administered and updated by Astrodienst at www.astro. com/astrodatabank. This, together with biographical material and links to Wikipedia and discussion sites, comprises a singularly helpful source for astrological research.

Astrotheme – www.astrotheme.com

CR – my own records/files.

Other specific sources are listed alongside names.

All data for private clients has been withheld for confidentiality.

Adie, Kate, 19 September 1945, time unknown, Sunderland, England. Source: Wikipedia.

Alexander, Roy, 15 August 1931, 9:58 BST, Manchester, England. Source: CR.

Ali, Muhammad, 17 January 1942, 18:35, Louisville, Kentucky, USA. Source: Clifford.

Ashmole, Elias, 5 June 1617, 3:28 LMT, Litchfield, England. Source: Astrodatabank.

Austen, Jane, 16 December 1775, 23:45, Steventon, England. Source: Astrodatabank.

Bacharach, Burt, 12 May 1928, 1:15, Kansas City, USA. Source: Astrodatabank.

Baker, Josephine, 3 June 1906, 11:00, St. Louis, Missouri, USA. Source: Astrotheme.

Barrie, J.M., 9 May 1860, 6:30, Kirremuir, Scotland. Source: Astrodatabank.

Berlusconi, Silvio, 29 September 1936, 5:40, Milan, Italy. Source: Astrodatabank.

Bernstein, Leonard, 25 August 1918, 13:00, Lawrence, MA, USA.
  Source: Astrodatabank.
Bishop, Beata, 8 June 1924, 16:00 CET, Budapest, Hungary. Source: CR.
Blake, William, 28 November 1757 NS, 19:45 LMT, London, England.
  Source: SF7/Visual Arts.
Branson, Sir Richard, 18 July 1950, 7:00, Blackheath, London, England.
  Source: SF7/Corporate.
Brown, Gordon, 20 February 1951, 08:40 GMT, Giffnock, Scotland.
  Source: AA.
Brunel, Isambard Kingdom, 9 April 1806 NS, 00:55 LMT, Portsmouth,
  England. Source: SF7/Science.
Bush, George W, 6 July 1946, 7:26 EDT, New Haven, CT, USA.
  Source: SF/Politics.
Byron, Lord, 22 January 1788, 14:00, London, England. Source: SF7/
  Literature.
Cameron, David, 9 October 1966, 6:00, Wantage, England. Source: AA.
Capa, Robert, 22 October 1913, time unknown, Budapest, Hungary.
  Source: Wikipedia.
Carnegie, Andrew, 25 November 1835, time unknown/unsure,
  Dunfermline, Scotland. Source: Astrodatabank.
Carter, Jimmy, 1 October 1924, 07:00 CST, Plains, Georgia, USA.
  Source: Astrodatabank.
Cartier-Bresson, Henri, 22 August 1908, 14:51, Chanteloup, France.
  Source: Astrodatabank.
Chanel, Coco, 19 August 1883 NS, 16:00, Saumur, France.
  Source: Clifford.
Charles, HRH Prince, 14 November 1948, 21:14, London, England.
  Source: AA.
Churchill, Winston, 30 November 1874 NS, 1:35 UT, Woodstock,
  England. Source: AA.
  Note: Since I had always thought of Churchill's chart as having the
  first degree of Libra rising, it was with a little alarm that I discovered
  most databases record a 1.30 am birth time which gives a 29°+ Virgo
  Ascendant. However, it is likely that the birth was recorded in Local
  Time which, at longitude 1W21, would equate to five minutes of time.
  The chart is therefore set for 1.35 am UT showing 1° Libra rising. I am
  grateful to Chester Kemp for his assistance in discussion about, and
  checking the technicality of, this point.

Clark, Jim, 4 March 1936, 15:25, Cupar, Scotland. Source: Astrodatabank.

Clegg, Nick, 7 January 1967, 5:30, Chalfont St. Giles, England.
Source: AA.

Cooke, Alistair, 20 November 1908, time unknown, Salford, England.
Source: BBC Press Office.

Cromwell, Oliver, 5 May 1599, 3:00, Huntingdon, England.
Source: SF7/Politicians, Statesmen.

Dalai Lama XIV, His Holiness, 6 July 1935, 4:38, Tengster Village, Tibet.
Source: Astrodatabank.

Davis, Bette, 5 April 1908, 21:00, Lowell, MA, USA.
Source: Astrodatabank.

Diana, Princess of Wales, 1 July 1961, 19:45 BST, Sandringham, Norfolk,
England. Source: AA.

Dickens, Charles, 7 February 1812, 19:50, Portsmouth, England.
Source: Astrodatabank.

Disraeli, Benjamin, 21 December 1804 NS, 5:30 LMT, London, England.
Source: SF7/Politics.

Doyle, Sir Arthur Conan, 22 May 1859, 4:55 UT, Edinburgh, Scotland.
Source: Marjorie Orr:www.star4cast.com

Dylan, Bob, 24 May 1941, 21:05 CST, Duluth, USA. Source: AA.

Einstein, Albert, 14 March 1879, 11:30, Ulm, Germany. Source: AA.

Eliot, George, 22 November 1819, 5:00, Nuneaton, England.
Source: SF7/ Literature.

England, Coronation William I, Christmas Day, true noon, 1066.
Source: Charles E.O. Carter, *An Introduction to Political Astrology*, L.N.
Fowler and Co. Ltd, 1951.

Farage, Nigel, 3 April 1964, 16:30, Farnborough, Kent, England.
Source: CR.

Federer, Roger, 8 August 1981, 8:40, Basle, Switzerland.
Source: Astrotheme.

Fleming, Ian, 28 May 1908, 00:10 UT, London, England.
Source: Astrotheme.

Frank, Anne, 12 June 1929, 7:30, Frankfurt am Maim, Germany.
Source: AA.

Gandhi, Mohandas, 2 October 1869 NS, 07:45 LMT, Porbandar, India.
Source: SF7/Politics.

Gates, Bill, 28 October 1955, 22:00 PST, Seattle, WA, USA.
Source: Astrodatabank.

Gershwin, George, 26 September 1898, 11:09, Brooklyn, NY, USA.
Source: Astrodatabank.

Gladstone, William, 29 December 1809, 8:15 LMT, Liverpool, England.
Source: Astrodatabank.

Greer, Germaine, 29 January 1939, 6:00, Melbourne, Australia.
Source: SF7/Literature.

Hahnemann, Samuel, 10 April 1755 NS, 23:59, Meissen, Germany.
Source: Astrotheme.

Hancock, Tony, 12 May 1924, 10:09 GMT, Birmingham, England.
Source: AA. (Time given as 10:00 am but subsequently rectified by Roy
Alexander to 10:09 am.)

Hari, Mata, 7 August 1876, 13:00, Leewarden, Netherlands.
Source: Astrotheme.

Harrison, George, 24 February 1943, 23:42, Liverpool, England.
Source: SF7/Entertainment.

Harry, HRH Prince, 15 September 1984, 16:20 BST, London, England.
Source: Buckingham Palace announcement.

Henry VIII, King, 7 July 1491 (Gregorian), 8:45, Greenwich, England.
Source: Astrodatabank.

Herschel, William, 15 November 1738, Hanover, Germany, time
unknown. Source: Astrodatabank.

Hillman, James, 12 April 1926, Atlantic City, USA, time unknown.
Source: Wikipedia, although Charles Harvey and Michael Harding
show a chart with Asc 17.49 Gemini, MC 4.59 Pisces in *Working with
Astrology*, Arkana, 1990, p.268 et seq.

Hitler, Adolf, 20 April 1889, 18:30, Braunau am Inn, Austria.
Source: Astrodatabank.

Holly, Buddy, 7 September 1936, 15:30, Lubbock, Texas, USA.
Source: SF7/Clifford.

Howe, Elias, 9 July 1819, Spencer, Massachusetts, USA, time unknown.
Source: Wikipedia.

Icke, David, 29 April 1952, 19:15, Leicester, England.
Source: SF7/Clifford.

Jackson, Michael, 29 August 1958, 12:00 CDT, Gary, Indiana, USA.
Source: Astrodatabank, (although time is thought to be very
uncertain).

Jacobi, Sir Derek, 22 October 1938, 04:00, London, England. Source: AA.

Jagger, Mick (Sir Michael), 26 July 1943, 2:30, Dartford, Kent, England.
Source: Astrodatabank.

John, Sir Elton, 25 March 1947, 16:00 BST, Pinner, England.
Source: Astrodatabank.

Jung, C.G. 26 July 1875, 19:32, Kesswil, Switzerland.
Source: AA/Astrodatabank.

Kahlo, Frida, 6 July 1907, 08:30 LMT, Coyoacan, Mexico.
Source: SF7/Visual Arts.

Keller, Helen, 27 June 1880, 4:02, Tuscumbia AL, USA, (time uncertain).
Source: Astrodatabank.

Kepler, Johannes, 6 January 1572, 14:37, Weil der Staft, Germany.
Source: Astrodatabank.

King, Dr. Martin Luther, 15 January 1929, 12:00 CST, Atlanta, Georgia,
USA. Source: SF/Politics.

Krishnamurti, J, 12 May 1895 NS, 00:23, Mandanapalle, India.
Source: Astrodatabank.

Kubler Ross, Elisabeth, 8 July 1926, 22:45 CET, Zurich, Switzerland.
Source: Astrodatabank.

Kyi, Aung San Suu, 19 June 1945, time unknown, Rangoon, Burma.
Source: Press reports various.

Lawrence, D.H., 11 September 1885, 09:45, Eastwood, Nottingham,
England. Source: AA.

Lennon, John, 9 October 1940, 18:30 BST, Liverpool, England.
Source: AA.

Lennox, Annie, 25 December 1954, 23:10 GMT, Aberdeen, Scotland.
Source: birth certificate via Aaron Fischer, Deborah Houlding, *The
Mountain Astrologer*, Dec.2007/Jan.2008.

Linares, Pedro, 29 June 1906, time unknown, Mexico City, Mexico.
Source: *En Calavera*, Susan N. Masuoka, UCLA Fowler Museum of
Cultural History, 1994.

Lloyd George, David, 17 January 1863, 7:55, Manchester, England.
Source: Astrodatabank.

Locke, William John, 20 March 1863, Georgetown, British Guiana
(Guyana), South America, time unknown. Source: Wikipedia.

Lynn, Dame Vera, 20 March 1917, 7:35, London, England. Source: AA.

McClure, James, 9 October 1939, 5:30, Johannesburg, South Africa.
Source: CR.

McEnroe, John, 16 February 1959, 22:30, Wiesbaden, Germany.
Source: Astrodatabank.

Major, John, 29 March 1943, Sutton, Surrey, UK, time unknown.
Source: AA.

Mandela, Nelson, 18 July 1918, 14:54 EET, Umtata, S.Africa.
Source: Astrodatabank, (although time thought to be very uncertain).

Margaret, HRH Princess, 21 August 1930, 21:22, Glamis, Scotland.
Source: AA.

May, Rollo, 21 April 1909, 2:20 CST, Adia, Ohio, USA.
Source: originally Michael Harding, *Hymns to the Ancient Gods*,
Arkana 1992, p.348, (listed as March but subsequently agreed as April
in CR discussion with the author).

Menuhin, Yehudi, 22 April 1916, 23:30 EST, New York, USA.
Source: CR.

Milne, A.A., 18 January 1882, London, England, time unknown.
Source: Wikipedia.

Montessori, Maria, 31 August 1870, 02:40 GMT, Chiaravalle, Italy.
Source: Astrodatabank.

Mozart, Wolfgang Amadeus, 27 January 1756, 20:00, Salzburg, Austria.
Source: AA.

Nijinsky, Vaslav, 11 March 1888, 22:30, Kiev, Russia.
Source: Astrodatabank.

Nureyev, Rudolph, 17 March 1938, 13:00, Irkutsk, Russia.
Source: Astrodatabank (time uncertain).

Obama, Barack, 4 August 1961, 19:24 AHST, Honolulu, Hawaii, USA.
Source: Astrodatabank.

Orwell, George, 25 June 1903, 11:30, Motihari, India. Source: AA.

Paine, Thomas, 29 January 1737, 11:30, Thetford, England.
Source: Astrodatabank.

Pasteur, Louis, 27 December 1822 NS, 02:00 LMT, Dole, France.
Source: Astrodatabank.

Peck, M. Scott, 22 May 1936, New York City, USA, time unknown.
Source: www.mscottpeck.com

Picasso, Pablo, 25 October 1881, 23:15, Malaga, Spain.
Source: Astrodatabank.

Pilger, John, 9 October 1939, time unknown, (chart set for noon), Bondi,
Sydney, Australia. Source: www.johnpilger.com

Popejoy, Emily Jane, 4 July 1880 NS, 05:15, Bagshot, Surrey, England.
  Source: Charles Carter.

Presley, Elvis, 8 January 1935, 4:35, Tupelo, Mississipi, USA, Source: AA.

Queen, HM Elizabeth II, 21 April 1926, 2:40 BST, London, England.
  Source: AA.

Ram Dass, 6 April 1932, 10:40 EST, Boston, USA.
  Source: Zipporah Dobyns.

Rhodes, Zandra, 19 September 1940, London, England, time unknown.
  Source: Wikipedia.

Rogers, Carl, 8 January 1902, Oak Park, Illinois, USA, time unknown.
  Source: Wikipedia.

Rubinstein, Arthur, 28 January 1887, Lodz, Poland, time unknown.
  Source: Wikipedia.

Rudhyar, Dane, 23 March 1895, 00:32, Paris, France. Source: AA.

Savage, Jon, 2 September 1953, 21:00, London, England. Source: CR.

Shackleton, Sir Ernest, 15 February 1874, 05:00 LMT, Athy, Kilkea,
  Ireland. Source: Astrotheme.

Silkwood, Karen, 19 February 1946, 21:50, Longview, Texas, USA.
  Source: SF7/Politics.

Sinatra, Frank, 12 December 1915, 3:00 EST, Hoboken, NJ, USA.
  Source: AA.

Thatcher, Margaret, 13 October 1925, 9:00, Grantham, England.
  Source: AA.

Trump, Donald, 14 June 1946, 9:51, Queens, NY, USA.
  Source: Astrodatabank.

Turner, Tina, 26 November 1939, 22:10, Nutbush, Tennessee, USA.
  Source: Clifford.

United Kingdom, Act for Union of Great Britain and Ireland, 1 January
  1801, 00:00, Greenwich, England. Source: Charles E.O. Carter, *An
  Introduction to Political Astrology*, L.N. Fowler and Co. Ltd, 1951.

Van Gogh, Vincent, 30 March 1853, 11:00 LMT, Zundert, Netherlands.
  Source: Astrodatabank.

Victoria, Queen, 24 May 1819, 4:15 LMT, London, England. Source: AA.

Whicker, Alan, 2 August 1925, 5:30, Cairo, Egypt.
  Source: SF7/Entertainment.

White, Gilbert, 18 July 1720, time unknown, Selborne, England.
  Source: Times Newspapers Online.

Wilberforce, William, 24 August 1759, Hull, Yorkshire, England, time
    unknown. Source: CR.
William, HRH Prince, 21 June 1982, 21:03 BST, London, England.
    Source: Buckingham Palace Announcement.
Winfrey, Oprah, 29 January 1954, 4:30 CST, Kosciusko, Mississippi, USA.
    Source: Astrodatabank.
Wonder, Stevie, 13 May 1950, 16:15, Saginaw, MI, USA.
    Source: Astrodatabank.

Bibliography and Recommended Reading

Alexander, Roy, *The Astrology of Choice: A Counseling Approach*, Samuel Weiser Inc.,1983.

—— *Meet Your Planets*, Lewellyn Publications, 1997.

Anderton, Bill, *Life Cycles*, Quantum Books, 1990.

Arroyo, Stephen, *Astrology, Psychology and the Four Elements*, CRCS Publications, 1975.

—— *Astrology Karma and Transformation*, CRCS Publications, 1978.

—— *Relationships and Life Cycles*, CRCS Publications, 1979.

—— *The Practice and Profession of Astrology: Rebuilding Our Lost Connections with the Cosmos*, CRCS Publications, 1984.

Assagioli, Roberto, *Psychosynthesis*, Psychosynthesis Research Foundation/ Turnstone Books, 1965.

Attenborough, Sir David, *The Private Life of Plants*, Princeton University Press, 1995.

Baring, Anne and Cashford, Jules, *The Myth of the Goddess*, Penguin/ Arkana, 1993.

Birkbeck, Lyn, *Divine Astrology*, O Books, 2005.

Busteed, Marilyn and Wergin, Dorothy, *Phases of the Moon: A Guide to Evolving Human Nature*, American Federation of Astrologers Inc., 1976.

Calle, Carlos I., *Coffee with Einstein*, Duncan Baird Publishers, 2008.

Cashford, Jules, *The Moon: Myth and Image*, Cassell Illustrated/Octopus Publishing Group Limited, 2003.

Clark, Brian, *The Sibling Constellation: The Astrology and Psychology of Sisters and Brothers*, Penguin/Arkana, 1999.

Cunningham, *Healing Pluto Problems*, Samuel Weiser Inc., 1986.

Eliade, Mircea, *Patterns in Comparative Religion*, University of Nebraska Press, 1996.

Elwell, Dennis, *Cosmic Loom: The New Science of Astrology*, The Urania Trust, 1999, and 3rd edition The Wessex Astrologer, 2008.

Filbey, John and Peter, *Astronomy for Astrologers*, The Aquarian Press, 1984.

George, Demetra, *Mysteries of the Dark Moon*, Harper Collins, 1992.
_____ *Finding Our Way Through the Dark*, ACS Publications, 1994.

Goldsmith, Martin, *Moon Phases: A Symbolic Key*, Whitford Press,1988.

Grebner, Bernice Prill, *Everything Has a Phase*, American Federation of Astrologers Inc., 1992.

Greene, Liz, *Saturn: A New Look at an Old Devil*, Weiser Books, 1976.

Grof, Christina and Grof, Stanislav, *The Stormy Search for the Self*, Tarcher/Penguin, 1990.

Heath, Robin, *Sun, Moon and Earth*, Wooden Books Ltd, 1999.

Hill, Lynda, *360 Degrees of Wisdom*, Plume Books/Penguin Group, 2004.

Janov, Arthur, *Imprints: The Lifelong Effects of the Birth Experience*, Coward-McCann, Inc., 1983.

Jinnie and Joanne (Virginia Ewbank and Joanne Wickenburg), *The Spiral of Life*, The Digested Astrologer, 1974.

Johnson, Robert A., *She: Understanding Feminine Psychology*, Harper and Row, 1977.
_____ *He: Understanding Masculine Psychology*, Harper and Row, 1977.

Jones, Marc Edmund, *The Sabian Symbols in Astrology*, Shambhala Publications Inc., 1953.

Kornfield, Jack, *After the Ecstasy, the Laundry*, Bantam Books, 2000.
_____ *The Wise Heart*, Bantam Books, 2008.

May, Rollo, *The Courage to Create*, Bantam Books, 1975.

Meyer, Michael R., *A Handbook for the Humanistic Astrologer*, Anchor/Doubleday, 1974.

Pottenger, Maritha, *Healing With The Horoscope*, Astro Computing Services, 1982.

Rael, Leyla and Rudhyar, Dane, *Astrological Aspects*, Aurora Press Inc., 1980.

Reinhart, Melanie, *Chiron and the Healing Journey*, Penguin/Arkana, 1989.

Robertson, Marc, *Cosmopsychology I: The Engine of Destiny*, American Federation of Astrologers, 1975.
_____ *Critical Ages in Adult Life: The Transit of Saturn*, American Federation of Astrologers, Inc., 1976.

Rogers, Carl, *On Becoming a Person*, Constable, London, 1967.

Roose-Evans, James, *Inner Journey Outer Journey: Finding a Spiritual Centre in Everyday Life*, Darton Longman and Todd, 1987.

Rosenblum, Bernard, M.D., *The Astrologer's Guide to Counseling*, CRCS Publications, 1983.

Rudhyar, Dane, *The Astrology of Personality*, Lucis Publishing Company, 1936.

—— *The Pulse of Life*, Servire-Wassenaar, 1963.

—— *The Lunation Cycle*, Servire-Wassenaar, 1967, and Aurora Press, 1978.

—— *The Practice of Astrology*, Penguin Books Inc., 1968.

—— *An Astrological Mandala*, Vintage Books/Random House, 1974.

—— *From Humanistic to Transpersonal Astrology*, The Seed Center, 1975.

—— *Person-Centred Astrology*, ASI Publishers Inc., 1976.

—— *New Mansions for New Men*, Hunter House, 1978.

—— *The Astrology of Transformation*, Theosophical Publishing House, 1980.

Ruperti, Alexander, *Cycles of Becoming*, CRCS Publications, 1978.

Sasportas, Howard, *The Gods of Change: Pain, Crisis and the Transits of Uranus, Neptune and Pluto*, Penguin/Arkana, 1989.

—— *The Twelve Houses*, The Aquarian Press, 1985.

Somers, Barbara with Gordon-Brown, Ian, *Journey in Depth*, Archive Publishing, 2002.

—— *The Fires of Alchemy*, Archive Publishing, 2004.

Storr, Anthony, *The Integrity of the Personality*, Penguin Books, 1960.

—— *The Art of Psychotherapy*, Martin Secker and Warburg, 1979.

—— *Solitude: A Return to the Self*, Harper Collins, 1989.

Szanto, Gregory, *The Marriage of Heaven and Earth*, Penguin/Arkana, 1985.

Tarnas, Richard, *Cosmos and Psyche: Intimations of a New World View*, Plume/Penguin, 2007.

Teftt, J.C., *The Christ is Not a Person: The Evolution of Consciousness and the Destiny of Man*, iUniverse, USA, 2008.

Thompson, Damian, *The End of Time*, Sinclair-Stevenson/Reed International Books Ltd, 1996.

Tierney, Bil, *Dynamics of Aspect Analysis*, CRCS Publications, 1983.

Tompkins, Peter and Bird, Christopher, *The Secret Life of Plants*, Allen Lane, 1973.

Waram, Marilyn, *The Book of Neptune*, ACS Publications, 1989.

Wilber, Ken, *Quantum Questions*, Shambhala Publications Inc., 1984.

Index

Also by The Wessex Astrologer

Patterns of the Past
Karmic Connections
Good Vibrations
The Soulmate Myth: A Dream Come True or Your Worst Nightmare?
The Book of Why
Judy Hall

The Essentials of Vedic Astrology
Lunar Nodes - Crisis and Redemption
Personal Panchanga and the Five Sources of Light
Komilla Sutton

Astrolocality Astrology
From Here to There
Martin Davis

The Consultation Chart
Introduction to Medical Astrology
Wanda Sellar

The Betz Placidus Table of Houses
Martha Betz

Astrology and Meditation
Greg Bogart

The Book of World Horoscopes
Nicholas Campion

Life After Grief : An Astrological Guide to Dealing with Loss
AstroGraphology: The Hidden Link between your Horoscope and your Handwriting
Darrelyn Gunzburg

The Houses: Temples of the Sky
Deborah Houlding

Through the Looking Glass
The Magic Thread
Richard Idemon

Temperament: Astrology's Forgotten Key
Dorian Geiseler Greenbaum

Nativity of the Late King Charles
John Gadbury

Declination - The Steps of the Sun
Luna - The Book of the Moon
Paul F. Newman

www.wessexastrologer.com

Astrology, A Place in Chaos
Star and Planet Combinations
Bernadette Brady

Astrology and the Causes of War
Jamie Macphail

Flirting with the Zodiac
Kim Farnell

The Gods of Change
Howard Sasportas

Astrological Roots: The Hellenistic Legacy
Joseph Crane

The Art of Forecasting using Solar Returns
Anthony Louis

Horary Astrology Re-Examined
Barbara Dunn

Living Lilith
M. Kelley Hunter

The Spirit of Numbers: A New Exploration of Harmonic Astrology
David Hamblin

Primary Directions
Martin Gansten

Classical Medical Astrology
Oscar Hofman

The Door Unlocked: An Astrological Insight into Initiation
*Dolores Ashcroft Nowicki and
Stephanie V. Norris*

Understanding Karmic Complexes
Patricia L. Walsh

Pluto Volumes 1 & 2
Jeff Green

Essays on Evolutionary Astrology
Jeff Green Edited by Deva Green

Planetary Strength
Bob Makransky

All the Sun Goes Round
Reina James

The Moment of Astrology
Geoffrey Cornelius

Lightning Source UK Ltd.
Milton Keynes UK
UKOW041835270613

212920UK00008B/586/P